Captives of War

This is a pioneering history of the experience of captivity of British prisoners of war in Europe during the Second World War, focussing on how they coped and came to terms with wartime imprisonment. Clare Makepeace reveals the ways in which POWs psychologically responded to surrender, the camaraderie and individualism that dominated life in the camps and how, in their imagination, they constantly breached the barbed wire perimeter to be with their loved ones at home. Through the diaries, letters and logbooks written by seventy-five POWs alongside psychiatric research and reports, she explores the mental strains that tore through POWs' minds and the challenges they faced upon homecoming. This book tells the story of wartime imprisonment through the love, fears, fantasies, loneliness, frustration and guilt these men felt, shedding new light on what the experience of captivity meant for these men both during the war and after their liberation.

Clare Makepeace is an Honorary Research Fellow at Birkbeck, University of London.

Studies in the Social and Cultural History of Modern Warfare

General Editor
Jay Winter, *Yale University*

Advisory Editors
David Blight, *Yale University*
Richard Bosworth, *University of Western Australia*
Peter Fritzsche, *University of Illinois, Urbana-Champaign*
Carol Gluck, *Columbia University*
Benedict Kiernan, *Yale University*
Antoine Prost, *Université de Paris-Sorbonne*
Robert Wohl, *University of California, Los Angeles*

In recent years the field of modern history has been enriched by the exploration of two parallel histories. These are the social and cultural history of armed conflict, and the impact of military events on social and cultural history.

Studies in the Social and Cultural History of Modern Warfare presents the fruits of this growing area of research, reflecting both the colonization of military history by cultural historians and the reciprocal interest of military historians in social and cultural history, to the benefit of both. The series offers the latest scholarship in European and non-European events from the 1850s to the present day.

A full list of titles in the series can be found at: www.cambridge.org/modernwarfare

Captives of War

*British Prisoners of War in Europe in the
Second World War*

Clare Makepeace

Birkbeck, University of London

CAMBRIDGE
UNIVERSITY PRESS

CAMBRIDGE
UNIVERSITY PRESS

University Printing House, Cambridge CB2 8BS, United Kingdom

One Liberty Plaza, 20th Floor, New York, NY 10006, USA

477 Williamstown Road, Port Melbourne, VIC 3207, Australia

4843/24, 2nd Floor, Ansari Road, Daryaganj, Delhi – 110002, India

79 Anson Road, #06–04/06, Singapore 079906

Cambridge University Press is part of the University of Cambridge.

It furthers the University's mission by disseminating knowledge in the pursuit of education, learning, and research at the highest international levels of excellence.

www.cambridge.org
Information on this title: www.cambridge.org/9781107145870
DOI: 10.1017/9781316536247

First published 2017

Printed in the United Kingdom by TJ International Ltd. Padstow Cornwall

A catalogue record for this publication is available from the British Library.

Library of Congress Cataloging-in-Publication Data
Names: Makepeace, Clare, author.
Title: Captives of war : British prisoners of war in Europe in the Second World War / Clare Makepeace.
Other titles: Captives of war, British POWs in Europe in the Second World War | British prisoners of war in Europe in the Second World War
Description: New York : Cambridge University Press, [2017]
Identifiers: LCCN 2017026031 | ISBN 9781107145870
Subjects: LCSH: World War, 1939–1945 – Prisoners and prisons, German. | Prisoners of war – Great Britain. | Prisoners of war – Europe. | Prisoners of war – Diaries. | World War, 1939–1945 Personal narratives, British.
Classification: LCC D805.E85 M35 2017 | DDC 940.54/7243092241–dc23
LC record available at https://lccn.loc.gov/2017026031

ISBN 978-1-107-14587-0 Hardback

For my parents, Alan and Penelope Makepeace and my other half, Richard Stokoe

Contents

Illustrations

Acknowledgements

This book originated as a doctoral dissertation, submitted to Birkbeck College, University of London, in 2013. I am grateful, first and foremost, to my PhD supervisor, Professor Joanna Bourke, for being an untiring source of advice, support and enthusiasm. My gratitude also goes to the Arts and Humanities Research Council for funding three years of my research.

A number of other scholars and former postgraduate colleagues were very generous in discussing my ideas with me, providing advice about sources and methodologies and sharing their own research: Dr Gilly Carr, Professor Sears Eldredge, Dr Kent Federowich, Dr Anna Hájková, Professor Paul MacKenzie, Dr Carmen Mangion, Professor Mark McDermott, Professor Bob Moore, Professor Panikos Panayi, Meg Parkes, Dr Matthias Reiss and Dr Helen Smith.

Colleagues, friends and family very generously undertook highly considered reads of draft chapters. They are Dr Bernice Archer, Suzanne Bardgett, Dr Hazel Croft, Dr Chris Dillon, Dr Alex Dowdall, Midge Gillies, Dr Barbara Hately, Dr Alan Makepeace, Penelope Makepeace, Richard Makepeace, Professor Mark McDermott, Dr Lizzie Oliver, Victoria Powell, Dr Jen Purcell, Dr Keith Rathbone, Richard Stokoe, the late Rod Suddaby and Dr Janet Weston. Great scrutiny came from my PhD examiners, Dr Heather Jones and Professor Michael Roper. The anonymous readers at Cambridge University Press also provided extremely helpful reports, which served to push my thinking a great deal further. An extra word of thanks must also go to close family and friends who re-read sections of the manuscript just before it went into press: thank you to my parents, my uncle, Hazel and Rich for your help and patience. Thanks also to Rich for his last-minute work on the illustrations. All comments and criticisms were invaluable in shaping the content and direction of this book. Needless to say, any errors that remain are my responsibility alone.

I am grateful to the following archives and archivists for allowing me access to their documents and aiding me in my research: Maria Anthony,

Simon Offord, Tony Richards and the late Rod Suddaby in the Department of Documents at the Imperial War Museum, London; Anne Wickes at the Second World War Experience Centre, West Yorkshire; and Fabrizio Bensi and Daniel Palmieri at the International Committee of the Red Cross, Geneva. Thanks are also due to Sandra Stokoe for her hospitality during various research trips to Leeds.

I would like to thank the following persons and organisations for permission to quote extracts from collections to which they hold copyright: Edney Abbott, Ken Abbott and Helen Scott for the diary of Private E. W. Abbott; Mrs D. Armitage for the correspondence of Squadron Leader D. L. Armitage; the Army Medical Services Museum for the RAMC papers; Pat Athawes for the diary of Driver G. Didcock; Judy Avery for the logbook of Gunner C. G. King; Mrs G. V. Barnard for the diary and correspondence of Captain J. W. M. Mansel; Diane Barrington for the diary of Corporal E. Barrington; Stephen Barter for the diary of Dispatch Rider L. F. Barter; Peter Beddis for the logbook of Flight Sergeant J. Beddis; the family of Greaser C. E. Bloss for his correspondence; Vicky Briggs for the correspondence of Warrant Officer H. L. Hurrell; Alexis Penny Casdagli and Cylix Press for the diary of Major A. T. Casdagli; Wendy Coles for the logbook of Lieutenant C. L. Coles; John Cunningham for the logbook of Flight Lieutenant P. A. Cunningham; the family of Regimental Sergeant Major J. F. Dover for his diary; Nancy Fairclough for the correspondence of Flight Lieutenant R. Fairclough; Veronica Forwood for the letters of Lieutenant J. Phillips; Dr Mary Gibbens for the thesis of Lieutenant T. Gibbens, lodged at the University of Cambridge; Garth Graydon for the logbook of 5th Engineer R. A. Graydon; Wing Commander John Grogan (rtd) and Kerry Grogan for the diary of Flying Officer R. J. Grogan; Mrs Sandra Hawarden-Lord and Mr G. O'Brien for the diary of Sergeant Major A. Hawarden; Roger Hewitt for the logbook of Trooper J. Scott and Private J. Hewitt; Colin Howard for the logbook of Apprentice A. C. Howard; Peter Jenkins for the diary of Captain J. E. Jenkins; James Johnson for the logbook of Lieutenant R. G. Johnson; David Kausmann for the logbook of Flying Officer A. G. Edwards; Jean Kemp for the diary of Sergeant L. D. Pexton; Robin Craig Kennedy for the logbook of Flying Officer J. F. Kennedy; the trustees of the Liddell Hart Centre for Military Archives, King's College London, for the Adam papers; John Lightfoot for the correspondence of Lance Corporal F. G. Blyth; Andrew William Macey and Alison Mary Campbell for the logbook of Petty Officer H. C. Macey; the trustees of the Mass Observation Archive, University of Sussex; Professor Mark McDermott for the logbook of Cadet L. McDermott-Brown; Margaret Millard for the diary of Canon J. H. King; the council of the National Army Museum, London, for the correspondence of Second Lieutenant A. R. Jabez-Smith; Charlotte Oxley for the diary, logbook and correspondence of Sub-lieutenant H. R. Taylor; Jane Preese for the letters of Wing Commander N. C. Hyde; the trustees of the Second World War Experience Centre for the logbook of Warrant Officer A. Clague, the diary of Lieutenant R. G. M. Quarrie and the letters of Warrant Officer D. H. Webster; Gillian Stein for the letters of Major G. B. Matthews; John Stewart for the papers of Second Lieutenant F. J. Stewart; Dr Simon Stoddart for the letters and diary of Lieutenant K. B. Stoddart; Paul Tipple for the logbook of Able Seaman E. Tipple. I would also like to thank the trustees of the Imperial War Museum and the Second World War Experience Centre for access to each of the copyright holders.

Every effort has been made to contact copyright holders for the material used in this book, but, if anyone holds the intellectual rights to any images or text whose copyright holder could not be established, they are invited to make themselves known to either the author or the publisher. The author and the Imperial War Museum would be grateful for any information which might help to trace the families of 4th Mate C. W. G. Allen, Captain R. L. Angove, Lance Corporal L. A. Bains, Sergeant E. G. Ball, Lieutenant W. M. G. Bompas, Major E. Booth, Rifleman A. G. Brook, Second Lieutenant B. A. Brooke, Gunner D. R. Cooper, Warrant Officer A. J. East, Rifleman J. Eldridge, Lieutenant J. W. Evans, Flying Officer R. J. Fayers, Driver J. K. Glass, Sergeant Navigator G. Hall, Warrant Officer H. M. C. Jarvis, Lance Corporal E. G. Laker, Commander G. T. Lambert, Reverend J. S. Naylor, Sergeant D. Nell, Gunner E. E. Parker, Private W. Richards, Leading Telegraphist H. F. Shipp, Lance Bombardier E. C. Stirling, Corporal J. G. White, Reverend R. D. F. Wild and Signalman N. R. Wylie. The author and the Second World War Experience Centre would be grateful for any information which might help to trace the families of Second Lieutenant F. J. Burnaby-Atkins and Driver P. Hainsworth. The author and the National Army Museum would be grateful for any information which might help to trace the family of Second Lieutenant A. R. Jabez-Smith. The author and the University of Leeds, Special Collections would be grateful for any information which might help to trace the families of Lance Bombardier S. Campbell and Warrant Officer G. B. Gallagher.

Chapter 4 incorporates material and arguments that first appeared in Clare Makepeace, 'Living beyond the barbed wire: the familial ties of British prisoners of war held in Europe during the Second World War', *Historical Research*, 86 (2013), 158–77. I would like to thank the editors of *Historical Research* for permission to reproduce this material.

The final word must go to my family who show me so much support and love. I am indebted to my parents, Alan and Penelope Makepeace, for continuing to provide me with an endless supply of support and encouragement, taking care of me when I needed it, and always being there for me. My partner, Richard Stokoe, has been more closely involved in this research than any other person and deserves the greatest thanks. At one point in my thesis, probably when, yet again, I had become engrossed in my thoughts, Richard mused whether, if I had to choose between him and it, which I would opt for. I was, of course, aghast that he could possibly think this choice would present me with a dilemma. I repeat now what I told him then: 'You make it all worthwhile.'

Abbreviations

In text

Campo PG	Campo concentramento di prigionieri di guerra, meaning 'prisoner of war camp'
CRU	Civil Resettlement Units
Dulag	Short for *Durchgangslager*, meaning transit camp
Dulag Luft	Short for *Durchgangslager der Luftwaffe*, meaning transit camp for captured air crew
ICRC	International Committee of the Red Cross
Kriegie	Short for *Kriegsgefangener*, meaning prisoner of war
Marlag	Short for *Marine-Lager*, meaning a camp for naval seamen
Milag	Short for *Marine-Internierten-Lager*, meaning a camp for merchant seamen
MI9	Military Intelligence Section 9
NCO	Non-commissioned officer
Oflag	Short for *Offizierslager*, meaning a camp for officers
OKW	Oberkomando der Wehrmacht, meaning 'German High Command'
POW/PW	Prisoner of war
RAChD	Royal Army Chaplain's Department
RAF	Royal Air Force
RAMC	Royal Army Medical Corps
SBO	Senior British Officer
SHAEF	Supreme Headquarters Allied Expeditionary Force
SS	*Schutzstaffel*, meaning protection squadrons
Stalag	Short for *Stammlager*, meaning main camp or root camp (as opposed to branch camps or work camps that were attached to these main camps but located elsewhere)
Stalag Luft	Short for *Stammlager Luftwaffe*, meaning main camp for captured aircrew
YMCA	Young Men's Christian Association

In footnotes

ACICR	Archives of the International Committee of the Red Cross
ADM	Admiralty
AIR	Air Ministry
AMD	Army Medical Department
CUST	Boards of Customs
DAP	Directorate of Army Psychiatry
DPW	Directorate of Prisoners of War, War Office
FO	Foreign Office
HC	House of Commons
HMSO	His/Her Majesty's Stationary Office
IWM	Imperial War Museum
IWM Art	Imperial War Museum Art Department
IWM Pst	Imperial War Museum Poster
LAB	Ministry of Labour
LHC	Liddle Hart Centre for Military Archives, King's College, London
Liddle	Liddle archive, Leeds University Library
Marlag	Short for *Marine-Lager*, meaning a camp for naval seamen
Milag	Short for *Marine-Internierten-Lager*, meaning a camp for merchant seamen
M. D.	Doctor of Medicine
NAM	National Army Museum
Oflag	Short for *Offizierslager*, meaning a camp for officers
PIN	Ministry of Pensions
P.W.2	Section two of the Directorate of Prisoners of War, War Office
RAF	Royal Air Force
RAMC	Royal Army Medical Corps
SBO	Senior British Officer
SHAEF	Supreme Headquarters Allied Expeditionary Force
SOFO	Soldiers of Oxfordshire Museum
Stalag	Short for *Stammlager*, meaning main camp or root camp (as opposed to branch camps or work camps that were attached to these main camps but located elsewhere)
Stalag Luft	Short for *Stammlager Luftwaffe*, meaning main camp for captured aircrew
SWWEC	Second World War Experience Centre, West Yorkshire
T	Treasury
TNA	The National Archives, London
WO	War Office

Introduction

Signalman Andrew Makepeace, my grandfather, was taken prisoner, along with more than 10,000 other men in the 51st Highland Division, at St Valery-en-Caux on 12 June 1940. It was often said in our household that a veteran's silence on the war was a direct reflection of how much he had suffered. My parents regularly invoked this maxim to explain why my grandfather rarely talked about his experiences. From a very early age, I struggled to reconcile this: how could my kind, gentle, patient grandfather have gone through things so dreadful they had rendered him mute when it came to discussing these five years of his early adult life? Very occasionally, and unexpectedly, something would break his silence. I remember wearing a pair of clogs one day: I was about twelve years old. He looked at them and then looked at me. 'Dreadful things', he said in a distant voice. I watched his eyes fill with anguish over, what seemed to me, up until that point, to be the most harmless of items.[1]

After my grandmother died, my grandfather started to speak a little more freely but still would talk suddenly about captivity on the most unanticipated of occasions. We once met at the newly opened Roman baths in south-west England. I am not sure what triggered the recollection, but suddenly I found myself being told about Russian prisoners of war (POWs) resorting to cannibalism. It was shocking, profound and slightly awkward. We were in the midst of hordes of people, but mentally my grandfather had disappeared elsewhere.

---

[1] My grandfather had been a prisoner of Stalag XXB in Marienburg in East Prussia. In May 1942, it held the second-largest contingent of British Commonwealth POWs, 9,555, all of them English except for ten Canadians and five Australians. The vast majority of these men, including my grandfather, was spread amongst some 450 work camps. A chief worry of the camp leaders was the footwear these prisoners were given to work in. An order of the Stalag forbade them being issued with leather boots during the summer. This meant many of the prisoners had to work on railways or in the field (where my grandfather worked) wearing excruciating wooden clogs or shoes with wooden soles, Arieh Kochavi, *Confronting Captivity: Britain and the United States and Their POWs in Nazi Germany* (Chapel Hill: University of North Carolina Press, 2005), p. 36.

Figure 0.1: Signalmen Andrew Makepeace (far right) and Frank Marshall (second left) in captivity. Signalmen Andrew Makepeace and Frank Marshall were called up together, served together, were captured together, laboured on farms in Poland together and did The Long March. They remained firm friends for the rest of their lives.
    Source: Author's collection

During my grandfather's final years, my family and I started to encourage him to write down his story. My grandfather had now moved from Bristol to Hertfordshire to be closer to his sons and granddaughters. We saw him more often, and he was providing us with more and more snippets of his life as a POW. He had also started to speak regularly to his best friend, Frank Marshall. He and my grandfather had been called up together, had served together, had been captured together and had laboured on farms in Poland together [Figure 0.1]. During the final months of the war, they supported each other through The Long March, when POWs were forced to walk across Europe ahead of Russian advances. Frank and my grandfather developed a routine: one phone call on a Wednesday evening, two on a Saturday and two on a Sunday. He was talking more and more about the war.

My grandfather continued, however, to resist all our persuasions to record his experience. He thought he could not possibly add to the existing accounts. Ex-POWs from the Second World War have been, quite possibly, more forthcoming than any other group of veterans in composing their memoirs, and my grandfather had read many of them.[2] He also considered his memories would be uninteresting to us, let alone the lay reader. I thought he was being too modest. He was so intelligent and articulate that I knew my grandfather would tell his story with so much insight and reflection that it would make a valuable addition to the others that had been written. I kept on urging him. I felt a need to convince him that his past mattered as much as anyone else's, and people would want to hear about it.

In the autumn of 2008, my haranguing came to an abrupt end. I had, yet again, been encouraging my grandfather to write a memoir. I even suggested getting a Dictaphone. Perhaps, I mooted, it would make the task easier. This time, he gave me a different reason for his resolve. 'Why would I record my story?' he asked, immediately answering himself with: 'It would just be one long tale of humiliation.' At that moment, I realised an incongruity lay between him and me. I was so proud of my grandfather. I thought he was incredible for what he had been through, for what he had survived and witnessed, and for who he had become as a result. He, meanwhile, seemed embarrassed and ashamed. My attitude was, no doubt, informed by the contemporary society in which I lived: an era when the war victim or sufferer had become a heroic figure, and when the masculine ideal was far from synonymous with martial prowess. I wanted to understand my grandfather's perspective. So I scoured the books written on POWs. Those histories of captivity described in great detail what life was like for the 142,319 men taken prisoner whilst serving in the armed forces of the United Kingdom in the war against Germany and Italy.[3] They were structured chronologically and often drew upon the first-hand accounts of POWs themselves. They started with the chaos with which life in captivity commenced for those captured in 1940, described the conditions in various POW camps spread throughout the Third Reich and set out the activities these men participated in whilst behind barbed wire. For example, their escape attempts, the educational and exam systems they developed or the theatrical productions they put on. These histories also explored what life was like for men, such as my grandfather, who were forced to labour for their captors. In addition, they

---

[2] On the abundance of POWs' memoirs, see Philip Towle, 'Introduction', in Philip Towle, Margaret Kosuge and Yoichi Kibata (eds.), *Japanese Prisoners of War* (London: Hambledon Press, 2000), p. xi.

[3] 'Table 9. Total number of prisoners of war of the armed forces of the United Kingdom captured by the enemy as reported to 28th February 1946', in *Strength and Casualties of the Armed Forces and Auxiliary Services of the United Kingdom 1939 to 1945* (London: HMSO, 1946), p. 9.

described POWs' mental and physical state, the food they received and the extent to which they were protected by the 1929 Geneva Convention, which set out the rights and safeguards which prisoners of war as a whole should be accorded and to which Britain, Germany and Italy were all signatories. These accounts often ended with The Long March across Europe, and then gave brief attention to POWs' homecoming and their subsequent lives.[4]

Yet they did not provide me with the understanding I was looking for. Knowing what these men did in captivity, and what happened to them, was not enough. I wanted to understand how it felt to be in captivity, how POWs psychologically responded to the experience, how they coped with it and how they came to terms with it. My desire to understand the experience in these ways was undoubtedly driven by what I had witnessed of my grandfather. It was also driven by my interest in cultural history. Cultural historians do not just focus on what people did in the past, but also explain why they did it; how, that is, they ascribed meaning to their lives.[5]

I began to understand why a cultural approach might be a particularly pertinent one to apply to prisoners of war. Humans order their lives through binary categories, that is, we often classify people, concepts and behaviour into distinct and opposite groups.[6] The POW experience seemed to slip between many of the categories we use to define and interpret, and so give meaning to, people's experiences of war. Their surrender, for example, meant they had given up much of their combatant status, but they were not civilians again either. POWs were no longer on the front line, but nor were they on the home front. They fitted neither of the oppositions of heroic victor nor glorious dead. Their daily interactions with their captors potentially undermined the distinction between friend and foe. They also reversed behaviours in war that are perceived as having

---

[4] See, for example, David Rolf, *Prisoners of the Reich: Germany's Captives 1939–1945* (Sevenoaks: Coronet, 1989); S. P. MacKenzie, *The Colditz Myth: British and Commonwealth Prisoners of War in Nazi Germany* (Oxford: Oxford University Press, 2006). Far fewer histories have been written on the lives of captives in Italy, for one exception, see Adrian Gilbert, *POW: Allied Prisoners in Europe, 1939–1945* (London: John Murray, 2007). Some books have focussed on specific periods of captivity; see for example, Sean Longden, *Dunkirk: The Men They Left Behind* (London: Constable, 2008); John Nichol and Tony Rennell, *The Last Escape. The Untold Story of Allied Prisoners of War in Germany, 1944–45* (London: Viking, 2002).

[5] Joanna Bourke, 'New Military History', in Matthew Hughes and William J. Philpott (eds.), *Modern Military History* (London: Palgrave, 2006), p. 263; Jay Winter and Blaine Baggett, *The Great War and the Shaping of the 20th Century* (London: Penguin Studio, 1996), p. 11.

[6] Thomas Kühne, *Belonging and Genocide. Hitler's Community, 1918–1945* (New Haven, CT: Yale University Press, 2010), p. 59.

highly gendered connotations: the male role of fighting and the female role of waiting at home.[7] Given their unclear status in the discourses of war how, then, did British POWs make sense of their wartime imprisonment? This is the central question addressed in *Captives of War*.

This book is the first cultural history written about British POWs held in Europe in the Second World War. Through its focus on how POWs made sense of their experience, it tells a new story: one replete with loves, fears, fantasies, frustrations, guilt and mental strains. Unlike other histories, *Captives of War* explores these men's experiences, not by narrating what is happening in the camps, as if observing prisoners' behaviour and activities from the barbed-wire perimeter, but instead, this book reaches into their interior and intimate worlds, to look at how they mentally and emotionally responded to their wartime imprisonment. The primary way in which their worlds are accessed is through the personal narratives they composed whilst they were in captivity: their letters home, diaries and logbooks. My grandfather never kept a diary during captivity and most of the letters he sent home were, lamentably, discarded during a loft clear-out. Instead, at the centre of this study are seventy-five other men who did compose, and then preserve, personal narratives whilst they were held prisoner of war. The thoughts, topics and activities about which they commonly wrote have directed the focus and contents of this book.

Historiography

Captives of War seeks to improve our understanding of British POWs held in Europe in the Second World War, as well as contributing, more

---

[7] Other historians have reflected on how POWs and civilian internees failed to fit into these dichotomies of war; see Annette Becker, 'Art, Material Life and Disaster. Civilian and Military Prisoners of War', in Nicholas J. Saunders (ed.), *Matters of Conflict. Material Culture, Memory and the First World War* (London: Routledge, 2004), p. 28; Christina Twomey, *Australia's Forgotten Prisoners. Civilians Interned by the Japanese in World War Two* (Cambridge: Cambridge University Press, 2007), p. 16; Brian K. Feltman, 'Letters from Captivity: The First World War Correspondence of the German Prisoners of War in the United Kingdom', in Jennifer D. Keene and Michael S. Neiberg (eds.), *Finding Common Ground. New Directions in First World War Studies* (Boston: Brill, 2011), p. 90; Heather Jones, *Violence against Prisoners of War in the First World War: Britain, France, and Germany, 1914–1920* (Cambridge: Cambridge University Press, 2012), p. 10. Historians have also pointed out the inadequacy of such binarisms as interpretative strategies for other combatants and civilians, see Angela Woollacott, 'Sisters and Brothers in Arms: Family, Class, and Gendering in World War I in Britain', in Miriam Cooke and Angela Woollacott (eds.), *Gendering War Talk* (Princeton, NJ: Princeton University Press, 1993), p. 143; Carol Acton, 'Writing and Waiting: First World War Correspondence between Vera Brittain and Roland Leighton', *Gender and History*, 11, 1 (1999), 56; Eric Leed, *No Man's Land. Combat and Identity in the First World War* (Cambridge: Cambridge University Press, 1979), pp. 17–18.

broadly, to the field of literature on captivity in the two World Wars. So far, histories on this group of British POWs have mainly been written from two perspectives.

The first consists of histories exploring the policies of governments and neutral observers. Two sets of neutral observers were involved in the lives of British POWs in Europe: the International Committee of the Red Cross (ICRC), whose principal functions included visiting camps and reporting on the conditions in which POWs lived, investigating the state of health of sick or wounded prisoners and conveying letters and parcels to prisoners, plus providing medical relief. The other observer was the Protecting Power, a neutral state, nominated by a belligerent government, who also visited prisoners of war and monitored their incarceration.[8] The majority of historians working in this area, foremost amongst them being historians Bob Moore, Kent Fedorowich and Neville Wylie, have been largely concerned with understanding how warring nations negotiated the treatment received by captured men.[9] Historian Barbara Hately, meanwhile, explores government policy from a different angle: its treatment of the families of British POWs. As she points out, in history books and memoirs, POWs' relatives are rarely discussed – an omission that *Captives of War* also addresses.[10]

The second set of histories have been written from the perspective of British prisoners of war and what they went through whilst they were in Italian or German hands. Some of the most scholarly work has been written to correct the image, put forward in films, television programmes and the most prominent POW memoirs, that captivity was a game for POWs, dominated by their schemes to outwit, evade and escape from their captors.[11] Historians David Rolf, Adrian Gilbert and Paul MacKenzie have each documented what life was like for the great mass

---

[8] Kochavi, *Confronting Captivity*, pp. 3, 81; Peter Monteath, 'POW "Holiday Camps" in the Third Reich', *European History Quarterly*, 44, 3 (2014), 490; Prisoner of War Enquiry Centre, *A Handbook for the Information of Relatives and Friends of Prisoners of War* (London: HMSO, 1943), p. 4. The Protecting Power for British POWs was first the United States and then, after it entered the war, Switzerland. Prisoners were also entitled to write to the representatives of the Protecting Power in order to draw attention to points on which they had complaints.

[9] See, for example, Bob Moore and Kent Fedorowich (eds.), *Prisoners of War and Their Captors in World War II* (Oxford: Berg, 1996); Neville Wylie, *Barbed Wire Diplomacy. Britain, Germany, and Politics of Prisoners of War, 1939–1945* (Oxford: Oxford University Press, 2010).

[10] Barbara Hately-Broad, *War and Welfare: British Prisoner of War Families, 1939–45* (Manchester: Manchester University Press, 2009).

[11] See, for example, Eric Williams, *The Wooden Horse* (London: Collins, 1949); Paul Brickhill, *The Great Escape* (London: Faber & Faber, 1951); Patrick Robert Reid, *The Colditz Story* (London: Hodder & Stoughton, 1952); *The Colditz Story*, directed by Guy Hamilton (Ivan Foxwell Productions, 1955); *The Great Escape*, directed by John

of British POWs who did not escape, and how their experiences varied between camps, working parties and at different times of the war.[12]

These numerous histories provide a comprehensive picture of imprisonment but, by adopting a cultural approach, *Captives of War* moves beyond them in a variety of ways. At the centre of this study is a consideration of how these prisoners of war made sense of their experiences *as men*. Numerous aspects of wartime imprisonment demand that the experience of captivity be studied as a gendered one. With conceptions of masculinity being so strongly linked to performance in battle in societies, past and present, POWs had to contend with the possibility that their capture had raised questions over their manhood.[13] The imprisoned conditions under which they lived could also be emasculating. As historian Stephen Garton puts it, the 'enforced passivity conjures up a feminised condition'.[14] POWs existed in homosocial environments, and those who did not work for their captors had highly limited, if any, contact with the opposite sex. Yet, so far, only a handful of histories, focussing on other wars or spheres of captivity, have considered how expectations and understanding of masculine behaviour affected the ways in which captivity was experienced.[15]

Sturges (MGM Studios, 1963); *Colditz*, Series 1 and 2, first broadcast between 1972 and 1974 by the BBC (BBC and Universal TV, 1972–4).

[12] Rolf, *Prisoners of the Reich*; MacKenzie, *The Colditz Myth*; Gilbert, *POW*.

[13] Joshua S. Goldstein, *Gender and War: How Gender Shapes the War System and Vice Versa* (Cambridge: Cambridge University Press, 2001), pp. 252, 331; Robin Gerster, *Big-Noting: The Heroic Theme in Australian War Writing* (Melbourne: Melbourne University Press, 1987), p. 228.

[14] Stephen Garton, *The Cost of War: Australians Return* (Melbourne: Oxford University Press, 1996), p. 210.

[15] Bernice Archer, *A Patchwork of Internment. The Internment of Western Civilians under the Japanese, 1941–1945* (London: RoutledgeCurzon, 2004); Joan Beaumont, *Gull Force. Survival and Leadership in Captivity 1941–1945* (Sydney: Allen & Unwin, 1985); Frank Biess, *Homecomings: Returning POWs and the Legacies of Defeat in Postwar Germany* (Princeton, NJ: Princeton University Press, 2009); Brian K. Feltman, *The Stigma of Surrender. German Prisoners, British Captors, and Manhood in the Great War and Beyond* (Chapel Hill: University of North Carolina, 2015); Juliette Pattinson, Lucy Noakes and Wendy Ugolini, 'Incarcerated Masculinities: Male POWs and the Second World War', *Journal of War and Culture Studies*, 7, 3 (2014), 179–90; Iris Rachamimov, 'The Disruptive Comforts of Drag: (Trans)Gender Performances among Prisoners of War in Russia, 1914–1920', *American Historical Review*, 111, 2 (2006), 362–82; Iris Rachamimov, 'Camp Domesticity. Shifting Gender Boundaries in WWI Internment Camps', in Gilly Carr and Harold Mytum (eds.), *Cultural Heritage and Prisoners of War. Creativity behind Barbed Wire* (New York: Routledge, 2012), pp. 291–305; Matthias Reiss, 'The Importance of Being Men: The Afrika-Korps in American Captivity', *Journal of Social History*, 46, 1 (2012), 23–47; Matthew Stibbe, 'Gendered Experiences of Civilian Internment during the First World War: A Forgotten Dimension of Wartime Violence', in Ana Carden-Coyne (ed.), *Gender and Conflict since 1914. Historical and Interdisciplinary Perspectives* (Basingstoke: Palgrave Macmillan,

Captives of War also moves beyond existing histories written on British POWs held in Europe in its treatment of personal narratives. Instead of drawing upon the narratives that POWs wrote during and after captivity as if they provide a window onto these men's experiences, these narratives are considered both as records of experience and as interacting with, shaping and altering those experiences. Historian Christina Twomey is one scholar of wartime imprisonment who thinks critically about captives' narratives. She has researched the links between wider cultural discourses of captivity and the construction of memoirs when analysing the writings of Australian Far East ex-POWs and civilian internees.[16] Another is historian Iris Rachamimov in her analysis of the narratives constructed in the letters and memoirs written by POWs in the First World War on the eastern front.[17] In *Captives of War*, the personal narratives POWs composed in captivity are not just analysed for the words they contain, but also for the images or other paraphernalia that they carry. Analysing POWs' records in this way follows a very recent development in captivity studies, spearheaded by archaeologist Gilly Carr, which looks at the material culture of civilian and military prisoners, particularly their creativity behind barbed wire.[18]

The focus on the emotions of POWs, rather than their material lives, has led to certain aspects of captivity featuring prominently in *Captives of War* that are largely absent in other histories. A key theme that appears throughout the following pages is the presence of loved ones at home in the lives of British prisoners of war.[19] This follows Michael Roper's work on British soldiers in the First World War, which did much to alter the parameters of the way in which a combatant's warring life should be

---

2012), pp. 14–28; Christina Twomey, 'Double Displacement: Western Women's Return Home from Japanese Internment in the Second World War', *Gender and History*, 21, 3 (2009), 670–84; Christina Twomey, 'Emaciation or Emasculation: Photographic Images, White Masculinity and Captivity by the Japanese in World War Two', *Journal of Men's Studies*, 15, 3 (2007), 295–310.

[16] Christina Twomey, '"Impossible History": Trauma and Testimony among Australian Civilians Interned by the Japanese in World War II', in Joy Damousi and Robert Reynolds (eds.), *History on the Couch. Essays in History and Psychoanalysis* (Melbourne: Melbourne University Press, 2003), pp. 155–65. See also Frances Houghton, '"To the Kwai and Back": Myth, Memory and Memoirs of the "Death Railway" 1942–1943', *Journal of War and Culture Studies*, 7, 3 (2014), 223–35.

[17] Iris Rachamimov, *POWs and the Great War: Captivity on the Eastern Front* (Oxford: Berg, 2002).

[18] G. Carr and H. Mytum (eds.), *Cultural Heritage and Prisoners of War. Creativity behind Barbed Wire* (New York: Routledge, 2012).

[19] Oliver Wilkinson also recognises how British POWs in the First World War stayed close to those at home, Oliver Wilkinson, 'Diluting Displacement. Letters from Captivity', in Sandra Barkhof and Angela K. Smith (eds.), *War and Displacement in the Twentieth Century. Global Conflicts* (London: Routledge, 2014), pp. 70–88.

understood. He demonstrated that the connections between home and war fronts were a central part of the experience of battle.[20]

The psychological disturbances that POWs experienced also receive much attention in the following pages and, since the emotional experience of captivity continued well beyond liberation, *Captives of War* also explores POWs' homecoming. Unlike studies of other spheres of incarceration, neither of these aspects of the wartime imprisonment of British servicemen in Second World War Europe has been explored systematically as part of the wider captivity experience.[21] The most thorough research in this regard has emanated from historians of psychiatry.[22]

As a cultural history, *Captives of War* also contributes to our understanding of Britain in the Second World War and the twentieth century. Compared to the First World War, there is still much research to be carried out. Only two historians have put masculinity centre stage in their monographs on British servicemen: Martin Francis's *The Flyer*, which examines the lives of RAF personnel and their representation in literary and cinematic texts, and Emma Newland's *Civilians into Soldiers*, looking at how military authorities sought to control and transform male bodies.[23] More attention has been paid to non-combatant men who remained on the home front in the Second World War, whose masculinity, because they did not wear a military uniform, was more visibly contested.[24] By considering how prisoners of war reacted to their capture, the extent to which gender roles were maintained in captivity and how

---

[20] Michael Roper, *The Secret Battle. Emotional Survival in the Great War* (Manchester: Manchester University Press, 2009). See also Ilana R. Bet-El, *Conscripts. Forgotten Men of the Great War* (Stroud: Sutton Publishing, 1999). Stéphane Audoin-Rouzeau also demonstrates the connection between home and front through his reading of a different literary source: trench newspapers, Stéphane Audoin-Rouzeau, *Men at War, 1914–1918. National Sentiment and Trench Journalism in France during the First World War*, translated by Helen McPhail (Oxford: Berg, 1992).

[21] For other spheres of incarceration that explore the return of POWs, see, for example, Megan Koreman, 'A Hero's Homecoming: The Return of the Deportees to France', *Journal of Contemporary History*, 32 (2007), 9–23; Biess, *Homecomings*.

[22] Edgar Jones and Simon Wessely, 'British Prisoners-of-War: From Resilience to Psychological Vulnerability: Reality or Perception', *Twentieth Century British History*, 21, 2 (2010), 163–83; Ben Shephard, *A War of Nerves: Soldiers and Psychiatrists in the Twentieth Century* (Cambridge, MA: Harvard University Press, 2001).

[23] Martin Francis, *The Flyer. British Culture and the Royal Air Force, 1939–1945* (Oxford: Oxford University Press, 2008); Emma Newlands, *Civilians into Soldiers. War, the Body and British Army Recruits, 1939–45* (Manchester: Manchester University Press, 2013).

[24] Sonya O. Rose, *Which People's War?: National Identity and Citizenship in Britain 1939–1945* (Oxford: Oxford University Press, 2003); Penny Summerfield and Corinna Peniston-Bird, *Contesting Home Defence. Men, Women and the Home Guard in the Second World War* (Manchester: Manchester University Press, 2007); Linsey Robb, *Men at Work: The Working Man in British Culture* (Basingstoke: Palgrave Macmillan, 2015).

men transgressed from them, *Captives of War* sheds light on what it meant to be a British man in the mid-twentieth century.

The focus on the psychological disturbances that POWs experienced during captivity and ex-POWs' difficulties in readjusting to civilian life also enables *Captives of War* to contribute to other under-researched aspects of Britain in the Second World War. Between 1939 and 1945 military psychiatrists were handed unprecedented new powers and, for the first time, radical new social treatments were put in place, which took their therapeutic value not from drugs and other medical interventions, but from the study of social relationships.[25] It is surprising, therefore, that only a few monographs have been written on war neurosis in this period, particularly so considering the vast literature on shell-shock in the First World War.[26] *Captives of War* contributes to this limited literature by exploring both how men experienced psychological disturbances in the Second World War and how army psychiatrists conceived of them. This book also adds to our understanding of the return and reintegration of British service personnel at the end of the war. Historian Alan Allport's work, *Demobbed*, shows how ex-servicemen's homecoming in Britain was often clouded with ambivalence, regrets and fears. He includes a limited discussion of ex-POWs.[27]

Finally, *Captives of War* speaks to, and has drawn upon, a body of literature that is vast but less easy to delineate. It includes studies of

---

[25] Nafsika Thalassis, 'Treating and Preventing Trauma: British Military Psychiatry during the Second World War', unpublished PhD thesis, University of Salford (2004), pp. 4, 191.

[26] Thalassis, 'Treating and Preventing Trauma'; Hazel Croft, 'War Neurosis and Civilian Mental Health in Britain during the Second World War', unpublished PhD thesis, Birkbeck College, University of London (2016); Michal Shapira, *The War Inside. Psychoanalysis, Total War, and the Making of the Democratic Self in Postwar Britain* (Cambridge: Cambridge University Press, 2013). Studies tend to look at specific aspects of military psychiatry in the Second World War or treat the subject as part of a more general examination of war neuroses in the twentieth century. For specific aspects, on personnel selection, see Jeremy A. Crang, *The British Army and the People's War* (Manchester: Manchester University Press, 2000); on psychiatrists' role in controlling combatants' fear reactions, see Joanna Bourke, 'Disciplining the Emotions: Fear, Psychiatry and the Second World War', in Roger Cooter et al. (eds.), *War, Medicine and Modernity* (Stroud: Sutton Publishing, 1998), pp. 225–38; on the work of the Tavistock Group and practitioners of group therapy, particularly at the Northfield Military Hospital, see Tom Harrison, *Bion, Rickman, Foulkes and the Northfield Experiments. Advancing on a Different Front* (London: Jessica Kingsley Publishers, 2000), p. 266. For general histories, see Hans Binneveld, *From Shellshock to Combat Stress. A Comparative History of Military Psychiatry* (Amsterdam: Amsterdam University Press, 1997); Wendy Holden, *Shell Shock* (London: Channel 4 Books, 1998); Edgar Jones and Simon Wessely, *Shell Shock to PTSD. Military Psychiatry from 1900 to the Gulf War* (Hove: Psychology Press, 2005); Shephard, *A War of Nerves*.

[27] Alan Allport, *Demobbed: Coming Home after World War Two* (New Haven, CT: Yale University Press, 2009). See also Julie Summers, *Stranger in the House: Women's Stories of Men Returning from the Second World War* (London: Simon and Schuster, 2008).

mental landscapes, emotional experiences, subjectivities and personal narratives or, in the words of Iris Rachamimov, studies that explore how 'reality is subjectively perceived and interpreted' by individuals, as accessed through their personal writings or recollections.[28] Historian Alexandra Garbarini's analysis of how Jewish people used diaries to make meaning of and understand their experiences of the war, plus the work of literary scholar Carol Acton on wartime diaries as a site for understanding an individual's experience of war, has been particularly relevant to this study.[29]

In these ways, *Captives of War* contributes to histories of captivity, the cultural history of warfare and studies of personal narratives. The way in which I have approached and analysed POWs' personal narratives, as the basis of this book, is discussed more fully in the next section.

The Personal Narratives of British Prisoners of War

The personal narratives that British POWs composed whilst imprisoned fall into three broad genres. The first is correspondence. Article 36 of the 1929 Geneva Convention stipulated that 'each of the belligerents shall fix periodically the number of letters and postcards which prisoners of war of different categories shall be permitted to send per month.'[30] Following the efforts of the ICRC to ensure POWs were allowed to send a 'reasonable' monthly quota of letters and postcards, each was entitled to a minimum of two letters and four postcards from 1940 until the end of the war. Each letter-form consisted of twenty-six lines; a postcard of seven [Figure 0.2]. German censorship of POWs' letters and postcards required them to refrain from any mention of their camp conditions, otherwise these sections were liable to be blacked out.[31] The letters and postcards POWs sent home often covered a variety of subjects. Those recurring included: the weather, activities in captivity, health, reassurances over their living conditions, housekeeping matters, longing for home, their reticence to fully express themselves (since censors would be reading

---

[28] Rachamimov, *POWs and the Great War*, p. 17.

[29] Alexandra Garbarini, *Numbered Days. Diaries and the Holocaust* (New Haven, CT: Yale University Press, 2006); Carol Acton, '"Stepping into History": Reading the Second World War through Irish Women's Diaries', *Irish Studies Review*, 18, 1 (2010), 39–56; see also Carol Acton and Jane Potter, '"These Frightful Sights Would Work Havoc with One's Brain": Subjective Experience, Trauma, and Resilience in First World War Writings by Medical Personnel', *Literature and Medicine*, 30, 1 (2012), 61–85.

[30] Article 36, 'Convention Relative to the Treatment of Prisoners of War', Geneva, 27 July 1929, www.icrc.org/ihl.nsf/FULL/305?OpenDocument, last accessed 8 February 2013.

[31] 'Camp Standing Orders Oflag VIIIB', September 1942, in NAM 2001-09-300, private papers of Second Lieutenant A. R. Jabez-Smith.

Figure 0.2: Letters and postcards sent home by Major George Matthews. Each prisoner of war was entitled to send home a minimum of two letters and four postcards from 1940 until the end of the war. Each letter-form (shown on the left) consisted of twenty-six lines and was then folded up into an envelope (top right). A postcard consisted of seven lines (middle right), with the address on the opposite side (bottom right).

Source: IWM 03/12/1, Major G. B. Matthews, letters to his family. Reproduced with permission from Gillian Stein.

the letters) and not knowing what to write about. POWs would also often list the letters and postcards they had so far received plus the parcels that had arrived in the camps. British POWs received four types of parcels. Red Cross food parcels were supplied from Britain, the United States and all the Commonwealth countries. These, as well as bulk supplies delivered from the British community in Argentina, brought them perishables, such as condensed milk, biscuits, sugar, jam, tea and oats.[32] Next-of-kin parcels, sent from the United Kingdom once every three months, included items such as blankets, books, toothpaste, soap and chocolate.[33] Cigarette parcels could be sent to British POWs through any English firm which held a government permit for such exports, as well as the Red Cross.[34] Those who had the money and contacts, which were mostly officers, could also purchase additional food parcels and have them sent from neutral countries.[35]

The second genre of personal narrative written in captivity was the logbook, which was akin to a scrapbook [Figure 0.3]. These almost always took the form of a small, hard-backed notebook, consisting of 112 pages, with the title 'A Wartime Log' on its cover. They were issued to many British POWs by the Young Men's Christian Association (YMCA) in Geneva in the final year of the war: prior to this, Canadian and American editions had been distributed in POW camps. Inside the logbook was a letter suggesting several ways in which the logbook might be used: to write a diary, short stories or letters to loved ones; to draw sketches or caricatures of important personalities; to store recipes; to record sporting achievements; to collate poetry and jokes or to collect autographs of fellow POWs. The logbooks could also be used to hold photographs. These might be of loved ones at home, which relatives were permitted to post to POWs, or of fellow prisoners and other aspects of camp life, which had been taken by the Germans and were given to prisoners for them to send home (see, for example, Figures 0.1, 0.3, 3.4, 3.5, 3.6).[36] The Germans realised that pictures of POWs enjoying themselves or looking healthy made good

---

[32] W. Wynne Mason, *Prisoners of War. Official History of New Zealand in the Second World War 1939–45* (London: Oxford University Press, 1954), p. 99; Gilbert, *POW*, pp. 100–1, Peter Doyle, *Prisoner of War in Germany* (Oxford: Shire Publications, 2008), p. 17.

[33] TNA CUST 106/369, 'Communication with Prisoners of War Interned Abroad', General Post Office, December 1940. For a full list of permissible and prohibited items, see 'Communication with Prisoners of War and Civilians Interned in Europe (Leaflet P 2280E)', General Post Office, May 1943, in IWM 61/161/1, private papers of Warrant Officer H. L. Hurrell.

[34] Mason, *Prisoners of War*, p. 47; Doyle, *Prisoner of War in Germany*, p. 23.

[35] For a summary of the various schemes that enabled POWs to do this, see Wylie, *Barbed Wire Diplomacy*, pp. 98–100.

[36] On photographs posted to prisoners of war from home, see Chapter 4.

Figure 0.3: Logbooks POWs kept in captivity. Many POWs kept
'A Wartime Log' in captivity. These small, hard-backed notebooks
consisted of 112 pages. They were used for a variety of purposes. Here
can be seen how Lieutenant Robert Johnson used one page for a sketch
of his camp (top left). There were cardboard pages in the middle of the
logbook to hold photographs (bottom left).

Source: (from top left clockwise) IWM Documents.9020, Lieutenant
R. G. Johnson, logbook; IWM 61/157/1, Flight Sergeant J. H. Beddis,
logbook; IWM 61/161/1, Warrant Officer H. L. Hurrell, logbook.
Reproduced with permission from James Johnson, Peter Beddis and
Vicky Briggs.

propaganda.[37] There were cardboard pages in the middle of the logbook to hold these photographs, and mounting-corners were provided

[37] Doyle, *Prisoner of War in Germany*, p. 38; Bob Moore and Barbara Hately, 'Captive
Audience: Camp Entertainment and British Prisoners-of-War in German Captivity,
1939–1945', *Popular Entertainment Studies*, 5, 1 (2014), 61.

in a pocket attached to the back cover. This pocket, as well as small envelopes on the last page, could also be used to store clippings and souvenirs of life in the camps.

Whilst there is, of course, individual variation between the contents of letters that POWs wrote home and the logbooks they kept, there is much consistency within each of these two genres. All POWs' letters cover broadly similar topics and their intended audience is clear, as they were written to named individuals. Almost all the contents of logbooks conformed to the suggestions made by the YMCA and they were largely compiled for posterity, whether for the future self or an external audience to read. By contrast, the final genre of personal narrative kept by POWs during captivity, the diary, is far more heterogeneous. A diary is defined here as a personal narrative in which dated entries were written progressively.[38] Very few POWs kept diaries prior to capture and many started writing them in the weeks or months following their capture, or at some other stage of their imprisonment, the significance of which will be discussed in the next chapter. The contents of POW diaries vary so extensively, due both to the writers' purposes for keeping them and the audiences for which they were written, that, possibly, they should not even be described as a single genre.[39] POWs' diaries can be grouped into three very different types.

The first type is what I call unvarnished diaries. In these diaries, individual entries are brief and often consist of a few incomplete sentences. The POW provides a largely objective record of daily events in the camps, such as when he woke up, had appell (a daily or twice-daily roll call), his rations, the arrival of letters and parcels, the weather, the latest rumours, war news and his working detail. The activities of captivity being recorded are almost entirely uninterpreted. Events are briefly stated, even when they cry out for further comment, such as the 27 March 1942 entry in Gunner Donald Cooper's diary, which is one of the diaries drawn upon in this book: 'Man from 20 Batt. shot dead for refusing to wheel a barrow which he considered too heavy.'[40] These

---

[38] This definition allows for the fact that often diary writers do not record the events of a day on the same day as they occurred, but often write up entries for a number of days in one sitting, a practice that POWs also took part in, Garbarini, *Numbered Days*, p. 16.

[39] On the need for scholars to start considering diaries as a form which can be further divided into a number of genres, see Rebecca Hogan, 'Engendered Autobiographies: The Diary as a Feminine Form', in Shirley Neuman (ed.), *Autobiography and Questions of Gender* (London: Frank Cass & Co. Ltd, 1991), p. 97. On the significance of a diary's audience, see Margo Culley, 'Introduction', in Margo Culley (ed.), *A Day at a Time. The Diary Literature of American Women from 1764 to the Present* (New York: The Feminist Press at the City University of New York, 1985), pp. 11–12.

[40] IWM Department of Documents, 75/71/1, Mrs D. Cooper, D. R. Cooper, diary entry, 27 March 1942.

diaries are also very private. The diarist often does not provide any context to his entry, nor introduce the characters being referenced, indicating he is only writing for himself and not with an external audience in mind.[41]

The second type of diary is the documentary-style diary. In this diary, entries tend to be long, descriptive and written for a wide audience. They often describe how the diarist was initially captured, the conditions he endured during his first weeks or months in captivity, the physical environment of the camp and the activities taking place there. These diaries are written in a manner that is designed to inform a reader ignorant of POW life. Often the dated entries are also given headings, indicating the diarist's attempt to help his audience navigate the diary's contents. This type of diary frequently occurs when entries are written up retrospectively, from a time later on in captivity. Like the unvarnished diary, there is very little explicit reflection on the meaning or significance of the events or aspects of captivity being recorded.

Conversely, the final type of diary kept by prisoners of war consists of what I call reflective diaries. In these, the diarist often used his entries not just to describe what is happening in captivity, but to comment and reflect on it. For example, when explaining the rations POWs received, the diarist might have also discussed his longing for food or, when noting the arrival of letters or parcels, articulated their importance in POWs' lives. The subject matter in reflective diaries is not confined to the present conditions of camp life: these diarists often mused on past experiences, both in captivity and prior to it, and they imagined how their future life would unfold, or wondered what their friends and family, outside the barbed wire, were doing in the present.

More so than the unvarnished diaries, these reflective diaries were written for an audience, but the audience is more variable than in the documentary-style diary. Some reflective diaries are explicitly written for a relative to read and, in these cases, the tone and content of the diary entries are not dissimilar from letters. Second Lieutenant Francis Stewart is the author of one such diary cited frequently in *Captives of War*. He addressed the preface of his diary to his parents and sister, telling them:

---

[41] On unvarnished diaries, see Lynn Z. Bloom, '"I Write for Myself and Strangers": Private Diaries as Public Documents', in Suzanne L. Bunkers and Cynthia A. Huff (eds.), *Inscribing the Daily: Critical Essays on Women's Diaries* (Amherst: University of Massachusetts Press, 1996), pp. 25–7. There are similarities between this type of diary and the 'ordinary' diary; see Alison Twells, '"Went into Raptures": Reading Emotion in the Ordinary Wartime Diary, 1941–1946', *Women's History Review*, 25, 1 (2015), 143–60.

Knowing only too well that I am not an Evelyn or a Pepys I can start off with the certainty that my innermost thoughts will not be laid before the public gaze for all to mock. ... My intention is mainly to write a diary addressed personally to you. ... As you know, with the number of letters I'm allowed to write I can never tell you half of what I want to, so, if you like, you can regard this as a day to day letter.[42]

Others personify their diary, writing in it as if they were speaking to a neutral confidante to whom they were able to open up candidly. In these cases, the diary can be considered, as literary scholar Helen Wilcox describes it, one of the 'most intimate of written forms'.[43] These prisoners told their diaries things that they would not or could not tell another human being.

This variation within POWs' diaries has dictated which individual personal narratives have been used in *Captives of War*. Out of the three types of diary, I most frequently selected reflective ones, since they provide the greatest access to POWs' inner worlds. The others occasionally feature. The brief and objective entries of the unvarnished diary might initially appear unenlightening, but, when examined in the context of the entire narrative, individual entries can take on a particular significance or meaning. For example, on the rare occasion that the diarist accorded a particular topic a few words of reflection, or when he used a different type of formatting for a specific entry, or when the same subject was discussed across a number of entries, it reveals much about the importance of that aspect of captivity to the diarist. It is also important to point out that diaries do not consistently fall into one of these types. Often the POW kept a different type of diary during different periods of his incarceration, a practice explored later in this book.[44] Since there is much more consistency within the genres of correspondence and logbooks, I selected those that feature in *Captives of War* on a more random basis, although I did choose collections of correspondence where there was a large number of letters written by the same POW, since this would enable a better picture of that individual's life, both inside and outside captivity, to be built up.[45] These collections tended to be written to a wife

---

[42] IWM 88/20/1, Second Lieutenant F. J. Stewart, diary, preface.

[43] Helen Wilcox, 'Civil War Letters and Diaries and the Rhetoric of Experience', in Laura Lunger Knoppers (ed.), *The Oxford Handbook of Literature and the English Revolution* (Oxford: Oxford University Press, 2012), p. 243.

[44] See Hogan, 'Engendered Autobiographies', p. 97.

[45] Of the collections of correspondence that form the basis of this book, the most substantial collection is that of Captain Mansel, who wrote 286 letters to his family, then Greaser Bloss' 223 letters to his newly wedded wife, followed by Major Matthews's 176 letters to his wife and two daughters. The shortest run of letters was written by Squadron Leader Armitage to his mother, numbering just eleven. This discrepancy will be due more to how

or a parent or, more occasionally, to a sweetheart, a sibling, or a son or daughter back home.

Drawing upon reflective diaries, as well as logbooks and the more substantial collections of correspondence, has resulted in this book focussing more on officers, warrant officers and senior non-commissioned officers (NCOs) than junior NCOs and privates, or those of equivalent status.[46] There is a number of reasons for this. Officers were entitled to send more letters home than the other ranks. Those below the rank of officer sent two letters and four postcards home a month; officers were allocated an extra one or two. Protected personnel – those men who had been captured whilst engaged exclusively in non-combatant duties, namely medical and religious personnel – were given double the number due to a combatant of equivalent rank.[47] As a result of this, and because more letters written by officers seem to have been preserved in public archives, officers were the correspondents in more than half of all the collections of letters I have explored, despite making up a small minority of all British prisoners.[48] Reflective diaries and logbooks were also more likely to be written by officers: a significant reason for this was that they, along with warrant officers and senior NCOs, had time to write these narratives as, according to the Geneva Convention, they were not permitted to be put to work.[49] There may be a few other reasons why officers predominate as the authors of reflective diaries. Their better education and literary abilities probably enabled them to be more articulate. Their senior ranking might also have granted them a greater sense of self-worth: literary scholar Margo Culley has argued that keeping a diary always begins with a 'sense of self-worth,

___

many letters were preserved by Armitage's family or subsequently handed over to the SWWEC than how many he actually wrote.

[46] For a list of the ranks in the British Army, RAF, Royal Navy and Merchant Navy, and how the POWs who feature in *Captives of War* fit into these hierarchies, see Appendix 1.

[47] *Report of the International Committee of the Red Cross on Its Activities during the Second World War*, September 1939 to 30 June 1947, vol. I (Geneva: International Committee of the Red Cross, 1948), pp. 348–9; letter from Swiss Legation, acting as Protecting Power to British Man of Confidence, Stalag IVC, 15 May 1943 in IWM 01/8/1, private papers of R. A. Hilton.

[48] This figure ranges from 4.5 per cent to 8 per cent. For the 4.5 per cent figure, see TNA PIN 15/3444, 'Medical Examination of Repatriated Prisoners of War', letter from War Office to General Officers Commanding-in-Chief and General Officers Commanding, 21 December 1944; for the 8 per cent figure, see TNA WO 32/10757, Secret Working Paper (44) 456, War Cabinet, 'Rehabilitation of Returned Prisoners of War', Memorandum by the Secretary of State for War, 22 August 1944.

[49] Of the logbooks drawn upon in this research, eleven were written by officers, four by warrant officers, three by senior NCOs, two by junior NCOs and five by servicemen without rank. Of the diaries: sixteen were written by officers, four by warrant officers, three by senior NCOs, six by junior NCOs and eleven by servicemen without rank.

a conviction that one's individual experience is somehow *remark*able.'[50] This sense of self-worth would explain why officers, compared to other ranks, were more likely to write diaries aimed at a public audience. In other words, they were more likely to write a reflective or documentary-style diary than an unvarnished one. If we also consider that officers in the Second World War were most likely to be drawn from the middle or upper classes, this discrepancy might also be attributed to a reflective life being a predominantly middle-class ideal during this era whilst amongst the working class, there was a tradition of keeping the most intimate matters hidden in the narrative form.[51]

This focus on officers, warrant officers and senior NCOs has resulted in many of the experiences described in this book taking place in central POW camps, rather than the work or satellite camps, where prisoners led a very different existence. There were 248 central camps in Germany and seventy-two in Italy.[52] In both countries, they tended to take one of two physical forms. Some were purpose-built constructions of barrack huts surrounded by a double barbed-wire fence, dotted with observation towers [Figure 0.4].[53] This type of construction is famously depicted in the film *The Great Escape*. These camps typically housed many thousands of men, the largest being divided into compounds.[54] Other permanent camps were located in commandeered buildings, such as regional palaces, schools, convents, fortresses and castles. The most famous of these was Oflag IVC, more commonly known as Colditz Castle, located in Saxony in eastern Germany. The capacity of these buildings was often then augmented by adding sub-camps, huts and other temporary structures. Immediately upon capture, officers were separated from NCOs and privates and segregated in different camps throughout their imprisonment. The central camps in Germany that housed officers were known as Oflags (short for *Offizierlager*, meaning a camp for officers); Stalags (short for *Stammlager*, meaning 'main camp' or 'root camp') housed those without commissions. These camps were usually defined by a Roman numeral and a letter: the Roman numeral indicated the military district to which the camp was attached, with the letter differentiating the various camps in the same district. Some had an Arabic number, either because they were situated

---

[50] Culley, 'Introduction', p. 8.

[51] Historians have made this argument regarding the First World War, and my analysis of POW diaries suggests it could be applicable to the Second; see Woollacott, 'Sisters and Brothers in Arms', pp. 142–3, Jessica Meyer, *Men of War: Masculinity and the First World War in Britain* (Basingstoke: Palgrave Macmillan, 2009), p. 48.

[52] Gilbert, *POW*, p. 66.

[53] Doyle, *Prisoner of War in Germany*, pp. 9–11; Gilbert, *POW*, p. 69.

[54] MacKenzie, *The Colditz Myth*, pp. 265–6.

Figure 0.4: Stalag 383 (Hohenfels) in Bavaria, south-eastern Germany, c. 1943. Purpose-built camps consisted of barrack huts. The barbed-wire fencing and guard towers can be seen in the distance.
Source: Australian War Memorial.

outside the Reich's military districts or so they could be shifted from district to district with ease, though commonly they stayed put.[55] In Italy, central camps were referred to as campo PG, short for *Campo concentramento di prigionieri di guerra*. Each camp was initially distinguished by its place name, but, from early 1942, they were given an Arabic number as well.[56] In Italy, some camps were assigned for officers, but, in other cases, officers were separated from other ranks by being placed in different compounds within the same camp.[57]

On average, each prisoner who appears in this book passed through four main camps whilst in captivity. Consequently, a significant number of these central camps is mentioned in this book (Figure 0.5). The twenty-two men appearing in the following pages, who spent their first few months or years in captivity in Italy, were held in one quarter of

---

[55] For example, in October 1943, Stalag VIIIB in Lamsdorf became Stalag 344, and the designation 'VIIIB' was passed to another camp at Teschen in the same military district; see Peter Monteath, *P.O.W. Australian Prisoners of War in Hitler's Reich* (Sydney: Macmillan, 2011), p. 142.

[56] Mason, *Prisoners of War*, p. 112.

[57] Mason, *Prisoners of War*, p. 112; Gilbert, *POW*, pp. 66–7.

Figure 0.5: Map showing German and Italian prisoner-of-war camps, 1939–45. In total, there were seventy-two camps in Italy for Allied POWs and 134 camps in Germany which housed British and American prisoners.

Source: CartoGIS, College of Asia and the Pacific, The Australian National University.

the seventy-two camps for Allied POWs.[58] The seventy-three POWs in Germany experienced almost half of the 134 camps that could have potentially housed them.[59] Together, these seventy-five men composed forty diaries, twenty-five logbooks and twenty-six collections of correspondence during their time in captivity, which form the basis of Chapters 1 to 6.[60] The contents of these chapters explore not the aspects of captivity that I thought were most interesting or important, but the experiences and features of wartime imprisonment that most commonly recur in these personal narratives and, therefore, were most interesting or important to the captive men.

This book draws only upon POWs' personal narratives composed at the time of captivity. For a number of reasons, these narratives provide us with an insight into how prisoners of war experienced captivity as they lived through it, in a way in which memoirs and oral histories do not. Diaries, letters and logbooks were written as the experience unfolded, at a series of moments, over a period of time, whilst these men were in the midst of both a shifting war situation and changing personal relationships, without an awareness of how the war would finally end.[61] As a result, these narratives capture all that was important, interesting and significant about captivity for their authors, even as this changed from month to month.[62] Memoirs, by contrast, are written from a vantage point of knowing how the experience unfolded and eventually ended. Their contents almost always have a clear, linear chronology and they document only what was important about captivity from the vantage point from which they were written. This latter point is illustrated by the way in which POWs' attitude towards homecoming features in their memoirs. Chapter 1 discusses the highly optimistic attitude POWs held during captivity towards their release: they believed they would return home imminently, following an Allied victory. In memoirs, this optimism is frequently replaced by pessimism, with ex-prisoners emphasising the indefinite nature of their imprisonment, because they, unlike the POWs

---

[58] In Italy, by September 1943, seventy-two POW camps held Allied POWs, of which British and Commonwealth POWs made up the bulk; see Gilbert, *POW*, p. 66.

[59] There were 248 in Germany, 134 of which housed British and American prisoners; see Gilbert, *POW*, p. 66.

[60] In the case of fifteen POWs, more than one of their personal narratives have been included. Appendix 2 lists all the men whose letters, diaries and logbooks have been drawn upon in this book and provides details of their background, date and place of capture and POW camps in which they were held.

[61] Acton, 'Stepping into History', 40, 48; Harriet Blodgett, 'Preserving the Moment in the Diary of Margaret Fountaine', in Suzanne L. Bunkers and Cynthia A. Huff (eds.), *Inscribing the Daily. Critical Essays on Women's Diaries* (Amherst: University of Massachusetts Press, 1996), p. 156.

[62] Hogan, 'Engendered Autobiographies', pp. 103–5.

who were writing at the time of captivity, knew how protracted their imprisonment ultimately was.[63]

The ways in which diaries and letters 'touch time' also means they recorded certain details of captivity that are almost always absent in retrospectively written POW narratives. Sociologist Michael Flaherty's theoretical interpretation of the lived experience of time sets out how individuals who pass what can be described as 'empty' time actually fill it with thoughts, feelings or fantasies about their circumstances.[64] The reflective diaries of POWs are filled precisely with such musings. These are then both impossible and pointless to recall. Two diaries, kept by Corporal Eric Barrington and Captain Richard Angove, which feature heavily in this book, illustrate this point. As mentioned, and discussed more fully in Chapter 1, many POWs wrote up their initial few weeks or months in captivity retrospectively, often starting their contemporary account when they reached their first permanent camp or when they first had access to paper. In such cases, there is a clear shift in the type of diary they wrote. The first nine months of Barrington's diary were written retrospectively and take the form of a documentary-style diary. From 1 January 1943, when he is writing contemporaneously, the diary becomes reflective.[65] In other words, even diarists who had a tendency and desire to write reflectively did not do so retrospectively. Also, part of the reason why reflective diarists recorded their thoughts, feelings or fantasies was to help them to manage the experience of captivity. Angove, as will be shown in Chapter 4, regularly used his diary to fantasise about returning home. This allowed him to 'get away from the atmosphere' of his POW camp. Yet, one day after writing about one such fantasy, he described his entry as 'drivel'.[66] Just twenty-four hours later, he thought the diary entry was nonsense. It is highly unlikely, therefore, thirty or forty years on, he would have chosen to highlight those same thoughts in a memoir.

The ways in which diaries, letters and logbooks could interact with the experiences being recounted also sets them apart from retrospectively

---

[63] This finding is based on a random sample of fifty memoirs held at the Imperial War Museum, London.

[64] Michael G. Flaherty, 'The Erotics and Hermeneutics of Temporality', in Carolyn Ellis and Michael G. Flaherty (eds.), *Investigating Subjectivity. Research on Lived Experience* (Newbury Park: Sage Publications, 1992), pp. 147, 152–3. On diaries 'touching time', see Philippe Lejeune, *On Diary*, edited by Jeremy D. Popkin and Julie Rak, translated by Katherine Durnin (Manoa: University of Hawaii, 2009), p. 209.

[65] IWM 88/58/1(P), Corporal E. Barrington, diary. See also IWM 86/89/1, Lieutenant W. M. G. Bompas, diary: the first section (contained in 'A Wartime Log') is a retrospective documentary-style diary written for friends and families. When Bompas started writing his diary contemporaneously from 29 August 1944, it became reflective.

[66] IWM 66/174/1, Captain R. L. Angove, diary entries, 30–1 August 1942.

written narratives. Confiding to a reflective diary, as Chapter 3 discusses, could be therapeutic, a means of venting exasperations, which then made communal living more bearable.[67] The same chapter shows how log-books were a site where male bonding took place. Writing a letter or a diary entry that was addressed to a loved one at home, as Chapter 4 reveals, made POWs feel closer to them. In this way, the act of keeping a personal narrative in captivity could alter the actual experience of captivity as it happened and shape the relationships contained within it.[68]

Memoirs may also offer the historian unique insights into how wartime imprisonment was experienced, whether because censorship prevented a full and frank discussion of life in captivity or because, with the passage of time, the author became able to better articulate and construct a coherent narrative of what he went through.[69] However, it is impossible to separate any such insights that memoirs offer from how those events have subsequently been interpreted through the filter of memory. Individuals come to think about periods of their past in different ways from how they did at the time, whether because they now know how those episodes ended or because of the experiences they had and the knowledge they gained in the intervening years.[70] Individual memories also evolve in dialogue with the wider cultural context. In relation to British POWs in Europe, that context, influencing individual memories, has been domi-nated by a plethora of books, films and television series on POW escapes.[71] Psychologists agree that the principal function of a memory may not even be to record the past, but to enable an individual to generate meaning in life in the present.[72] These functions of memory not only influence the shape and contents of memoirs, but can also lead memoir-ists to misremember the past. For these reasons, if memoirs were to be used in this study, they would need to be analysed as sources that are revealing both for life in captivity and life afterwards, with an awareness that the two sometimes mesh together in indiscernible ways.

---

[67] For the act of writing sometimes being 'therapeutic', see Acton and Potter, 'These Frightful Sights Would Work Havoc with One's Brain', 74.

[68] Culley, 'Introduction', p. 14.   [69] Roper, *The Secret Battle*, p. 21.

[70] Alan Allport, *Browned Off and Bloody-Minded: The British Soldier Goes to War 1939–1945* (New Haven, CT: Yale University Press, 2015), p. xvii.

[71] Joan Beaumont, Lachlan Grant and Aaron Pegram, 'Remembering and Rethinking Captivity', in Joan Beaumont, Lachlan Grant and Aaron Pegram (eds.), *Beyond Surrender. Australian Prisoners of War in the Twentieth Century* ([e-book] Carlton, Victoria: Melbourne University Press, 2015), unpaginated. Amongst such films are *The Wooden Horse* (Canal +, 1950), *The Colditz Story* (Ivan Foxwell Productions, 1955), *The Great Escape* (MGM Studios, 1963) and *Colditz* (BBC and Universal TV, 1972–4).

[72] Martin A. Conway, Lucy V. Justice and Catriona M. Morrison, 'Beliefs about Autobiographical Memory . . . and Why They Matter', *The Psychologist*, 27, 7 (2014), 505.

As *Captives of War* is concerned with understanding how POWs experienced captivity at the time of imprisonment, I have drawn only upon personal narratives composed during wartime incarceration. As a result, this book highlights a number of aspects of the POW mind-set that have, so far, been misunderstood, side-lined or overlooked by the histories that do not distinguish between contemporary and retrospective sources. *Captives of War* also seeks to convey these men's experiences with some of the rawness and emotion that comes through so palpably in personal narratives composed during captivity, written whilst these men were vulnerable to their conditions, as compared to memoirs, which were composed in the knowledge that they had survived them.

POWs' personal narratives form the basis of Chapters 1 to 6. Alongside these, I have drawn upon contemporary psychiatric research and reports written by other POWs, military personnel and the ICRC and Protecting Powers.[73] Since POWs ceased writing their personal narratives around the time of liberation, Chapter 7, which explores the homecoming of POWs, is based almost entirely on medical papers and reports psychiatrists produced during the war and in its immediate aftermath. As explained in this chapter, it would be wrong to assume that the medical officers and psychiatrists' observations and diagnoses provide accurate portrayals of the attitudes of ex-prisoners of war, but they do provide insight into some of the emotional difficulties these men faced.

Chapter Outline

Chapter 1 explores the moment of capture. It sets out when and how the majority of British POWs, including the men who feature in *Captives of War*, were taken prisoner, and examines how they made sense of the moment of their surrender. It looks first at the moment of capture as signalling an end to combat duties, and demonstrates POWs' need to impress upon their readers that they were not personally culpable for their defeat. It then examines capture as the start of these men's imprisoned existence. Only retrospectively did British POWs come to see their

---

[73] Some caution does need to be exercised regarding the accuracy of these reports written on the individual POW camps. As the war progressed, the expectations of the ICRC and Protecting Power delegates who visited the camps were reduced; thus what might have been unsatisfactory became good, but as historian Vasilis Vourkoutiotis has pointed out, no other source of information provides as comprehensive a coverage of the camps over the course of the war years. The standards to which inspectors were prepared to hold the detaining powers also slid downwards and inspectors themselves also had to balance varying pressures from the home power, detaining power and even their own organisation, Vasilis Vourkoutiotis, *Prisoners of War and the German High Command: The British and American Experience* (Basingstoke: Palgrave Macmillan, 2003), pp. 8–9.

capture as creating a permanent rupture in their lives. The chapter shows how these men held a remarkably optimistic view: of the war ending imminently following an Allied victory.

Chapters 2 to 5 focus on different themes of imprisonment. Chapter 2 explores how POWs made sense of being incarcerated by their enemy. It initially examines how British POWs responded to being out of the war and controlled by their enemy and goes on to show how POWs made sense of some of the other outstanding features of their confinement: living in enemy territory as well as existing in a restricted space, under impoverished conditions and facing empty time. The chapter presents the upbeat view of captivity POWs formed in their personal narratives; how they defied the captor–captive power relationship, how they followed 'normal' routines and activities in captivity as well as how they created their own unique identity. But, even within this positive picture, there are hints that these men did not feel as empowered as they suggest. These intimations are built on in the final section of the chapter. By highlighting POWs' use of metaphors of emasculation, the moments when they con-cluded the experience had been worthless and declared it would never be understood, the chapter also paints a bleaker picture of how these men came to terms with their predicament of being imprisoned servicemen.

The next chapter, 'Bonds between Men', examines how POWs responded to their crowded, all-male society. First, it looks at the personal relationships prisoners formed with each other and how these were strained by captivity. Then, it turns to how POWs bonded at a broader level, and argues the hardships these men suffered whilst behind barbed wire did not create group solidarity. Both sections also demonstrate the different ways in which the writing of letters, diaries and logbooks helped POWs to make sense of their relationships, and so shaped, rather than simply recorded, their experience of captivity. Finally, the chapter looks at how POWs responded specifically to the homosocial environment of captivity by focussing on their reactions to female impersonators. These responses demonstrate the fluidity of heterosexual and homoerotic rela-tions, both in captivity and in society beyond.

Chapter 4, 'Ties with Home', argues one of the primary ways in which POWs made sense of their captivity was to look beyond the barbed wire and to turn towards their loved ones at home. Home provided British POWs with a crucial source of emotional and physical strength, through the photographs, letters and parcels sent into camps, as well as through fantasies prisoners created. Yet, at the same time, the very dependence POWs had on home resulted in a reconfiguration of familial and gender roles. Loved ones at home made POWs conscious of how they had shed their masculine roles of protector, provider and procreator. This chapter shows how prisoners' emotional proximity to their loved ones helped them to endure captivity, but also hindered them in their ability to make sense of their imprisonment.

Chapter 5 looks at what happened to POWs when, in a sense, they could find no meaning in their experiences: at those who went 'round the bend', as these men referred to it. The chapter initially provides a brief overview of the research carried out into the mental effects of captivity during the First World War to understand how they were initially recognised and conceived. It then goes on to explore the psychological disturbances experienced by British POWs held in Germany and Italy in the Second World War. It looks at the causes and symptoms of these disturbances, their prognosis and finally the treatment of those who were either mildly or more acutely affected. At least a significant minority of POWs suffered some form of psychological disturbance during their time in captivity, and a remarkably sympathetic and permissive context developed in the POW camp. This enabled POWs to refer to how they were going 'round the bend', but their disturbances remained very ill-defined.

A brief chapter on liberation then concludes this examination of life during captivity. It sets out how prisoners represented, in their diaries, their final few months of imprisonment and the difficulty these men had in articulating the feelings that accompanied their release; instead, their excitement can be found in the way in which they formatted their diary entries. The chapter also looks at how and when these men ended their diaries, and so how they brought their narratives on their captive lives to a close.

Chapter 7 examines POWs' lives after captivity. The chapter shows that some of the ways in which POWs had coped with and made sense of captivity caused them difficulties once back in their military service or when they returned to their civilian lives. These were compounded by practical problems, such as demotion and reallocation. There were few psychiatric casualties amongst ex-POWs, and evidence even suggests that those men who attended Civil Resettlement Units, set up by the government to help former POWs adjust to civilian life, showed greater adaptability and co-operation in their relationships than those who had not experienced captivity. However, overall, the consequences of captivity were not well acknowledged and shrouded with ambiguity, in the language used by officials and psychiatrists, as well as by POWs themselves.

This monograph ends with a brief concluding chapter that draws out a number of historical lessons. These relate to how historians might revise the ways in which they consider the experience of captivity, draw upon personal narratives, approach the cultural history of warfare more generally and their current understandings of social and gender conventions in mid-twentieth-century Britain.

*****

In 2012 my grandfather died. During the final three years of his life, he commented on early drafts of some of my chapters. He affirmed a number of my findings, but, quite quickly, it became apparent to me that the story I was telling had very little to do with him. 'Never heard of it' was a response I all too frequently got, even though I had read numerous accounts of that particular aspect of captivity in other POWs' testimonies. My grandfather never saw a theatre production put on in captivity, let alone a female impersonator. He was shocked at the number of parcels that some men received. He was staggered that I had found diaries in which POWs had written lengthy entries for practically every day they spent in captivity. 'What on earth did they write about?' he asked. His responses made me acutely aware, from early on, that this history of captivity could never presume to be representative of the experiences of all prisoners of war. Nor would I claim it to be representative of the experiences of those POWs whose narratives I have read. To do that, each would require a book of his own. *Captives of War* does, however, highlight aspects of the experience of captivity that have so far been under-researched, and so gives us a greater understanding of what it meant to be a prisoner of war, both during captivity and immediately afterwards.

1   Capture

> [S]o here we are captured within sight of home. I can honestly say
> without shame that I had tears in my eyes when I looked across that
> narrow stretch of water a prisoner of war after 3 weeks attempting to get
> home.

Private Ernest Abbott wrote these words at Calais on 20 June 1940,
following his capture at 3.30 p.m.[1] He was, quite literally, in sight of
home. His wife and two sons lived in the village of Capel-le-Ferne,
situated above the White Cliffs between Dover and Folkestone on the
Kent coast. Abbott, who had been recalled to the Army Reserve at the
outbreak of war, had spent the three weeks prior to 20 June in retreat,
along with the rest of the British Expeditionary Force, as it withdrew to
the beaches of northern France after Germany's successful invasion of
Western Europe.[2] Abbott went on to spend almost five years as a prisoner
of war. Abbott's diary entry is unique amongst those that feature in
Captives of War. Not only had he started keeping a diary before being
taken prisoner, but he provides some indication as to how he felt at the
moment of surrender. The majority of others started their diaries only
after having entered imprisonment and, in their accounts of capture, few
give any explicit indication of their feelings.

Initially this chapter sets out when and how the majority of British
POWs, including the men who feature in *Captives of War*, were taken
prisoner. It then examines how these men made sense of this moment.
Capture both signalled the end of one phase of the servicemen's war
experience and the start of another. When looked at as an end to their
combat duties, POWs' diaries reveal their need to demonstrate they were
not personally culpable for their defeat. When considered as the start of
something new, the structure of these men's personal narratives demonstrates how they came to see their capture as a rupture, or point of
transformation, in their lives. Yet to think of this transformation as

---

[1] NAM 2001-01-352-1, Private E. W. Abbott, diary entry, 20 June 1940.
[2] The British Expeditionary Force was the home-based British army forces that went to
northern France at the start of the Second World War.

happening at the point of surrender misunderstands the mentality of British servicemen captured in Europe. British POWs had a remarkably optimistic attitude towards the length and outcome of the war. They believed it would end imminently following an Allied victory.

Surrender in the Second World War

Harold Shipp, a leading telegraphist in the Royal Navy, was captured on 9 January 1940. He was thirty-one years old. His ship, HMS *Starfish*, was attacked by a German minesweeper during a war patrol in the North Sea. Shipp was one of just a few hundred British servicemen to be captured during the first few months of the Second World War, or what is known as the Phoney War, because there was little fighting during this period. By mid-April 1940, approximately fifteen other ranks from the army had been captured, twelve officers and twenty-four airmen from the Royal Air Force (RAF), and thirty-three officers and 182 ratings from the Merchant Navy and Royal Navy.[3]

In his first two years of captivity, Shipp was moved between six POW camps before finally being sent to Marlag-Milag Nord (Marine-Lager und Marine-Internierten-Lager), a camp specifically established to accommodate seafaring POWs, located in Westertimke in north-western Germany and run by the German navy. Shipp was held in Marlag, which accommodated those from the Royal Navy; Milag held those from the Merchant Navy. The Marlag and the Milag were physically separate, although on the same complex.[4] In 1944, Shipp compiled a logbook of his time behind barbed wire. Out of all the POWs whose personal narratives feature in the following pages, Shipp was the first to be taken prisoner. His logbook is one of twenty-five to be drawn upon in *Captives of War*.

The number of British servicemen taken prisoner dramatically changed with the end of the Phoney War. Norway was the first victim of Germany's Blitzkrieg, or lightning war, in Western Europe. During the winter of 1940, Germany had been flouting Norwegian neutrality by transporting Swedish iron ore, vital for the German war effort, from the port of Narvik to German North Sea ports. In response, Britain warned Norway that it planned to lay mines in her waters to force these German

---

[3] In February 1945, it was recorded that 266 British POWs who had been in captivity in mid-April 1940 were still in captivity. The actual number of men in captivity at this time is likely to be higher because some would probably have been repatriated by February 1945, see TNA, WO 32/10746, 'Prisoners of War Captured before 14 April 1940, Repatriation of Prisoners of War Who Have Been a Long Time in Captivity'.

[4] Monteath, *P. O. W.*, p. 155.

ships out to where they could be attacked. In February 1940, sailors from a British destroyer also violated Norwegian neutrality by boarding a German supply ship sheltering in Norwegian waters.[5] Adolf Hitler decided to pre-empt any Allied move in the area, and invaded Norway by sea and air on 9 April 1940. In response British forces were sent to Norway. This saw the first large cohort of British men taken prisoner. Amongst them were a naval officer, Lieutenant Commander Peter Buckley, and a merchant seaman, Greaser Claude Bloss. Buckley was captured after HMS *Shark*, which was under his command, was attacked whilst on patrol off the south-west of Norway. Buckley's logbook is another of the twenty-five drawn upon in this book, which he, like Shipp, compiled from the confines of Marlag. Bloss was captured on 8 June 1940, near Narvik. Being a civilian rather than a serviceman, he was not technically a prisoner of war but, like all merchant seamen captured by the Germans and Italians, was treated as such.[6] The letters and postcards Bloss wrote home and received during the following five years – 223 to his wife and 558 from her – form one of the twenty-six sets of correspondence referenced in *Captives of War*.

Germany's attacks on France, Belgium, the Netherlands and Luxembourg, which commenced on 10 May 1940, saw many more British servicemen fall into German hands. Approximately one third of all those who would ultimately find themselves behind barbed wire in Europe in the Second World War were captured during May and June 1940.[7] A similar proportion of the personal narratives that feature in the following pages were written by men taken prisoner at this time.[8] Amongst them was Captain John Mansel. Captured on 21 May 1940, Mansel started writing a diary ten days later. Over the following five years, he filled ten volumes of pocket diaries, exercise books and logbooks [Figure 1.1], and wrote more than 250 letters and postcards home, the vast majority addressed to his mother. The commentary Mansel produced whilst behind barbed wire, written in miniscule but beautiful manuscript, is, quite possibly, the most self-reflective of any prisoner of war. On days of

---

[5] Martin Gilbert, *The Second World War. A Complete History* (London: Phoenix, 2009), pp. 37, 42.

[6] TNA WO 366/26, Col. H. J. Phillimore, 'Prisoners of War', 1949, p. 70.

[7] Forty-four thousand eight hundred British men were captured at this point, out of a total of 142,319 men serving in the armed forces of the United Kingdom who were captured by Germany and Italy during the Second World War, Wylie, *Barbed Wire Diplomacy*, p. 68; 'Table 9. Total number of prisoners of war of the armed forces of the United Kingdom captured by the enemy as reported to 28th February 1946', in *Strength and Casualties of the Armed Forces*, p. 9.

[8] Twenty men whose personal narratives have been drawn upon in this book were taken prisoner at this point.

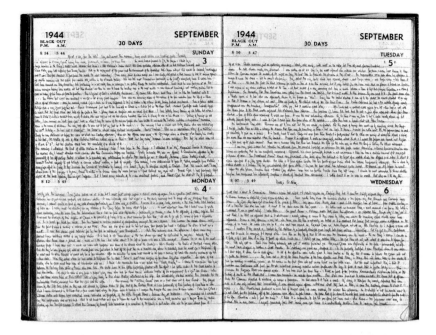

Figure 1.1: Pages from the diary of Captain John Mansel. Mansel, captured in May 1940, filled ten volumes of pocket diaries, exercise books and logbooks with miniscule but beautiful manuscript. His thoughts on captivity feature more prominently than any other prisoner in *Captives of War*.

Source: IWM 99/68/1, Captain J. W. M. Mansel, diary entries, 3–6 September 1944. Reproduced with permission from Gilly Barnard.

no particular note other prisoners would ask Mansel, 'what on earth has happened which can fill the page of [his] diary.' Mansel's response, written in his diary, was 'that people who can find nothing of which to write have no imagination, in fact I am sorry for them, because it must make this life even more empty than it cannot help being.'[9] Mansel's thoughts on captivity feature more prominently than any other man's in this book.

Others captured at this time, whose names appear frequently in the following pages, include Sergeant Major Andrew Hawarden. At forty-four years old, he was the oldest man to enter captivity out of all those who feature in *Captives of War*. He had previously served with the Royal Field Artillery in the First World War. Hawarden wrote a diary entry every day

---

[9] IWM 99/68/1–2, Captain J. W. M. Mansel, diary entry, 8 November 1941.

for the 1,790 days he spent behind barbed wire, except for a two-month period when he was suffering from bronchial pneumonia. Canon John King was captured shortly after Hawarden. He was serving as a chaplain to the 51st Highland Division and taken prisoner on 12 June 1940, as part of the divisional surrender at St Valery-en-Caux. King's diary is one of three personal narratives written by chaplains to the army that feature here.

Men taken prisoner during the fall of France faced highly testing conditions over the following days, weeks and months. They were forced to trek through France and Belgium in the heat of the summer, with minimal food, shelter and inadequate sanitation. They were then trans-ported to their permanent camps in packed barges or cattle trucks.[10] The officers' journeys were less unpleasant than those undergone by the other ranks. Most officers were ferried, at least part of the way, across France and the Low Countries by vehicle, rather than going exclusively on foot.[11] Mansel, for example, along with other British officers, was put in a lorry three days after his capture, and travelled by truck through Belgium. He arrived at his first permanent camp just twelve days after his capture.[12] Reaching their camps often resulted in little improvement in prisoners' circumstances, particularly for those in the other ranks. As author Sean Longden puts it, 'conditions experienced by the prisoners within the stalags varied in everything but awfulness.' Accommodation was ramshackle, food was scarce, the supply of Red Cross parcels had been halted as new supply routes were found, and organised activities in the camps were rudimentary.[13]

The German invasion of Greece and Yugoslavia on 6 April 1941, to protect Romanian oilfields and secure a south-eastern flank ahead of the planned invasion of the Soviet Union, led to the next large intake of POWs. British forces were sent to aid Greece but, by 28 April, Axis troops had pacified most of the mainland. British forces then withdrew to the island of Crete. In mid-May, German paratroopers landed there and again, after heavy fighting, defeated British forces. Twenty-five thousand British and Commonwealth servicemen surrendered.[14] Amongst them were five soldiers. Rifleman J. Eldridge and Lieutenant Louis Upshall were captured on the Greek mainland in April 1941;

---

[10] For details of these conditions, see MacKenzie, *The Colditz Myth*, pp. 64–77; Longden, *The Men They Left Behind*, pp. 263–315; Rolf, *Prisoners of the Reich*, pp. 26–33.

[11] MacKenzie, *The Colditz Myth*, p. 71.

[12] Mansel, diary entries, 23–6 May and 2 June 1940.

[13] Longden, *The Men They Left Behind*, pp. 325, 317–53; MacKenzie, *The Colditz Myth*, pp. 161, 165.

[14] Wylie, *Barbed Wire Diplomacy*, p. 70.

Major A. T. Casdagli, Lieutenant John Phillips and Lieutenant Richard Quarrie were captured in Crete on 1 June 1941. The diaries, correspondence and logbooks these men subsequently wrote inform this book. Due to a lack of transport, POWs captured at this point in the war often spent long periods of time in overcrowded, temporary transit cages. Almost all eventually passed through the notorious Dulag 183 (short for *Durchgangslager*, meaning transit camp), at Salonika in Greece.[15] Its buildings were filthy, dilapidated and infested with lice. Men slept on floors without blankets. Sanitation was poor and there was a lack of food and water. Those in the ranks below that of sergeant were forced to do heavy physical work in intense heat.[16] Historian Peter Monteath sums Salonika up as 'a hellhole'.[17] Some POWs stayed there only twenty-four hours; others had to wait several months before their move to Austria or Germany. They were transported in wagons, where cramped conditions, heat and the length of the journey made travel particularly trying.[18]

North Africa was the last sphere of operations in the war against Germany and Italy that saw large numbers of British servicemen taken prisoner. Three campaigns were waged from September 1940 to May 1943: the Western Desert campaign, which took place in Egypt and eastern Libya; Operation Torch in Algeria and Morocco; and the Tunisia campaign. During the course of these campaigns, some 68,000 British and Commonwealth troops were taken prisoner, and the personal narratives that eighteen of these men subsequently wrote feature in the following pages.[19] Amongst those taken prisoner in Libya was Angove, captured at Tobruk. One month into captivity, on 20 July 1942, Angove decided to keep a diary that took the form of letters to his mother. It was a way of keeping note of 'little things and incidents' for his mother to subsequently read.[20] Angove wrote these letters, or diary entries, every few days. His lengthy entries, which provide a highly intimate account of his imprisoned existence, have been drawn upon heavily in *Captives of War*.

---

[15] MacKenzie, *The Colditz Myth*, p. 77; Gilbert, *POW*, p. 47.

[16] MacKenzie, *The Colditz Myth*, pp. 79–81; Mason, *Prisoners of War*, pp. 78–9.

[17] Monteath, *P. O. W.*, p. 101.

[18] Peter Monteath, 'Beyond the Colditz Myth: Australian Experiences of German Captivity in World War II', in Joan Beaumont, Lachlan Grant and Aaron Pegram (eds.), *Beyond Surrender. Australian Prisoners of War in the Twentieth Century* ([e-book] Carlton, Victoria: Melbourne University Press, 2015), unpaginated.

[19] According to Gilbert, just over 68,000 British and Commonwealth troops made up the bulk of the POW population in Italy, and the vast majority of them would have been captured in North Africa (*POW*, p. 66). Wylie states that the loss of Tobruk in June 1942 alone saw the capture of 33,000 British men (*Barbed Wire Diplomacy*, p. 128).

[20] Angove, diary entry, 20 July 1942.

Many of these prisoners had surrendered to German forces, but they were placed under the custody of the Italian government once in captivity, since they had been captured on Italian soil. Libya had become a unified colony of Italy in 1934 and the Western Desert campaign began when Italy launched an attack from bases in Libya on British forces in western Egypt. Britain defeated the Italian attack and instead drove deep into Libya but, following this, German General Erwin Rommel was sent to Libya to take command of troops sent to reinforce Germany's Italian allies. The German units were rapidly expanded and renamed the German Afrika Corps. Prisoners taken in Tunisia were captured on the soil of Vichy France, but they were also removed to Italy.[21]

Just as for those captured in Greece, the journey of these men out of North Africa and into Italy involved being held in a number of transit camps. Derna, in eastern Libya, was one of the largest to which these prisoners were taken. Here they were housed in tents and the Italian commandant kept prisoners short of water and allowed guards to loot and bully.[22] Benghazi was the other main transit camp in the area. It consisted of twenty-five acres of desert and low bivouac tents. It was grossly overcrowded and had no working sanitation and only limited food supplies [Figure 1.2].[23]

On their journeys to Italy, these prisoners endured vastly different conditions depending on their ranks. Some were placed in the holds of Italian warships or Axis cargo or passenger vessels for seventy-two hours. Barrington, who had been captured in Libya at the fall of Tobruk, retrospectively recorded in his diary that he was held in a hold of about twelve yards square, along with 550 other men. Almost all the officers, meanwhile, were transferred to Italy by plane.[24] Reverend John Naylor, another chaplain whose diary features in the following pages, was flown from North Africa to Italy. Once in Italy, he travelled to his permanent camp by first-class train, six to a compartment.[25]

In the Second World War, of all the men serving in the UK forces who were taken prisoner, the greatest proportion came from the army.[26] The vast majority of them entered imprisonment at the dates and in the places listed earlier. Similarly, forty-four of the authors of the personal narratives drawn upon in *Captives of War* were written by soldiers,

[21] Mason, *Prisoners of War*, p. 139.   [22] Mason, *Prisoners of War*, p. 196.
[23] Gilbert, *POW*, p. 50; Mason, *Prisoners of War*, p. 199.
[24] Mason, *Prisoners of War*, p. 202.
[25] IWM P382 (+ Con Shelf), Reverend J. S. Naylor, logbook, pp. 79–81.
[26] Soldiers made up 88 per cent of all those captured in the war against Germany, 'Table 14. Casualties suffered during the war by the Armed Forces, Auxiliary Services and Merchant Navy', in *Statistical Digest of the War. Prepared in the Central Statistical Office* (London: HMSO, 1951), p. 13.

Figure 1.2: 'Six prisoners of war from camp 116 in Benghazi, Libya'. Taken by H. R. Dixon in 1942. These prisoners had been living in these barren conditions for about three months. Their bivouac tents stretch into the distance.
  Source: DA-10602, Alexander Turnbull Library, Wellington, New Zealand.

and all but two of them entered captivity in these three spheres of operations.[27]

The second highest proportion of all those taken prisoner came from the RAF: almost 10,000 men or 7 per cent of the British POW population.[28] Eighteen, captured in Europe or North Africa, feature in *Captives of War*. The first of them was Warrant Officer Harold Hurrell. He was taken prisoner on 15 October 1940. Seventy-four letters and fifty-five postcards he subsequently wrote to his parents and sweetheart have informed this book. The last was Flight Lieutenant Paul Cunningham. He was forced to bail out during a raid over Scholven-Buer in Germany

[27] Lance Corporal F. G. Blyth was taken prisoner in Italy in September 1943. It is unclear where Lieutenant R. G. Johnson was taken prisoner.
[28] 'Table 14. Casualties suffered during the war by the Armed Forces, Auxiliary Services and Merchant Navy', in *Statistical Digest of the War*, p. 13.

on 23 June 1944. He was then taken to Stalag Luft III, a camp set up for air force prisoners in Sagan, western Poland, from where he compiled a logbook on his captivity. The most senior officer to feature in this book also came from the RAF: Wing Commander Noel Hyde. Shot down at the age of thirty on 9 April 1941, thirty-seven of the letters he wrote to his wife have been drawn upon here.

Far smaller proportions of British POWs were captured whilst at sea. Just over 4 per cent came from the Royal Navy. In addition to Shipp and Buckley's, the logbooks, letters and diaries of five other naval seamen are featured in this work. The Merchant Navy accounted for the smallest proportion of British POWs: just 3 per cent. The logbooks written by five of them have been drawn upon here, in addition to the letters written by Bloss.

Capture as an End

What was it like, for these seventy-five men, to have to surrender to their enemy? How did they make sense of this ending to their war? Accounts of capture can most consistently be found in prisoners' diaries. The length of the letter form, the censorship of letters and the fact that they were sent to relatives and friends whom POWs often tried not to worry, meant only fleeting references to the moment of capture were made in POW correspondence. Given the diverse purposes for which logbooks were used, a report on surrender was not necessarily a relevant item to include. In the diary, in which dated entries were progressively written, an account of capture lent itself well to inclusion.

As mentioned in the previous chapter, in most of these diaries, the moment of capture was not written about as it happened. The majority of POWs who feature in *Captives of War* only started writing their diaries in the days, weeks, months or years after they entered captivity. Only four of these men record having kept diaries prior to being taken prisoner, but these seem to have been thrown away or destroyed as they entered enemy hands.[29] Five continued their diaries into captivity but, it seems, there was little opportunity, or perhaps willingness, to write lengthy, reflective entries specifically about their surrender.[30]

As a result, the accounts of capture were generally retrospectively written, with an external audience in mind. They differ in the stories they tell of the orders, incidents, events and circumstances that led to

---

[29] These four are Corporal E. Barrington, Driver J. K. Glass, Lance Corporal E. G. Laker and Reverend J. S. Naylor.
[30] These five are Private E. W. Abbott, Flying Officer R. J. Fayers, Lance Bombardier E. C. Stirling, Corporal J. G. White and Signalman N. R. Wylie.

each man's surrender. Their length varies, with some writing just one paragraph and others much more: notably Second Lieutenant Anthony Jabez-Smith, who filled three exercise books with his account of his capture at Calais in May 1940.[31] But what these accounts do have in common is the way in which they almost entirely consist of descriptions of the external events that led up to each man's surrender. Probably in part due to the time lag between their experience of capture and writing about it, they contain very little explicit articulation about how it felt to surrender.[32]

In a few places, these descriptions are punctuated by rhetorical devices, such as repetition, metaphor or calls for the reader's attention. These are insightful. These sentences stand out above the rest of the account to reveal which aspects of capture the diarist felt most emphatic about. Across these diaries, rhetorical devices are used to impress two main points. The first is these soldiers' helplessness in the battles that led to their surrender. This point frames Driver John Glass's sixteen-page account of his capture in Libya. He calls on the reader – 'you' – to consider the vulnerable position his work in the Petrol Section, which involved suppling petrol, ammunition and rations to the front line, put him in: 'When you consider that our convoys were unaccompanied by any A. F. V's [armoured fighting vehicles] and were dependent solely on each man's .303 [the standard British military cartridge] and perhaps a machine – or Tommy – gun, you will see how exposed we were to enemy action and air activity.'[33] Quarrie demonstrates his desire to point out the disadvantaged position he, along with the rest of the 7th Commandos, was in, prior to capture at Crete, by his intervention in his own narrative. 'It was the old, old story', he wrote, 'of not only lack of air-support but complete absence! However, I don't intend to write about that campaign in these pages.'[34] The animal similes used by others indicate their powerlessness. 'For eight days before our arrival at Mechili', Rifleman Arthur Brook described, 'we had been hounded about the Desert like a fox in the hunt.'[35] Of his capture near Tebourba

[31] This compares to Rachamimov's finding: that when prisoners tell their story of captivity, they often describe the moment of their capture in great detail and that this narration device, of allocating much space to 'what is often in reality just a few minutes in a saga of years', indicates that 'the moment of capture is the crucial pivot of the whole plot; the moment in which the narrator assumes a new identity as a POW and the real beginning of the story' (*POWs and the Great War*, p. 44).

[32] For example, see IWM Documents.2483, Second Lieutenant B. A. Brooke, notebook.

[33] IWM 95/30/1, Gunner J. K. Glass, diary entry, 11 November 1941–22 January 1942.

[34] SWWEC 2009.21, Lieutenant R. G. M. Quarrie, diary entry, 1 June 1941.

[35] Brook also describes himself as being rounded up like a 'herd of cattle' (IWM 80/38/1, Rifleman A. G. Brook, diary entry, pp. 3–4).

in Tunisia, Lieutenant William Bompas wrote that his revolver had 'disappeared', so he took an 'unobtrusive back seat' and 'came like a lamb when some Jerries about two yards away asked us to come.'[36]

The other aspect of capture, where rhetorical devices appear, is in relation to the mind-set of these servicemen. They are used to impress the idea that these men had never considered the possibility of being captured. Lance Corporal Eric Laker opened his diary with a digression in order to make this point:

I am in Italy. A prisoner of war. Funny that really, because whoever I speak to agrees with me that that is the last thing that enters one's head when going into action. The thought that you may stop a fatal one occurs to you, and also that you get wounded either more or less severely, but that you may be captured never enters your head. Maybe it is just as well. But I am digressing.[37]

Barrington made the same point repeatedly. In the space of just fifteen pages within his account of capture, he emphasised firstly: 'I still did not give it a thought as it was not in the realms of possibility to be taken prisoner'; then he absolved all his comrades of culpability by writing, 'no one that I can remember ever suggesting the possibility of being taken prisoner', and, finally, he commented, 'at last we resigned ourselves to our fate which at the best would be to be taken prisoner of war, something which in all my service I had never visualized [sic]'.[38] Meanwhile, Brook used rhetorical questions to command the reader's attention. 'Captured?' he asked,

Prisoners of War? Was it possible that this could happen to us, a Rear H. Q. of Armoured Division? Whilst we had known that the enemy had been on our tail for the past two or three days it never occurred to us that we would be caught. . . . It was all so unexpected and somehow the last mishap which a soldier expects to befall him.[39]

These examples all indicate that these diarists wanted to impress on their readers that they bore no personal responsibility for their fate.[40] The first set highlights how POWs stood little chance in their battles;

---

[36] Bompas, diary entry, pp. 7–8.
[37] IWM 85/18/1, Lance Corporal E. G. Laker, diary entry, p. 1. For a similar example, see IWM 44/43/1, Canon J. H. King, diary entry, 20 April 1941.
[38] Barrington, diary, unpaginated.   [39] Brook, diary entry, p. 4.
[40] This finding is similar to that of Rachamimov, who argues that, 'Seen from below, captivity never appears to have been a matter of personal choice.' The 'abundance of detail' in the POW narrative has the important function of 'exculpat[ing] the narrator in the eyes of his readers. It is through details that a prisoner seeks to refute (or pre-empt) accusations of personal failure, cowardice or treason [and] construct an accepted version of what took place in order to diminish their personal responsibility' (POWs and the Great War, p. 44).

the second that surrender was not something these men had anticipated or planned for in lieu of making the ultimate sacrifice. Such a conclusion is substantiated by the observations of psychiatrists who interviewed returned POWs in the summer of 1945. They recorded how few POWs appeared to have thought they might be captured, but had considered the possibilities of being wounded or killed. A governmental adviser in psychiatry, Lieutenant Colonel R. F. Barbour, wondered if there was some deeper significance to this: 'Capture provides an escape from a situation which every man desires escape from. Some men do admit guilt over being captured – is the surprise of the others a mask to cover their sense of relief?'[41]

Historians have also written at length about how combatants, in other wars and spheres of incarceration, saw surrender as tarnishing their sense of honour, carrying an 'emasculating stigma', or as a renunciation of one's claim to manhood.[42] In the POW narratives examined here, it was not being captured in itself that was the issue at stake for their honour. These men's use of rhetorical devices reveals a more unconscious awareness of the need to address the possibility that the circumstances of their capture might be seen as dishonourable.[43] This was a point psychiatrists also made at the time. A report for army psychiatrists, Technical Memorandum 13, compiled in Britain in 1944 from interviews with POWs who had escaped or been repatriated, noted that

many have marked degrees of unrecognised or partly unrecognised guilt over capture. It must be stressed that this important feature is, as a rule, partly or completely unrecognised by repatriates. ... Direct questioning in consequence does not reveal the extent of this feeling. Its existence will not, however, be doubted by any who have had dealings with prisoners of war, whether repatriated or not.[44]

Only one of the men who feature in *Captives of War* consciously expresses guilt over his capture and, unlike other diarists, who confined their account of capture to the opening pages of their diary, he constantly dwells on this moment throughout captivity. 'Could I have

---

[41] TNA WO 32/10757, Interim Report on Returned Prisoners of War by Lt-Col R. F. Barbour, RAMC, 29 August 1945.

[42] Robert C. Doyle, *Voices from Captivity. Interpreting the American POW Narrative* (Lawrence: University of Kansas Press, 1991), p. 115; Feltman, *The Stigma of Surrender*, p. 2; Gerster, *Big-Noting*, p. 143.

[43] Guilt over capture was also recorded by medical officers at the time (TNA WO 32/10757, The Repatriate Prisoner of War from the Medical Aspect, Australian Military Forces, undated).

[44] TNA WO 32/10757, Directorate of Army Psychiatry. Technical Memorandum No. 13. The Prisoner of War Comes Home. Notes Prepared for the Information of Army Psychiatrists, prepared by DAP, May 1944.

prevented this capture?' Mansel asked in his diary on 13 March 1941. 'I shall only know this by discussion after the war. It is a terrible feeling and one of which I feel I shall never be rid.' On 10 January 1942, he recounted a dream, where he had been given a 'cold reception' by various officers from his regiment for having been taken prisoner. It would cause him to 'go over again and again in my mind the events leading up to my capture on the 21st May 1940'. 'Oh God', he was still asking on 29 November 1943, 'why didn't some better sort of plan occur to me that evening of May 20th 1940, so that I could get my meagre Company out?'[45] Mansel, as explained earlier, was unique in the extent to which he reflected on captivity in his diary. He may, therefore, have also been unusual in dwelling so heavily on his capture and, consequently, feeling such levels of guilt. But, unlike the other accounts of capture, which were written with a public audience in mind, these diary entries were primarily written for Mansel. He often, as the rest of this book will show, confided thoughts in his diary that he could not share with others. It is possible, therefore, that other prisoners shared Mansel's feelings of guilt, but were not willing to explicitly acknowledge them to a broader audience.

All these extracts are taken from the diaries of soldiers; no similar justifications of surrender appear in the diaries of sailors or flyers. Generally, the circumstances of capture for servicemen in the navy or RAF were very different from those from the army. Soldiers were the most likely to consciously effect their surrender. Even if they fought until there was no possible further resistance, still there was a moment when most of them had to deliberately lay down their arms. The alternative to imprisonment for sailors was drowning with their sinking ship or, for aircrew, being killed in their doomed planes.[46] Perhaps, in part, for this reason, 5th Engineer Robert Graydon, Apprentice Anthony Howard and Able Seaman Edwin Tipple represented capture in their logbooks in a very unequivocal way. They compiled lists of ships sunk in the Second World War that were represented by POWs imprisoned at Milag.[47] These appear as if rolls of honour. There was no need for these merchant seamen to justify how they entered captivity.

---

[45] Mansel, diary entries, 13 March 1941, 10 January 1942, 29 November 1943.
[46] Mason, *Prisoners of War*, p. vii; Rolf, *Prisoners of the Reich*, pp. 22, 25.
[47] IWM Documents.2996, 5th Engineer R. A. Graydon, logbook, pp. 27–36; IWM 88/5/1, Apprentice A. C. Howard, logbook, pp. 170–2; IWM 79/32/1 Able Seaman E. Tipple, logbook, pp. 37–47. Being merchant seamen, these men may also not have felt the same concern over the circumstances of their capture as those in the armed forces.

Capture as a New Beginning?

As well as signalling an end to their combat duties, the moment of capture also ushered in a new phase of these men's war experience. With hindsight, we know that, for many British POWs, this was lengthy: the majority spent more time in captivity than they did in combat.[48] The same can be said of most of the prisoners who feature in this book.[49] Historians, writing of POWs in other wars and spheres of incarceration, have conceived of the moment of capture as the start of something new. Historian Robert C. Doyle, in his wide-ranging analysis of captivity narratives since the seventeenth century, described it as 'a process of transformation and initiation'.[50] In Brian Feltman's history of German military prisoners in the First World War, it is called 'an identity crisis'.[51] Similarly, Iris Rachamimov, in her study on POWs on the eastern front in the First World War, has written about this moment, and the period immediately following capture, as one when servicemen assumed a 'new identity'.[52]

Eventually, British POWs captured in the 1939–45 war in Europe came to see the moment of capture in this way. Major Edmund Booth articulated it as such, one year after being taken prisoner. He described how the first few weeks

seem like a nightmare that could not possibly have happened in real life; then comes a period of coma during the beginning of captivity followed by a gradual awakening, as though in an operation the anaesthetic were applied too late to save the patient pain and from which he gradually was aroused to a state of consciousness.[53]

The majority of POWs who feature in this book similarly indicate the moment of capture was a point of transformation in their lives but, rather than articulating this, they reveal it through the structure of their diaries. Literary scholars and historians have identified how writing a diary can be a means of helping individuals control catastrophes or life-changing events.[54] A diary is necessary, as literature specialist Felicity Nussbaum put it, 'at the point when the subject begins to believe that it cannot be intelligible to itself without written articulation and representation.'[55]

---

[48] Available figures indicate that of 103,000 British POWs, 58,000 spent more than three years in captivity (TNA WO32/10757, British ex-Prisoners of War. Rehabilitation of those Returning to Civil Life. A. G. 16 August 1944).
[49] Sixty-two spent at least half the war in captivity.
[50] Doyle, *Voices from Captivity*, p. 89.   [51] Feltman, *The Stigma of Surrender*, p. 3.
[52] Rachamimov, *POWs and the Great War*, p. 44.
[53] IWM P370, Major E. Booth, diary entry, pp. 26–7.
[54] Carol Acton, 'Stepping into History', 50; Culley, 'Introduction', p. 8.
[55] Felicity Nussbaum, 'Toward Conceptualizing Diary', in James Olney (ed.), *Studies in Autobiography* (New York: Oxford University Press, 1988), p. 135.

As discussed previously, most of the POWs who feature in *Captives of War* started writing a diary only after they had entered captivity and the majority commenced their narrative by writing retrospectively from the moment of capture, or from the events that led up to it.[56] Through their narrative form, they indicate that they, retrospectively, needed to make their lives intelligible to themselves from when they were taken prisoner, rather than from when they entered the war, or from another earlier point in their lives.

Yet to think of this transformation as happening at the very moment of capture, as other historians have represented it, is to misunderstand the mentality of British servicemen captured in Europe. When these men were captured, they did not immediately come face to face with the prospect that surrender would be a moment of transformation in their lives. Almost all POWs who feature in *Captives of War*, along with those with whom they were imprisoned, possessed a remarkable optimism. From the moment of their capture and, for some, during the subsequent five years, they experienced captivity not as something that would last indefinitely, but as something that would end imminently, in the context of the Allies winning the war. This mentality is crucial, both for under-standing how the moment of surrender was experienced, along with the rest of captivity.

Being Liberated

In July 1940, two months after he had been captured during the BEF's evacuation from Dunkirk, Hawarden wrote in his diary of the 'fantastic' rumours circulating in Stalag XXA, a camp located at Thorn in northern Poland, to which he, along with thousands of other British prisoners, was initially sent:

It's surprising how many Tommies lap it up when they hear anything – like we've broken through the Gerry lines and have retaken Brussells [*sic*]. Being captured two or three days later than some of our fellows, I was able to tell them that the BEF had been withdrawn from France and Belgium. This they wouldn't believe.[57]

In September 1940, Sergeant L. D. Pexton, captured during the same month as Hawarden, charitably expressed in his diary his 'pity' for 'the

---

[56] Of thirty POWs who started keeping diaries only after they had entered captivity, seven wrote their entries from the date at which they started keeping their diary; one started his narrative at a moment prior to capture, and then continued his entries until he was writing his diary contemporaneously; twenty-two retrospectively began their accounts at the moment of, or with the events that directly led to, capture.

[57] IWM 66/132/1, Sergeant Major A. Hawarden, diary entry, 2 July 1940.

last war's prisoners having four years of it. Dont know how they stuck it.'[58] In April 1941, writing from Oflag IXA/H in Spangenberg in Hesse in central Germany, Mansel described one POW, in a diary entry, as 'bar none the greatest pessimist I have ever met. He is now putting September 1942 as the end of the war.'[59] In summer 1941, Canon King recorded he had contemplated buying a French horn in order to get into the new dance band at Oflag VIID in Tittmoning in Bavaria, south-eastern Germany, but was deterred partly by the expense and partly by the 'effect which the new Russian campaign may have on the duration of the war'.[60] Writing six months after his capture in Libya in June 1942, Lance Corporal L. A. Bains recalled how he and his fellow captives had discussed 'whether it would be better to try to be amongst the first to be sent to Derna, or to hang back for the possibility of recapture'. He passed through Derna that day and, having spent a night in a compound attached to a fort, he noted, 'Quite a number of men had been in the compound for several days, presumably hanging on in the hope of recapture.'[61] At Christmas 1942, Captain John Jenkins recorded how his roommates, at Campo PG 21 at Chieti, southern Italy, had been trying to give it a festive air. They used toffee wrapping 'saved over a period of some months by a pessimistic member of the room.'[62] In July 1943, from Campo PG 53 at Sforzacosta in eastern Italy, Glass wrote of how he did not 'profess to be a super-optimist, but I certainly don't uphold the opinions of one or two of the boys – and old soldiers at that – that we can't possibly expect to see home again within 18 months. I think people like that want isolating.'[63] At the start of 1944, Hawarden wrote of how at Stalag 383, at Hohenfels, in Bavaria, there was 'something in the air – everyone here is expecting startling developments to commence shortly on a new western front.'[64] After the Allied invasion of German-occupied France, Lieutenant Kenneth Stoddart, captured two years earlier at Tobruk, recorded 'great hopes' at Oflag 79, near Brunswick, in Lower Saxony, north-western Germany, that

[58] IWM 86/89/1, Sergeant L. D. Pexton, diary entry, 18 September 1940.

[59] Mansel, diary entry, 7 April 1941; see also diary entry, 21 March 1941. When the capacity of camps located in commandeered buildings needed to be augmented, sub-camps, huts or other temporary structures were added. The two areas of accommodation were distinguished in the camp name. An 'H' would be added, which referred to the main camp, or *Hauptlager*, a 'Z' referred to the hutted sub-camp, *Zweiglager* (Doyle, *Prisoner of War in Germany*, pp. 10, 13; Gilbert, *POW*, p. 69).

[60] King, diary entry, 19 July 1941.

[61] IWM Documents.883, Lance Corporal L. A. Bains, diary entries, 9 and 10 June 1942. For similar hopes that British troops might reach POWs before the Italians could take them away, see Laker, diary entry, p. 5; SWWEC 2001.1048, Driver P. Hainsworth, accounts of capture, pp. 10, 27–8.

[62] SWWEC 99.201, Captain J. E. Jenkins, diary entry, 23 December 1942.

[63] Glass, diary entry, 31 July 1943.   [64] Hawarden, diary entry, 6 January 1944.

the war would be ending 'anytime', although adding, 'it is odd to me how some people can go on for three years saying the war will be over in two months.'[65] In December 1944, Angove, also captured at Tobruk in June 1942, acknowledged in his diary how he had 'refrained from asking for books & chocolate for so long, thinking it would be all over very soon'.[66]

These men did not see their capture as a signal for the start of a wartime incarceration lasting an indefinite but lengthy duration, as numerous historians, sociologists and psychologists have suggested.[67] The vast majority of personal narratives consulted in *Captives of War* indicate that POWs made sense of their entry into captivity, and its indeterminate duration, not by thinking of it lasting an interminable length of time, but ending imminently, with almost no one considering the possibility that the Allies might actually lose the war.[68]

Certain groups of these prisoners had particularly good reason for believing they would soon be home. One was the protected personnel. The Geneva Convention included a provision for protected personnel, as well as sick or wounded POWs, to be repatriated or sent to a neutral

---

[65] The private collection of Simon Stoddart, Lieutenant K. B. Stoddart, diary entry, August/September 1944.

[66] Angove, diary entry, 30 December 1944.

[67] Erving Goffman, *Asylums: Essays on the Social Situation of Mental Patients and Other Inmates* (Harmondsworth: Penguin, 1968), p. 67; Gilbert, *POW*, p. 224; Wylie, *Barbed Wire Diplomacy*, p. 95; Bob Moore and Barbara Hately-Broad, 'Living on Hope and Onions: The Everyday Life of British Servicemen in Axis Captivity', *Everyone's War: The Journal of the Second World War Experience Centre*, 8 (2003), 42. Official historian of New Zealand prisoners of war, Wynne Mason, acknowledges this optimism of prisoners of war (*Prisoners of War*, p. 103). Historians Midge Gillies and David Rolf cite some evidence of prisoners' optimistic attitudes, although Rolf also concludes one of the 'hardest things' of captivity was having no end in sight (Gillies, *The Barbed-Wire University. The Real Lives of Prisoners of War in the Second World War*. London: Aurum Press Ltd, 2011, p. 75; Rolf, *Prisoners of the Reich*, pp. 87–90). Historian Paul Fussell has noted that 'consolatory rumours' providing 'hope without facts' were widespread amongst captives, and combatants more generally, in the Second World War (*Wartime. Understanding and Behaviour in the Second World War*. Oxford: Oxford University Press, 1989, pp. 43–5). Also see Amia Lieblich's study of oral histories of ten Israeli POWs in Egypt. She acknowledges how 'at every single moment', these POWs 'might have been liberated and returned home, yet in the same vein, they might have been held in jail forever' (*Seasons for Captivity. The Inner World of POWs*. New York and London: New York University Press, 1994, p. 11).

[68] Only three prisoners whose personal narratives have been drawn upon in this book contemplated an interminable sentence; see IWM 03/10/1, Rifleman J. Eldridge, diary entries, 11 October and 12 December 1941, 18 February 1942, 23 March 1943; SWWEC 2006.690.3–5, Sub-lieutenant H. R. Taylor, diary entries, 24 August and 23 October 1942; IWM PP/MCR/215, Sergeant D. Nell, diary entry, 14 January 1943. Only one discussed Britain losing the war; see IWM 83/33/1, Signalman N. R. Wylie, diary entry, 29 September 1940. Other historians have noted soldiers' belief in victory and their optimism of an early end to the war; see David French, *Raising Churchill's Army. The British Army and the War against Germany 1919–1945* (Oxford: Oxford University Press, 2000), p. 130.

country, if no agreement was formed between the belligerents to the contrary. The types of injuries and illnesses which entitled prisoners to repatriation were agreed between the enemy governments.[69] Such repatriations were typically carried out in the form of exchanges between eligible prisoners from the two warring sides.[70] As a chaplain to the forces, this provision was relevant to Canon King. Having spent just seven weeks in captivity, he received news from a German doctor, the American embassy in Berlin and the Red Cross that plans were afoot for this group's repatriation. A further fifteen months later, he, along with 1,500 others, commenced his passage home.[71] King's diary entries setting out this journey were written retrospectively on 14 December 1941. His inability to keep his diary contemporaneously during this two-month period possibly underlines the difficulty he had in coming to terms with what was happening to him. He explained how, on 2 October 1941, the group travelled by train across Europe. At Liège station, in Belgium, overcome with exuberance at the idea of being in England within twenty-four hours, they showered civilians with food tins from their Red Cross parcels.[72] On 3 October, they arrived at Rouen in France, and lined up '100 yards from the quay.' Confidently, they threw away their remaining bread ration, were given their 'Boat number' labels, and waited to set sail.[73] King then described how, on 9 October, his fellow prisoners were 'too depressed for words. It really was heartbreaking', he wrote: 'We had come so near, and were now so far.' Negotiations between Britain and Germany had broken down three days earlier. King languished at Rouen for a further two months, only to return to captivity in Poland.[74]

Repatriation rumours continue to litter King's diary. On 20 April 1942, he wrote, 'Two years ago I left England for France', and then asked, 'Shall I cross the channel again before two more years from now?' On 13 July 1942, he recorded the repatriation question had 'become nauseating to us all. We never mention R. by name: but refer to it as

[69] Article 68, 'Convention Relative to the Treatment of Prisoners of War'; Article 12, 'Convention for the Amelioration of the Condition of the Wounded and Sick in Armies in the Field'; Prisoner of War Enquiry Centre, *A Handbook for the Information of Relatives and Friends of Prisoners of War*, p. 9.

[70] Monteath, *P. O. W.*, p. 371.

[71] King, diary entries, 25 and 31 July 1940, 25 September 1941. For details on the government machinations behind this move, see Wylie, *Barbed Wire Diplomacy*, p. 86.

[72] King, diary entry, 2 October 1941.

[73] King, diary entry, 3 October 1941. King's narrative implies these men were to board a boat there and then, but the plan was to move them to Dieppe when news of the ship's arrival had been confirmed (Wylie, *Barbed Wire Diplomacy*, p. 86).

[74] King, diary entries, 9 October and 19 December 1941. Other POWs had to wait almost two further months before being returned to POW camps (ACICR B G 14, box 413, file IV, note pour M. Pictet de Marti, Délégue du CICR, 30 janvier 1942).

"the ugly head" or "the broader issue".' By November 1942, he had had enough. He requested his name be removed from the exchange list. On 20 April 1944, he went back and annotated the question he had asked in his diary exactly two years previously with the words: '(No, you poor fool!, 20/4/44)'.[75] This note reveals the extent to which these repatriation rumours defined King's experience behind barbed wire. By replying to a previous diary entry in this way, King demonstrated how he saw this earlier self, the one who had possessed a hopeful attitude towards an early homecoming, as an entirely different person.[76]

King was freed with the vast majority of British POWs held in Europe in the spring of 1945. Others had more success. Eight exchanges were eventually carried out between Italy, Germany and Britain. There were four Anglo–Italian repatriations. The first took place at Smyrna in Turkey in April 1942. The second occurred a year later at Lisbon in Portugal and Smyrna. The third and fourth were also held at Smyrna in May 1943 and June 1943. A fifth should have taken place in September 1943, but was disrupted by the armistice. There were four exchanges between Germany and Britain. The first one took place at Gothenburg in Sweden, Oran in Algeria and Barcelona in Spain in October 1943; the next at Barcelona in May 1944; the third at Gothenburg in September 1944 and the final at Kreuzlingen in Switzerland in January 1945.[77]

Amongst those repatriated were two POWs who feature in *Captives of War*: Major George Matthews and Lieutenant John Evans. Matthews returned to Britain in September 1944, but he had had his hopes raised years earlier. He was captured on 28 May 1940 whilst serving in the Royal Army Medical Corps (RAMC). In April 1942, Matthews was working in the lazarett attached to Stalag XIIIC in Hammelburg, Bavaria. Lazaretts were small military hospitals attached to main POW camps, but often located at some distance from them.[78] When Matthews was given notification that he would soon be leaving his medical duties there, to be sent to an oflag instead, he told his wife that he could not help wondering whether it was 'a step towards repatriation'.[79] His confusion is understandable given that medical personnel in both Italy and Germany were

[75] King, diary entries, 20 April and 13 July and 5 November 1942.
[76] Wendy J. Wiener and George C. Rosenwald, 'A Moment's Moment: The Psychology of Keeping a Diary', in R. Josselson and A. Lieblich (eds.), *The Narrative Study of Lives*, volume 1 (London: Sage, 1993), p. 49.
[77] *Report of the International Committee of the Red Cross*, vol. I, pp. 378–82. See also Monteath, *P.O.W.*, pp. 372–6.
[78] Kochavi, *Confronting Captivity*, p. 29.
[79] IWM 03/12/1, Major G. B. Matthews, letter to his wife, 15 April 1942. For another example, see IWM 66/185/1, Reverend R. D. F. Wild, letter to his wife, 5 September 1943.

randomly selected for inclusion in a repatriation exchange, as opposed to according to their length of time or type of employment in captivity.[80] When Matthews was repatriated, he was given minimal notice of his departure.[81]

Evans was repatriated as one of the sick or wounded. He does not allude to his repatriation in the letters he wrote to his wife, but reports produced by the ICRC show that the sick or wounded, who were eligible for repatriation, also faced uncertainty. It was one thing to be selected by the camp's medical officer or a senior prisoner to go before the Mixed Medical Commission, which examined prisoners of war and decided which sick or wounded were entitled to be repatriated, but it was something quite different to actually reach home.[82] Many of the sick or wounded had to wait a year before getting a chance to even see the Commission. Once they had passed it, some then had their records lost and needed to be re-examined. This problem was most widely faced by POWs who were passed by the Italian Mixed Medical Commission, but were then transported to Germany following the Italian armistice. Others had to wait months before their move could commence, watching an exchange come and go without them. Some were left behind due to diplomatic wrangling or an administrative error.[83]

[80] ACICR, C SC, Germany, Zweiglager du Stalag XXID/Z, 6 octobre 1943; ACICR, B G 14, box 426, file R.I, 'Some Notes on the Treatment of Prisoners of War', Major G. J. Dean, 24 April 1942; ACICR, B G 14, box 414, Dr A. Cramer, membre du CICR, 'Note sur la Question du Rapatriement', 20 janvier 1944; ACICR, B G 14, box 414, D. A. Cramer, 'Note pour la Délégation du CICR à Berlin', 4 février 1944.

[81] With thanks to Gillian Stein for this information.

[82] The Mixed Medical Commission consisted of three doctors; two members were from a neutral country and one was appointed by the detaining power.

[83] On waiting to see the Mixed Medical Commission, see ACICR, B G 14, box 414, letter from Senior British Medical Officer at Stalag VIIIB to the Protecting Power, 7 October 1943; ACICR, B G 14, box 414, letter from A. S. Greenwood, Man of Confidence, Reserve Lazarett, Freising, to the Secretary, ICRC, 5 September 1943. On records being lost, see ACICR, B G 14, box 414, letter from Senior British Medical Officer at Stalag VIIIB to the Protecting Power, 7 October 1943; ACICR B G 14, box 427, R.IV, letter from the SBO of Oflag IXA/Z to ICRC, 9 November 1942. On being passed by the Italian Mixed Medical Commission and then being moved to Germany, see ACICR, B G 14, box 427, R.IV, lettre de Dr A. Cramer, membre du CICR, à Monsieur H. B. Livingston, Consul Britannique, 9 juin 1944; ACICR, B G 14, box 427, R.IV, lettre de 'Commando der Wehrmacht' au CICR, 23 août 1944. Prisoners at Stalag 383 (Hohenfels) who passed the Commission in October 1943 had to wait a further six months before they commenced their move (Hawarden, diary entry, 17 April 1944). Two thousand POWs passed by the Commission were not repatriated in May 1944 because of the policy of exchanging the sick or wounded on a per capita basis (ACICR, B G 14, box 424, letter d'Erlach à A. Cramer, membre du CICR, 22 mai 1944). One hundred and eighty-three POWs missed the exchange at Gothenberg because the doctor of their camp did not understand the orders he was given (ACICR, B G 14 box 424, Dr Rubli et Dr Waldhart, 'Commission Médicale Mixte en Allemagne (avril 1944)', 15 mai 1944).

Eventually, some 10,000 British and Commonwealth sick or wounded or protected personnel were repatriated in this way.[84] Long-term prisoners of war was the most sizeable group of all those captured who had good grounds for believing their return home would take place before the end of the war, yet to absolutely no avail. By March 1945, 41,000 British POWs had spent more than four years in German hands; amongst them were thirty-three POWs featuring in *Captives of War* who, from the middle years of the war, recorded being surrounded by hopes of an imminent homecoming.[85] Booth, captured in May 1940, noted that when the wounded started to leave Germany in October 1943, there was 'much talk of the three year old kriegies [short for *Kriegsgefangenen*, meaning prisoners of war] going to a neutral country'; Hawarden recorded hearing similar rumours, which affected 'a very large number' from Stalag 383 (Hohenfels).[86] At the end of that year, Mansel wrote of how he put 'absolutely no faith' in these rumours, but he was aware of 'lots of four year old prisoners who are literally banking on it ... going as far as to get rid of food etc.'[87] Mansel's faith in such hearsay would not have been totally misplaced. Around this time, the British and German governments were contemplating a mutual repatriation of able-bodied, long-term POWs, which was discussed in the House of Commons in November 1944.[88]

Although these optimistic expectations were, in every single case, either excessively premature or never realised, they served a vital function: faith was invested in them because they aided men in their ability to cope with captivity. This point was recognised by Lieutenant Trevor Gibbens, who worked as a medical officer in a number of camps throughout his five years of imprisonment. After the war, Gibbens submitted a Doctorate of Medicine thesis on 'The Psychology of the Prisoner-of-War' to the University of Cambridge, the observations in which have been drawn upon throughout *Captives of War*, and used extensively in Chapter 5. One

---

[84] According to *The Times*, in the exchanges with Germany, more than 7,500 British and Commonwealth sick or wounded and some 2,200 British and Commonwealth protected personnel were repatriated. The ICRC figures indicate 6,890 British POWs were repatriated in the exchanges with Italy and the first exchange with Germany. For the last three exchanges with Germany, the ICRC only provides a figure for all Allied POWs, this being 6,103 ('Exchange of War Prisoners. German Answer to Latest Approach', *The Times* (18 April 1945); *Report of the International Committee of the Red Cross*, vol. I, pp. 378–82).

[85] TNA WO 32/10757, British ex-Prisoners of War. Rehabilitation of those Returning to Civil Life. A. G. 16 August 1944.

[86] Booth, diary entry, 12 October 1943; Hawarden, diary entries, 2 and 4 May 1944.

[87] Mansel, diary entry, 29 December 1944.

[88] Negotiations with the Germans on this issue commenced in April 1944 and continued until the end of March 1945; see Kochavi, *Confronting Captivity*, pp. 148–68; Hansard HC Deb., 17 November 1944, vol. 404 col. 2352–70.

of Gibbens' findings was that the uncertainty of the duration of captivity had been 'greatly over-emphasised'. According to him, 'Both the convicted prisoner and the prisoner of war ... have a tendency to blind themselves to the future and elaborate false hopes.'[89] The same point is made in these POWs' personal narratives. Signalman Norman Wylie, captured at St Valery, and the only one to contemplate Britain losing the war, recorded in his diary entry of 7 October 1940 having a 'cheery chat' with one sergeant major, who believed 'something' would happen 'soon'. Wylie added, 'I take this to heart just to give myself a few moments of happiness.'[90] Brook acknowledged that, of the rumours reaching them at Derna, such as the Germans being driven back from Tobruk, 'there could have been little foundation ... but they did assist in keeping our spirits up in these early days of our captivity.'[91] Barrington similarly reflected in his diary on the 'Benghazi rumours' that circulated in that transit camp, where he spent ten days. He recalled:

during those miserable days they did definitely help us to bear our troubles & give us some light in our darkness. We would be feeling tired, hungry, and depressed & suddenly we would hear a rumour that the invasion had started or that the 10th Army was on its way to release us, & we would cheer up wonderfully, discuss the news cheerfully forgetting our surroundings & go to bed hoping we should not be moved before our army could catch us up! Silly I know now, but many of those nights we slept better on a full stomach of rumours.[92]

Barrington's nutritional metaphor, that prisoners 'slept better on a full stomach of rumours', is a highly significant choice for a POW whose life was often dominated by hunger. Similarly, Driver Peter Hainsworth and Mansel, during their imprisonment, placed their homecoming anticipations on a par with physical sustenance when they respectively wrote of how prisoners were living 'on hope + onions' and 'on stew and rumours'.[93]

Ironically, only during the final few months of the war did many of these POWs abandon their misplaced confidence. Noting in December 1944 of how he had deprived himself of books and chocolates throughout captivity, Angove finally declared in his diary: 'in future I am going to ignore the time element & just ask for what I want, to be sent irrespective of apparent

[89] Trevor C. N. Gibbens, 'The Psychology of the Prisoner-of-War', unpublished M. D. thesis, University of Cambridge (1947), p. 18. See also E. R. C. Walker, 'Impressions of a Repatriated Medical Officer', *The Lancet*, 243, 6249 (15 April 1944), 514.

[90] Wylie, diary entry, 7 October 1940; see also diary entry, 29 September 1940.

[91] Brook, diary entry, pp. 28–9.   [92] Barrington, diary entry, unpaginated.

[93] SWWEC 2001.1048, Driver P. Hainsworth, letter to his mother, 31 January 1943; Mansel, diary entry, 25 March 1941. For a similar metaphor, see IWM 88/22/2, Flying Officer R. J. Fayers, diary entry, 11 January 1944.

" Now Do You Believe it ?! "

Figure 1.3: 'Now do you believe it!!' This POW is so disbelieving that the war has ended that he has to be carried in his bed to the ship that will take him home.

Source: SWWEC 2008.134, Warrant Officer A. Clague, logbook, p. 45. Reproduced with permission of the trustees of the Second World War Experience Centre.

conditions prevailing at the time.'[94] The following month, Glass confessed to his diary

from the occasional English news I hear, things are looking very favourable and we might be home any time within the next five years. Naturally after three years of guessing and hoping and unrealised expectations, it is excusable that one no longer feels really optimistic over the best of good news. I thought when I was first captured, the Tommies would get me released in a few hours, at the most a few days – and it's been going on like that ever since.[95]

Warrant Officer Alexander Clague captured the feeling of hopelessness that pervaded some prisoners in a drawing in his logbook entitled 'Now do you believe it!!' [Figure 1.3]. A POW has become so sceptical that the war could have ended that he has to be carried in his bed to the ship that

[94] Angove, diary entry, 30 December 1944.   [95] Glass, diary entry, 30 January 1945.

will take him home. Two months before the end of the war in Europe, Sergeant David Nell, who had been captured almost three years earlier, recorded the same mentality but with less humour: 'lessons of unjustified optimism have been learned in the past. Now I'm cynical. I really expect nothing good. I dare not. I've got to the stage when disappointment is too hard to bear.'[96]

Conclusion

The moment of capture in the lives of prisoners of war signified both the end of their combat duties and the start of a period of wartime incarceration of an unknown duration. In their accounts of capture, POWs did not explicitly identify the act of surrendering to their enemy with shame or dishonour, but their use of rhetorical devices to renounce any personal culpability in their fate, plus the observations of psychiatrists at the time, indicates an unconscious awareness that dishonour surrounded this end to their war. Rarely, in their accounts, did POWs write about the moment of capture as a point of transformation, but their retrospective dating of their diaries from that juncture suggests they came to see the moment in this way. To think of this transformation as happening at the point of surrender is to misunderstand the mentality of British servicemen captured in Europe. POWs had a remarkably optimistic attitude, and considered their captivity would end imminently, following an Allied victory.

Chronologically, it may seem strange to discuss POWs' attitude towards homecoming at the start of this book, but this mind-set is important, not just for fully understanding how the moment of capture was experienced, but also the rest of these men's wartime imprisonment. Different aspects of this are examined in the next four chapters. The first of these turns to how British POWs made sense of being imprisoned by the enemy and being confined at a time of war.

---

[96] Nell, diary entry, 19 March 1945; see also diary entry, 6 March 1945.

2   Imprisoned Servicemen

I feel here ... that I have come off a football field after a one-sided match and a poor game, the loser, but perfectly set for a beer party with my immediate opponents at any moment – stupid and unpatriotic it may seem, but frank.[1]

Mansel's comparison of prisoners of war to defeated, ineffective football players, written on 11 March 1941, provides an insight into the peculiar role he had now assumed whilst the war was still waging. Mansel had lost his game, or his particular battle. All he could do now was wait for others to finish their matches. He no longer belonged to the team for which he had played. He also perceived himself as having developed an inappropriately jovial relationship with his adversaries. Knowledge of Mansel's other activities in captivity makes his neat analogy particularly interesting. There is no reference of it in his diary or letters, but we know from other sources that, from July 1940 to September 1944, Mansel worked with various escape committees in his capacity as a forger of escape documents, gaining the title of 'Forger No. 1' in two of the camps in which he was imprisoned.[2] He was also one of eleven main coded-letter writers at Oflag VIIB located in Eichstätt, Bavaria, who passed to the War Office information on the German war machine.[3] In other words, Mansel was far from out of the war, but he still considered himself defeated, idle and unpatriotic.

This chapter explores how British POWs made sense of being imprisoned by their enemy. It looks at how POWs responded to being out of the

---

[1] Mansel, diary entry, 11 March 1941.

[2] Mansel forged identity and other official documents, as well as personal correspondence that supported the escapee's 'nationality' and supposed occupation, 'Editor's Foreword', in Ted Beckwith (ed.), *The Mansel Diaries. The Diaries of Captain John Mansel, Prisoner of War and Camp Forger in Germany 1940–45* (London: Wildwood House, 1977), p. ix. See also T. C. F. Pritte and W. Earle Edwards, *South to Freedom. A Record of Escape* (London: Hutchinson & Co., 1946), p. 233.

[3] These code-writers passed back information on German oil production, factory production, the effects of air raids on production and on the railway system, German manpower generally, defences in north-east Poland, German morale and unrest in Austria (TNA WO 208/3291, Secret Camp Histories, Oflag VIIB Eichstätt).

war and under the control of their foe and how they made sense of some of the other salient features of their imprisonment: living in enemy territory as well as existing in a restricted space, under impoverished conditions and facing empty time. When referring in their personal narratives to these aspects of their imprisonment, POWs presented an upbeat view of captivity: one in which they defied the captor–captive power relationship, followed 'normal' routines and activities in captivity and formed what might be called a 'Kriegie identity'. Yet, within this positive picture, there are also traces of POWs not feeling as spirited as they suggested. This chapter concludes by showing the ways in which these men lamented their imprisoned existence.

'Out of the War'

As soon as a British serviceman surrendered on German territory, he immediately came under the control of the German High Command – OKW (Oberkomando der Wehrmacht).[4] Below the OKW sat the department established to administer prisoner-of-war affairs and, under it, seventeen military districts responsible for the oflags and stalags, along with many smaller satellite camps and work units in that area.[5] In the second year of the war, the *Luftwaffe* (the German air force) and *Kriegsmarine* (the German navy) set up their own facilities for air force and navy prisoners. Seven permanent camps, called Stalag Lufts, were set up by the German air force. The German navy ran a compound at Stalag XB at Sandbostel in Lower Saxony until the number of prisoners warranted the opening of Marlag-Milag Nord at Westertimke.[6] POW camps in Italy were spread across six military districts, but, since the vast majority of POWs in Italy were from the army, camps were not separately run by different branches of service.[7]

In both Germany and Italy, whilst the higher authorities in the OKW and military districts made policy decisions and drafted regulations for captivity, German or Italian officers and NCOs, who were in charge of individual camps, had the most influence over POWs' day-to-day lives. In accordance with the Geneva Convention, each camp was in the charge of a commanding officer or Commandant.[8] Often a deputy and a number of camp officers undertook general administrative duties, but it was their camp guards with whom POWs most frequently came into contact.[9]

---

[4] Rolf, *Prisoners of the Reich*, p. 50.
[5] These military districts were identified with Roman numerals I to XXI, but there were no military districts XIV, XV, XVI or XIX; see Monteath, *P.O.W.*, p. 141.
[6] MacKenzie, *The Colditz Myth*, p. 94.   [7] Gilbert, *POW*, pp. 66–7.
[8] MacKenzie, *The Colditz Myth*, p. 108.   [9] Gilbert, *POW*, p. 67.

Numbers and functions of guards varied according to the size and importance of the camp concerned. For example, certain camps contained
high-value prisoners, persistent escapers and other troublesome individuals, such as Oflag IVC at Colditz Castle in Saxony, in eastern
Germany, and its Italian equivalent, Campo PG 5 at Gavi in northern
Italy. On average, there was one guard for every seven to ten prisoners
from the army and one for every four from the air force. RAF prisoners
had more guards as they were considered a higher escape risk.[10]

The Commandant and staff of central camps controlled the physical
movement of POWs. They had to ensure POWs stayed within the peri-
meters of their camp. Prisoners would be watched by guards who sat in
towers on the outskirts of the camp as well as by those who patrolled on
foot. The guards also carried out regular searches on the prisoners.
In Italy and Germany, specialist security officers would roam around
the camps looking for anything suspicious that indicated a planned escape
or act of sabotage or resistance.[11] POWs were subjected to one or two roll
calls each day, and were expected to abide by a set of orders and regulations that listed unacceptable behaviour and prohibited items.[12] Those
caught disobeying the regulations were subject to disciplinary punish-
ments, which normally involved time in solitary confinement.[13]

How these men responded to being out of the war and under the power
of their foe is a difficult question to answer through personal narratives
written at the time of captivity. As mentioned in the Introduction, censorship of POWs' letters required they refrain from referencing their camp
conditions, otherwise those sections were liable to be redacted.[14] Their
diaries and logbooks were also subject to seizure during a snap search,
which could take place at any time, day or night. If taken away, but
deemed safe and innocuous by their captors, the diary or logbook would
be stamped by the camp censors and returned to its author. If the contents
irritated the Italian or German authorities, or revealed behaviour that
broke the rules, these narratives could be confiscated or the author
severely punished.[15]

Consequently, these personal narratives can be both unenlightening
and even downright misleading when discussing prisoners' relationships
with their guards or any major acts of rebellion in captivity, such as

---

[10] MacKenzie, *The Colditz Myth*, pp. 108–9; Gilbert, *POW*, pp. 67, 71.
[11] Gilbert, *POW*, p. 67.
[12] Vourkoutiotis, *Prisoners of War and the German High Command*, p. 84.
[13] Gilbert, *POW*, p. 242.
[14] 'Camp Standing Orders Oflag VIIIB', September 1942, in the private papers of Jabez-
Smith.
[15] IWM 66/132/1, Sergeant Major A. Hawarden, notebook 9.

escape, sabotage or other activities, which were explicitly prohibited. Angove, for example, chose to omit all discussion of his feelings towards his captors. On several occasions, he explicitly stated there were no 'disparaging remarks' about them in his diary, and that he would not write anything that could 'compromise' himself or his 'hosts'.[16] He repeated these assurances so many times that they appear to be aimed at the censors, in order to hasten the return of his diary should it have been removed for examination (which it eventually was).[17] Casdagli's diary, which was kept carefully hidden throughout his time in captivity, makes no reference to his work as a coded-letter writer.[18] Mansel often included a deprecatory note about escapers in his diary, intended to act as a smoke-screen for his forging activities. On one occasion when four POWs tried to escape from Oflag VIB, located just outside Warburg in north-western Germany, he wrote, 'How the hell they thought they could get out God knows. I thought you required all sorts of papers to get out of a gate.'[19] One can imagine the mischievous smile that crossed Mansel's face as he penned these misleading lines.

Despite these censorship restraints, there is evidence in POWs' perso-nal narratives to indicate that acts of rebellion were key in giving meaning to their existence. Warrant Officer Alexander East demonstrates this through his impatience to inform the readers of his diary of the secret radio they had at Stalag IVB, a camp that held predominantly British POWs, near the town of Mühlberg in the east of Germany. At the earliest possible opportunity, that is, the day he and the camp were liberated, he could proudly announce,

without indiscretion that we have been supplied with news for the last twelve months or more by two secret radio sets . . . Apart from a few odd breakdowns and security silences we had a broadcast read out to us most nights and during the last few hectic days, several news flashes were read out each day.[20]

During captivity, POWs also resisted or defied their captors through smaller acts of self-assertion and insubordination contained in their per-sonal narratives.[21] A number, for example, reference what subsequently

---

[16] Angove, diary entries, 30 August and 17 November 1942, 6 December 1943.

[17] Angove, diary entry, 17 February 1944.

[18] A. T. Casdagli, *Prouder Than Ever. My War + My Diary + My Embroideries*, compiled by Alexis Penny Casdagli (London: Cylix Press, 2014), p. 203, fn 3 p. 222; TNA WO 208/3295, 'Secret Camp Histories. Oflag XIIB, Hadamar'.

[19] Mansel, diary entry, 2 February 1942; 'Editor's Foreword' in E. G. C. Beckwith (ed.), *The Mansel Diaries*, p. vii.

[20] IWM 87/34/1, Warrant Officer A. J. East, diary entry, 23 April 1945.

[21] For the concept of resistance broadening out to include not only major acts of rebellion, but smaller acts of self-assertion and insubordination, see S. Alexander Haslam and

became popularly known as 'The Great Escape'. In March 1944, at least 200 men attempted an escape from Stalag Luft III (Sagan), with the prime aim of causing maximum disruption throughout Germany.[22] In the event, seventy-six escaped, seventy-three were recaptured and, of these, fifty were murdered by the Gestapo. The logbooks of POWs held at Stalag Luft III (Sagan) record the mass escape by variously listing the names of those who died, including a drawing of a tomb erected in the officers' honour and pasting in newspaper cuttings on the episode.[23]

The importance of escaping to prisoners of war is also reflected through flyers, pasted into numerous logbooks, which were distributed by the German authorities in the middle of 1944.[24] With the deteriorating military situation, the increase in number of POW escapes and, then, the mass escape from Stalag Luft III (Sagan), Hitler and Heinrich Himmler became more concerned with the potential security threat that prisoners of war and foreign workers posed to the Third Reich. A greater range of forces was employed to prevent further mass breakouts and Himmler and the SS (Schutzstaffel) took over responsibility not only for capturing escaped POWs, but also preventing escapes.[25] The flyer advised POWs that 'The escape from prison camps is no longer a sport!' It informed them that escapees would be shot on sight and they should, instead, 'Stay in the camp where you will be safe!' Some prisoners annotated the flyer, informing their audience of when it was distributed; others took the time to copy it into their logbooks and colour it in.[26] Tipple and Sergeant Navigator Geoffrey Hall indicate why these men made a record of it. Tipple's logbook includes a drawing of a POW amidst barbed wire, under the title of 'Escaping is no longer a sport. Sez who?' [Figure 2.1].[27] Hall, meanwhile, explained in his diary, on 18 October 1944, that the writer of the flyer, of which there were 'several copies . . . now circulating in the camp',

---

Stephen D. Reicher, 'When Prisoners Take Over the Prison: A Social Psychology of Resistance', *Personality and Social Psychology Review*, 16, 2 (2012), 165.

[22] Gilbert, *POW*, p. 270.

[23] See, for example, IWM 85/50/1, Gunner C. G. King, logbook, pp. 59, 70–3; IWM 61/157/1, Flight Sergeant J. H. Beddis, logbook, p. 44; IWM Documents.8127, Flying Officer A. G. Edwards, logbook, pp. 48–9; IWM Documents.172, Sergeant Navigator G. W. Hall, diary entry, 9 April 1944; Flying Officer J. F. Kennedy, logbook, p. 44.

[24] Monteath, *P. O. W.*, p. 300.

[25] Wylie, *Barbed Wire Diplomacy*, p. 230; Monteath, 'POW "Holiday Camps" in the Third Reich', 491; Monteath, 'Beyond the Colditz Myth', unpaginated.

[26] For annotated flyers, see IWM 95/3/1, Petty Officer H. C. Macey, logbook, p. 74; Quarrie, diary, p. 132. For copied-out flyers, see Edwards, logbook, p. 50; Allen, logbook, pp. 38–9. For others who included this flyer, see IWM P308, Leading Telegraphist H. L. Shipp, logbook, unpaginated; Bompas, logbook, back pocket.

[27] Tipple, logbook, p. 81.

Figure 2.1: 'Escaping is no longer a sport. Sez who?' This drawing in Able Seaman Edwin Tipple's logbook indicates that POWs were not prepared to abide by the instructions contained in 'The escape from prison camps is no longer a sport!' flyer, which was handed out towards the end of the war. This is one example of how POWs appropriated something that was intended to quell them and turned it, instead, into a symbol of their defiance. Styling the POW to look like the 1930s cartoon character Popeye is a nod to Tipple's seafaring background.
    Source: IWM 79/32/1, Able Seaman E. Tipple, logbook, p. 81. Reproduced with permission from Paul Tipple.

points out that in the past, escapers when caught were, for the most part, dealt with tolerantly; escaping was regarded as a battle of wits between prisoners and German security. Now, with Germany fighting on several fronts, manpower is depleted, every available fit man being needed to fight the evil powers of capitalism on the one hand and the monstrous ogre of Soviet communism on the other. Therefore, he goes on to say, there is no-one to spare for rounding up escaped prisoners. In future, if any are found, they will be handed over to the Gestapo for severe punishment, perhaps death.[28]

In fact, the flyer says nothing of the sort. Hall's incorrect paraphrasing of it suggests the significance inferred by POWs: that escapers consumed German manpower and so hindered the war effort and that, henceforth, they were liable to be murdered by the Gestapo. Tipple's defiant drawing in his logbook, meanwhile, indicates that he thought the Germans had no right to prevent what was seen as a duty of British officers. This drawing and diary entry suggest other POWs preserved the flyers as a record of their insubordination: that they would not succumb to this unfair order from the Germans and their belief that their escapes had served to hinder the German war effort. The preservation of this flyer also provides an example of how POWs appropriated something that was intended to quell them and turned it, instead, into a symbol of their defiance.

Prisoners of war also demonstrated defiance in their narratives when they were caught up in reprisal episodes. Reprisals were retaliatory measures carried out by Germany in response to real or supposed misdeeds committed by the British government against German POWs.[29] There were nine of these episodes over the course of the war that affected POWs' daily lives. The most serious and extensive was the 'shackling crisis'.[30] Following a large-scale seaborne raid on the port of Dieppe in France, in August 1942, by Canadian and British forces, there was evidence that German prisoners taken in this action were tied up and blindfolded and, in a smaller commando raid on Sark, in October 1942, German prisoners were shackled and a few were later found shot dead whilst still tied.[31] In response to this, in October 1942, 3,000 POWs, mainly at Oflag VIIB (Eichstätt), Stalag VIIIB, located near Lamsdorf in south-western Poland

---

[28] Hall, diary entry, 18 October 1944.

[29] For this definition of reprisals, see Matthew Stibbe, *British Civilian Internees in Germany: The Ruhleben Camp, 1914–1918* (Manchester: Manchester University Press, 2008), p. 127.

[30] S. P. Mackenzie, 'The Shackling Crisis: A Case Study in the Dynamics of Prisoner-of-War Diplomacy in the Second World War', *International History Review*, 17, 1 (1995), 78–98. For details of these reprisal episodes, see MacKenzie, *The Colditz Myth*, pp. 243–8. There was one reprisal incident between the British and Italians, in relation to messing charges; see Mason, *Prisoners of War*, p. 260.

[31] Mason, *Prisoners of War*, pp. 245–6.

and Stalag 383 (Hohenfels) were put into shackles.[32] Six of the authors of personal narratives drawn upon in *Captives of War*, who were involved in this episode, explain in their diaries that, rather than be broken by these measures, being handcuffed actually made their lives better. Booth described how being forced to wear handcuffs not only improved POWs' relationships with each other, but also gave them a welcome respite from preparing food and enabled them to avoid the crowded conditions of camp life. 'I have been in handcuffs now for ten days and in many ways it has been a very enjoyable period', Booth announced in his diary on 9 November 1942.

> Common misfortune invariably leads to good temper and companionship. ....
> The full story of handcuffing will have to be told later, but suffice it to say that the inconveniences are slight (one's hands get used very quickly to following each other round) and the advantages many, for ... it is a great blessing to have an evening meal brought to you without all the fuss and bother of preparing it. ....
> We can now go outside when we like but are not allowed to mix with the rest of the camp, consequently we are cut off from camp entertainments and such attractions, but we lead on the whole a more peaceful and quieter life.[33]

Towards the end of the war, Booth wrote 'a short account' of some of the other reprisals POWs had experienced. An earlier one, on 30 September 1942, at Oflag IXA/H (Spangenberg), involved personal items being confiscated from Commonwealth POWs in the camp, including towels, razors, scissors and all utensils. Camp orderlies were also to be taken away and moved elsewhere.[34] This was in response to the alleged confiscation of the personal possessions of German officer POWs whilst they were on a transport ship travelling from Egypt to South Africa.[35] Booth described how POWs celebrated the consequences of losing their razors by holding competitions for the longest and silkiest beards. He concluded that the reprisal incident had 'just petered out with no particular harm done to anyone and certainly no good done to the Germans.'[36] Casdagli was involved in it. He recorded, whilst the reprisal was being

---

[32] MacKenzie, *The Colditz Myth*, p. 246.

[33] Booth, diary entry, 9 November 1942. For similar examples, see Hawarden, diary entry, 13 December 1942; IWM 01/25/1, Corporal J. G. White, diary entry, 22 November 1943; NAM 2001-09-300, Second Lieutenant A. R. Jabez-Smith, letter to his father, 20 August 1942; Quarrie, diary, pp. 80–5. Lambert was also involved in the handcuffing episode, but his reaction is harder to discern (IWM 90/19/1, Commander G. T. Lambert, letters to his wife, 24 September 1942, 20 April 1943).

[34] MacKenzie, *The Colditz Myth*, p. 245.

[35] Jonathan F. Vance, 'Men in Manacles: The Shackling of Prisoners of War, 1942–1943', *Journal of Military History*, 59 (1995), 484.

[36] Booth, diary entry, 22 February 1945.

enforced, that 'our spirits are <u>very high</u> and everyone is getting very proud of his beard!'[37]

One other common expression of defiance appearing in these personal narratives relates to the British Free Corps. In 1942, the German Foreign Office and the SS had taken up the idea of raising a unit from British prisoners of war to fight on the eastern front. In June 1943, the Foreign Office established two 'holiday camps' or 'luxury camps', as POWs described them, where the normal privations and restrictions of POW life were removed and prisoners were exposed to subtle propaganda to identify those who might be recruited into the unit.[38] At the start of 1944, the British Free Corps came into existence under the wing of the Waffen-SS (the armed wing of the SS). As part of its recruitment drive, leaflets encouraging POWs to join were distributed to them.[39] Nine logbooks contain these leaflets, all kept by men who were held at Marlag-Milag Nord at Westerminke. The leaflet made the points that the British Free Corps had been conceived and created by British subjects from across the empire, that it condemned the war against Germany and desired peace in Europe, and that it would not wage war against Britain or the British Crown. Shipp annotated his leaflet with the words: 'Needless to say they went empty handed from our camp'; Lieutenant Charles Coles with 'No volunteers!' [Figure 2.2]. Howard recorded a different story. He wrote of men from Milag joining the Corps, adding that their roommates 'immediately burnt all the culprits' gear.' Howard then made his feelings clear on the subject: 'I can't understand any man turning pro-German and I only hope they are treated for their treachery after the war.'[40] In the event, the British Free Corps membership peaked at twenty-seven in January 1945, with some of these recruits joining in the belief that the leaflet had been issued with the authority of the British government, whilst one had the express purpose of wrecking it from within.[41] Just as with the flyer 'The escape from prison camps is no longer a sport!' and the confiscation of razors at Oflag IXA/H (Spangenberg), these nine POWs, who included the British Free Corps leaflet in their logbooks, took what

---

[37] Casdagli, diary entry, 12 October 1942, in Casdagli, *Prouder Than Ever*, p. 97; see also Casdagli, diary entry, 19 November 1942, in Casdagli, *Prouder Than Ever*, p. 100.

[38] Mansel, diary entry, 15 October 1944; Booth, diary entry, 8 July 1944. For more details on these camps see Monteath, 'POW "Holiday Camps" in the Third Reich', 480–503.

[39] MacKenzie, *The Colditz Myth*, pp. 303–5.

[40] Shipp, logbook, p. 59; SWWEC 2001.927, Lieutenant C. L. Coles, logbook, p. 14; Howard, logbook, pp. 129–33. For others who included this leaflet in their logbooks, see Tipple, logbook, p. 54; IWM 81/5/1, Lieutenant P. N. Buckley, logbook, p. 54; Macey, logbook, p. 53; Allen, logbook, pp. 27, 37; SWWEC 2006.690.3–5, Sub-lieutenant H. R. Taylor, logbook, unpaginated.

[41] MacKenzie, *The Colditz Myth*, pp. 304–5.

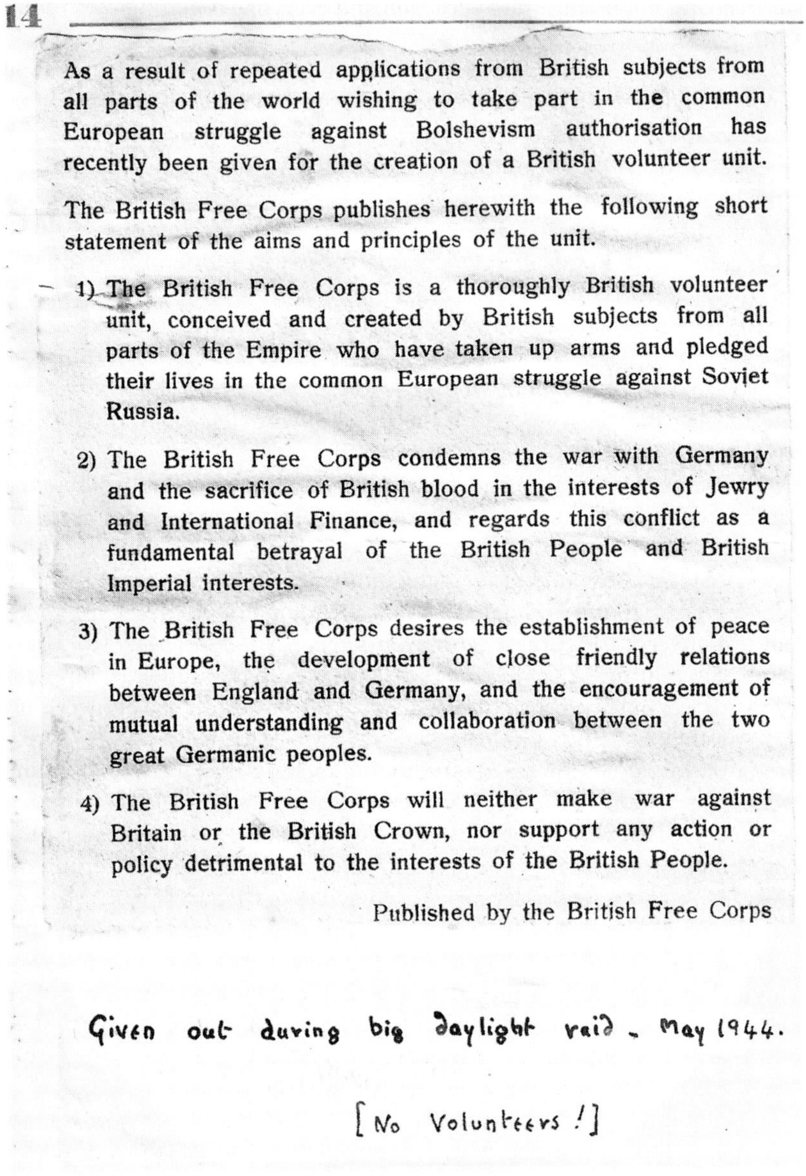

14

As a result of repeated applications from British subjects from all parts of the world wishing to take part in the common European struggle against Bolshevism authorisation has recently been given for the creation of a British volunteer unit.

The British Free Corps publishes herewith the following short statement of the aims and principles of the unit.

1) The British Free Corps is a thoroughly British volunteer unit, conceived and created by British subjects from all parts of the Empire who have taken up arms and pledged their lives in the common European struggle against Soviet Russia.

2) The British Free Corps condemns the war with Germany and the sacrifice of British blood in the interests of Jewry and International Finance, and regards this conflict as a fundamental betrayal of the British People and British Imperial interests.

3) The British Free Corps desires the establishment of peace in Europe, the development of close friendly relations between England and Germany, and the encouragement of mutual understanding and collaboration between the two great Germanic peoples.

4) The British Free Corps will neither make war against Britain or the British Crown, nor support any action or policy detrimental to the interests of the British People.

Published by the British Free Corps

Given out during big daylight raid – May 1944.

[No Volunteers !]

Figure 2.2: The British Free Corps leaflet in the logbook of Lieutenant Charles Coles. In 1944, POWs were given leaflets to encourage them to join the British Free Corps. Including them in their logbook, as Coles did, illustrates how British POWs took what was intended to compromise them and appropriated it instead as a symbol of their defiance.
   Source: SWWEC 2001.927, Lieutenant C. L. Coles, logbook, p. 14. Reproduced with permission from Wendy Coles.

the Germans intended would compromise or quell them but appropriated it instead to illustrate their defiance.

These acts of self-assertion reinforce contemporary understandings as to how individuals challenge authority. According to scholars of psychology Alexander Haslam and Stephen David Reicher, individuals are most inclined to work together to resist domination where the relationship between the subordinated group and those in power could be construed as illegitimate.[42] In each example cited earlier, one can easily see how the actions of the Germans were perceived as illegitimate, and so garnered POWs' defiance. The shooting of the fifty prisoners involved in The Great Escape, for example, was seen as cold-blooded murder. 'The escape from prison camps is no longer a sport!' flyer took away a duty and a right of British officers. Attempts to recruit prisoners into the British Free Corps were perceived as an unreasonable attempt to compromise the British serviceman's loyalty to his nation. Reprisals saw British POWs penalised for actions in which they had no involvement. Casdagli made the very point of reprisals being unjust. When, on 28 November 1942, the reprisal ended and POWs at Oflag IXA/H had their personal items returned to them, Casdagli recorded in his diary how the 'Germans considered that we, the officers of this Oflag, had been "sufficiently punished" – what had we done anyway!!'[43]

One can also see in these acts of defiance another key finding of social psychologists: where individuals share the view that the authority being exerted on them is unjust, then this encourages them to work together to resist domination.[44] In the examples cited earlier, POWs defined their situation as unjust on a collective level. A number of them pasted into their logbooks the British Free Corps recruitment leaflets or 'The escape from prison camps is no longer a sport!' flyers. Booth reports how prisoners became more united when wearing handcuffs, and both he and Casdagli described men at Oflag IXA/H (Spangenberg) collectively responding to reprisals by taking pride in their beards.

One other sign of POWs' collective defiance mentioned in these personal narratives is the wearing of military uniform. Numerous men record in their diaries the imperative of looking smart and being well turned out; others wrote to their wives asking them to send service caps, battle dresses and regimental buttons so they could distinguish themselves in captivity.[45] Their dress was a means by which POWs could continue to

---

[42] Haslam and Reicher, 'When Prisoners Take Over the Prison', 157.
[43] Casdagli, diary entry, 28 November 1942, in Casdagli, *Prouder Than Ever*, p. 101.
[44] Haslam and Reicher, 'When Prisoners Take Over the Prison', 157.
[45] Angove, diary entry, 30 August 1942; IWM P 382 (+ Con Shelf), Naylor, diary entry, 6 July 1942; King, diary entry, 10 March 1945; Mansel, diary entries, 6 September 1940,

act as a recognised military body, and not dissolve into an unmilitary mess of unkempt men. Those in the RAF, in particular, also used their log-books to highlight their attachment to their branch of service. Their logbooks contain illustrations of various Allied planes, the RAF coat of arms as well as poetry about the work of the air force.[46] This close identification can probably be explained both by the RAF consisting of an elite group of personnel and their being grouped together in particular camps.[47]

These personal narratives reveal one other way in which prisoners commonly made sense of being under the power of their enemy. Far from rueing or bemoaning their now subservient position, throughout these narratives POWs asserted themselves as the equal or superior of their captors. Most commonly, and almost uniformly, POWs who were taken prisoner in North Africa record their Italian captors as being their inferiors. Barrington described them as 'only an apology for a soldier, far different from Jerry'. He was 'extremely annoyed' at being given a next-of-kin card that described him as an Italian prisoner. He used his diary to correct this insult. 'In fact' he wrote, 'we had not seen an Italian till hours after we were captured, & not yet had we seen one who looked capable of taking a prisoner.'[48] The suggestion that he might have surrendered to the Italians appears to have been such a slur for Nell that, almost two years after his capture and now a POW in Germany, he was adamant in his diary that one of the repatriated medical personnel 'must tell [my fiancée] that I was captured by Germans and not the Italians as I think she might believe.'[49] Both Brook and Glass, meanwhile, derided the Italians for their brutish behaviour. Brook, upon his arrival at Derna, likened them to 'wild animals', and contrasted them with the Germans, who had received

---

22 March 1941, 15 and 16 November 1943; Barrington, diary entry, 6 March 1943; Matthews, letters to his wife, 2 December 1940, 26 October and 31 December 1941; Hyde, letter to his wife, 31 December 1941.

[46] Six logbooks contain illustrations of Allied planes; see, for example, Beddis, logbook, p. 3; five logbooks carry the RAF coat of arms; see, for example, Edwards, logbook, inside front cover; four logbooks carry poetry; see, for example, SWWEC 2008.134, Warrant Officer A. Clague, logbook, pp. 17, 25, 27. To a lesser extent, naval officers and seamen, and then those from the army, carry similar markers of identifications with their branch of service.

[47] For the RAF flying personnel being an elite group, see Francis, *The Flyer*, p. 13.

[48] Barrington, diary entry, 19 February 1943 and diary entry, unpaginated. For a similar example, see Bains, diary entry, 8 June 1942.

[49] Nell, diary entry, 29 April 1944. Seumas Spark also writes that Australian POWs 'had scant regard for the fighting abilities of Italian personnel, and some felt shame at being a captive of the Italians' ('Australian Prisoners of War of Italy in World War II: Public and Private Histories', in Joan Beaumont, Lachlan Grant and Aaron Pegram (eds.), *Beyond Surrender. Australian Prisoners of War in the Twentieth Century*, [e-book] Carlton, Victoria: Melbourne University Press, 2015, unpaginated).

the prisoners with 'cool preserve'. Glass distinguished between the Germans who captured him, who he believed would have given him more rations if able, and the Italians, who had 'scientifically laid down' a process for POWs' starvation. 'For each of these meals', he explained, 'we queued up, insufficiently clothed and in the bitter cold for a period of from 1 ½ to 2 ½ hours, depending on the whim of the ~~swine~~ Italian Commandant.' Glass' replacement of the word 'swine' with 'Italian' suggests he saw the Commandant's cruel behaviour as a part of his nationality.[50]

The report for army psychiatrists, Technical Memorandum 13, noted this attitude towards the Italians and attributed it to their 'petty sadism', which made it easier for prisoners to 'despise' them. Technical Memorandum 13 also noted that British POWs found it 'more difficult' to 'despise' the Germans. In these personal narratives, British POWs do not express the same universal contempt for their German captors.[51] They still undermined the captor–captive power relationship, but in more varied and, sometimes, counterintuitive ways.

One way in which POWs did this was by portraying themselves as better off than their guards. These men comment on how they were the envy of their captors when it came to material goods. The parcels POWs received in captivity gave them access to food and commodities that were impossible for Germans to obtain, even on the black market.[52] POWs wrote in their diaries of how their captors pestered them for their better-quality cigarettes, or described the great lengths to which guards would go to in order to bring items into the camps that POWs demanded in exchange for the goods in their parcels.[53] Under a section in his logbook entitled 'Bribery of Germans', Howard explained that, once cigarette parcels began to arrive from home, the 'real barbaric manners' of the German guards altered, and they started to

quieten down … all because they saw that they had a chance of a cigarette. So whether it was pity on the part of the 'gef' [POW] seeing a German guard

---

[50] Brook, diary entry, p. 20; Glass, diary entry, 27 January 1942–5 February 1942; see also diary entry, 17 September 1943.

[51] TNA WO 32/10757, Directorate of Army Psychiatry. Technical Memorandum No. 13. The Prisoner of War Comes Home. Notes Prepared for the Information of Army Psychiatrists, prepared by DAP, May 1944. On British soldiers being impressed by those in the German Army, see Allport, *Browned Off and Bloody-Minded*, pp. 228–9.

[52] East, diary entry, 18 December 1943.

[53] On cigarettes, see King, diary entry, 30 April 1941; Barrington, diary entries, 12 May and 25 July 1943. Glass provides a counter-example of POWs at Campo PG 65 following officers and guards around the camp, and collecting the butts they threw away, Glass, diary entry, Chapter XIII, 'Food and cigarettes'. On guards bringing goods into the camps, see Hawarden, diary entries, 31 August and 23 October 1943.

without a smoke or whether it was for bribery reasons in order to lead a life of peacefulness, smokes were given to barrack guards and guards on the wire.[54]

British POWs also undermined the captor–captive power relationship by portraying prisoners and guards as the equals of one another. Historian Matthias Reiss has studied the experiences of German prisoners of war from the Afrika Corps, some 135,000 of whom had surrendered to the Allies at the end of the Tunisian campaign in May 1943 and subsequently were shipped to the United States and interned there for up to three years. He argues that fraternisation on the basis of social equality indicates that American guards and German POWs saw themselves as part of the same race. Reiss highlights how the friend/foe dichotomy in prisoner-of-war camps could be undermined through showing understanding, having shared experiences or cooperation.[55] Each of these actions is also referred to in these narratives, often appearing in extremely unlikely circumstances.

Understanding between POWs and guards is expressed in the context of reprisal episodes, which is curious given these brought into the POW camp a dispute being fought out between the belligerents at the most senior level. The 1942 'shackling crisis', for example, saw both Hitler and Winston Churchill's intervention.[56] Stewart was caught up in the final reprisal measure of the war, which took place in January 1945. In response to news that German prisoners in a British-run POW transit camp in Egypt were forced to sleep on sand by Jewish guards, all the bedding and furniture in Oflag VIIB (Eichstätt), Stalag VIIIC (Sagan) and Stalag 357 in Fallingbostel, Lower Saxony, was removed, plus the theatre and canteen closed.[57] When all the furniture was taken out of Stewart's hut in Oflag VIIB (Eichstätt), he noted how his guards

admitted that they thought reprisals were a very poor method of retaliation ... the inevitable result has always been that the Germans have become much more sympathetic & friendly. At first they obviously feel shifty about it & expect us to be rude to them, but we all realise that they aren't individually responsible and treat them as though nothing has happened and they appreciate it.

Not only did Stewart conceive of the guards as sympathetic to the position in which POWs had been placed, but he also portrayed the guards as grateful for the understanding that POWs, in turn, showed.[58]

---

[54] Howard, logbook, pp. 120–1.
[55] Matthias Reiss, 'Bronzed Bodies behind Barbed Wire: Masculinity and the Treatment of German Prisoners of War in the United States during World War II', *The Journal of Military History*, 69, 2 (2005), 502; Reiss, 'The Importance of Being Men', 37.
[56] Monteath, 'POW "Holiday Camps" in the Third Reich', 490.
[57] MacKenzie, *The Colditz Myth*, p. 248.
[58] Stewart, diary entry, 15 January 1945. For similar examples, see Hall, diary entry, 1 February 1945; Hawarden, diary entry, 17 January 1943. Vance also notes that during

One of the shared experiences singled out in these men's personal narratives appears in another unlikely context: escape attempts. This is surprising given that escapes were the prime threat to camp security. POWs describe their guards as interested in and almost admiring of their escape efforts. 'I have a sneaking belief that the Commandant was rather intrigued by the effort', wrote Nell of a tunnel found at Stalag IVB (Mühlberg). He then added: 'He was a prisoner himself in the last war. He is not a bad sort of bloke really. It is the shower of bastards under his command who are the trouble.'[59] When two Frenchmen escaped from Oflag VIID (Tittmoning), Canon King declared the prisoners to be in soaring spirits and 'G's took it pretty well. It had been a brilliant effort. The home-made disguises had been perfect, & are much sought for by the G's for their escapist museum.'[60] It is very questionable whether there was such a thing as an escapist museum, but the fact that King considered it might exist indicates the high regard he thought the Germans held for such initiative.

The most explicit way in which captors and captives are perceived as equals in these personal narratives is in relation to their efforts towards co-operation. Both King and Casdagli describe, in great detail, the ways in which POWs and their guards worked together for mutual benefit, but they reacted to it in opposite ways. King wrote in his diary of the 'entente' at Oflag VIID (Tittmoning).[61] On one occasion, he described how it was strengthened by prisoners helping to clean the camp ahead of a German general's visit. In return for the prisoners' efforts, the senior British officer (SBO), who led other prisoners in the camp and was the point of contact between captors and captives, had secured a promise that no more prisoners would be sent to the camp, as well as permission to obtain better furniture and more orderlies. The German staff, meanwhile, had received praise for their camp being clean and well-run. This co-operation left everyone, as King described it, 'purring'. The following month, King recorded British POWs being allowed to go bathing outside the camp whilst on parole, that is, they gave their word that they would not try to escape. He described the beneficial effects on one occasion. 'Like Sunday School children', he wrote, 'we rambled home. ... We felt years' [*sic*] younger and strangely free.'[62]

In contrast, when POWs gave their parole at Oflag XIIB, at Hadamar in western Germany, and promised not to escape during Christmas 1944,

---

the shackling crisis, prisoners believed the guards found the matter distasteful; see Vance, 'Men in Manacles', 486.

[59] Nell, diary entry, 7 July 1944.

[60] King, diary entry, 21 August 1941; see also diary entry, 4 February 1941. For a similar example, see Nell, diary entry, 7 July 1944.

[61] King, diary entry, 28 March 1941.   [62] King, diary entries, 13 May and 17 June 1941.

Casdagli responded with virulent opposition.[63] 'In MY opinion this is a very wrong action', he wrote in his diary

> because it is being done solely for our comfort (which is NOT one of the reasons sanctioned by the War Office); secondly, the Germans can reduce their guards for this period and are free from responsibility of our escaping; we should keep them at full pressure at all times.

Casdagli stated his objection to the SBO, but was advised he had to obey this direct order. He retorted in his diary,

> Although others I spoke to FULLY AGREE with my view and my ACTION, only one ... had the GUTS to do the same – so the laissez-faire spirit wins again – it is ABSOLUTELY INFURIATING. What can the action of two people do out of two hundred and sixty – had fifty or sixty gone he would have HAD to change his orders and NOT give parole for the camp. My VIEWS are very STRONG on this.[64]

Casdagli's words make his fury clear, emphasised further through his use of capital letters.

These ways in which POWs responded to being under the power of their enemy demonstrate how their relationships with their German guards were characterised by more than antagonism or animosity, but it should also be remembered that this is the view of captivity these POWs wanted to project. Whether or not portraying themselves as the equals or superiors of their enemy actually made POWs feel empowered in their captive state is more difficult to assess, although King's choice of simile might provide one answer. The entente may have improved prisoners' material lives, but King's comparison of POWs to 'Sunday School children' suggests a recognition that it had undermined them both as men and as combatants. Not only were they now like children, but well-behaved children at that. The insights such a metaphor offers are returned to in the final part of this chapter.

A Kriegie Way of Life

Being under the power of their captors was just one of the hallmarks that defined imprisonment by the enemy. There were many others: living in enemy territory, existing in a restricted space and in impoverished conditions and not knowing when the end of the war might come. POWs, particularly those who, under the Geneva Convention, could not be forced to work for the Third Reich, also faced unoccupied time stretching out ahead of them. The previous chapter indicated how British prisoners

---

[63] For an example of the form POWs signed when they gave their parole, see Figure 2.5.
[64] Casdagli, diary entry, 22 December 1944, in Casdagli, *Prouder Than Ever*, pp. 164–5.

of war made sense of facing an indeterminate sentence of imprisonment: by anticipating the war's imminent end. The rest of this chapter explores how POWs responded to these other challenges.

One of the core means by which POWs made sense of their imprisoned existence was by representing themselves as continuing to lead 'normal' lives. Examples of this appear repeatedly in personal narratives. The idea that POWs kept themselves occupied in captivity is, most broadly, reflected in references to their daily routines. For example, numerous logbooks and diaries and, more commonly, letters detail how, despite their empty time, POWs adhered to a schedule of activities. Shortly after his capture, Matthews informed his wife that

A typical day is: – rise at 6.15am, a few gentle exercises, shave, & cold shower. 7.0 coffee only & then complete dressings, make bed, tidy room, & out of it by 8.45. 9.5 [sic] parade & roll call & afterwards there is usually something to do. 11.0 cereal soup & potatoes 12.0 classes, reading, writing, & walking round our small field. 5.0pm cereal soup & potatoes. 6.0 canteen. 7.0 lecture of general interest, concert &c &c 8.0 supper from food saved from previous meals 9.0 prayers, voluntary but well attended. 9.15 bridge &c in our rooms. 10.30 bed.[65]

Setting out these daily routines indicated to those at home that POWs were disciplined, active and occupied in the camps, a point Matthews emphasised when he stated that prayers were 'voluntary' but still 'well attended'.

The logbooks and diaries of non-working POWs also elaborate on the various activities that occupied much of their time, whether through descriptions of the different types of sports played in captivity, such as football, rugby, cricket and boxing, or discussions of the lectures and classes they taught and participated in, as well as the exams they took.[66] These narratives carry accounts and photos of camps' orchestras, bands and concerts.[67] They were also a place where some POWs showcased their art.[68]

Two activities feature particularly prominently in these narratives. One is reading. Books were supplied to camps from autumn 1940 by the Red

[65] Matthews, letter to his wife, 23 July 1940. Nine other personal narratives set out such daily routines.
[66] On sports, see Naylor, logbook, pp. 62–6; Quarrie, diary, pp. 63, 116, 118, 120, 130; Bompas, diary entry, p. 19. On education, see Quarrie, diary, pp. 90, 92; East, diary entry, 1 November 1943; Hall, diary entry, 15 May 1943. For both, see McDermott-Brown, logbook, p. 54; Kennedy, logbook, p. 30.
[67] Bompas, diary entry, pp. 20–1; Kennedy, logbook, p. 32; IWM 05/3/1, Lieutenant L. G. F. Upshall, logbook, unpaginated; Shipp, logbook, unpaginated; IWM 89/16/1–89/16/2(P), Warrant Officer H. C. M. Jarvis, scrapbook; East, diary entry, 1 November 1943.
[68] Clague titled two pages in his logbook 'Some early efforts at painting' (Clague, logbook, unpaginated).

Cross and St. John Indoor Recreations Section. By the time the war ended, it had supplied 239,500 volumes. The YMCA also sent more than a million books on behalf of the U.S. Red Cross.[69] Numerous POWs compiled long lists in their diaries and logbooks of all the books they read.[70] Reading was undoubtedly a form of escapism for these men, but, by tallying up the books they had read, POWs were also able to show how profitably they had spent their time.[71] It was a point Stewart, who read about 350 books in nearly five years of captivity, articulated towards the end of the war.

Early on in this diary I claimed that though in many ways we may have deteriorated in prison, in some ways we have definitely progressed. Reading & the instruction & thought resulting from it is probably the most obvious example of this & certainly the most universal. No prisoner, I suppose, can deny that he has read more & over a wider field in prison than he would have done at home, even if there hadn't been a war on.[72]

Stewart's final sentence also hints at another reason for the compilation of these lists. Reading could be undertaken more productively in wartime captivity than any other setting: it was a way of demonstrating that POWs could excel at something whilst imprisoned.

The other activity that features most prominently in these personal narratives is theatrical productions. These were common in camps and, over time, became highly organised affairs. For example, by 1944, Oflag 79 (Brunswick), which housed just over 2,000 POWs, had two separate stages, each with its own theatre companies; similarly at Stalag 383 (Hohenfels), which had two stages with several hundred seats, each of the 6,000 prisoners could look forward to watching a show every fortnight.[73] POWs' diaries describe these entertainments; their logbooks often list the shows performed in various camps, some illustrated with sets, stages and audiences.[74] Logbooks and diaries also contain photographs of theatrical productions.[75] Hawarden recorded how, by 1944, all

[69] Gillies, *The Barbed-Wire University*, pp. 256–7.
[70] Brook, diary, unpaginated; Mansel, see end of 1943 diary; Naylor, logbook, pp. 38–9; Edwards, logbook, p. 101.
[71] On escapism, see Gillies, *The Barbed-Wire University*, p. 257.
[72] Stewart, diary entry, 10 March 1945.
[73] MacKenzie, *The Colditz Myth*, p. 210; ACICR, C SC, Germany, Oflag 79, 19 September 1944. For further details on theatrical entertainments, see Moore and Hately, 'Captive Audience', 58–73.
[74] For descriptions, see Bompas, diary entry, pp. 20–1, 29, 32; Howard, logbook, p. 77; McDermott-Brown, logbook, p. 54. Nine personal narratives list shows; see, for example, McDermott-Brown, logbook, pp. 168–71. Macey lists the shows, and includes a note about the play and the part he held for each one (Macey, logbook, pp. 37–40). Three personal narratives provide illustrated lists; see, for example, Edwards, logbook, pp. 64–5.
[75] Ten personal narratives contain photos; see, for example, Upshall, logbook, unpaginated.

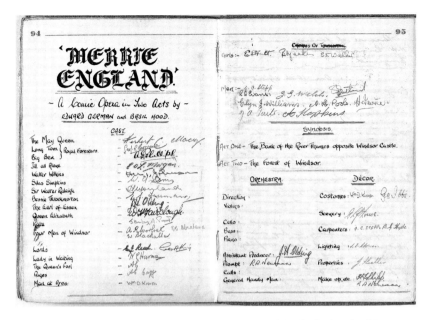

Figure 2.3: Programme of 'Merrie England' in the logbook of Petty Officer Herbert Macey. The time and care taken in copying out programmes and collecting signatures, as Macey did in his logbook, demonstrates the importance of these theatrical productions for prisoners of war.

Source: IWM 95/3/1, Petty Officer H. C. Macey, logbook, pp. 94–5. Reproduced with permission from Andrew William Macey and Alison Mary Campbell.

the shows at Stalag 383 (Hohenfels) had photos taken of them and several POWs had produced 'very fine albums ... hoping to get them home as souvenirs.'[76] Programmes of these various performances were also pasted into these narratives.[77] Some men even took the time and care to copy them out.[78] Others went a step further: not only did they write out the programme, but also gathered signatures from the cast and production team [Figure 2.3].[79]

[76] Hawarden, diary entry, 25 March 1944.
[77] Nine personal narratives contain programmes; see, for example, Upshall, logbook, unpaginated.
[78] IWM 05/57/1, Sergeant E. G. Ball, logbook, pp. 12–13; Buckley, logbook, pp. 51–2; Bompas, diary entry, unpaginated.
[79] Shipp, logbook, p. 107; Macey, logbook, pp. 94–5.

The time and manpower required to produce a performance, plus the distraction an actual performance offered, explain why theatre productions were recorded so prominently. During the actual performance, those watching could imagine themselves elsewhere; those who participated could temporarily become someone other than a prisoner of war and experience different material comforts from those available in captivity, such as when a set enabled them to sit on a couch or at their own personal desk. Preparing for performances probably involved a greater number of POWs, and more of their time, than other activities. In addition to rehearsal time for the cast, prisoners were involved in the building of theatres, including designing and constructing the set; costume creation and make up; the production of programmes, tickets and advertising posters; and dressing the actors and serving as ushers and programme sellers.[80]

It is also likely that POWs kept records of these theatrical productions as tokens of what they achieved in captivity. In their diaries, POWs highlighted how these performances, along with other activities pursued in captivity, were equal to anything produced on civvy street. For example, of the arts and crafts exhibition at Campo PG 73, located in Carpi in northern Italy, Barrington wrote that the works 'would not have disgraced an art gallery in peace time.'[81] Of the dance band at Stalag 383 (Hohenfels), Hawarden said it was 'as good as any provincial dance band at home', whilst Corporal Jack White gave a back-handed compliment to the Sunday 'Concert at 13': it 'was terrific, have seen several worse in Blighty.'[82] Angove went even further. He excitedly wrote, in his diary to his mother, of the shows put on at Campo PG 35 in Padula, south-western Italy, that 'quite seriously they are good enough for the West End stage & in some cases are better than shows I have seen in town', although when Angove moved to Campo PG 19 at Bologna, northern Italy, he recognised the standard of performance at his previous camp had been particularly high.[83]

POWs' keenness to demonstrate their achievement in recreating a normal society is also commonly reflected in their references to their own inventiveness. These diaries and logbooks contain diagrams and photos of their creations, which enabled them to brew beer, make tea or cook.[84] A number explicitly emphasises prisoners' resourcefulness. Squadron Leader Dennis Armitage wrote home in October 1941, 'Until you have lived

---

[80] These benefits are also recorded in Feltman, *The Stigma of Surrender*, p. 128.

[81] Barrington, diary entry, 19 June 1943.

[82] Hawarden, diary entry, 21 November 1942; see also diary entry, 30 May 1943; White, diary entry, 11 January 1942.

[83] Angove, diary entries, 8 May and 24 August 1943. For similar examples, see East, diary entry, p. 15; Kennedy, logbook, p. 32.

[84] Eight personal narratives highlight these inventions; see, for example, IWM 61/161/1 Warrant Officer H. L. Hurrell, logbook, p. 9 and unpaginated.

with people who have been Prisoners of War for a year or so, you can have no idea at all of what the word "improvise" means.'[85] When all the furniture was removed from Stewart's hut in Oflag VIIB (Eichstätt), during the final reprisal episode of the war, he commented that two tables and four benches were quickly constructed out of 'locker doors & bits of chair', adding 'Everything is back to normal again. There's no denying that prisoners are resourceful'.[86]

These examples indicate how POWs represented their daily lives as normal and productive. They paint a picture of prisoners mastering the challenges of boredom, inactivity and impoverishment by undertaking activities commensurate with life at home. By highlighting in their personal narratives how they continued to carry out these normal forms of work, sport and entertainment, POWs also re-instated their masculinity.[87] They still possessed the attributes frequently associated with men: being active, productive and resourceful.

At the same time, however, these personal narratives indicate that POWs were equally keen to highlight the unique aspects of their existence. Logbooks and diaries, for example, explain certain facets of their new world to their readers. They describe the daily roll calls and the physical environment of the camps, and contain photos and drawings of different aspects of them, plus plans of the camp layout [Figure 2.4].[88] They contain physical traces taken directly from their captive world, including camp money issued by the Germans and Italians, along with other tokens of these men's imprisoned existence, such as POW identity cards and discs; parole forms [Figure 2.5]; cuttings from *The Camp*, the German propaganda paper issued to British POWs; and even samples of German tea and coffee.[89]

---

[85] SWWEC 99.117, Squadron Leader D. L. Armitage, letter to his mother, 29 October 1941.

[86] Stewart, diary entry, 15 January 1945. For similar examples, see Taylor, logbook, unpaginated; East, diary entry, p. 15.

[87] For this argument, see Gill Plain, 'Before the Colditz Myth: Telling POW Stories in Postwar British Cinema', *Journal of War and Culture Studies*, 7, 3 (2014), 281.

[88] For roll calls, see Bains, diary entry, 5 August–17 October 1942; Hall, diary entry, 4 May 1943. For physical environment, see Hall, diary entries, 26 April and 10 July 1943; IWM Documents.2483, Second Lieutenant B. A. Brooke, diary entries, 6 October–4 November 1940 and 8–15 June 1941; Bompas, diary, p. 32; East, diary, p. 15; Kennedy, logbook, pp. 28, 41; McDermott-Brown, logbook, p. 54; Taylor, logbook, unpaginated. Fifteen personal narratives contain drawings or photos of the camp; see for example, Macey, logbook, p. 106; Beddis, logbook, pp. 30–1; Jarvis, scrapbook, unpaginated. Eleven narratives contain plans of the camp; see, for example, Tipple, logbook, pp. 52–3; Graydon, logbook, p. 68.

[89] Sixteen narratives have camp money pasted into them; see, for example, Shipp, logbook, pp. 56–67; Hurrell, logbook, pp. 1–3. For identity discs, see Allen, logbook, p. 113. For identity cards, see Kennedy, logbook, unpaginated. For parole forms, see Naylor, logbook, unpaginated. For 'The Camp', see Quarrie, diary, pp. 64, 66. For tea and coffee, see Liddle RAF 042, Warrant Officer G. B. Gallagher, logbook, p. 112.

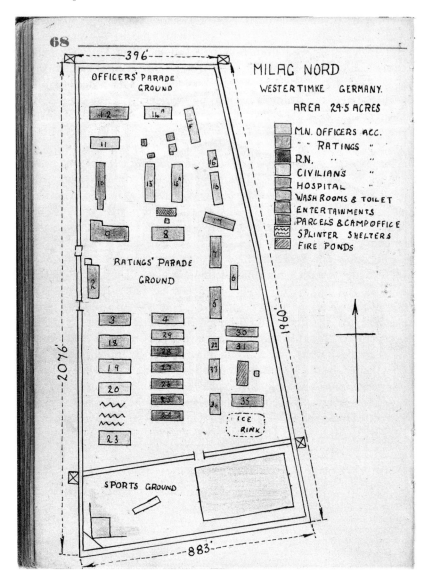

Figure 2.4: Plan of Milag Nord in the logbook of 5th Engineer Robert Graydon. Including plans of their camp's layout in their personal narratives, as Graydon did in his logbook, was one way in which POWs highlighted the unique aspects of their existence.

Source: IWM Documents.2996, 5th Engineer R. A. Graydon, logbook, p. 68. Reproduced with permission from Garth Graydon.

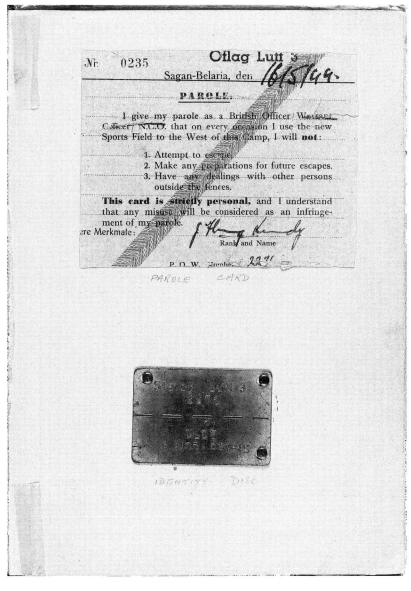

Figure 2.5: Identity disc and parole form in the logbook of Flying Officer John Kennedy. POWs also highlighted the unique aspects of their existence by including, in their logbooks, physical traces taken directly from their captive world. Kennedy did this by pasting into his logbook his identity disc and parole form. Kennedy obtained these items after he and others raided the German administration block after the guards had fled as the Russians approached their camp.

Source: IWM Documents.16311, Flying Officer J. F. Kennedy, logbook, unpaginated. Reproduced with permission from Robin Craig Kennedy.

These narratives also emphasise how POWs occupied the unique space of living in enemy territory. They do this in a variety of ways. They contain diagrams and maps, tracing the routes that POWs took from their point of capture to their permanent POW camps, sometimes with subsequently added routes of their journey across Europe back out of captivity. They carry mementoes of German life, from banknotes to military emblems.[90] A number of logbooks contains the silver strips, known as 'window', which the Allies dropped to interfere with German radar. These were pasted in, and annotated accordingly 'Found in North Compound, Stalag Luft II', in Barth in northern Germany, explained Gunner Cyril King, 'Thousands of them – perhaps 10 tons of them on one raid. Originally with a black background, this silver paper is dropped by bombing aircraft in order to counteract German detection apparatus, ie radar.'[91] In these ways, POWs also represented themselves as witnesses to life in Nazi Germany and to events in war-torn Europe.

The aspect of British POWs' unique existence that receives the greatest attention in these personal narratives is their food. Article 11 of the 1929 Geneva Convention demanded that 'the food ration of prisoners of war shall be equivalent in quantity and quality to that of the depot troops.'[92] By and large, both Germany and Italy failed to meet this requirement.[93] Hunger is a frequent theme in these men's diaries.[94] They also set out in their diaries and logbooks what food was issued at which times of the day and provide lists of the different rations they received from their captors, often giving precise quantities of each foodstuff, and how these varied at particular times during the war.[95] These lists are striking: they indicate that, for some POWs, writing about their hunger was insufficient. They wanted their personal narratives to carry objective proof of their famished existence. Some annotated their lists to this effect. In case his readers misunderstood the frugality of the foodstuffs issued per week at Oflag

---

[90] Twelve personal narratives set out these routes; see, for example, Graydon, logbook, pp. 86–7. Three logbooks contain banknotes; see, for example, Tipple, logbook, pp. 49, 51. Eleven logbooks contain cuttings from the German press; see, for example, IWM Documents.19672, Flight Lieutenant P. A. Cunningham, logbook, p. 43. Four logbooks contain stamps; see, for example, Hurrell, logbook, unpaginated. Two logbooks contain emblems from uniforms; see, for example, Kennedy, logbook, unpaginated.

[91] King, logbook, p. 21. Five other logbooks contain anti-radar strips.

[92] Article 11, 'Convention Relative to the Treatment of Prisoners of War'.

[93] Kochavi, *Confronting Captivity*, p. 23.

[94] See, for example, Glass, diary entry, 28 June 1943; Jenkins, diary entry, 24 July 1942; Fayers, diary entry, 31 March 1945; Hall, diary entry, 9 May 1943.

[95] Twenty-two personal narratives detail issues of food; see, for example, Laker, diary entry, pp. 12–13. For how POWs set out the exact quantities of each foodstuff they received, see Coles, logbook, pp. 22–3. For how these varied at different times of the war, see Allen, logbook, pp. 9–12.

VIIB (Eichstätt), between 1942 and 1944, Lieutenant Robert Johnson circled one set of ingredients in his logbook with the words, 'This is all that is supplied to produce soup or some meat dish on 5 days.' He then summarised: 'The above scale works out at 1644 calories per man per day. A working man at Home should have at least 3600 calories, an invalid on light diet 1800 and an elderly person doing little work 2000 to 2500 calories!'[96]

Along with the lists of German rations, these logbooks and diaries also show the contents of Red Cross food parcels, often comparing how they differed according to which nation supplied them.[97] These lists signify how precious parcels were to POWs: a point that 4th Mate C. W. G. Allen emphasised both through words and art. His logbook contains detailed illustrations of each of the items included in these parcels; written beside them is 'God bless the Red Cross, they saved us from starvation' [Figure 2.6].[98] These drawings were a way of honouring the Red Cross: the time and care spent in creating these illustrations being an indication of the high esteem in which the organisation was held.[99] Leslie McDermott-Brown, who served as a cadet, meanwhile, suggests the parcels were so important that he developed an emotional attachment to them. After setting out the contents of one, he described it as 'the PoW's friend'.[100]

These descriptions of camp life, the lists of rations and food contained in Red Cross parcels and the mementos pasted in these logbooks all hint at a broader way in which British POWs made sense of their captivity: they indicate these men were creating, whilst in captivity, a 'Kriegie identity' out of the unique aspects of their experience. Far from being ashamed or humiliated by their imprisonment, these men wanted to communicate their distinctive life to the outside world. As well as documenting this new life that had been thrust upon them, POWs also acknowledged their unique existence through references to how they adapted to their new-found conditions. Diaries and logbooks indicate that a specific language arose in captivity. East was one of many POWs to

[96] IWM Documents.9020, Lieutenant R. G. Johnson, logbook, p. 110. For similar examples, see Barrington, logbook, pp. 32–3; Macey, logbook, pp. 9–10; Quarrie, diary, p. 32.

[97] Nineteen personal narratives list Red Cross food parcels; see, for example, Shipp, logbook, unpaginated.

[98] Allen, logbook, unpaginated. For illustrations of both Red Cross parcels and German rations, see Kennedy, logbook, pp. 144–5. For others who similarly annotated their lists of parcels, see Quarrie, diary, p. 58; Howard, logbook, p. 103.

[99] On POWs honouring individuals who had assisted them, see Feltman, *The Stigma of Surrender*, p. 181.

[100] McDermott-Brown, logbook, p. 59.

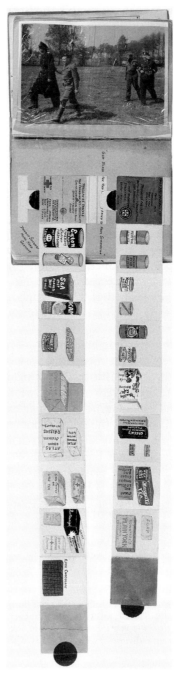

Figure 2.6: 'God bless the Red Cross, they saved us from starvation' in the logbook of 4th Mate C. W. G. Allen. This illustration in Allen's logbook shows each item in a Red Cross parcel. The time and care spent

include a number of definitions in his diary of the new words these men
had invented to describe their life, such as:

Mossing   to store up food for a rainy day is to moss and a 'mosser' is
            looked down upon.
Mucker   one who shares one's parcel, and 'muck in' with the cooking.
To bash   to eat up in one go.

Quarrie also listed some POW vocabulary in his diary, and then showed
its remoteness to the outsider by quoting an example of a sentence formed
from it. 'A question overheard at VIIB', he wrote: 'Have you seen the new
doover the whackos have got for their smokeless?' This, he explained,
meant, 'Have you seen the new contraption the Australian officers have
adapted for their special portable heating stoves for tea brewing
purposes?'[101]
   These personal narratives also suggest POWs developed a 'Kriegie
identity' through the many references they contain to the peculiar way
of life prisoners had developed. These allusions appear in all sorts of
contexts, both through words and drawings, but are always infused with
humour, making light of POWs' situation through self-mockery. Flying
Officer Arthur Edwards, for example, in his logbook, ridiculed
POWs' hopeful attitude regarding an early end to the war, through
a drawing titled 'The optimist' [Figure 2.7].[102] The calendar shows
6 June 1944, the first day of the Allied landings on the Normandy
beaches, otherwise known as D-Day. In front of it stands a POW. His
bags are already packed and he is shaving, in preparation for his imminent
return home. POWs' obsession with escape attempts are shown in

---

Caption for Figure 2.6: (cont.)

in creating this drawing indicates how vital these parcels were to
prisoners, and the high esteem in which the Red Cross was held for
providing them.
   Source: Documents.3746, 4th Mate C. W. G. Allen, logbook,
unpaginated.

[101] East, diary entry, 26 January 1945; Quarrie, diary, pp. 60–1 and 12 October 1941. For
similar examples, see Coles, logbook, pp. 16–17; Taylor, logbook, unpaginated;
Gallagher, logbook, p. 57; Scott, logbook, p. 113, held in IWM 86/35/1, the private
papers of J. D. Hewitt; IWM 99/68/1–2, Captain J. W. M. Mansel, letter to his mother,
10 June 1943.
[102] Edwards, logbook, p. 13.

Figure 2.7: 'The optimist'. POWs developed a 'Kriegie identity' through the peculiar way of life they developed in captivity. Their references to these ways of life are always infused with humour and self-mockery. This drawing, in Flying Officer Arthur Edwards' logbook, ridiculed POWs' optimistic attitude towards their liberation and homecoming.

Source: Flying Officer A. G. Edwards, logbook, p. 13. Reproduced with permission from David Kausmann.

"IT WON'T BE LONG NOW, GEORGE.!! "

Figure 2.8: 'It won't be long now, George!!' Warrant Officer Harold Hurrell's logbook is one of many to contain this drawing of an escape. It illustrates one other aspects of the captives' lives that POWs mocked: their obsession with escape attempts.
  Source: IWM 61/161/1, Warrant Officer H. L. Hurrell, logbook, p. 11. Reproduced with permission from Vicky Briggs.

a number of drawings in logbooks, which all follow the same theme of two POWs in a tunnel extending beyond the barbed wire. One says to the other, 'It won't be long now, George!!' Above them, where the tunnel is about to emerge, a German guard waits for them [Figure 2.8].[103] POWs also highlighted and laughed at their peculiar way of life by suggesting, in extreme ways, that they might continue to exhibit some of their strange habits once back at home. A few referred to this possibility in their letters. In November 1943, Reverend Robert Wild wondered to his wife 'if, when I get home, I shall keep looking out of the window to see if the guard has been changed.'[104] Angove suggested in a diary entry in June 1943 that, when he arrived back, he would

---

[103] Hurrell, logbook, p. 11. This cartoon features in nine logbooks; see also, for example, Gallagher, logbook, p. 11; Beddis, logbook, p. 23.
[104] Wild, letter to his wife, 7 November 1943. For a similar example, see SWWEC 1999.14, Second Lieutenant F. J. Burnaby-Atkins, letter to his mother, 11 April 1944.

be leaping on to the window sill with a brew tin in one hand & a box of wood & paper in the other & shall crouch there kindling a fire for a cup of tea & again will be seen walking round & round in circles in the garden. . . . In the mornings about half-past nine I shall probably be found dashing into the garden for roll call & being quite unable to eat unless the bugle has sounded.[105]

Others used art to portray such peculiar habits. Flying Officer John Kennedy's logbook contains a series of such illustrations. One is of an ex-POW who has forgotten how to have conjugal relations. It shows him and his wife lying in bunk beds. His wife sits in the lower bunk, naked. The POW is in the top, wearing pyjamas, drinking tea and reading a book. 'Twelve o'clock!' he calls out. 'Your turn to put the lights out, Darling!'[106] His wife looks less than impressed.

The other feature of these personal narratives that suggests a 'Kriegie identity' was created in captivity is the appearance of an 'out-group'. Social identity theorists have shown how identity is formed of in-groups and out-groups. The in-group is the social group with which a person identifies; the out-group, by being different, confirms the in-group's shared identity by its difference from and lack of understanding of what the in-group is experiencing.[107] The replication of what were known in captivity as 'mail bag splitters' suggests POWs forged an in-group identity against people at home not understanding what life in captivity was like.

Mail bag splitters were extracts from letters purportedly sent to POWs from friends and relatives at home. Either they were printed anonymously and pinned up on camp notice boards, or they were circulated through camps by rumour. POWs then copied lists of them into their diaries and logbooks, often giving them titles such as 'The things they say!! [see Figure 2.9]' or 'Extracts from "kriegie mail"'.

The 'mail bag splitters' are notable for their insensitivity and obtuseness. A number belittles prisoners' contribution to the war effort, such as:

I am sorry our engagement is ended. I would rather marry a 1943 hero than a 1941 Coward.[108]

So glad you were shot down before flying became dangerous.[109]

---

[105] Angove diary entry, 18 June 1943.

[106] Kennedy, logbook, p. 141. For similar examples, see Beddis, logbook, pp. 9, 67; Gallagher, logbook, p. 35. Such cartoons appear to have been popular amongst POWs as they are contained in magazines produced in different POW camps; see cartoon by E. J. Scolley (1942) reproduced in E. C. G. Beckwith (ed.), *Selections from The Quill. A Collection of Prose, Verse and Sketches by Officers Prisoner-of-War in Germany, 1940–1945* (London: Country Life, 1947), p. 125; Padula Parade, February 1943, held in IWM 66/174/1, private papers of Captain R. L. Angove.

[107] Henri Tajfel, 'Experiments in Intergroup Discrimination', *Scientific American*, 223 (November 1970), 96–102.

[108] Shipp, logbook, p. 66.   [109] Beddis, logbook, 'Some of the things they wrote', p. 108.

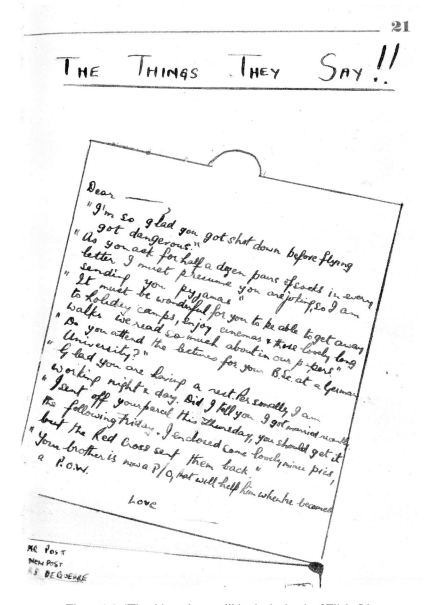

Figure 2.9: 'The things they say!!' in the logbook of Flight Lieutenant Paul Cunningham. 'Mail bag splitters' were extracts from letters, purportedly sent to POWs from friends and relatives at home, which were insensitive to the conditions POWs were enduring.

Others demonstrate a gross ignorance of the restrictions and hardships of captivity with which POWs had to live, for example:

Joe is in Stalag VIIIB, Can you pop round and see him.[110]
It must be wonderful for you to be able to get away to holiday camps, enjoy cinemas & those lovely walks we read so much about in the papers.[111]

Many others show insensitivity towards POWs locked up in captivity whilst their wives and sweethearts at home were free:

(from wife to POW, who had been a prisoner 3 years). Darlingest, I've just had a baby, but don't worry, the American officer is sending you cigarettes regularly.[112]
The popular song amongst the girls here is now 'Roll me over, lay me down + do it again'.[113]

Whether or not people at home actually said such cruel things is of less significance here, although it is likely many were written at one time or another; MI9 recorded a number as 'true extracts'.[114] More noteworthy is that numerous POWs in different camps took the time and care to copy them out. They show a 'Kriegie identity' was formed against those outside captivity misunderstanding life in it. Hall specifically refers to how these 'mail bag splitters' served to increase solidarity amongst prisoners of war. In his diary entry of 22 May 1944, he explained how they were sometimes exhibited publicly on bunk ends and concluded, 'I suppose in this way the hurt shared and the subsequent ribaldry – never the agony-prolonging collusion of sympathy – acts as a therapy.'[115]

Caption for Figure 2.9: (cont.)

Cunningham was one of many to copy these extracts into his logbook. These 'mail bag splitters' show a 'Kriegie identity' was formed against those outside captivity having a profound misunderstanding of life in it.
     Source: IWM Documents.19672, Flight Lieutenant
P. A. Cunningham, logbook, p. 21. Reproduced with permission from John Cunningham.

---

[110] Gallagher, logbook, 'Choice Bits from Letters to Kreigies', pp. 96–7.
[111] Cunningham, logbook, 'The Things They Say!!', p. 21.
[112] Macey, logbook, 'Some extracts of letters to POWs printed and placed on noticeboard', pp. 82–3.
[113] Shipp, logbook, pp. 60–6.
[114] See IWM 74/22/1, private papers of Miss Mary Trevor.
[115] Hall, diary entry, 22 May 1944.

These mail bag splitters offer one other insight into the POW mind-set. Many of these extracts deal with sensitive subjects, such as the shame of capture or sexual betrayal. However obtuse these comments, however much POWs copied them out in jest, they also reveal POWs were vulnerable to attack in these areas, and so suggest these men had feelings of inadequacy, as soldiers or as sexual partners. So stung, for example, was one POW by the quote, 'I would rather marry a 1943 hero than a 1941 Coward' that an entire poem was written as a rebuttal. This poem must have then been circulated through POW camps as both Warrant Officer Hilary Jarvis and Shipp, who were held in different camps throughout the course of the war, copied it into their logbooks.[116] The psychiatrists who wrote Technical Memorandum 13 similarly commented on the significance of POWs' copying out these 'mail bag splitters':

in the stalags accusations of cowardice were not uncommonly read into vague, careless or, on occasion, malicious statements in mail from this country. A single chance remark often struck home, not only to the man to whom it was written, but to very large groups within the stalag.

They went on to explain why these statements struck such a strong chord: 'It can therefore be said that partly unrecognised guilt is a widespread phenomenon.' They added, drawing upon Freudian thinking, why 'mail bag splitters' might have been particularly wounding:

The most obvious reason for the soldier's taking up arms is to defend those he holds nearest and dearest. In consequence, the narcissistic function of the ego holds them in part responsible for its plight and inevitably, therefore, it attacks them. This completely unrecognised (ie deeply unconscious) process is productive of much guilt; and as a result the prisoner of war constantly pictures himself forsaken by all at home or as a 'forgotten man', and has many similar depressive thoughts. The depressive attacks on all he holds dear, and the isolation which he has thus unwittingly inflicted on himself, produce a profound mourning reaction.[117]

In other words, the replication of 'mail bag splitters' was a manifestation of the blame POWs had for those at home whom they unconsciously thought were partly responsible for their fate. This, in turn, induced feelings of guilt and furthered POWs' feelings of isolation and fear of being forgotten.

---

[116] Jarvis, scrapbook, unpaginated; Shipp, logbook, p. 66.
[117] TNA WO 32/10757, Directorate of Army Psychiatry. Technical Memorandum No. 13. The Prisoner of War Comes Home. Notes Prepared for the Information of Army Psychiatrists, prepared by DAP, May 1944.

The Kriegie Lament[118]

In addition to the phenomenon of guilt, psychiatrists who worked with repatriated or escaped POWs during the Second World War recorded POWs as having a 'brittle self-respect', a 'loss of self-respect', and being 'low in morale'.[119] So far, this chapter has presented an upbeat view of how British POWs mastered imprisonment by their enemy but, even amongst the examples cited earlier, evidence lurks of the negative effects of captivity that psychiatrists noted. The comparisons of POWs' achievements during their incarceration to life at home, for example, could also suggest POWs' presumption that their lives would be seen as inferior. The way in which they spelt out their daily rations might also indicate they thought their hardship would be underestimated. Laughing at their peculiar way of life was a means of making sense of captivity, by making light of it, but within these humorous drawings and descriptions are also undercurrents of POWs' fear that they would have difficulty readjusting to their home lives, plus feelings of self-derision and self-deprecation.[120]

POWs' loss of self-respect is also spelt out more specifically in their narratives, most commonly through metaphors of emasculation. These occur time and again, and in relation to many aspects of POWs' confinement. The physical restrictions inherent in camp life caused numerous POWs to equate themselves to caged animals.[121] Canon King even reduced POWs below the status of animals when he described how the barbed-wire fence made it impossible to enjoy the view outside Oflag VIID (Tittmoning). Oflag VIID was a hill-top medieval castle on the Salzach river. 'It is a pity that the designers of Kriegsgefangenerlager did not study Hagenbeck's humane method of giving his animals at least the illusion of freedom', he wrote in his diary on 9 February 1941. Three decades earlier, Carl Hagenbeck had created a revolutionary zoological

---

[118] This is the title of a poem that sets out a sarcastic response to some of the miserable aspects of POWs' existence. The poem was copied into a number of logbooks; see, for example, Kennedy, logbook, p. 99; Jarvis, scrapbook, unpaginated; Clague logbook, p. 7.

[119] TNA WO 32/10757, Directorate of Army Psychiatry. Technical Memorandum No. 13. The Prisoner of War Comes Home. Notes Prepared for the Information of Army Psychiatrists, prepared by DAP, May 1944; TNA WO 32/10757, Extract from 'Report on Interviews with Escaped and Repatriated Ps of W', 8 June 1944.

[120] Twomey has similarly identified Australian male internees in the Far East using stories of captivity and cartoons to make light of their situation, but these often contained 'an undercurrent of contradiction and discomfort', suggesting some found their situation emasculating (*Australia's Forgotten Prisoners*, p. 113).

[121] Barrington, diary entry, 1 April 1943; 89/16/1–89/16/2(P), Warrant Officer H. C. M. Jarvis, letter to his parents, 4 April 1943; King, diary entries, 15 and 18 July and 8 September and 4 October 1940, 7 April 1945; Mansel, diary entry, 28 November 1943; Cunningham, logbook, p. 33.

park by moving wild animals out of their cages and into 'natural land-scape'. King then added, 'But they have not the same commercial incentive to keep their captives in the pink of condition.'[122] The same language appears in the context of POWs having their physical movements controlled. Upon being transferred from camp to camp or compound to compound, they described themselves as being 'herded' and treated like 'sheep'.[123]

With respect to other aspects of confinement, POWs invoked similar metaphors. Their unoccupied time, in the early months of captivity, led Canon King to compare POWs to living 'humdrum cow-like lives.'[124] Shortages of food towards the end of the war resulted in Stoddart describing POWs as 'waiting ... in a queue like unemployed'.[125] At a time when being the breadwinner was a key component of masculinity, Stoddart's simile indicates how being so dependent for food left his manhood wanting. The insanitary camp conditions caused Barrington to describe British soldiers using basic latrines, consisting of a single plank balanced over a hole in the ground, as 'being perched like a row of roosted fowls.'[126] During the first reprisal episode of the war, Mansel repeatedly associated himself with various animals. He was one of 256 officers sent to live in Fort 15 at Stalag XXA (Thorn) between March and June 1941, following reports of German officers imprisoned in Canada being held in primitive conditions. At this time, Stalag XXA was principally composed of five forts that housed predominantly British prisoners: Forts 11, 13, 13A, 14 and 15.[127] Conditions were poor at Fort 15. There was great overcrowding with resultant insanitary conditions, including large numbers of vermin.[128] The darkness of their rooms caused Mansel to sympathise with the 'pit pony' when he entered daylight, except Mansel then realised even the pit pony was better placed than he, for its blindness meant it would not find the light so troubling. In the context of the dark, enormous passages in the fort being like sewers, Mansel equated POWs to a 'plague

---

[122] King, diary entry, 9 February 1941; Nigel Rothfels, *Savages and Beasts. The Birth of the Modern Zoo* (Baltimore, MD: John Hopkins University Press, 2008), p. 8.

[123] Barrington, diary entry describing journey into captivity; Angove, diary entry, 29 September 1943; Quarrie, diary, p. 9; Booth, diary entry, 2 April 1941; Lambert, letter to his wife, 11 July 1943. In the same context, Didcock uses a metaphor of infantilisation, IWM 10/6/1, Driver G. Didcock, diary entry, 6 July 1943.

[124] King, diary entry, 1 October 1940; see also diary entry, 3 May 1941.

[125] Stoddart, diary entry, February/March 1945.

[126] Barrington, diary entry describing journey into captivity. For a similar example, see Didcock, diary entry, 28 November 1942.

[127] ACICR, C SC, Germany, Stalag XXA, 7 September 1941.

[128] TNA FO 916/38, Telegram from American Embassy at Berlin, 25 March 1941; MacKenzie, *The Colditz Myth*, p. 243.

of rats'. Of their living conditions, he both likened them to the elephant house at a zoo, and described them as vastly inferior to a pigsty.[129]

'Metaphors', as historian Joanna Bourke explains, 'are particularly useful when people are attempting to convey experiences most resistant to expression.' The use of these metaphors by POWs indicates they tried to make their experiences known to the external world by describing them as something belonging to those that were less than human, or wanting in their manhood.[130] Comparing themselves to caged animals is hardly surprising: it does not require any great stretch of the imagination to understand why men held behind barbed wire came to think of themselves in such a way.

More remarkable are the occasions when, in the context of various aspects of captivity, POWs drew parallels between their experiences and those of explorers and adventurers. When discussing POWs' diet, Naylor recorded that 'There is a close similarity between the articles of our Red Cross Parcels and the rations used by the 1933 Everest climbers when getting to high altitudes, where weight was an all important factor, & food had to be nutritious and beneficial whilst occupying small compass and weighing little.'[131] Mansel compared his impoverished living conditions at Oflag VIB (Warburg), which was probably the worst camp for officers from a physical standpoint, to those conquering the Arctic. At 8.30 P.M., on 15 October 1941, the lights were turned out suddenly in his hut, which prevented Mansel from completing his diary entry. The following day he described the scene that had unfolded in the darkness:

I sat for a bit of chatting in a corner rather cosily arranged with an upturned box as a table and a speise fat candle. There was also a gramophone going of dance music which was rather pleasant in the dark. The whole scene was very much what I always imagine an Arctic hut to be like. People huddled round stoves and the hut absolutely full of smoke.[132]

In the context of POWs being unfamiliar with the world into which they would emerge from captivity, Canon King wrote, on the fourth anniversary of his capture:

when we do at last get home I shall experience for myself the answer to a question that used to intrigue me: what would Scott & Wilson & Oates feel like if the

---

[129] Mansel, diary entries, 15 and 17 March 1941; see also diary entries, 7 April and 16 May 1941.

[130] Joanna Bourke, 'Pain: Metaphor, Body, and Culture in Anglo-American Societies between the Eighteenth and Twentieth Centuries', *Rethinking History*, 18, 4 (2014), 477.

[131] Naylor, diary entry, p. 84

[132] Mansel, diary entry, 16 October 1941; MacKenzie, *The Colditz Myth*, p. 98.

scientists brought them out of cold storage at the Pole, massaged their hearts back to life, & let them loose in a newer world?[133]

These men were not the first to draw links between the experiences of POWs and polar explorers. A surgeon and Swiss embassy official, Adolf Lukas Vischer, who visited British camps holding German combatant and civilian internees during the First World War, wrote of the similarities between these two groups in his 1918 publication, *The Barbed Wire Disease. A Psychological Study of Prisoners of War*, which is discussed more fully in Chapter 5.[134] Vischer wrote of the two groups having a comparable 'psychical experience', through the monotonous days they endured, their fixation on returning home and living in the constant presence of others.[135] Such parallels may, in part, explain why these men drew such unlikely comparisons. There is also, perhaps, a more negative reason. During this era, explorers and adventurers were celebrated in British popular culture for their hyper-masculinity: they were seen to extol the manly virtues of heroism, sacrifice and fortitude through their endurance of testing conditions.[136] Comparing themselves to such men may have been a means by which POWs, unconsciously or otherwise, bolstered up their own masculinity. Canon King indicated as much when he explained how POWs interchanged metaphors depending on how they felt. 'Tucked away in our bunks at night we look', he wrote at Oflag VIIC, at Laufen in south-eastern Bavaria, 'if one is feeling in good form – like sailors snug in a fo'c'sle, or even like Arctic explorers in winter quarters. If one is feeling not so well, then we resemble, both in looks & in raison d'etre, rabbits in a hutch.'[137]

In addition to noting POWs' guilt or lack of self-respect, War Office officials and British and Australian army officers who studied repatriated prisoners of war recorded another emotion: 'even with the distractions provided by such opportunities for work as may arise or by communal activities, expression of good morale as they are, he [the POW] will find it difficult to escape from a pervading feeling of futility.'[138] This observation

---

[133] King, diary entry, 12 June 1944.
[134] A. L. Vischer, *Barbed Wire Disease. A Psychological Study of Prisoners of War* (London: John Bale & Co., 1919); Panikos Panayi, *Prisoners of Britain. German Civilian and Combatant Internees during the First World War* (Manchester: Manchester University Press, 2012), p. 124.
[135] Vischer, *Barbed Wire Disease*, pp. 71–80.
[136] Martin Francis, 'A Flight from Commitment? Domesticity, Adventure and the Masculine Imaginary in Britain after the Second World War', *Gender and History*, 19, 1 (2007), 164–6.
[137] King, diary entry, 18 July 1940.
[138] TNA WO 32/10757, The Repatriate Prisoner of War from the Medical Aspect, Australian Military Forces, undated.

is also echoed in these personal narratives. Whilst POWs described in their diaries, letters and logbooks the active and productive life they led behind barbed wire, when they reflected on their time in captivity as a whole, from a significant moment in their imprisonment, they concluded the experience had, in fact, been barren. Eldridge is an exemplar of many others when he counted up the time that had passed since his capture – two years and four months in his case – and wrote, 'This is no life but just an existence ... (? Existence)'. His bracketed caveat suggests he considered even *existence* too generous a term.[139] Others came to the same conclusions on certain annual occasions. Spending a second birthday in captivity prompted Casdagli to momentarily abandon his usually spirited attitude and record 'Life drags on and the wasted days pass.'[140] On New Year's Eve 1943, Nell concluded in his diary that 'The lot of a POW is a hard one. Conditions aren't really bad but this idle useless existence of ours rots the very soul.' More ominously, he added, 'I shall never allow myself to be taken prisoner again. The misery is too much for a sensitive person to bear.'[141] Hurrell's letter to his future wife, written as he looked back on the four Christmases he had spent in captivity, and whilst contemplating future ones, was equally desolate. He wrote, on 8 December 1944, 'I honestly wish I hadn't bothered to leave that aircraft – its an awful thought I know but whatever happens I can never recapture these wasted years of previous youth – and a guy is certainly not expected to be gay and irresponsible at 30. I do believe I'm beginning to feel sorry for myself – what a confession.' His final sentence indicates he was aware that such divulgences were improper, but he was unable to restrain himself.[142]

Such melancholic musings on landmark occasions are reminiscent of 'anniversary reactions', which are primarily understood by psychologists to be the result of inadequate or incomplete mourning of a traumatic loss.[143] Reflecting on the anniversary of their capture in these bleak ways may indicate POWs conceived of their incarceration, overall, as a period of loss that they had not yet fully come to terms with. An anniversary

---

[139] Eldridge, diary entry, 16 September 1943. For similar examples, see Fayers, diary entry, 26 November 1944; Kennedy, logbook, pp. 94–5; Laker, diary entry, 16 January 1943; Mansel, letter to his mother, 20 May 1943.

[140] Casdagli, diary entry, 10 April 1943, in Casdagli, *Prouder Than Ever*, p. 109; see also diary entry, 31 December 1944, in Casdagli, *Prouder Than Ever*, p. 165. For a similar example, see Jabez-Smith, letter to his family, 20 June 1944.

[141] Nell, diary entry, 31 December 1943.

[142] Hurrell, letter to Pamela (his future wife), 8 December 1944. For a similar example, see Angove, diary entry, 1 January 1945.

[143] Martha A. Gabriel, 'Anniversary Reactions: Trauma Revisited', *Clinical Social Work Journal*, 20, 2 (1992), 189.

reaction can also occur at times of festivities, with the first Christmas after bereavement or trauma often being hardest.[144] Christmases spent in captivity becoming progressively more difficult for POWs to bear illustrates that, instead of gradually coming to terms with their situation, they increasingly felt defeated by it. Meanwhile, the despondence they showed, on their birthdays or New Year's Eve, indicates their realisation that they had little to look forward to whilst they spent another year imprisoned.[145]

The final lament that recurs in these personal narratives is that the experience of captivity would never be understood by those who had not lived through it. Again, this point is invoked in relation to a variety of aspects of POWs' confinement. Booth recorded of his first parole walk outside the barbed wire: 'Only someone who has been shut in a cage for 3 ½ years could realise the excitement … of seeing women and children going about their normal and ordinary affairs and of being away from the Khaki clad mass of one's fellows.'[146] The self-discipline needed when it came to rationing their stores of food could, according to Stoddart, 'only be imagined by a person who has really been short of food, & felt weak over a period of time. The average person', he asserted, 'has no conception – luckily.'[147] On the monotony of their lives, Gunner Edward Parker wrote to his sweetheart that it was 'something which you can only appreciate when you are locked up'.[148] Similarly Sub-lieutenant Ray Taylor advised his wife, 'Time here has just no meaning. The days go leaving the past further behind but getting no nearer the future. It's difficult for anyone to understand who hasn't "done time".'[149] More broadly, Stewart explained to his family, 'I can describe the actual room we live in in detail but still you won't be able to realise the life as a whole. Only experience and, above all, time could do that.'[150] Despite the logbooks, the documentary-style diaries, the letters home, which all tried to convey what it was like to be imprisoned at a time of war, these men were also aware that no one would really be able to comprehend it.

---

[144] Katherine Fair Donnelly, *Recovering from the Loss of a Parent* (New York: Berkley Publishing, 1993), pp. 94–5.

[145] Katherine Fair Donnelly, *Recovering from the Loss of a Parent*, p. 93.

[146] Booth, diary entry, 22 November 1943. For similar examples, see Angove, diary entry, 23 January 1945; King, diary entry, 19 July 1940; Stewart, diary entry, 4 January 1945.

[147] Stoddart, diary entry, pp. 39–40.

[148] IWM 85/20/1, Gunner E. E. Parker, letter to his sweetheart, 31 May 1944.

[149] SWWEC 2006.690.3–5, Sub-lieutenant H. R. Taylor, letter to his wife, 19 September 1943.

[150] Stewart, diary entry, 9 January 1945. For a similar example, see Booth, diary entry, 10 August 1944.

Conclusion

This chapter has shown how British POWs made sense of being imprisoned by their enemy. Instead of being cowed by their captors, in their personal narratives these British captives paint a picture of continuing to fight the war from behind barbed wire. Their defiance comes to the fore on the occasions when the power exerted over them could be perceived as unjust and echoes contemporary understandings of how individuals resist oppression. POWs also undermined the captor–captive power relationship by portraying themselves as the superiors or equals of their enemies. Their Italian captors are almost uniformly conceived as British prisoners' inferiors. POWs did not express, in their personal narratives, the same universal contempt for their German captors. Instead, they undermined the power dynamic with their German captors in more varied and, sometimes, counterintuitive ways, such as by portraying POWs as materially better off than their guards, or by creating shared experiences and understanding between the two groups in the unlikely contexts of escapes or reprisals.

These personal narratives present an upbeat image of POWs standing up to their captors; this assured image also appears in relation to these men mastering other aspects of their confined existence. In their letters, diaries and logbooks, POWs both conceive of and represent themselves as continuing to lead 'normal' lives. By setting out their daily routines and elaborating on the activities that consumed much of their time, such as their sports, educational activities, reading and entertainments, POWs demonstrated that they remained disciplined, active and occupied in the camps. By alluding to their achievements in captivity – the number of books they had read, the excellence of their entertainments or their inventiveness – they also showed their captive lives were far from inferior versions of those they lived at home.

At the same time, POWs also highlighted the uniqueness of their existence, suggesting that they were forging, whilst in captivity, a unique 'Kriegie identity'. In their diaries and logbooks, they illustrated the new life that had been thrust upon them, most commonly by describing the quantities of food they were given and how they adapted to their unusual conditions. The frequent replication of 'mail bag splitters' also illustrates the formation of a 'Kriegie identity', against a perceived out-group of people who did not understand their life.

There are contained, however, even within this positive picture, hints that these men did not feel as empowered as they suggested. In other places, prisoners' personal narratives demonstrate this more comprehensively. POWs' use of metaphors, in relation to aspects of their confined conditions, indicates their sense of emasculation. Whilst prisoners presented themselves as active and productive, their anniversary reactions reveal that, as a whole, they could also conclude their time in captivity had been worthless. Despite the logbooks, the documentary-style diaries and the letters home all trying to convey what it was like to be imprisoned at a time of war, some declared it could never be understood.

In addition to the features of wartime imprisonment focussed on in this chapter, another was significant. These men lived in crowded, all-male environments, often amongst hundreds or thousands of other prisoners. It is to the relationships they formed within these conditions that I now turn.

3 Bonds between Men

Gefangenschaft
A period of great trials and tribulations
Great hopes and great disappointments, of
Endless waiting, of standing in queues.
A series of searches for tools, hooch
Wireless sets, bugs, fleas and end of the war
A period of worry and doubt of hunger and
(sometimes) draught – a time at which man's
Initiative is put to the test and one's sense
Of humour increases vastly or becomes nil.
Also one of the world's closest views of human
nature that one can experience.[1]

'Gefangenschaft', meaning 'captivity', is one of the many poems on the experience of wartime imprisonment that prisoners of war composed and copied into their personal narratives. This one appears in Howard's logbook. It describes many of the themes covered in the previous chapters – the hopes and disappointments of an early homecoming, being at the mercy of their captors, the hunger and the sense of humour often used to overcome these hardships. The final two lines invoke the aspect of POWs' lives that is the focus of this chapter: the relationships prisoners formed with each other and how they lived within their crowded, homosocial environment.

This chapter examines the friendships, or lack of them, that arose in captivity and looks at how bonding amongst POWs was affected by certain aspects of wartime imprisonment. Writing logbooks, letters and diaries affected the ways in which POWs made sense of the relationships formed in captivity and two of the most significant challenges of wartime imprisonment – length of time in captivity and food – failed to instil group solidarity. Another aspect of captivity that affected men's relationships in captivity was their all-male environment. This chapter concludes by examining how POWs negotiated this by focussing on the female impersonator. The POWs' reactions to men in drag demonstrate that the

---

[1] Howard, logbook, p. 174.

boundaries between heterosexual and homoerotic relations were blurred, both in captivity and in society beyond.

Personal Bonds

On 19 August 1944, Angove handed over a blue exercise book to one of his fellow POWs, Roy, in Oflag XIIB (Hadamar). Angove's exercise book contained thirty-three contributions, consisting of drawings, poems, short writings and signatures, with some from highly eminent POWs, including the most senior-ranking British prisoner in captivity in Germany, Major-General Victor Fortune, and George Haig, the son of the First World War commander. When Roy wrote in Angove's exercise book, he was clearly conscious of the esteemed company he was about to keep amongst its pages. He wrote that he 'could only conclude on looking through [it] that you've handed it to me out of pure friendship'. Roy then referenced how he would remember Angove: through his ability at table tennis and the piano, his role in the theatre and:

> the good talk which it would at present be heresy to set down, but which we both know to be good sense; & the companionship of which no second can remain but in the mind. I hope + believe these will continue when this one meal a day, one thought a day existence is over + done with – when we can recall by name about 20 fellow prisoners, + only meet them when we want to. That'll be the day Dick, that'll be the day!

He signed it 'your sincere friend'.[2]

The friendships that POWs developed in captivity are not revealed through written diary entries, in which a particular prisoner describes how much others meant to him, but, instead, through such signatures, sketches and vignettes. They are less a description and more a physical imprint of the bonds that developed amongst these men. In their most anodyne form, these imprints take the form of autographs and the home addresses of fellow POWs. Page upon page of logbooks and diaries are filled in this way.[3] They are indications of the friendships formed in captivity and a desire to maintain them once back at home. Tipple and Kennedy [Figure 3.1] decorated the pages of their logbooks containing these signatures. The time and care

---

[2] Angove, exercise book, unpaginated. For a similar example, see Ball, logbook, p. 76.

[3] Ball, logbook, pp. 100–3; Buckley, logbook, pp. 15–21, 24; Macey, logbook, pp. 60, 110–13; Trooper John Scott, logbook, pp. 59–60, held in private papers of J. D. Hewitt; Howard, logbook, pp. 176–7; Bompas, diary entry, pp. 56–7; Shipp, logbook, pp. 84–5; Graydon, logbook, pp. 21–3, 70; Hurrell, logbook, pp. 55–72; Edwards, logbook, pp. 105, 107; McDermott-Brown, logbook, pp. 17, 55–108; Taylor, logbook, unpaginated; Gallagher, logbook, pp. 104–9, 110–11; Clague, logbook, pp. 54, 148.

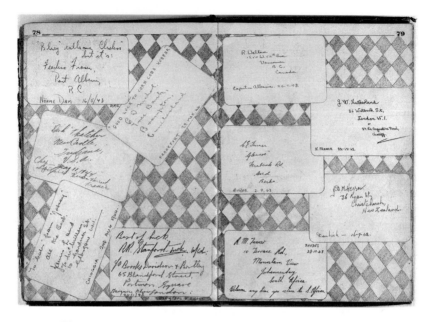

Figure 3.1: Autographs and addresses of fellow POWs in the logbook of
Flying Officer John Kennedy. Page upon page of POWs' logbooks are
filled with autographs and home addresses of fellow inmates. Kennedy's
decoration of these pages in his logbook is an indication that the
signatures and addresses were valued for more than just the practical
information they contained.

   Source: IWM Documents.16311, Flying Officer J. F. Kennedy,
logbook, pp. 78–9. Reproduced with permission from Robin Craig
Kennedy.

they took in doing so is an indication that these names and addresses were
valued for more than just the practical information they contained.[4]

   Many autographs were also accompanied by a message. Often, these
referenced an aspect of life in captivity that had helped forge the friendship. Steve's signature in Kennedy's logbook was accompanied by
a verse titled 'Ode to the Day's Bread Ration'. Keith drew a guard in
a watchtower into McDermott-Brown's logbook and wrote, 'This scene
that we know so well may serve to bring back memories of a happy
friendship that I shall never forget.'[5] Most commonly these messages

---

[4] Tipple, logbook, pp. 18–23; Kennedy, logbook, pp. 73–86.

[5] Kennedy, logbook, p. 133; McDermott-Brown, logbook, p. 11. For a similar example, see
   Stoddart, diary entry, p. 55.

refer to the camp entertainments, indicating again the valued part they played in captive life.[6] Those who wrote in Petty Officer Herbert Macey's logbook repeatedly referenced the roles he played in theatre productions in Marlag 'M', the smaller of the two compounds which made up Marlag and which housed an elite group of officers and orderlies.[7] Macey, who was in both of the compound's two opera companies, appeared in all the musical shows put on in the camp.[8] In tribute to his performance in May 1944, as one of the three 'little maids' in 'The Mikado', Johnson addressed his message 'To the finest "Peep Bo" in Marlag'.[9] The Padre of Marlag 'M' signed his name with thanks for the 'service you have rendered this camp, through entertainments', whilst Wilfred composed an extra verse that he added to the end of Rudyard Kipling's 'If':

> 'If' it should be possible to recall a single
> Pleasant instance from a 'dump' like 'MARLAG'
> I hope (should you be the Producer?) that you include on the
>   set, as a principal, of course.
> Your Very Sincere Friend.[10]

POWs' letters also demonstrate how much friendships in captivity were valued, not through descriptions they contained, but through the messages they carried home.[11] POWs wrote directly to the relatives of their fellow captives, with the intention of reassuring them of their sons or husbands' well-being.[12] Their support and care for their fellow captives extended to supporting and caring for their relatives at home. Loved ones were also invited to contact each other, therefore, mirroring outside captivity the networks established within. Lance Corporal Frederick Blyth told his wife that his 'mucker' was a 'good cook, better than me',

---

[6] Shipp, logbook, pp. 69, 110–11; Buckley, logbook, p. 41; McDermott-Brown, logbook, p. 15.

[7] The other compound, Marlag 'O', accommodated petty officers and leading seamen (Monteath, *P.O.W.*, p. 155).

[8] IWM Sound Archive 4790/6, oral history interview with H. C. Macey, recorded 1981.

[9] Macey, logbook, pp. 22, 38.

[10] Macey, logbook, pp. 3, 70–1. For a similar example, see Buckley, logbook, p. 41.

[11] These findings support Carol Acton's analysis of how, in circumstances of grief in the First World War, letters exchanged between combatants and those at home 'created a community of mourners who sustained and supported each other, even in instances where there had been no prior connections' (*Grief in Wartime. Private Pain, Public Discourse*. Basingstoke: Palgrave Macmillan, 2007, p. 10). Michael Roper also draws a link between families at home and comradeship fostered through the sharing of news from home or relating family histories ('Nostalgia as an Emotional Experience in the Great War', *The Historical Journal*, 54, 2 (2011), 439–40).

[12] See, for example, letter from F. G. Metcalfe to Miss Figg, 15 August 1943 in IWM (not yet catalogued), private papers of Bombardier T. A. Figg; Mansel, letter to Mrs Stubbs, 28 June 1942; Mansel, letter to Mrs Drummond, 25 June 1944.

and then offered: 'You can write and tell his wife that if you like.'[13] These relationships took on a greater significance when relatives visited one another. When Booth and his fellow POW received letters from their respective wives on consecutive days, informing them of how they had met, Booth wrote that he was 'delighted that this new link has been forged.'[14] Relatives also helped POWs to maintain their bonds after two friends had been physically separated. When Warrant Officer Donald Webster was evacuated from Stalag IVB (Mühlberg) towards the end of the war, his mother and father became responsible for maintaining the relationships he had formed there: his 'POW pal' requested of Webster's parents, 'Please keep us in touch.'[15] The same happened following repatriation. Flight Lieutenant Robert Fairclough wrote to his wife in October 1944 that 'Joe should have reached England by now. I hope you've seen him. . . . If you're in touch with him tell him we all wish to be remembered to him + want to know if his grandmother is keeping him from freezing this winter.'[16] Ever the reflective one, Mansel, alone, specifically enunciated in his diary the importance of this correspondence for POWs' relationships. He developed an arrangement with his friend, Eric, to read each other's mail, which lasted until the end of the war. They introduced their respective mother and wife to each other, who would meet to exchange news and eventually developed a 'four-cornered correspondence'. Mansel described how this arrangement 'cemented a friendship'.[17] In fact, it was through a telephone conversation between Mansel's mother and Eric's wife, and then Eric's wife sending a letter about it to her husband, that Mansel learnt of his younger brother's death in the war.[18]

---

[13] IWM 05/57/1, Lance Corporal F. G. Blyth, letter to his wife, 5 November 1944. For similar examples, see Mansel, letter to his mother, 20 June 1943, Mansel, diary entry, 21 November 1943.

[14] Booth, diary entry, 19 February 1941. For similar examples, see Mansel, diary entry, 21 July 1941; SWWEC 2003.2426, Flight Lieutenant R. Fairclough, letters to his wife, 6 February and 14 May 1943; Wild, letter to his wife, 28 June 1942; Lambert, letter to his wife, 23 September 1943.

[15] Letter from Steve, who calls himself 'Don's POW pal', to Webster's parents, 28 February 1945 in SWWEC 2007.158, private papers of Warrant Officer D. H. Webster. For similar examples, see Matthews, letter to his wife, 1 February 1942.

[16] Fairclough, letter to his wife, 7 October 1944. For similar examples, see NAM 2001-09-300, Second Lieutenant A. R. Jabez-Smith, diary entry, 2 August 1944; Wild, letter to his wife, 16 January 1944; Dennis Norton, letter to Burnaby-Atkins' parents, 19 September 1944 in SWWEC 1999.14, private papers of Second Lieutenant F. J. Burnaby-Atkins. Such visits appear to have been common: army medical officers noted that repatriated prisoners of war spent part of their leave visiting the relatives of their comrades who remained in captivity (TNA WO 165/129, Medical Diaries, AMD 11, January to December 1943, Memorandum for Deputy Director of Medical Services, Eastern Command, 10 January 1943).

[17] Beckwith (ed.), *The Mansel Diaries*, fn † p. 71; Mansel, diary entry, 30 November 1944.

[18] Mansel, diary entry, 27 July 1944.

Beyond these individual friendships, POWs' diaries and logbooks also carry traces of the bonds established amongst small groups of men. Tipple pasted numerous photographs of Milag, loved ones at home and POWs into his logbook, but, tellingly, the only ones he labelled were given the heading 'Fellow Boarders at Milag', 'More Fellow Boarders' and 'Room mates for 4 years'.[19] Around Shipp's photograph of '6 Room, 5 Block' at Marlag, each man signed his name and wrote his date of capture, whilst Warrant Officer G. B. Gallagher's logbook includes a drawing of each of the twenty-three men, along with one of himself, with whom he shared his room 'K8' at Stalag Luft VI, near the town of Heydekrug, in former East Prussia.[20] Others used poetry to express these communal bonds. The act of writing a poem demonstrates the importance of these friendships to each man; one can also imagine the pleasure derived when all those referred to in the poem came to read it. Stephen Bellen's poem, 'Room 4', copied into Graydon's logbook, at Milag, devoted a couplet to each of the room's fourteen inhabitants whilst 'Kriegie Camarden', in Kennedy's logbook, contained seventeen verses, each dedicated to a different man who 'shared my messing place' at Stalag Luft III (Sagan).[21]

Edwards provided much more detail on his fellow captives in his logbook. Across ten pages there are pen and picture portraits of twenty-five men with whom he lived in Stalag Luft III (Sagan). The first two pages contain full-page portraits of the camp's SBO and adjutant; the third page is dedicated to his seven 'Room Mates' in North camp; on the final three pages he grouped POWs under the headings of '"Kriegie" friends' [Figure 3.2], 'More "kriegie" friends', 'Still more kriegie friends'. The existence of these men in Edwards' logbook is indicative of his affection for them: grouping a number onto a single page was a representation of their collective solidarity.[22]

Edwards' commentary focussed on factual information about each prisoner: when that POW had been shot down, what he had done before the war and for what he was best known at Stalag Luft III (Sagan). Very occasionally, Edwards offered his own view. Onto the description of one fellow captive, he added, for example, 'One of the most interesting men I've ever met.'[23] Trooper John Scott also devoted one page in his logbook

---

[19] Tipple, logbook, unpaginated.

[20] Shipp, logbook, unpaginated; Gallagher, logbook, pp. 80–5. For similar examples, see Barrington, diary; Cunningham, logbook, pp. 77–80. Other signatures were grouped together by mess; see Kennedy, logbook, pp. 72–86.

[21] Graydon, logbook, p. 44; Kennedy, logbook, pp. 88, 90, 92.

[22] Edwards, logbook, pp. 78–87. For a similar example, see a Christmas menu card at Marlag, where drawn onto each man's menu card was a picture of him and his 'peculiarities' (Shipp, logbook, unpaginated). Campbell also included pen portraits at the back of his diary.

[23] Edwards, logbook, pp. 86, 78–87.

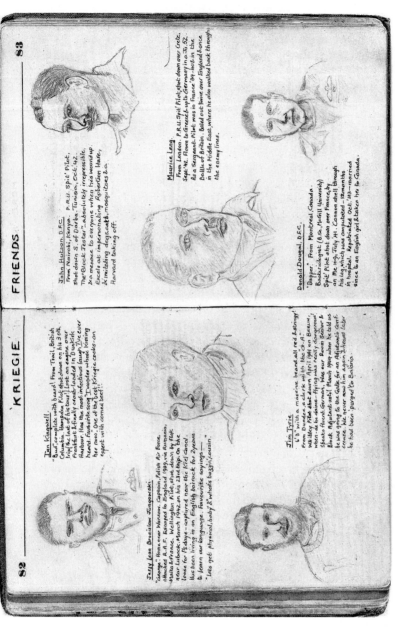

Figure 3.2: "'Kriegie" friends' in the logbook of Flying Officer Arthur Edwards. Across ten pages of this logbook, Edwards provided portraits and commentaries of his senior officers, friends and roommates in captivity. It shows the bonds established amongst small groups of men.

Source: IWM Documents.8127, Flying Officer A. G. Edwards, logbook, pp. 82–3. Reproduced with permission from David Kausmann.

to each of twenty POWs. He variously set out a brief biography and description of their physiques, plus their hobbies, skills, likes and also, in almost half of the cases, his personal opinion of them. Scott described one as 'a very clean living and honest fellow, very good natured', whilst less positive was his assessment of another: 'My opinion of him is that he is a very lazy sod and will swing work on to anybody if they don't look out.' His greatest appreciation was reserved for Jack Hewitt: 'He is, in my opinion, one of the only two genuine fellows among us.' Hewitt subsequently inherited Scott's logbook, suggesting that the logbook itself became a testament to the bond between these two men. Scott also enclosed a brief biography of himself amongst these pages.[24] These drawings and accounts were not just a record by which Scott could remember his fellow captives, but their presence on these pages reinforced these friendships: Scott needed to figure amongst the others on the page, just as he did in real life. This is similar to the grouping of POWs onto particular pages of Edwards' logbook. We do not know whether, in practice, these men existed as a tight-knit set, but the fact that they were represented as such was a way of reinforcing, or even creating, that effect.

Scott's personal opinion of each of these men hints at another way in which these pen portraits could strengthen the bonds between POWs. This is illustrated most explicitly in Canon King's diary. Chapter 1 discussed the 'heart-breaking' few months that King spent at the end of 1941, when he travelled to Rouen ahead of his anticipated repatriation. From 14 October 1941 to 14 December 1941, King broke his normal practice of writing a diary entry every few days, and completed just one for this two-month period. Those eight weeks, he wrote, were 'so monotonous in their routine, interests & boredom, that one day was indistinguishable from another.' This made prisoners' 'personal relationships' the 'biggest thing' in their lives. King used this one diary entry to describe each of the ten men with whom he shared 'Hut 4'. As well as setting out their backgrounds, attributes and achievements, he also detailed the personality traits of each man that affected the harmony of their lives. Cecil, for example, 'was a good person to lean on', whilst King described Fred as 'one of the most generous people with food & property'. Of another Fred, who was a regular soldier, he recorded that they all 'got a little tired of his strident voice & "When I was in Karachi"', but King added, 'at heart he is a very humble shy soul.' Left until last in this list was the person for whom King had the 'greatest respect'. Edward was complimented as being 'one of the men whom I'm thoroughly glad to have been a POW in order to meet; & whom I hope to keep in touch with

---

[24] Scott, logbook, pp. 2–22, held in the private papers of J. D. Hewitt.

after we get home.' Together, King summed them up as a 'happy crowd', but added this qualification:

like everyone else our behaviour was adversely affected by the continuous nervous strain under which we lived. To be uprooted from 18 months settled living in an oflag and dumped suddenly within smells of England, to be told daily that we might be going home at a moment's notice – all this is fatal to an equable frame of mind; and many tempers, my own not least, became uncertain.[25]

King used his diary to demonstrate to his audience the strength of these men's relationships in captivity and the qualities that each brought to Hut 4 and, by doing so, he also reinforced these bonds. In telling his diary's audience of each man's positive attributes, he was reminding himself of them, the need for which is apparent in those final few sentences, which set out the tensions under which these men lived.

Many difficulties POWs faced put these bonds under a great deal of strain. King refers to the imminent prospect of returning home as one such challenge. He detailed another in his diary: the 'lack of home news'. 'Nothing', he wrote, 'puts a man off his oats or makes him more scratchy with his friends'.[26] Food, or rather lack of it, also altered friendships. In the middle years of the war, White commented in his diary how the atmosphere had changed at his working camp now that prisoners had more food and cigarettes. 'Everyone has more time for each other', he commented, 'say good night at lav. etc.'[27] By contrast, in early 1945, when rations were so short that food had to be issued with 'hair-splitting exactness', Nell wrote of how 'fellows lose their tempers and fight over silly little things which they would normally laugh at.'[28]

Other aspects of captivity were a more constant source of strain. Noise was one. Canon King titled his diary entry, of 24 November 1944, 'On Silence'. He conjures up the rowdy environment in which these men had to live. 'Within the huts', King wrote,

noise is inescapable. Boots or clogs clump on wooden floors. Tinware for cooking and eating clatters on the tables. And everybody shouts. Why worry to cross the room to speak, if shouting is less trouble? . . . And in the discussions that roll like the tide of battle up and down the room, victory goes to him who can succeed in shouting down the other fellow, preferably on a subject about which neither of them really know anything.[29]

---

[25] King, diary entry, 14 October–14 December 1941.
[26] King, diary entry, 14 October–14 December 1941. For a similar example, see Nell, diary entry, 20 January 1943.
[27] White, diary entry, 28 April 1942. For a similar example, see Glass, diary entry, 23 November 1943.
[28] Nell, diary entry, 1 February 1945.   [29] King, diary entry, 24 November 1944.

Lack of personal space was another challenge. Angove tried hard 'to remain placid under all circumstances', but, 'sometimes it is very difficult, as people are very exasperating to live with.' He went on to explain:

Cigarette ash over everything, stools left in the middle of the room, tables cluttered up with dirty cups & plates, to-day's newspapers used as tablecloths & covered in jam before one has read them & so on ad infinitum. It takes one all one's time to keep a hold on oneself & not give way to exasperation.[30]

Such were the challenges of noise and lack of privacy that being sent to solitary confinement became, for some, a reward instead of the intended punishment. Booth spent seven days in the 'cooler' (solitary confinement) at Oflag VIIB (Eichstätt) having been found with his handcuffs off during the shackling reprisals episode. On the 'credit side' of the experience was a 'wonderful sense of privacy and quiet'. It was the first time in nearly three years where, for a week, he could

spend practically the whole of every day in a 'room' by myself; I can read without continual interruptions, without constantly being jostled in my chair, without being reminded that it is time to do this or that, to collect a parcel or fetch the soup. I can indulge my thoughts without having those of others thrust upon me.[31]

Spending so much time with the same group of men also led to an increased sensitivity towards peculiar characteristics or behaviours. On 6 February 1941, Mansel's diary entry was filled with frustrations of his fellow prisoners' 'idiosyncracies [sic]', to the extent that they read as if they were spilling out, almost uncontrollably, from his pen. One prisoner had two types of voice. It was either 'a) pansy and stage, lecturing' or 'b) conversational, blasphemous and lavatory'. Both irritated Mansel. Another he described as a 'selfish snob'; of a third, he wrote his 'Bank Counter "Yers" and "Er-er" are v. trying'; whilst a fourth had become 'up-stage'.[32]

The lack of food and privacy, the noise and living in close proximity with the same people made another of the challenging aspects of captive life all the more likely: quarrelling. Canon King compared arguing POWs to 'the violent tempestuous lovers & hatreds which make Monkey Hill at the Zoo so entertaining.'[33] In December 1943, Eldridge confided in his

---

[30] Angove, diary entry, 26 January 1944. For similar examples, see King, diary entry, 8 March 1942; Eldridge, diary entry, 10 February 1942.

[31] On the 'debit side' was the loss of exercise and missing his 'usual occupations', such as playing the gramophone and recorder (Booth, diary entry, 31 March 1943). Mansel was also envious of those who had been so punished (Mansel, diary entry, 28 March 1941).

[32] Mansel, diary entry, 6 February 1941. For a similar example, see Eldridge, diary entry, 16 October 1943.

[33] King, diary entry, 20 August 1940.

diary how he was 'tired of petty jealousies and intrigues amongst us here. Sometimes it is difficult to believe that men could behave as they do, just like children.'[34] Angove remarked to his mother, in his diary entry of 14 June 1944, 'I should like you to hear the scandal & catty remarks going on in this room at the moment. . . . Never believe men aren't catty, take it from me that POWs at least are as catty bad as the worst of women.'[35] The ways in which Eldridge, Angove and King described quarrelling POWs as like animals, children or women are noteworthy. Historian Thomas Kühne has written of how 'in every culture the institution of male bonding fulfilled an important role regarding carrying out and maintaining male supremacy'.[36] These quarrelling prisoners brought the male gender into disrepute.

These entries also show how POWs used their diaries as a 'subversive space', to borrow a description from literary scholar Carol Acton.[37] They were a place where prisoners of war could safely criticise their fellow captives. Mansel explicitly noted that describing his fellow captives' idiosyncrasies helped him to 'work off steam'.[38] A month later, he explained, 'a diary is a great thing as you can get things off your chest and feel much better for it without hurting anybody's feelings, a situation which must never arise in this place unless you are prepared to risk it being permanent for the duration.'[39] By using his diary in this way, Mansel made communal living more bearable. However, it seems after two further years of captivity, the practice had become redundant. Recalling, in April 1943, how he used to write down his opinions of people, he added, 'If I did this now I would never stop and it is a dangerous practice. I'm not nearly so tolerant now as I used to be then.'[40] Writing a diary entry still had the potential to affect his actual relationships, but, after three years of captivity, rather than contain Mansel's feelings, such a practice was liable to explosively unleash them.

Captive Bonds

Whilst these diaries and logbooks conjure up the intense emotions experienced by POWs living in close proximity, there is very little to learn from

---

[34] Eldridge, diary entry, 22 December 1943; see also diary entry, 29 November 1942.

[35] Angove, diary entry, 14 June 1944. For a similar example, see Mansel, diary entry, 9 November 1944.

[36] Thomas Kühne, 'Comradeship: Gender Confusion and Gender Order in the German Military, 1918–1945', in Karen Hagemann and Stefanie Schüler-Springorum (eds.), Home/Front. The Military, War and Gender in Twentieth-Century Germany (Oxford: Berg, 2002), p. 235.

[37] Acton, 'Stepping into History', 43.   [38] Mansel, diary entry, 6 February 1941.

[39] Mansel, diary entry, 25 March 1941.   [40] Mansel, diary entry, 4 April 1943.

the simple and unsurprising fact that POWs in captivity invariably liked or disliked their fellow captives. Much more revealing, for both the captivity and wider war experience, are the broad lines along which unity or dissonance prevailed in the camps. The findings set out in Chapter 2, which show the ways in which British POWs created a 'Kriegie identity', might also be interpreted as an indication that a loose sense of community existed amongst prisoners of war. It is likely, for example, that 'mail bag splitters' garnered camaraderie between POWs, against the perceived incomprehension or unfaithfulness of women at home.[41] The formation of a 'Kriegie identity' could also be suggestive of prisoners forming, across camps, an 'imagined community', to adopt a term coined by historian and political scientist Benedict Anderson to describe how members of a nation who will never meet or even hear about each other perceive themselves as part of a single community.[42] The 'imagined community' of POWs could have been strengthened by the movement of prisoners between camps, and their being able to see that the cultural and social activities and reactions to captivity present in one camp also existed in others. In these personal narratives, three aspects or characteristics of captivity are specifically singled out as broadly shaping prisoners' relationships: date of capture, rank and allocation of food. Each will be discussed in turn for the insight it provides into how POWs made sense of captivity.

The first British men to be captured by Germany in the Second World War were Sergeant George Booth and Aircraftsman Larry Slattery, who were shot down in a bombing raid over Wilhelmshaven the day after Britain declared war on Germany.[43] Almost five years later, on 26 August 1944, from Stalag 357 (Fallingbostel), Slattery signed Clague's logbook. By this point, some 90,000 other British servicemen had joined him in captivity. Slattery signed his name with the words 'EVERY GOOD WISH ALEX FROM THE "FATHER" OF POWs. LARRY.'[44] Slattery's chirpily paternalistic metaphor suggests a family of prisoners of war existed behind barbed wire, in which the longer-term

---

[41] Other historians have noted how, more generally, comradeship amongst servicemen was galvanised by the incomprehension of women or by their unfaithfulness, Roper, *The Secret Battle*, p. 305; Stephen Garton, 'War and Masculinity in Twentieth-century Australia', *Journal of Australian Studies*, 56 (1998), 93.

[42] Matthew Stibbe also explores the link between cultural activities in captivity and solidarity amongst civilian internees in his study of the Ruhleben camp in the First World War, and he considers the extent to which they formed an 'imagined community' (*British Civilian Internees in Germany*, pp. 80–94, 102); Benedict Anderson, *Imagined Communities. Reflections on the Origins and Spread of Nationalism* (London: Verso, 1983).

[43] Tim Carroll, *The Great Escapers: The Full Story of the Second World War's Most Remarkable Mass Escape* (Edinburgh: Mainstream, 2004), p. 23.

[44] Clague, logbook, p. 5.

POWs provided the newly captured ones with fatherly care. The rest of these personal narratives suggest the opposite was the case. They indicate that POWs distinguished themselves into two groups: long-term prisoners and newly captured ones, who far from accorded each other loving protection. As Stewart, who had entered captivity on 15 June 1940, recorded, 'there can't be anything worse than a new prisoner having to meet an old one – except an old prisoner having to meet a new one.'[45]

The division resulted from their differing experiences of captivity. An anecdote Stewart copied into his diary portrays long-term prisoners of war as hardened captives, against the mollycoddled more recent ones. He wrote of a 'typical' story in which a 'new prisoner' told 'old prisoners' about his 'terrible experiences.' The new prisoner, Stewart explained, had been travelling in a cattle truck

when the train was bombed and the engine hit. The 20 people in his truck leapt out and ran up the bank beside the railway. The New Prisoner explained with great gusto and excitement how the sentries had thought they were escaping and had opened fire, killing or wounding 10 out of the 20. The Old Prisoner looked completely bored merely answered, 'Good Lord, d'you mean you only had 20 to a cattle truck?'[46]

Hall, meanwhile, provided the perspective of the 'new prisoner' in his diary. Shot down on 18 April 1943 during a bombing raid over Germany, he recorded, just over a month later, of how 'it is when the "new boys"', such as himself

grumble about rations and standing for hours on appel [sic] and the hardness of old straw palliasses, that the 'old uns' look at each other meaningly and say, 'Get some kriegie hours in! When I was at Lamsdorf in 1940 we were in an old fortress, in stinking cells! Not luxury hotel stuff like this. And food! One dish of skilly a day.'

'Even allowing for their exaggeration', Hall conceded, 'I detect a ring of truth in their stories particularly when confirmed independently by others', but he added, 'There still remains the annoyance which makes me want to say, "OK, so it was bad and I'm sorry, but it's not altogether a bed of roses here is it?"'[47]

Long-term POWs also differentiated themselves from newly captured ones due to their different experiences of fighting in the war. Those captured in 1940, Stewart explained, 'knew nothing about fighting & very few wanted to'. The new arrivals were

---

[45] Stewart, diary entry, 28 January 1945.

[46] Stewart, diary entry, 8 January 1945. For a similar example, see Johnson, logbook, p. 107.

[47] Hall, diary entry, 22 May 1943.

different. Since 1939 their only purpose has been fighting whether they have had actual experience of it or not. Their lives have of necessity been bound up in it, to the exclusion of everything else. They've been instilled with propaganda in favour of war & anything they've done or thought has been in relation to the war effort.[48]

Quarrie, captured in June 1941, portrayed a similar disconnect when fourteen servicemen, recently captured in Italy, arrived at Oflag VIIB (Eichstätt), in June 1944. He wrote of how these

boys of the 'Modern Army' usually want to tell us all about modern organisation and equipment of the army which bores us to tears and usually we sit back paying no attention at all with an occasional 'Really!', 'Is that so?' or just 'Yes.' They must think us very rude but then of course we are.[49]

The following month, Mansel put it more succinctly: they 'give one the impression of regarding you as a dead beat and . . . can talk of nothing but modern war.'[50]

So well-acknowledged were these different mentalities that sketches depicted long-term POWs meeting recently captured ones. One such sketch was included in Warrant Officers Robert 'Andy' Anderson and David Westmacott's series on prison camp life in Germany. Anderson and Westmacott were captured early on in the war, in May 1941 and June 1941, respectively. They described how it 'was something of a shock to the older prisoners, of from four to five years standing, to see youngsters of nineteen or twenty, who were still at school during the early years of the war, arriving in the camp.'[51] Their illustration portrays this meeting [Figure 3.3]. The long-term prisoner has aged dramatically. He has not moved for so long that he is wrapped in cobwebs. His slippers suggest he has become institutionalised, as does his armchair, made from Red Cross boxes. The new arrival, meanwhile, poses the painfully obvious, and so somewhat insensitive, question of 'Have you been here long?'

The second characteristic of captivity that shaped POWs' relationships was their rank. The segregation of POWs into different camps or compounds, depending on their rank, meant those from the other ranks and those with commissions rarely came into contact. There is, as a result, far less reflection from POWs on how rank altered their experience of captivity than might be expected in these personal narratives. One aspect of the rank

[48] Stewart, diary entry, 28 January 1945; see also diary entry, 24 January 1945.
[49] Quarrie, diary, p. 123.   [50] Mansel, diary entry, 7 July 1944.
[51] Robert Anderson and David Westmacott, *Handle with Care: A Book of Prison Camp Sketches Drawn and Written in Prison Camps in Germany* (Belper, Derby: JoTe Publications, 2005; first published in 1946), p. 63. For similar examples, see Cunningham, logbook, p. 37; 'The first and last Gefangener', in E. C. G. Beckwith (ed.), *Selections from The Quill. A Collection of Prose, Verse and Sketches by Officers Prisoner-of-War in Germany, 1940–1945* (London: Country Life, 1947), p. 184.

Figure 3.3: 'Have you been here long?' In Robert Anderson and David
Westmacott's *Book of Prison Camp Sketches*. This illustration, by Warrant
Officers Robert Anderson and David Westmacott, was part of their series
of sketches on prison camp life in Germany. It shows the divide between
long-term POWs and recently captured ones. The long-term POW is
shown to have aged dramatically in captivity. He has not moved for so
long that cobwebs have formed around him. His slippers and armchair,
made from Red Cross boxes, indicate he has become institutionalised.
The recently captured prisoner, dressed in a new uniform, asks him the
painfully obvious question 'Have you been here long?'
    Source: Robert Anderson and David Westmacott, *Handle with Care:
A Book of Prison Camp Sketches Drawn and Written in Prison Camps in
Germany* (Belper, Derby: JoTe Publications, 2005; first published in
1946), p. 63.

order is frequently singled out for comment: the armed forces' batmanning
system, through which other ranks were assigned to work for officers as
their personal servants. The preservation of the batmanning system in
captivity was established through an Anglo–German agreement of 1918,
which had allowed one orderly to be allocated to a group of seven imprisoned captains, one to a group of four field officers and one to each
general.[52] As a result, about 10 per cent of the oflag population in

---

[52] Joan Beaumont, 'Rank, Privilege and Prisoners of War', *War and Society*, 1 (1983), 71.

the Second World War was made up of orderlies.[53] They performed tasks similar to those carried out in the armed forces: waking officers with tea or coffee in the morning, bringing hot shaving water, cooking and serving food and doing their washing.[54]

Numerous officers recorded the success of this hierarchical system in their personal narratives.[55] Angove and Hyde did so by commenting on how it was reversed on special occasions, such as Christmas Day, when officers waited on the other ranks.[56] These were rituals of 'status reversal', as anthropologist Victor Turner called them, where the vertical order was reaffirmed by inverting it on a one-off occasion.[57] There are equally examples, in these same personal narratives, of how the batmanning system unravelled in captivity. Mansel frequently used his diary to reflect on the orderlies' idleness. 'We are getting rather fed up with the ill-manners of the majority of orderlies, who seem to have forgotten how to address an officer', he wrote.

They slop about and take not the slightest notice of you. They are sitting pretty here compared with the Stalag Forts and they seem to forget it. An instance is an orderly who came into our rooms yesterday, without knocking, leaned against the door without saluting, shouted across the room 'Is Capt. Stubbs there? Oh, the Sgt. Major wants you.' I ask you.[58]

Much later in the war, on the occasion of Major General Victor Fortune's arrival at Oflag XIIB (Hadamar) in May 1944, Angove was 'all for it. No doubt he will straighten up a lot of things.' The rest of his entry appears thus:

The staff is very slack in my opinion & do very little. We sweep over our own rooms & make our own beds & while that doesn't kill us, other ranks are sent here to do those jobs & I resent having to sweep a room & fetch tea, when I can look out of the window & see eight or a dozen of the staff sunbathing at half-past nine in the morning & when so much of my pay is stopped each month in order to pay the staff for jobs which I have to do for myself.[59]

---

[53] Gilbert, *POW*, p. 129.

[54] King, diary entry, 27 December 1941; Wild, letter to his wife, 21 September 1941; Booth, diary entry, 8 July 1941. On orderlies' tasks in the army, see Roper, *The Secret Battle*, pp. 137–8.

[55] Wild, letter to his wife, 21 September 1941; King, diary entry, 27 December 1941; Booth, diary entry, 8 July 1941.

[56] Angove, diary entry, Boxing Day 1944; Hyde, letter to his wife, 30 December 1942.

[57] Victor W. Turner, *The Ritual Process. Structure and Anti-structure* (London: Routledge & Kegan Paul, 1969), pp. 176, 166–203.

[58] Mansel, diary entry, 7 April 1941; see also diary entry, 25 December 1941.

[59] Angove, diary entry, 15 May 1944.

Even though these examples illustrate the failure of other ranks to adhere to the military hierarchy, the types of personal narratives in which these examples are contained point to how upholding the chain of command was one of the ways in which these imprisoned officers understood how POWs' relationships should be organised. According to historian Matthias Reiss, this is unsurprising: in the crisis situation of being in enemy hands, both 'military unity and discipline provide obvious advantages.'[60] Yet the extracts that discuss the successful operation of the batmanning system are taken from letters written home, or diary entries designed for family members or public audiences, whilst Angove and Mansel's entries on the failings of the system are quite different. Mansel appears to use his entry for the same personal purpose as when he was frustrated with his fellow prisoners: to vent his emotions. Angove has crossed out his diary entry. He did this on many occasions throughout his writings, retrospectively expunging sections at a later date. His actions indicate that the entry had a purpose at the time of writing, but the deletion that he considered it deserved no place in posterity. The continued functioning of the military hierarchy was the view of captivity these men wanted to project. These private musings indicate there were limits to its success.

The third aspect of captivity that shaped POWs' relationships was the distribution of food. In historian Rachel Duffett's study on the experience of food of British rank-and-file soldiers during the Great War, she identifies it as both an 'object around which acts of kindness, generosity and pleasures were constructed' and something which 'could also act as the focal point for less positive emotional states'.[61] In the POW camp, the scarcity and sporadic supplies of food only enhanced its affective powers. Generosity and pleasure were felt by those who could give to those in need. Booth, held at Oflag VIIC (Laufen) received, over just ten days, no fewer than six parcels from various companies and relatives around the world. He was 'revelling' in tobacco and cigarettes and explained, in his diary, how it was 'such a pleasure to be able to offer to one's friends.'[62] Stoddart, in January 1945, was on the receiving end of generosity on the occasion of his final birthday in captivity. At a time when food stocks were running low, he was given 'all kinds of odd things' to eat by his room-mates, 'which', he explained in a letter to his parents, 'is saying quite a bit

[60] Reiss, 'The Importance of Being Men', 24.

[61] Rachel Duffett, *The Stomach for Fighting: Food and the Soldiers of the Great War* (Manchester: Manchester University Press, 2012), p. 188. See also Roper, *The Secret Battle*, p. 126.

[62] Booth, diary entry, 11 December 1940; see also diary entry, 30 November 1940. For a similar example, see Lambert, letter to his wife, 19 November 1943.

just now.'[63] The equal sharing of food also created powerful friendships. 'Combines' were groups of POWs who pooled their food rations and culinary efforts to make the most of meals.[64] Allen captured simply but poignantly in his logbook how combines could fortify men emotionally, in addition to their nutritional benefits. He drew a border around a photograph of two prisoners of war; at the top he wrote, 'The combine', at the bottom, 'United we stand' [Figure 3.4].[65]

The relationships formed around food were further supported by the manner in which it was consumed. In Campo PG 19 (Bologna), where Angove got on 'splendidly' with a fellow prisoner, the two would, as Angove described it, 'share our parcels & our friends & books, we have someone round to our "flat" almost every day for a cup of tea & a chat.'[66] Mansel similarly found having people coming to his room's regular 'Sunday afternoon tea party' in Oflag VIB (Warburg) to be 'gratifying ... recapturing a hint of civilization.'[67] Cultural historian Joanna Bourke has argued that men taking on domestic tasks in homo-social institutions, which were otherwise carried out by mothers, sisters, friends and lovers, stimulated intimate male friendships during the First World War.[68] These examples of men inviting guests over, laying the table and cooking for one another illustrate how domestic duties furth-ered bonding in captivity. Writing about how comradeship was instilled in Nazi Germany, Kühne has similarly argued that, when German men, in exclusively homosocial institutions, took on 'female jobs', such as cooking and cleaning, it encompassed a powerful idea: that the male bond is independent of the rest of the world, in particular from women.[69] This might explain why numerous POWs wrote home describing their domes-tic prowess in their letters.[70] They wanted to demonstrate how effectively they continued their lives in the absence of women. As Nell put it in his diary, on 9 January 1945, 'our barracks are swept out every day and we scrub our tables. It would surprise the people at home if they could see

[63] Private collection of Simon Stoddart, Lieutenant K. B. Stoddart, letter to his parents, 22 January 1945.
[64] MacKenzie, *The Colditz Myth*, p. 170.   [65] Allen, logbook, unpaginated.
[66] Angove, diary entry, 24 August 1943.
[67] Mansel, diary entry, 11 January 1942. For similar examples, see Booth, diary entry, 26 July 1942; White, diary entries, 11, 13 and 16 April 1945.
[68] Joanna Bourke, *Dismembering the Male. Men's Bodies, Britain and the Great War* (London: Reaktion, 1999), p. 133. On how 'camp domesticity' enabled intimacy and male bonding amongst German-speaking and English-speaking POW officers and civilian internees in the First World War, see Rachamimov, 'Camp Domesticity', pp. 298–303.
[69] Kühne, *Belonging and Genocide*, p. 47.
[70] Mansel, letter to his mother, 18 December 1941; Jarvis, letters to his parents, letter no. 2 and 4 July 1943; Hurrell, letter to Pamela (his future wife), 4 October 1942; Fairclough, letter to his wife, 26 April (no year given).

Figure 3.4: 'The combine. "United we stand"' in the logbook of 4th Mate C. W. G. Allen. Allen's annotation of this photograph, contained in his logbook, showing his combine of two, reveals how pooling food created powerful friendships in captivity.
Source: Documents.3746, 4th Mate C. W. G. Allen, logbook, unpaginated.

how clean and well-mannered we are.'[71] It is important, however, to note these men boasted about their domestic achievements to their mothers and wives. This suggests they were not entirely independent.

All these references to donating or sharing food, or its consumption in a civilised environment, come from the letters POWs sent home or diaries entries that were written with a public audience in mind. This was the image of captivity these men wanted to establish for the outside world. This is unsurprising. As Duffett has also pointed out, 'there was something elemental in the sharing of food; to witness a neighbour's hunger in the presence of one's own plenty would have contravened every sensibility, whether anthropological, social or religious.'[72] Yet, by far and away, receiving the most comment and condemnation from prisoners of

[71] Nell, diary entry, 9 January 1945.   [72] Duffett, *The Stomach for Fighting*, p. 202.

wars, with the level of criticism differing depending on the audience of the diary, is how individualism also prevailed in the captivity.

Individualism was expressed in many ways. One was a POW's decision not to share out the contents of his personal food parcels. East and Hurrell, writing with public audiences in mind, criticised other nationalities for such selfish behaviour.[73] Mansel, meanwhile, focussed his anger in his diary on his compatriots. On 27 December 1941, he recorded how it was 'infuriating' at Oflag VIB (Warburg) 'to see pow's from other camps walking away daily from the parcel hut laden with personal parcels, having as much and more than they can cope with', whilst Mansel, and the others who had recently arrived from Oflag IXA/H (Spangenberg), were 'speedily reaching bedrock'.[74]

Trading was another way through which individualism became pronounced. This was a common and accepted aspect of most POW camps. The prices in some camps were controlled on a non-profit basis; in other camps, the system varied from profits being channelled into the escape fund to 'cigarette barons' reigning dominant.[75] In October 1944, Mansel again used his diary to bemoan the existence of a profit-making motive at Oflag VIIB (Eichstätt).[76] Similarly, Hawarden, after explaining what an 'exchange mart' was to his diary readers, recorded that 'Many foodstuffs out of the Red Cross Parcels find their way on to these marts', and then added, 'Our Officers have put their feet down regarding food out of Invalid Parcels.'[77]

Rackets provide a third example of individualism. They had been an 'outstanding feature' of Booth's four years in captivity. He explained a racket as 'any job that is taken on for the sake of the perks'. Numerous POWs refer to them, but, in those narratives written with a public audience in mind, they often do so in guarded, oblique or uncritical ways. For example, Booth qualified his comment on rackets, first by adding 'the cynical kriegie is quick to detect or imagine racketeering in every grade of official life', and then by anticipating his reader's reaction: 'I shall be accused of cynicism and, of course, I am deliberating only painting one side of the picture'.[78] In his documentary-style diary, under the heading of 'Black Market and Rackets', Howard absolved any personal blame by explaining, 'Now all hands have been or are in a racket so no one can moan.'[79] Whilst when Bains described that 'Tarhuma' [sic] transit camp

---

[73] East, diary entry, 24 March 1944; Hurrell, logbook, p. 31.
[74] Mansel, diary entry, 27 December 1941; see also diary entry, 8 September 1940.
[75] Gilbert, POW, p. 113; Rolf, Prisoners of the Reich, p. 182.
[76] Mansel diary entry, 23 October 1944; see also diary entries, 11 February 1941, 12 January and 15 November 1944.
[77] Hawarden, diary entry, 26 June 1943.   [78] Booth, diary entry, 10 August 1944.
[79] Howard, logbook, pp. 99–102.

in Libya was 'the worst example of corruption I have ever seen' and that the 'cookhouse staff . . . took an undue proportion of all the best', he blamed it on the lack of leaders or authorities present. When he was taken to a desert fort, the 'Food was much better . . . being well-cooked and honestly issued' because a sergeant of the South Nottinghamshire Hussars was in charge.[80]

The private diary entries are more explicit. White, in his unvarnished diary, declared on 14 October 1942, without context or excuses, 'Cooks charged with pinching & roasting meat, leads to new staff. . . . court held to be taken up again in Blighty. Leads to formation of Camp Police.'[81] Barrington, a junior NCO, used his reflective diary to vent his frustrations. His outrage is palpable on 29 April 1943, over the behaviour of the senior NCOs in the camp:

There have been a lot of complaints about our rations lately . . . a notice from the camp authorities appeared on the board to the effect that Officers were present when rations were checked in and 'therefore there could be no mistake'! & any further complaints would be received unfavourably!! . . . I think a Mutual Aid Committee could do a good job of work here, but those W.Os [Warrant Officers], frightened for their double rations for their purely nominal job, stand in the way of any effort to form one, & if . . . any . . . agitation merely get his marching orders on some pretext to another camp.[82]

Together, these narratives show not only the broad ways in which men's relationships were shaped in captivity, but also what they understood as a publicly palatable version of life behind barbed wire. By writing in their letters, as well as diaries and logbooks aimed at a public audience, of friendship, camaraderie, the upholding of the military hierarchy and the sharing of food, they show this was the image of their relationships behind barbed wire they wished to project.[83] The more private diaries, which provided their authors with a subversive space, tell a different story.

Female Impersonators

The performances of female impersonators made the physical absence of women in POW camps, simultaneously, most obvious and least visible.

---

[80] Bains, diary entries, 24 June–7 July 1942 and 7 July–1 August 1942.

[81] White, diary entry, 14 October 1942; see also diary entry, 20 May 1941.

[82] Barrington, diary entry, 29 April 1943. For similar examples, see Barrington, diary entries, 23 January and 13 and 15 February 1943.

[83] Wilkinson similarly analyses magazines produced by British POWs in the First World War for how they produced a 'publicly acceptable' version of captivity and one that emphasised the 'constructive aspects of camp life'; see Oliver Wilkinson, 'Captivity in Print. The Form and Function of POW Camp Magazines', in Gilly Carr and Harold Mytum (eds.), *Cultural Heritage and Prisoners of War. Creativity behind Barbed Wire* (New York: Routledge, 2012), pp. 227–43.

For example, the need for male POWs to imitate the opposite sex made women's absence most evident. POWs' successful mimetic performances, which minimised the difference between the female impersonator and a genetic woman, served, as this section will show, to obscure women's physical absence. POWs' written reactions to these impersonators, of which there are many, provide a useful lens through which to examine how POWs' all-male environment affected male bonding.

During this era, female impersonators were not an uncommon sight for British servicemen. In the First World War, division and battalion concert parties became a 'practically universal' feature of life on the western and eastern fronts, which, according to historian J. G. Fuller in his study on troop morale, acted to promote *esprit de corps*.[84] According to scholar David Boxwell, it was with 'startling frequency' that these plays featured military men in drag, which took cross-dressing from a marginal activity and placed it at the heart of this most public and mainstream of institutions.[85] Female impersonators, as historian Iris Rachamimov shows, were also central to POW camp life during the Great War.[86]

The tradition of cross-dressing continued in POW camps in the Second World War across the globe, from camps in the Far East holding Allied prisoners to those in the United States holding German ones.[87] In POW camps in Europe, female impersonators most commonly appeared in the camp theatre productions which, as Chapter 2 showed, were popular amongst POWs. They also appeared off-stage, in more informal settings, including hut or camp dances, fancy dress parties, New Year parties, and tea and sewing parties.[88]

The form of cross-dressing that elicited the most comment from POWs was that of mimesis, as opposed to mimicry. Mimesis occurs when female impersonators attempt to imitate women and make the difference between 'her' and a genetic woman as slight as possible. Mimicry is imitation with derision, or with the aim of creating a comic effect, as

---

[84] J. G. Fuller, *Troop Morale and Popular Culture in the British and Dominion Armies, 1914–1918* (Oxford: Clarendon Press, 1990), pp. 96, 102–3.

[85] David A. Boxwell, 'The Follies of War: Cross-Dressing and Popular Theatre on the British Front Lines, 1914–18', *Modernism/Modernity*, 9, 1 (2002), 4.

[86] Rachamimov, 'The Disruptive Comforts of Drag', 363.

[87] For an account of female impersonators in camps in the Far East, see Sears A. Eldredge, *Captive Audiences/Captive Performers: Music and Theatre as Strategies for Survival on the Thailand–Burma Railway 1942–1945* (Macalester College, 2014), pp. 516–41, http://digitalcommons.macalester.edu/thdabooks/24, last accessed 31 March 2016. Matthias Reiss also explores the role of female impersonators in German POW camps in the United States, Reiss, 'The Importance of Being Men', 23–47.

[88] Nell, diary entry, 1 January 1944; East, diary entry, 4 March 1944; Hawarden, diary entries, 9 and 26 November 1941, 6 December 1942; Jenkins, diary entry, 23 October 1942.

exemplified by the pantomime 'dame', who appears oversized and clumsy.[89] There are only three quotes amongst POWs who feature in *Captives of War* that suggest this effect was the intention of the cross-dressing in the performances they saw. For example, Webster wrote to his parents that the 'women' who appeared in the shows at Stalag IVB (Mühlberg) were 'most laughable, honestly', whilst Stewart recorded that 'all the female parts, of course, have to be played by men, and therefore have to be comic parts.'[90] Stewart's remark is puzzling. He was writing from Oflag VIIB (Eichstätt), where he had spent the previous two and a half years, and in which, as this chapter shows, there were some excellent mimetic performances by female impersonators. Perhaps it is an example of how the audience of Stewart's diary, his parents and sister, determined his observation more than what was happening in captivity.

In contrast to Stewart's assessment, all the other comments refer to mimetic performances.[91] These prisoners commented almost unanimously on how impressed they were by the results. Some premised their conviction of the excellence of these performers on the fact that they had not seen a woman for months. According to Commander Geoffrey Lambert, some of those on stage at Marlag 'O' (the other of the two compounds that made up Marlag: this one housed petty officers and leading seamen) 'make pretty good girls ... at least they look good to us who haven't seen a decent one for a long time.'[92] At the second theatre show Hyde saw at Stalag Luft III (Sagan), he commented on how 'The Popsie looked + spoke just like the real thing – or at least, as far as I can remember!'[93] Similarly, when Nell saw the play *Boy meets girl* at Stalag IVB (Mühlberg), he found 'the acting was very convincing. When a man is dressed as a woman he looks astoundingly like the authentic article. But none of us have been on speaking terms with a woman for some time: perhaps that is something to do with it.'[94] Others declared the brilliance of these female impersonators in more unequivocal terms. For East, also at Stalag IVB (Mühlberg), the 'feminine parts' of the Noël Coward play *Blithe Spirit* were taken 'with great accomplishment ... at

[89] Boxwell, 'The Follies of War', 13.
[90] SWWEC, 2007.531, Warrant Officer D. H. Webster, letter to his family, 1 December 1943; Stewart, diary entry, 11 January 1945. For a similar example, see Barrington, diary entry, 13 May 1943.
[91] Other scholars have emphasised this function of female impersonators in the First World War; see Boxwell, 'The Follies of War', 13; Fuller, *Troop Morale and Popular Culture*, pp. 105–6; Rachamimov, 'The Disruptive Comforts of Drag', 377.
[92] Lambert, letter to his wife, 7 February 1944; Monteath, *P.O.W.*, p. 155.
[93] Hyde, letter to his wife, 27 September 1943.
[94] Nell, diary entry, 5 February 1944. For a similar example, see IWM 05/57/1, Sergeant E. G. Ball, letter to his wife, 28 March 1943.

Figure 3.5: *Post-mortem* at Oflag VIIB (Eichstätt). Second Lieutenant Brian McIrvine was a female impersonator in a number of plays put on in oflags. Here, he can be seen on the left playing the protagonist's girlfriend in Noël Coward's gloomy and bitter anti-war play, *Post-mortem*.
Source: www.mgoodliffe.co.uk/

times we forgot that theirs was just impersonation.'[95] Mansel, after seeing *Pasquinade* at Oflag VIIB (Eichstätt), wrote of Second Lieutenant Brian McIrvine, who had been a professional actor before the war and was repeatedly cast in the female role in various oflag productions, 'I'm bloody sure if he was billed as a girl at a London Theatre no-one would question her sex. It's unbelievable.'[96] [Figure 3.5].

Perhaps the greatest compliment given to these performances is Hawarden's confused use of quotation marks in recording the success of a Gilbert and Sullivan collaboration put on at Stalag 383 (Hohenfels): 'Went to see "H. M. S. Pinafore" tonight – another marvellous show. I didn't know we had so many good singers in Camp. The "Male Part" of the chorus singing is very good – as good as I've heard at home. Five hundred handkerchiefs were used in making dresses for the six girls.'[97] Hawarden's

---

[95] East, diary entry, 18 December 1943.   [96] Mansel, diary entry, 26 February 1943.
[97] Hawarden, diary entry, 27 July 1943.

qualifying use of quotation marks for the wrong sex indicates how success-fully female impersonators switched the gender of prisoners of war.[98]

These comments fit in with the so-called safety valve interpretation of drag put forward by anthropologists. In this interpretation, drag provides men with a release from the abnormal state of a single-sex society.[99] This would also explain why POWs favoured mimetic performances: panto-mime dames would not have offered prisoners the same release from their homosocial environment because they draw attention to the fact that their impersonation is a performance.[100] Numerous POWs explicitly wrote in their personal narratives of how the function of female impersonators was to make their society a more normal one. Hawarden recorded how dances were held at Stalag 383 (Hohenfels) every Wednesday and Saturday and that 'As usual several lads dress as ladies to give it a proper atmosphere.'[101] At one performance of *Cinderella*, at Oflag XIIB (Hadamar), which Angove attended, an 'usherette & programme girl' as well as 'a dear old flower seller' worked at the theatre, 'all contributing to the creation of the right theatre spirit before the show started.'[102] Meanwhile, Mansel qualified his initial reaction to Brian McIrvine and one other female impersonator entering the canteen dressing room at Oflag VIIB (Eichstätt), when he wrote in his diary that they made him 'feel most uncomfortable – or comfortable?'[103]

In the 'safety valve' interpretation of drag, anthropologists generally agree that the basic societal order is not questioned. Historians Peter Boag and Emma Vickers have argued that cross-dressers affirm the two-gender/two-sex system by reintroducing a female element into an all-male environment.[104] Historian Natalie Zemon Davis explains how they can strengthen it: 'uses of sexual inversion ... are ultimately sources of order and stability in a hierarchical society. They can clarify the structure by the process of reversing it. They can provide an expression of, and a safety valve for, conflicts within the system. ... But, so it is argued, they do not question the basic order of society itself.'[105] This is very similar to the

---

[98] For the insight that the usage of quotation marks can provide in such contexts, see Rachamimov, 'Camp Domesticity', pp. 291–305.

[99] Rachamimov, 'The Disruptive Comforts of Drag', 375; Natalie Zemon Davis, *Society and Culture in Early Modern France. Eight Essays by Natalie Zemon Davis* (Cambridge: Polity Press, 1987), p. 130.

[100] Paul Baker and Jo Stanley, *Hello Sailor! The Hidden History of Gay Life at Sea* (London: Longman, 2003), pp. 134–5.

[101] Hawarden, diary entry, 6 November 1942.

[102] Angove, diary entry, 28 February 1945.   [103] Mansel, diary entry, 6 January 1944.

[104] P. Boag, *Re-dressing America's Frontier Past* (Berkeley: University of California Press, 2011), p. 17; Emma Vickers, *Queen and Country. Same-Sex Desire in the British Armed Forces, 1939–45* (Manchester: Manchester University Press, 2015), p. 98.

[105] Davis, *Society and Culture in Early Modern France*, p. 130.

inversion of the batmanning system discussed earlier. Prisoners of war also used these performances by female impersonators to assert the hierarchical gender order by declaring men were better at being female than women themselves. Mansel, for example, commented on how 'Citronella', again played by Brian McIrvine in Oflag VIB (Warburg)'s Christmas 1941 pantomime, 'is staggering and in a dance with the Prince, himself quite excellent, performs a dance at which the average girl would make but a poor attempt.'[106] Matthews similarly wrote to his wife, from Stalag XXIA, in Schildberg, in west central Poland, that the 'beauty chorus' in the musical comedy *Windbag the Sailor* did such a good job that 'When our "girls" come home the Tiller girls will have to take up Domestic Scenes!! As for our leading lady – well, that resection of Adam's rib was quite unnecessary.' On another occasion, now in Stalag Luft III (Sagan), he told his wife how, at one concert, 'the "ladies" were clad in the latest Paris models' and that 'when we come home we shall be very critical of how women play feminine parts.'[107]

There is, of course, a certain jocularity to these comments but, at the same time, embedded within them is the claim that men were better at being female than women themselves. These observations support the conclusions of other scholars and historians who have similarly noted how men in the past used cross-dressing to achieve dominance over women, by claiming they were better at being female than were genetic women.[108] In this way, although cross-dressers were praised for their femininity, they paradoxically enabled prisoners to uphold the traditional gender hierarchy and to assert their collective male superiority.

Historians and other scholars have also suggested that there are limits to this 'safety valve' interpretation of drag, arguing that cross-dressing can serve to destabilise gender identities.[109] As scholar David Boxwell writes on cross-dressing in the theatre on the British front lines during the First World War:

the form and content of the drag performer's 'act', strongly dependent as it was on multiple entendre, close physical contact with other men (both in and out of drag), and the illusion of eroticized, idealized and objectified femininity, disrupted the boundaries that contained the act as a necessary release in an all-male environment. A spectator's desiring and approving gaze on a soldier in drag was not simply

---

[106] Mansel, diary entry, 1 January 1942.
[107] Matthews, letters to his wife, 23 November 1941 and 13 December 1942.
[108] Sandra M. Gilbert and Susan Gubar, *No Man's Land, The Place of the Woman Writer in the Twentieth Century*, volume 2, *Sexchanges* (New Haven, CT: Yale University Press, 1989), pp. 334–5; Sharon R. Ullman, *Sex Seen: The Emergence of Modern Sexuality in America* (Berkeley: University of California Press, 1997), pp. 53–4.
[109] Rachamimov, 'The Disruptive Comforts of Drag', 364, 376; Eldredge, *Captive Audiences/Captive Performers*, p. 530; Boxwell, 'The Follies of War', 17.

a matter of pleasure in a 'surrogate' woman; rather, his gaze was directed at a fellow man in drag, a fellow soldier in his own military organization.[110]

In other words, when POWs showed admiration for female impersona-tors, it entailed the possibility that they were transgressing the boundaries of male heterosexual desire.[111] This is, perhaps, what Mansel referred to when he wondered whether the two female impersonators he saw in the canteen dressing room made him feel 'uncomfortable – or comfortable?'[112] Others were similarly unsettled by their admiration. When East attended an 'excellent party' put on by the army, where one of the 'fellows dressed as a girl and fooled the audience beautifully', he also commented that 'Many could be seen squirming in their seats.'[113] Whilst of 'Junior Booth', who was a female impersonator at Stalag Luft VI (Heydekrug), with 'flaxen hair, wide, baby-blue eyes, cheeks like rosy apples ... and a charming smile', Hall commented how gazing at him, when he was dressed as a woman, was 'both [a] pleasurable and haunting experience for hundreds of men'.[114]

These potential transgressions are also brought to the fore when these men discuss the personal attractiveness of the female impersonators in the camps. Hyde, in a letter home, described Dick Whittington's girlfriend as 'extremely popsie like and very attractive at that', whilst Angove said the 'usherette' and 'programme girl' at *Cinderella* were 'made up to kill'.[115] When Brian McIrvine or 'Lynda Swansdown', a character who regularly appeared in plays specially written in POW camps, opened the fun fair at Oflag VIB (Warburg) dressed in a two-piece costume, he was reported as looking 'simply ravishing!'[116] East used the same adjective to describe Stalag IVB's (Mühlberg) leading female impersonator, 'Sugar' Townley, who appeared in the musical show *Spring Time for Jennifer*.[117] Similarly, when referring to *Up the Pole*, a variety show performed at Stalag 383 (Hohenfels) in May 1944, White described the star, 'Pinky' Smith, as 'gorgeous'.[118]

Figure 3.6 shows 'Pinky' Smith. 'She' was photographed and turned into a camp pinup at Stalag 383 (Hohenfels) and, according to White,

---

[110] Boxwell, 'The Follies of War', 17. For a similar assessment of the role of cross-dressing in the armed forces, see Marjorie Garber, *Vested Interests. Cross-dressing and Cultural Anxiety* (New York: Routledge, 1992), pp. 55–6.

[111] For a discussion of this in relation to the performances of female impersonators in early twentieth-century America, see Ullman, *Sex Seen*, p. 54.

[112] Mansel, diary entry, 6 January 1944.   [113] East, diary entry, 27 November 1943.

[114] Hall, diary entry, 25 July 1943.

[115] Hyde, letter to his wife, 30 December 1942; Angove, diary entry, 28 February 1945.

[116] Mansel, diary entry, 3 January 1942; private collection of Andrew McIrvine, autobio-graphy of Brian McIrvine, unpaginated.

[117] East, diary entry, 12 December 1944.   [118] White, diary entry, 2 May 1944.

Figure 3.6: 'Pinky' Smith. Fourteen thousand orders were placed for a copy of this image of 'Pinky' Smith. He became a pinup in Stalag 383.
Source: IWM 66/12/1, the private papers of Sergeant Major A. Hawarden. Image reproduced with permission from Sandra Hawarden-Lord.

14,000 orders were placed for a copy of the image: an extraordinarily large number for a camp that contained approximately 4,700 prisoners.[119] Amongst 'her' admirers was Hawarden. He also recorded in his diary, in June 1944, that there was a 'big order' for a photograph of 'Pinky' Smith, 'even one for myself'. His order was fulfilled; the photograph is included in his papers held at the Imperial War Museum.[120]

In the 'safety valve' interpretation of drag, the cross-dressing contained in a performance is limited to that performance and, when the play ends, the female impersonators return to being and are again seen as men.[121] In this way, such performances did not threaten POWs' masculinity because they are temporal and bounded to the stage.[122] However, both the naming of 'Pinky' and 'her' being turned into a pinup indicate this impersonator continued to have a female presence off stage. Further evidence also shows that the behaviour of and effect created by female impersonators seeped beyond the boundaries of the theatre. Before performances at Oflag VIIB (Eichstätt), those POWs playing the female roles had their own separate 'ladies' dressing room in the canteen.[123] Similarly, at one debate, at Campo PG 35 (Padula), on 'This house believes in Father Xmas', Angove recorded in his diary how 'one of the "ladies" of the forthcoming pantomime' who spoke on behalf of the 'women's point of view . . . brought the house down & was very nearly mobbed at the end at the end of the show.'[124] Mansel similarly recorded how some POWs found the 'female artist' Brian McIrvine a 'great embarrassment' when he visited their room. One POW in particular could not 'refuse giving him anything he-she- has come to ask for.'[125]

These different examples illustrate that cross-dressing did not just provide POWs with temporary release from their all-male society but, instead, could result in prisoners breaching the boundaries of male heterosexual desire. On the occasions when POWs did note the presence of female impersonators entailed improper contraventions in male sexuality, they demonstrate contradictory attitudes in terms of what was considered acceptable behaviour and what was considered improper. East, for example, has already been cited as complimenting both the female impersonators in *Blithe Spirit* and 'Sugar' Townley.[126] Just after praising Townley, he also went on to write of how Townley was accused by other prisoners of 'being very effeminate as he puts polish on his nails and affects a long-bob

[119] White, diary entry, 11 May 1944; ACICR, C SC, Germany, Stalag 383, 16 April 1944.
[120] Hawarden, diary entry, 15 June 1944.
[121] Rachamimov, 'The Disruptive Comforts of Drag', 375.
[122] Vickers, *Queen and Country*, p. 92.   [123] Mansel, diary entry, 6 January 1944.
[124] Angove, diary entry, 23 December 1942.   [125] Mansel, diary entry, 21 January 1944.
[126] East, diary entries, 12 December 1944 and 9 February 1945.

hair style. In civvy life he was a beauty expert at a big Toronto department store'.[127] His description stops there. There is no disapproval from East of Townley's grooming habits. However, when East observed that the hut next door to him, in Stalag IVB (Mühlberg), was 'now holding sewing parties in which all members dress and make up in feminine garb' as well as 'tea parties with "waitresses"', he responded with incredulity: 'It is an extraordinary thing that some men have the inclination to impersonate women in these surroundings.'[128] Similarly, whilst Hawarden put in a request for a photo of 'Pinky' Smith, he responded negatively to one concert held at Stalag XXA (Thorn), where one of the lads was dressed as a waitress called Angela and would 'offer herself to be kissed by the highest bidder.' He considered this 'a little unsavoury', although clearly others did not, as the Welfare Fund benefitted from it by 400 marks, approximately £26, or £1,000 today.[129] However, as discussed earlier, Hawarden seems to have considered it acceptable for men to dress up as women at dances, but this form of male intimacy was frowned upon by the British authorities in another camp. Lieutenant Gibbens recorded that, in 1943, the custom of men 'holding dances, under shaded lights, in which half of them were dressed as women ... died out under official pressure'.[130]

Such contradictory attitudes indicate that ideas held by these prisoners of war about heterosexual and homoerotic behaviour were not clear-cut. This is further supported by the type of personal narrative in which these men comment on female impersonators. Almost all the quotes listed previously are taken from letters written to wives, or diaries written with a public audience in mind, the only exception being Mansel, whose entries are hard to discern between being written for a family member to read and written purely for himself. In other words, these prisoners of war do not show any compunction about discussing their reactions to female impersonators. This could indicate the extent to which attitudes around male sexuality altered in the homosocial POW camp, but it could also illustrate something broader about British society at this time.

Whilst in today's terms, sexuality is a crucial element of *all* men's identities and experiences, with the vast majority subscribing to a coherent sexual identity of homosexuality or heterosexuality, scholars have shown

---

[127] East, diary entry, 9 February 1945.   [128] East, diary entry, 4 March 1944.

[129] Hawarden, diary entry, 8 October 1941. It is difficult to establish a precise approximation for this value. Mansel indicates that 15 marks was the equivalent of £1 in 1941, and Jabez-Smith puts 400 marks as worth £36 in 1945, Mansel, diary entry, 9 August 1941; NAM 2001-09-300, Second Lieutenant A. R. Jabez-Smith, diary entry, 30 March 1945.

[130] Gibbens does not specify which camp this was, but, since he was there in 1943, he must be referring to either Oflag IXA/Z or Stalag 344, Gibbens, 'The Psychology of the Prisoner-of-War', p. 20.

that this was not always the case.[131] Historian Matt Houlbrook's work on *Queer London* explores homosex (sexual activity between men that makes no assumption about their sexual identity) and other intimate relationships that working-class men had with other men in the first half of the twentieth century. He demonstrates how these men could have such encounters without considering themselves – or being considered by other men – as anything other than 'normal'.[132] Covering a similar period, Helen Smith, in her study of men who desired other men in industrial England, has argued that for working men and their communities in the north, 'sexual fluidity' was common.[133] Sex between men was something ordinary: another form of human contact.[134] There was a 'tolerance' of or 'ambivalence towards' male same-sex desire in northern working-class communities.[135] Historian Emma Vickers, meanwhile, has shown how the Second World War fostered a '"for the duration" toleration' of same-sex desire 'and in some cases, acceptance'.[136] The unavailability of women plus the fear of contracting VD led to and legitimised the practice of homosex.[137] Same-sex activity was not officially accepted in the armed forces, but each ship, unit and squadron possessed its 'own, often implicit, guidelines' as to whether it was permissible, and whether an 'openly queer recruit was ostracised or accepted was subjective and often unit-specific'.[138] During the 1940s and 1950s, Houlbrook, Smith and Vickers all agree, sexual identity and sexual activity became much more firmly linked together, and the binary divide between 'homosexual' and 'heterosexual' became fixed, due to a variety of factors, including the advent of affluence and a consumer culture, the queer man becoming a scapegoat for social angst and fears about the influence of communism.[139]

These studies might help explain why POWs showed contradictory attitudes towards what was acceptable and unacceptable in terms of heterosexual and homoerotic desire. Ideas surrounding 'normal' male sexual behaviour at this time were much more fluid than they are today. They might also help explain the notable silence on homosexuality in the letters, diaries and logbooks consulted for this book. Only three POWs

---

[131] Helen Smith, *Masculinity, Class and Same-Sex Desire in Industrial England, 1895–1957* (Basingstoke: Palgrave Macmillan, 2015), p. 3.
[132] Matt Houlbrook, *Queer London. Perils and Pleasures in the Sexual Metropolis, 1918–1957* (Chicago: University of Chicago Press, 2005), p. 7.
[133] Smith, *Masculinity, Class and Same-Sex Desire in Industrial England, 1895–1957*, p. 14.
[134] Smith, *Masculinity, Class and Same-Sex Desire in Industrial England, 1895–1957*, p. 80.
[135] Smith, *Masculinity, Class and Same-Sex Desire in Industrial England, 1895–1957*, p. 3.
[136] Vickers, *Queen and Country*, p. 7.   [137] Vickers, *Queen and Country*, pp. 58, 61.
[138] Vickers, *Queen and Country*, pp. 62, 69.
[139] Vickers, *Queen and Country*, pp. 62, 155; Smith, *Masculinity, Class and Same-Sex Desire in Industrial England, 1895–1957*, p. 21; Houlbrook, *Queer London*, p. 270.

mention homosexuality, or homosex in the camps. One does so in extremely vague terms; the other two reference homosexuality only to point out that it was not encountered.[140] This does not necessarily mean that homosexuality was comparatively rare in the central camps, as other historians writing on captivity have concluded.[141] POWs may simply have chosen not to comment on it. Observations by psychiatrists and doctors suggest two reasons for this, both of which echo Smith and Vickers' findings. First, POWs might have been indifferent towards homosex in the camps. This is suggested in one report, based on the work of psychiatrists who interviewed almost 20 per cent of ex-POWs over the summer of 1945. It contains the conclusion that 'homosexualism [*sic*] although it did occur, does not seem to have been practised more frequently than in non-prison groups' and that 'on the whole a very realistic attitude would seem to have been adopted towards this side of life.'[142] The report does not explain what is meant by this 'realistic attitude': one interpretation might be that, in lieu of a female presence, such practice was considered acceptable. Imprisoned medical officer Captain Archie Cochrane seems to suggest this. He wrote that the 'extent of actual sodomy was very hard to judge', both because it was concealed from medical officers and because of 'its sporadic appearance: there would be a great deal in one working party, where it spread rapidly by a sort of infection, while neighbouring working parties would have none'. Overall, Cochrane concluded the general incidence of 'actual sodomy' was 'probably very low', but, where it did occur, there were two groups of cases. One group consisted of men who had been 'active homosexual[s]' before the war, one of whom told Cochrane that 'POWs were much more easily seduced than civilians.' The other group consisted of regular soldiers who turned to sexual activity when bored. The idea that POWs turned to homosexual activity when bored or were seduced into it suggests that such behaviour was regarded with a certain degree of pragmatism. 'In general', Cochrane concludes, 'homosexuals were treated more sensibly by P.O.W.s than by civilians.'[143]

---

[140] Blyth, letter to his wife, 4 June 1944; Mansel, diary entry, 10 February 1944; Hall, diary entry, 25 July 1943. The latter two comment on how they did not come across it.

[141] MacKenzie writes that the extent of active homosexuality amongst British POWs is open to debate, but most of the evidence he cites suggests it was uncommon. Gilbert concludes that in officer and other non-working camps, homosexual activity was minimal whilst in the larger other ranks' camps there were instances of quite overt homosexual behaviour (MacKenzie, *The Colditz Myth*, p. 213; Gilbert, *POW*, p. 118).

[142] TNA WO 32/10757, R. F. Barbour, 'Interim Report on Returned Prisoners of War', 29 August 1945.

[143] A. L. Cochrane, 'Notes on the Psychology of Prisoners of War', *British Medical Journal*, 1, 4442 (23 February 1946), 283.

The other reason for POWs' silence may lie in there being no clear language attached to same-sex experiences available to the general public at this time.[144] As Helen Smith has observed, 'Language is key to developing, categorising and solidifying sexual identities.'[145] In her research, she suggests that 'it is possible that homosexuality was not spoken of because there was no clear, widespread understanding in the community of what it meant as an identity.'[146] Instead, only men in London, where a homosexual subculture did exist that helped to create a distinctly homosexual self-identity, and those of the middle and upper classes outside the capital, with the ability to access London's nightlife and volumes written by sexologists, came into contact with new public discourses about homosexuality.[147] The idea that the word 'homosexuality' did not automatically signify a widely recognised sexual identity is reflected in the writing of medical officer Lieutenant Gibbens. He uses various adjectives to qualify the word. He wrote of 'visible homosexuality', which varied from camp to camp; 'emotional homosexuality', which was not common but regarded with 'unusual tolerance'; and, 'unconscious homosexuality', or 'intimate friendships', which was very widespread.[148] It is hard to know what Gibbens meant by these different types of homosexuality. 'Emotional homosexuality' might refer to when the sex act was accompanied by emotional meaning. These liaisons, according to Vickers, were deemed by authorities to be more harmful than those devoid of emotion, because they questioned the heterosexuality of the partners.[149] Perhaps this is why Gibbens points out they were viewed with 'unusual tolerance'. Either way, Gibbens' various types of homosexuality indicate no fixed meaning was attached to the word and that it could apply to both the act of sex and emotional attachment. In summary, this evidence of homosexuality, along with the contradictory ways in which POWs reacted to cross-dressers in captivity, indicates a fluidity in attitudes towards male sexuality during this era.

Conclusion

This chapter has explored the individual relationships that formed amongst prisoners of war. Their diaries, logbooks and letters carry

---

[144] Smith, *Masculinity, Class and Same-Sex Desire in Industrial England, 1895–1957*, p. 158.
[145] Smith, *Masculinity, Class and Same-Sex Desire in Industrial England, 1895–1957*, p. 186.
[146] Smith, *Masculinity, Class and Same-Sex Desire in Industrial England, 1895–1957*, p. 184.
[147] Smith, *Masculinity, Class and Same-Sex Desire in Industrial England, 1895–1957*, pp. 34, 80, 116, 161.
[148] Gibbens, 'The Psychology of the Prisoner-of-War', p. 21.
[149] Vickers, *Queen and Country*, p. 59.

physical imprints of their friendships through signatures, sketches and vignettes. POWs also used their letters to reinforce their friendships, by inviting loved ones at home to mirror outside captivity the networks that had been established within. The conditions of captivity also put these bonds under a great deal of stress. In such cases, diaries became a place where POWs could silently vent their frustrations and so make communal living more manageable.

Three aspects of captivity were singled out for broadly shaping prisoners' relationships: date of capture, rank and allocation of food. Two of the most significant hardships of imprisonment – length of time in captivity and shortage of food – divided as much as unified these men. Their pre-captivity military unity, based on rank, was one of the ways in which imprisoned officers understood POWs' relationships should be organised, but not all adhered to this hierarchy. Analysing how POWs discussed these aspects of their captive life in different types of personal narratives demonstrates what they understood as a publicly acceptable version of life behind barbed wire. By writing in their letters, as well as diaries and logbooks aimed at a public audience, of friendship, camaraderie, the upholding of the military hierarchy and the sharing of food, they show this was the image of their relationships behind barbed wire they wished to project. The more private diaries, which provided their authors with a subversive space, tell a different story.

This chapter also explored how prisoners of war negotiated their homosocial world through an analysis of their reactions to female impersonators. POWs' admiration for men in drag could be used to exert their collective male superiority, but it also shows a blurring of the boundaries between heterosexual, homosocial and homoerotic relations.[150] The contradictory attitudes that many showed towards female impersonators, as well as the readiness of POWs to discuss their equivocal reactions to them in letters home and diaries written with an external audience in mind, also indicates the fluidity of male sexuality in this era.

So far, *Captives of War* has explored the social world that POWs physically occupied and the relationships they formed within it. Yet they were also immersed in their imaginations in a totally different one. This is the focus of the next chapter, 'Ties with home'.

---

[150] Iris Rachamimov similarly concludes that drag in POW camps in Russia in the First World War could both reaffirm heterosexual masculinity and sanction homoerotic and transgender associations ('The Disruptive Comforts of Drag', 364).

4   Ties with Home

I've finished one life, am having a visit to hell where I'm learning and experiencing a lot that's good and, if I'm not careful, also a lot that's harmful, and afterwards I'll start a new life. Family ties, or shall I say loves, will be the only connection.[1]

Private Keith Panter-Brick wrote these words on 21 May 1944, upon entering his fifth year of captivity in Germany. He suggests in this letter home that the lives of captured servicemen could be divided into three phases: pre-captivity, the damnation of imprisonment and a future post-captive world. Those military relationships that predated captivity were often severed upon capture as a man's unit would be split into different camps; relationships formed in captivity, meanwhile, were constantly exposed to the risk of instant disruption with POWs being sent to join a new camp or working party. 'Family ties' remained the only link between these three existences.

This chapter shows how POWs made sense of captivity through their relationships with home. Through the arrival of letters and parcels into the camps, and fantasies created by prisoners of war, these men continued to achieve proximity with their loved ones. Feelings of being near to loved ones were also constantly primed through the plans that accompanied POWs' optimistic anticipations of an early homecoming. Yet there was a darker side to prisoners' attachment to loved ones: their dependence on them could alter and upset these men's familial and gender roles. Overall, this chapter demonstrates that whilst emotional proximity to their loved ones helped prisoners to make sense of their wartime imprisonment, it could also make captivity harder to bear.

Letters and Parcels from Home

Canon King spent his first few months in captivity eagerly anticipating the arrival of his wife's letters. He reached his first POW camp, Oflag VIIC

---

[1] Private Keith Panter-Brick, letter to his family, 21 May 1944, in Keith Panter-Brick, *Years Not Wasted 1940–1945. A POW's Letters and Diary* (Sussex: The Book Guild Ltd, 1999), p. 79.

(Laufen), on 7 July 1940, but it took until 23 September 1940 for mail for the 'St Valerie [*sic*] people' to begin to trickle through. On 7 October, the first large delivery of 700 letters arrived. Despite 'a 1–2 chance' of receiving some mail, King had 'no luck'. On 15 October 1940, a letter came for him from a friend in the United States. Receiving this, he wrote in his diary, had 'shaken' him 'more than I would have thought. The feel of a letter in my hands, and the news it brings, stirs up the mud.' Then, on 28 October 1940, his first two letters from friends in the United Kingdom arrived. These, he complained, were 'full of nothing but local domestic gossip. They assumed I have had plenty of letters already, so neither breathed a word to the anxious prisoner about his wife, children, parents or brother & sisters. Which is <u>most</u> provoking!' On 6 November 1940, he came back from lunch to find a letter on his bed addressed in his wife's handwriting. He 'swooped on it with a yell!' but the post office and censors had 'the laugh on [him] once more.' The envelope had merely been written by his wife, and inside was a letter from a friend. The envelope, however, was now his 'prize possession': it was King's first contact with his wife since he had entered captivity. He did not have long to wait for another. The following day, at noon, a letter written by his wife finally arrived. It was 'full of news', all of which King 'greedily devoured', but then, he concluded, the news 'seemed somehow the least important part'.[2]

The value of letters to prisoners of war is repeatedly emphasised in the strongest possible language. 'I do live for these letters', Taylor wrote in his diary, a few months after he had narrowly escaped death. He had spent fifteen hours in water, after his motor-torpedo-boat had been sunk and before the Germans picked him up off Calais, in July 1942.[3] 'I just live for your letters', Sergeant Ernest Ball told his wife, eleven months after he had been shot down near Aachen in Germany.[4] Summing up the attitude of all men in Stalag Luft I near Barth, the first permanent camp to which he was sent after he bailed out of his aircraft near Berlin, Hurrell informed his parents that 'we live for mail here.'[5]

However, as King suggests, the 'news' these letters contained was not of primary importance. This is unsurprising given the restrictions placed on relatives' correspondence in terms of quantity and censorship. Relatives were instructed by the General Post Office to write letters to POWs of no longer than two sides of notepaper and just once or twice a week. The British government also required that references to naval,

---

[2] King, diary entries, 23 September, 7 and 28 October, 7 November 1940.
[3] Taylor, diary entry, 28 December 1942.   [4] Ball, letter to his wife, 16 July 1942.
[5] Hurrell, letter to his parents, 12 May 1941. For similar language, see Angove, diary entry, 8 September 1942.

military, aerial, economic and political matters be avoided.[6] King found, instead, that the significance of his wife's letter lay in what it embodied as an object. Historians have frequently forgotten this other function of letters, but, as historian Martha Hanna has observed, 'the letter itself was a physical artefact that could cultivate intimacy by making the absent correspondent seem almost palpably present.'[7]

For prisoners of war, this is exactly what letters did: they bridged the hundreds of miles lying between them and home, enabling mothers, wives and sweethearts to join these men in captivity.[8] Fairclough, married just months before he was shot down in April 1942, found that his wife's character was expressed 'so vividly, naturally, + desirably' that he told her, even after more than two years apart, he had 'never . . . lost touch with you at all in the essentials.'[9] Lance Bombardier Stuart Campbell metaphorically described to his wife how her letters were living beings: they were 'breaths of hope and home', which he inhaled at Campo PG 70, located at Monte Urano in eastern Italy, his first permanent POW camp following his capture at Tobruk in 1942.[10] Meanwhile, of his mother's letters, Mansel similarly recorded, 'I can almost hear her voice, which adds infinitely to the joy of receiving letters'.[11] Using strikingly similar language, the value of next-of-kin parcels did not just lie in the sundries they contained. Having spent one year in Campo PG 65, located at Gravina, southern Italy, Glass wrote that 'the best thing of all' in his parcel was 'the breath of home it brought with it.' It was, literally, the mothering touch that affected this unmarried twenty-seven-year-old so strongly, for he later wrote in his diary, 'how close I feel to you when I see

---

[6] TNA CUST 106/369, 'Communication with Prisoners of War Interned Abroad', General Post Office, December 1940; TNA CUST 106/369, 'Communication with Prisoners of War and Civilians Interned Abroad', General Post Office, August 1941; 'Communication with Prisoners of War and Civilians Interned in Europe (leaflet P 2280E)' in SWWEC 2001.1048, private papers of Driver P. Hainsworth.

[7] M. Hanna, 'A Republic of Letters: The Epistolary Tradition in France during World War I', *The American Historical Review*, 108 (2003), 1348. For similar arguments see Margaretta Jolly, 'Love Letters versus Letters Carved in Stone: Gender, Memory and the "Forces Sweethearts" Exhibition', in Martin Evans and Ken Lunn (eds.), *War and Memory in the Twentieth Century* (Oxford: Berg, 1997), p. 115.

[8] Audoin-Rouzeau has drawn a similar conclusion in relation to French soldiers in the First World War. He characterises letters as 'permanent or occasional bridges' that 'materially and emotionally linked the front with the rest of the country' (*Men at War, 1914–1918*, p. 135); Annette Becker also describes letters as bringing the only female presence into the camps (*Oubliés de la Grande Guerre. Humanitaire et Culture de Guerre. Populations Occupées, Déportés Civils, Prisonniers de Guerre*. Paris: Noêsis, 1998, p. 131).

[9] Fairclough, letter to his wife, 6 June 1944.

[10] Liddle, ARMY 023, Lance Bombardier S. Campbell, letter to his wife, 17 November 1942.

[11] Mansel, diary entry, 27 February 1941.

all the things which not so long ago were being so carefully packed by you!'[12]

The presence of home was also evoked through the only item that could be enclosed within surface mail: 'snapshots or unmounted photographs of a personal nature'.[13] A photograph is, as critic Susan Sontag has pointed out, 'not only an image (as a painting is an image), an interpretation of the real; it is also a trace, something directly stencilled off the real'.[14] In captivity, these photos were framed and publicly displayed around POWs' beds. They embodied relatives back at home to such an extent that they were talked to and even replied back. For example, the 'gallery of portraits' above Matthews' bed in Stalag XXIA (Schildberg), where he was working in its isolation hospital, would, he wrote to his wife, 'greet me when I wake up & . . . bid me good-night.'[15] In the midst of one of Stalag Luft III's (Sagan) barracks, which Ball shared with about eighty other men, he would 'always say goodnight' to one particular portrait of his wife holding their son in her arms, a son to whom he was a 'posthumous parent', since he was born after Ball entered captivity.[16] So real were these photographs that they were sometimes physically experienced. Flying Officer Reginald Fayers referred to the photo of his wife as his first 'true-love' (his second was the library). This photo, he told his wife, was framed and placed at the head of his bed, with its proud caption suggesting it was there for all to admire: 'This is my only beloved, my wife, in whom I'm very well-pleased.' Retreating to his bunk bed, in one of the barrack rooms of Stalag Luft I (Barth), Fayers would daily turn to this photo and 'look at it foolishly and feel you leaning on me and smiling for me.'[17]

In these ways, letters and photographs could overcome the spatial divide that lay between POWs and their loved ones. Together they also

---

[12] Glass, diary entries, 3 February and 7 April 1943. For similar examples, see Barrington, diary entries, 19 and 21 May 1943; Liddle ARMY 023, Lance Bombardier S. Campbell, diary entry, 7 May 1944. For similar interpretations on the importance of parcels to combatants in the First World War, see Audoin-Rouzeau, *Men at War, 1914–1918*, p. 140; Becker, *Oubliés de la Grande Guerre*, p. 100; Duffett, *The Stomach for Fighting*, p. 197.

[13] CUST 106/369, 'Communication with Prisoners of War Interned Abroad', General Post Office, December 1940.

[14] Susan Sontag, *On Photography* (London: Allen Lane, 1978), p. 154.

[15] Matthews, letter to his wife, 18 June 1941. For a similar example, see Parker, letters to his sweetheart, 17 February and 10 November 1942.

[16] Ball, letter to his wife, 4 October 1942; ACICR, C SC, Germany, Luftlager III, 13 September 1942; For 'posthumous parent', see Guy Morgan, *Only Ghosts Can Live* (London: Crosby Lockwood & Son Ltd, 1945), p. 69.

[17] IWM 88/22/2, Flying Officer R. J. Fayers, letters to his wife, 4 February and 28 August 1944; ACICR, C SC, Germany, Stalag Luft I, 9 March 1944. For a similar example, see Fairclough, letter to his wife, 31 March 1943.

had the power to collapse the temporal gap that existed between the writing, and receiving, of a letter.[18] Due to the disorganisation and inadequacy of transport or the strain placed on the enemy powers' censors, it could take months for a letter to be delivered, but, when photographs were combined with letters, this delay was eradicated.[19] Parker would keep snapshots of his sweetheart in front of him when he wrote home, so it would, as he told her, 'feel as if Im [sic] telling you instead of writing because after every couple of words I write I stop and look at them'.[20] Equally, when Mansel read letters written by his parents and siblings with photographs alongside, it made 'letters seem so much more real and lessen the feelings of make-believe that one gets during the few moments it takes to read them'.[21]

The way in which letters provided POWs with a tangible connection with home is evidenced in other ways. Prisoners would repeatedly re-read a piece of mail, enabling them to prolong their proximity to loved ones.[22] POWs sent lists to their loved ones of the letters they had so far mailed through and invited them to do likewise.[23] Their lists indicate the symbolic value of the letter as an object, connecting two separated beings: it was as important to know that the other had written as it was to find out the contents of their letter.[24] Numerous men counted up their letters and proudly announced their cumulative totals in their correspondence and diaries, whilst others created meticulous tables at the back of their diaries, recording each one's date of arrival.[25] Such tables also appear in the

---

[18] Audoin-Rouzeau also argues that, for French combatants in the First World War, 'letters were unquestionably semi-magical objects. Navigating instruments for a voyage through time and space' (*Men at War, 1914–1918*, p. 141).

[19] On the delivery of letters, see *Report of the International Committee of the Red Cross*, vol. I, p. 350.

[20] Parker, letter to his sweetheart, 23 March 1943.

[21] Mansel, diary entry, 24 March 1941; ACICR, C SC, Germany, Stalag XXA, Camp pour officiers britanniques, 1 avril 1941.

[22] See, for example, IWM 66/132/1, Sergeant Major A. Hawarden, diary entry, 26 November 1940; Ball, letter to his wife, 24 December 1942; Matthews, letters to his wife, 18 November 1940, 14 December and 23 March 1941. For similar analysis with regard to criminal prisoners, see Anita Wilson, '"Absolutely Truly Brill to See from You": Visuality and Prisoners' Letters', in David Barton and Nigel Hall (eds.), *Letter Writing as a Social Practice* (Amsterdam: John Benjamins Publishing Co., 1999), pp. 182–3.

[23] Fairclough, letter to his wife, 13 May 1942; SWWEC 2007.158, Warrant Officer D. H. Webster, letter to his family, 26 October 1943; Matthews, letter to his wife, 6 July 1940.

[24] Luisa Passerini, *Europe in Love, Love in Europe. Imagination and Politics in Britain between the Wars* (London: I. B. Tauris Publishers, 1999), pp. 302–3.

[25] On counting up mail, see King, diary entry, 26 July 1941; Parker, letter to his sweetheart, 7 May 1942; Mansel, letter to his mother, 9 June 1943 and diary entry, 31 December 1941; Burnaby-Atkins, letter to his parents, 21 January 1941; Fairclough, letters to his wife, 3 April 1943 and 5 November 1944; Abbott, diary entry, 30 March 1943; Jarvis, letter to his parents, 21 March 1943. For examples of such tables,

unvarnished diaries. Whereas POWs' reflective diaries often contain loving musings, these were unsuited to the brief entries of unvarnished diaries, but such tables convey the importance of families and friends to these men.[26] Other diaries emphasise the way in which letters could bridge a gap by recording the non-arrival of mail, thus demonstrating the distance that lay between POWs and home in the absence of any correspondence.[27] Abbott's unvarnished diary consists of a couple of lines providing a very brief report of each day. However, he often used those words to note his lack of mail. Between 14 February 1941, when Abbott received his first letter from his wife, to the end of that year, out of 326 diary entries, 26 recorded the arrival of a letter from home whilst 91 entries stated that nothing had come. 'No mail yet', 'no mail', 'still waiting for mail', 'still no mail', he variously and repeatedly recorded.[28] Edwards, meanwhile, captured both the ebbs and flows of his letter and parcel arrivals, and thus the strength and weakness of his connection with home, through a line graph he diligently produced in the back of his logbook [Figure 4.1].

The arrival of mail was so important that, for some, it took precedence over the amenities and activities that had been established in the camps. From the well-organised camps of Oflag IXA/H (Spangenberg) and Marlag 'O' respectively, Mansel told his mother 'I ... don't live from day to day, but from postman to postman' and Taylor wrote to his wife of how 'life just seems to revolve round your letters'.[29] The arrival of letters also took precedence over the hardships of captivity. This point was noted by psychiatrists who interviewed escaped and repatriated POWs and concluded that, for some, 'anxiety over mail or food-parcels dwarfed physical comfort into insignificance.'[30] Similarly, when Abbott had the chance of leaving his 'rotten camp' in Willenberg in Poland,

see Glass, diary; Hawarden, diary book 10; Brook, diary; Brooke, diary; Barrington, diary; Cunningham, logbook.

[26] See, for example, IWM Documents.20269, Medical Officer A. M. Boyd, diary; IWM Documents.14385, Private L. Blakey, diary; IWM Documents.2728, Squadron Leader C. N. S. Campbell, diary; IWM Documents.2824, Corporal W. Kite, diary; IWM Documents.7927, Driver M. L. Jones, diary; IWM Documents.16596, Lance Sergeant H. Higton, diary; IWM Documents.17336, Driver A. J. Graham, diary.

[27] Steven Stowe, 'Making Sense of Letters and Diaries', *History Matters: The U.S. Survey Course on the Web*, http://historymatters.gmu.edu/mse/letters/, July 2002, last accessed 20 June 2016. See also Passerini, *Europe in Love, Love in Europe*, pp. 302–3.

[28] See, for example, Abbott, diary entries, 29 and 30 April and 1 and 3 May 1941.

[29] Mansel, letter to his mother, 11 August 1941; Taylor, letter to his wife, 25 April 1944. ACICR, C SC, Germany, Oflag IXA/H, 27 May 1941; ACICR, C SC, Germany, Marlag und Milag Nord, 28 June 1943.

[30] TNA WO 32/10757, Directorate of Army Psychiatry. Technical Memorandum No. 13. The Prisoner of War Comes Home. Notes Prepared for the Information of Army Psychiatrists, prepared by DAP, May 1944.

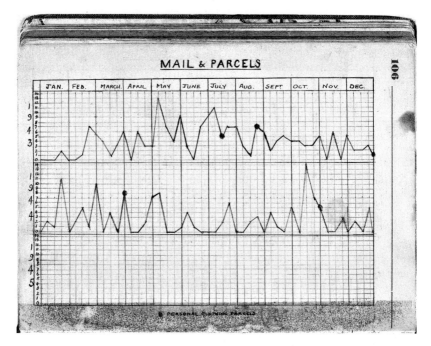

Figure 4.1: 'Mail & parcels' in the logbook of Flying Officer Arthur Edwards. The line graph shows how many letters and parcels Edwards received by month in 1943 and 1944. He was one of many prisoners of war to record the arrival of mail.

Source: IWM 99/82/1, Flying Officer A. G. Edwards, logbook, p. 106. Image reproduced with permission from David Kausmann.

where 'sleeping accommodation' was 'terrible', he greeted it by expressing, in his diary, the concern that it would 'mess up mail again'.[31] Matthews declared to his wife that, were it not for the ensuing arrears in mail and parcels, he would have been 'very glad to be leaving' Stalag XXIA (Schildberg), where there were 'things' of which he 'strongly disapprove[d]'.[32] Meanwhile, Campbell's reaction to becoming a prisoner of the Germans, after his Italian guards had left Campo PG 70 (Monte Urano), and to receiving orders to pack up ahead of a move to Germany, is particularly striking. He put his concern for his wife's letters ahead of his lost freedom. 'I feel completely adrift again', he wrote in his

[31] Abbott, diary entry, 15 June 1941.
[32] Matthews, letter to his wife, 2 February 1942. His disapproval may refer to the exceptionally strict discipline exercised over the camp; see ACICR, C SC, Germany, Stalag XXIA, 5 February 1942.

diary. 'The wretched story is to begin once more. No correspondence for either of us for weeks and weeks at least. And freedom had been in our grasp for a week.'[33]

When mail did arrive, it made these men's conditions of captivity much more bearable. As Hawarden described it, on 14 December 1940,

Somehow coffee seems a little better, you get up that little brighter, your soup is not too bad after all, you go about your job with a little lighter step and somehow your boots are not quite so heavy. In your company you might have one of the clever boys who cracks a joke at your expense. You just smile at him and when you get down to it at night, you go to sleep.[34]

Possibly most illustrative of how the arrival of letters affected prisoners are the metaphors of food they used to describe them: a highly significant choice for men whose lives were dominated by hunger.[35] Glass, who was concerned with the arrival, rationing and contents of parcels when held at Campo PG 65 (Gravina), announced in his diary entry of 2 July 1942 that the receipt of his mother's first letter was 'better than all the Red Cross Parcels and all the big feeds in the World.'[36] Barrington added in his diary entry, after complaining of the shortage of rations he was receiving from the Italians at Campo PG 73 (Carpi), where all supplies of milk and sugar were being depleted, that he 'forgot all about this on receiving a letter from home ... Wonderful how letters fill the stomach'.[37] Mansel, meanwhile, compared the arrival of letters in Oflag IXA/H (Spangenberg) to a feeding frenzy. He encouraged his mother to

Visualise feeding time at the Zoo and you have a fair picture of the scene here when the letters arrive – visualise also the poor animals that weren't thrusting enough & you can complete the scene with those, greedily eager a moment before, walking away despondent. Today I had a good meal – two from you ... one from George Banks, one from Tim.[38]

Visiting officials from the ICRC recorded Oflag IXA/H (Spangenberg), at this time, as the best camp in Germany for food rations, but Mansel was still preoccupied with food supplies when he wrote this diary entry,

---

[33] Campbell, diary entry, 23 September 1943.
[34] Hawarden, diary entry, 14 December 1940; see also diary entry, 10 November 1940. For similar examples, see Brooke, diary entry, 28 October–4 November 1940; King, diary entry, 2 February 1944.
[35] On letters being 'spiritual bread' that also sustained the body, see Becker, 'Art, Material Life and Disaster', pp. 27, 30.
[36] Glass, diary entry, 2 July 1942; see also diary entry, 23 September 1942.
[37] Barrington, diary entry, 31 January 1943. Matthews also wrote, 'letters mean more than food & physical comfort' (Matthews, letter to his wife, 16 July 1941).
[38] Mansel, letter to his mother, 27 October 1940.

indicating the importance letters held for these men.[39] Mansel's comparison of POWs to caged animals, and the connotations of subservience and subjection that such metaphors carried, as highlighted in
Chapter 2, also serves to emphasise how dependent these men were on
the arrival of correspondence. Elsewhere, the nutritional significance of
letters went beyond mere metaphor. When one of Fayers' pals got his
first mail, he was so excited that he passed his share of salmon from
a food parcel onto Fayers, and gave his pâté to someone else.[40]
At Stalag Luft VI (Heydekrug), a square of chocolate was put away
and given to the prisoner who had the least mail at the end of two
months.[41] The receipt of a letter in these instances was a literal sub-
stitute for food. Meanwhile, Nell described in his diary how letters
could be even more valuable. He repeatedly described them as 'spiritual food' and added that a letter from a loved one fed 'the spirit as no
food can.'[42]

Fantasies of Home

Whilst mail and photographs brought relatives into the camps, fantasies
allowed men to return home to their loved ones on civvy street. There
was, psychiatrists at the time noted, a 'great increase' in the fantasy life of
POWs, 'involving dreams of home and loved ones.'[43] Fantasies commonly occurred on familial occasions. According to historian Annette
Becker, writing about French POWs in the First World War, it was on
such occasions that prisoners' alienation from their loved ones was felt
most strongly.[44] At their most elementary level, prisoners spoke directly
to their relatives in their diaries, to wish them a happy birthday, Christmas
or New Year. 'It is Beryl's birthday on Saturday', wrote Glass on
25 May 1942, adding 'Many Happy Returns, Sis dear, in case
I overlook it later. I wish it was possible for me to be with you on

[39] ACICR, C SC, Germany, Oflag IXA/H, 16 October 1940. Mansel, diary entries, 8, 9 and
14 September 1940. Mansel's diary entries between mid-September 1940 and the end
of January 1941 are missing.
[40] IWM 88/22/2, Flying Officer R. J. Fayers, diary entry, 12 October 1944.
[41] IWM 95/39/1, Warrant Officer R. Watchorn, logbook, p. 35.
[42] Nell, diary entries, 10 and 22 August and 28 October 1944.
[43] TNA WO 32/10757, Directorate of Army Psychiatry. Technical Memorandum No. 13.
The Prisoner of War Comes Home. Notes Prepared for the Information of Army
Psychiatrists, prepared by DAP, May 1944. For further discussions on the importance
of fantasies for POWs and other prisoners, see Goffman, Asylums, p. 69; Robert J. Ursano
et al., 'The Prisoner of War', in Robert Ursano and Ann Norwood (eds.), Emotional
Aftermath of the Persian Gulf War. Veterans, Families, Communities, and Nations
(Washington, DC: American Psychiatric Press, 1996), p. 452.
[44] Becker, Oubliés de la Grande Guerre, p. 141.

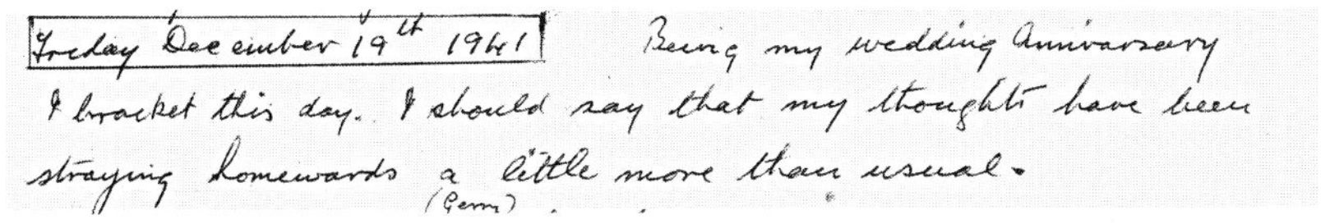

Friday December 19th 1941 Being my wedding anniversary I bracket this day. I should say that my thoughts have been straying homewards a little more than usual. (Pem)

Figure 4.2: Sergeant Major Andrew Hawarden's diary entry,
19 December 1941. Hawarden's wedding anniversary was
19 December. The brackets he put around the date shows how
Hawarden was mentally absent from Stalag XXA on this day. Numerous
POWs used their imaginations to join their loved ones at home,
particularly on familial occasions.
   Source: The private collection of Mrs Sandra Hawarden-Lord. Image
reproduced with permission from Sandra-Hawarden-Lord.

that day, perhaps the next one, eh?'[45] At a more elaborate level, these
fantasies would entail prisoners drifting out of their camps in all but body.
For example, Parker spent all of Christmas Day in 1941 thinking of his
sweetheart at home. He explained to her, in a letter written on
Boxing Day, how he 'imagined' he was at one of the Christmas parties,
a fantasy powerful enough for him to conclude, 'we all had a marvellous
time.'[46] For forty-four-year-old Hawarden, married for almost nine years
before he was captured, his wedding anniversaries were probably a well-
established part of his personal life. On the second one he spent in
captivity, the date of the diary is written in brackets [Figure 4.2].
Hawarden's diary rarely dwells on home. It was written for a public
audience, informing readers of the daily happenings in captivity.
On 19 December 1941, however, his mind had been far away from the
dank fifty-year-old fortress of Stalag XXA (Thorn), where he was imprisoned. The parenthesis around the diary date reflects the extent to which
Hawarden had been mentally absent from his physical surroundings on
that day.[47]
   Sundays were a particularly popular day for drifting home. Mansel
wrote in his diary of how going to church on a Sunday, in Oflag VIIB
(Eichstätt), was one of the 'few quiet places and few quiet opportunities of
really thinking of home 100% and the one place I can do it is home.' His
slip of the pen, writing 'home' instead of 'church', demonstrates the
extent to which those thoughts of home actually transplanted him to

[45] Glass, diary entry, 25 May 1942. For similar examples, see Mansel, diary entries,
   6 September 1940, 8 March and 25 December 1941, 1 January 1942.
[46] Parker, letters to his sweetheart, 26 December 1941 and 3 February 1942. For a similar
   example, see Fayers, diary entry, 26 February 1945.
[47] Hawarden, diary entry, 19 December 1940.

that physical place.[48] Similarly, on Sunday 16 August 1942, two months after he had been captured, Angove wrote in his diary, at 'half past eleven', of how his family would now be in chapel: 'I can picture it all so clearly in my mind, how I wish I could slip in quietly beside you.' The following Sunday, at church, he saw, 'dear old Mr Jenkin is in his seat & of course Miss Troureson as always is in hers, Mr & Mrs Whingales are there & Mr & Mrs George in their usual pew. I look up to the choir for Madeline, Kay & Gwen are in their old familiar places.' Later on, it was time for lunch, and he pictured: 'you all at home sitting down to your midday meal'.[49] One of the purposes Angove's reflective diary served was to provide a place where he could exist and survive in an alternative reality with his family.[50]

These alternative realities were openly acknowledged between prisoners of war as an aspect of life in captivity. Canon King recorded, on 15 September 1940, how one POW, Teddy, 'still spends Sunday at home – in his imagination.' Teddy would comment: 'It's just about the time when my Missus would come down the garden with a cup of tea to wake me after my afternoon nap.' King surmised: 'nearly everybody' at Oflag VIIC (Laufen) 'spends the day re-living an English Sunday.' As the years passed and POWs moved camps, this collective attitude persisted. On 8 March 1942, now in Oflag IXA/H (Spangenberg), King recorded,

On Sundays we write home: on Sunday afternoons we sleep: it seems immutable. And as a result, everyone is reminded more acutely than at other times that the proper place for an English gentlemen is in his English home. So Sunday evening is always the peak hour of the week's nostalgia.[51]

Since, during peacetime, Sunday had been the day most men spent at home with their families, it was easy for POWs to accurately imagine what their loved ones were doing at that time, so making their dreams of home more realistic.[52] Angove provides another reason as to why he would 'especially' picture his relatives on Sundays: 'it is the day when I know you have more time to think of me & wonder what I am doing & probably say "If Dick were here, wouldn't he enjoy this" & many other such

---

[48] Mansel, diary entry, 31 October 1943.
[49] Angove, diary entries, 16 and 23 August 1942.
[50] On this point, see Zoe Waxman, *Writing the Holocaust. Identity, Testimony, Representation* (Oxford: Oxford University Press, 2006), p. 76.
[51] King, diary entries, 15 September 1940 and 8 March 1942.
[52] A Mass Observation study of Sunday habits established that 'most people do, in fact spend not only Sunday morning but the entire day either in or around the home' (Mass Observation, *Meet Yourself on Sunday*. London: The Naldrett Press, 1949, p. 5, reproduced with permission of Curtis Brown Group Ltd, London on behalf of The Trustees of the Mass Observation Archive).

remarks.'[53] In other words, at the time when Angove was thinking of home, those at home were thinking of him. This is another form of fantasy POWs often refer to, and one that helped to bridge the temporal divide that lay between prisoners and their loved ones: synchronisation of thoughts.[54] This was orchestrated to occur at daily moments in order to help men overcome some of the trials of wartime imprisonment. Lieutenant John Evans was a thirty-three-year-old father of two who had joined the Royal Navy in 1928.[55] Despite having been away from home regularly, when in captivity he sought support from his wife through synchronisation. He wrote to her in February 1943: 'Think of me at 08.30, 12.30, 16.00 and 19.00 hrs. They are the most disappointing moments for me.'[56] He did not reveal to his wife why these times were so trying in Campo PG 70 (Monte Urano), which the ICRC had described as 'very good' verging on 'excellent'.[57] One assumes they were his meal times and, if so, it suggests another way in which the emotional support POWs received from home helped them overcome their material conditions. Meanwhile, the younger and only recently married Ball presumably had less melancholic thoughts in mind when he sent his wife similar instructions. He advised her that his bedtime in Stalag Luft III (Sagan) was 11 P.M., 'that will be ten in England so I hope you are in bed by then.'[58] Synchronicity was also popular on family occasions. On the birthdays that he spent in captivity, Second Lieutenant Frederick Burnaby-Atkins, only just beyond his teenage years, told his mother that he was 'having a wonderful birthday & thinking of you all as I know you'll be thinking of me.'[59]

Perhaps to reify these imaginings, others arranged with their loved ones to perform the same activity in unison. When Matthews wrote his 'regular Sunday letter' to his wife, he concluded how it was 'good to be writing to each other at about the same time.'[60] Canon King took his communion and said mass simultaneously with his wife, so he could keep her

---

[53] Angove, diary entry, 10 April 1943.

[54] On the use of synchronicity by soldiers in the First World War, see Roper, 'Nostalgia as an Emotional Experience in the Great War', 444; Duffett, *The Stomach for Fighting*, pp. 177–8.

[55] For a record of his naval service, see IWM 99/8/1–8, private papers of Lieutenant J. W. Evans.

[56] IWM 99/8/6, Lieutenant J. W. Evans, letter to his wife, 6 February 1943.

[57] ACICR, C SC, Italy, Campo PG 70, 15 November 1942.

[58] Ball, letter to his wife, 10 June 1942.

[59] Burnaby-Atkins, letter to his parents, 9 November 1944; see also letter to his parents, 10 November 1941. For similar examples, see Fairclough, letter to his wife, 18 September 1944; Matthews, letters to his wife, 10 November 1940 and 13 November 1941.

[60] Matthews, letter to his wife, 26 October 1941.

'company'.[61] On Mansel's birthday, he drank to his family's health at home and was 'sure they were drinking mine! – at 8.45pm prompt', whilst at Christmas, he expected his parents and sister to follow his lead by informing them in advance that he would 'drink your healths [*sic*] at 9.0 p.m. precisely here, but am far from certain what time this will be at home.'[62] In all these ways, synchronisation allowed POWs to have a simultaneous shared experience with their loved ones.[63]

One particularly striking feature of these thoughts of home is the way in which POWs conceived themselves as travelling back and forth between their captive and civilian worlds. Angove did this quite literally in his mental musings. They progress from a fly-on-the-wall fantasy, to Angove boarding a 'magic carpet', on which he 'flitted from place to place'. On one such occasion he wrote in his diary of how he had

breakfast with Madeline & Janet . . . We talked our heads off as you can imagine, then I went to see Mr & Mrs Street & enquired about the boys. I lunched with Kay & family & was surprised to see how the children had grown. . . . I had tea with Gwen & Doug and laughed until I cried at her for quips and sallies. Of course mother was with me on this magic carpet.[64]

When Angove re-read such entries, he subsequently described them as consisting of 'mostly drivel'. At some later date, he scored out this diary entry. But Angove also explained to his mother how these fantasies enabled him to 'get away from the atmosphere of this place & create an atmosphere of my own & I do that best when I write to you or in imagination come home & share the day with you'.[65] The atmosphere Angove was trying to escape was that of Campo PG 66 in Capua in southern Italy which, although one of the better camps in the country, held up to 8,000 British prisoners in an area of just 2 km by 400 m, with many housed in tents.[66]

Angove's fantasies might have provided him with a refuge, but they did not enable him to escape completely from the confines of captivity. For example, on one magic carpet ride, when he visited his sister Gwen, Angove had to explain how 'I was only on a brief flying visit in imagination from Capua & that I had to get back as quickly as possible or I shouldn't be allowed to come again'.[67] A similar pull came through in Naylor's

[61] King, diary entries, 27 September and 28 December 1940. For a similar example, see Mansel, letter to his mother, Boxing Day 1944.

[62] Mansel, diary entry, 2 August 1940; letter to his family, 14 November 1941.

[63] On this use of synchronisation, see David Fitzpatrick, *Oceans of Consolation. Personal Accounts of Irish Migration to Australia* (Cork: Cork University Press, 1994), p. 493.

[64] Angove, diary entry, 17 September 1944.   [65] Angove, diary entry, 31 August 1942.

[66] ACICR, C SC, Italy, Campo PG 66, 22 November 1942.

[67] Angove, diary entry, 4 September 1942.

dreams. Naylor was forty-two years old when he was captured in North Africa whilst serving as a Methodist Chaplain to the Forces, but had only recently married in between his evacuation from France in 1940 and his departure for duty in the Middle East. He recorded in his logbook a 'fairly common dream', which had been 'scattered over practically the whole period of captivity' of being back at home, but on leave from a POW camp. 'Never once was I quite free' he wrote

but always had to return. I went home once on leave for a week to be married, but remarked during our honeymoon that I should be going back to Italy at the weekend. During a fortnight's holiday at Saltburn [a seaside resort in Yorkshire] I told some friends I was shortly returning to a PoW Camp, and several times in dreams I informed people I was only on short leave. Even if I did not say so in so many words, I always knew I was coming back, or that my freedom was only a dream.[68]

Histories dealing with servicemen's relationship with home in the First World War have concluded that combatants imagined home as 'another world', an 'opposed world' or one that was 'distant' to the trenches.[69] These examples from Angove and Naylor indicate that POWs were unable to order and separate their captive and civilian existences in such ways, and instead lived them both simultaneously.

Hopes for Homecoming

It might have been easier for POWs to separate out their captive and civilian existences had they known of the date of their homecoming, since this would have enabled them to adjust more fully to captivity, but, as Chapter 1 demonstrated, POWs lived in constant anticipation of an imminent return home. In these expectations, prisoners demonstrated their attachment to their loved ones by conceiving the end of the war in terms of a wedding anniversary or birthday. In Oflag VIB (Warburg)'s 'end of war lottery', in which bets were placed at the start of 1942, Mansel put a guinea on hostilities ceasing on 6 September of that year, his father's birthday. If he had taken out a second bet, he would have chosen 12 June, his parents' wedding day.[70] When hopes ran high at the start of 1944 at Oflag XIIB (Hadamar), where many predicted the armistice would take place in February or March, Angove selected the date of 20 April 1944, 'for no other reason than the fact of it being mother's birthday.'[71] Over in Italy, meanwhile, at the beginning of 1943, Barrington had reckoned

---

[68] Naylor, logbook, p. 48. For a very similar dream, see Hall, diary entry, 2 November 1944.
[69] Roper, *The Secret Battle*, pp. 72, 122; Leed, *No Man's Land*, p. 189.
[70] Mansel, diary entry, 24 January 1942.   [71] Angove, diary entry, 1 February 1945.

1 June, his third wedding anniversary, would be his 'day of freedom'.[72] When 1 June 1943 arrived, it was also the day when Churchill's ultimatum to Italy expired and when Barrington had reached the end of the book into which he was writing his diary. 'Surely such a coincidence has some meaning', he willed. Barrington's conflation of the length of his diary with the duration of his confinement in captivity shows the extent to which composing a diary shaped his existence behind barbed wire.[73]

These men also framed their homecoming within a domestic context. Few wrote during captivity of how they wished they could resume their fighting roles whilst many stated how they looked forward to captivity ending in time for them to attend the next familial event.[74] In September 1943, Nell, at Campo PG 70 (Monte Urano), not unreasonably, given the Allied invasion of the Italian mainland, assumed he would soon be in England but wondered, in particular, if he could make it back in time for his fiancée's birthday.[75] Most hoped to be home by the following Christmas. Back in August 1942, Angove had originally confirmed to his loved ones in his diary how he was 'quite sure my dears that we shall have our Xmas Dinner together this year'.[76] One year later, Hainsworth in Italy, and Jarvis in Germany, wrote to their parents advising them to purchase big turkeys for Christmas, for they expected to be back home by then.[77] The Allied progress in the summer of 1944 caused Bloss to tell his wife, 'I can't see this country lasting another winter. Just think of it darling, you, baby and I will be together again before Christmas', whilst Regimental Sergeant Major John Dover recorded in his diary, 'We should at the outside be home for Christmas – hope this is not being over-optimistic.'[78] Reaching Christmas 1944 and still being in captivity caused some long-term prisoners of war to doubt their self-assurance. Dispatch Rider Leslie Barter contemplated his situation, 'We all have hopes of this being the last xmas out here. (Ive said the self

[72] Barrington, diary entries, 19 February and 30 April 1943.

[73] Barrington, diary entry, 1 June 1943; Culley 'Introduction', pp. 13–14. For another example of conflating a diary with time spent in captivity, see Hainsworth, diary, Forward.

[74] For those who wrote of their desire to return to the fighting, see, for example, Mansel, diary entries, 21 July 1940, 9 February and 11 December 1941, 3 January 1942; Panter-Brick, letters to his family, 16 March 1941, 15 November 1942, 3 November 1943; PP/MCR/408, Greaser C. E. Bloss, letter to his wife, 17 December 1943; Matthews, letter to his wife, 1 April 1942.

[75] Nell, diary entry, 9 September 1943.   [76] Angove, diary entry, 28 August 1942.

[77] Hainsworth, letter his mother, 13 August 1943; Jarvis, letter to his parents, 9 August 1943.

[78] Bloss, letter to his wife, 10 June 1944; IWM 99/82/1, Regimental Sergeant Major J. F. Dover, diary entries, 15 August and 14 September 1944. For a similar example see Nell, diary entry, 12 September 1944.

same thing for 5 years now, I must be right sometime).'[79] As Chapter 1 recorded, after repeated disappointments many, by this point, had lost faith. On 23 October 1944, Nell had 'ceased hoping to be home by Christmas ... It is all vain – hopeless' he wrote. On Christmas day he recorded, 'In the past we all said "Merry Christmas! – We'll be home next year!" but this morning I heard no one say that. "Hope you have a better one next year," took the place of "We'll be home next year." We're all afraid to mention next Christmas. We don't know how much longer the war will last.'[80]

POWs had also, often many years before the end of the war, made plans for how they would meet their loved ones, which was another way in which they remained close to them.[81] A full two years before he made it home, Barrington was already wondering where he would first see his wife: 'some railway station or convalescent camp, or perhaps on the doorstep of no.27?'[82] One month after he had been captured, Angove was choosing between sending a telegram home to announce his arrival, just walking in and surprising his family or telephoning them as soon as he landed. He followed these musings by setting out in detail how that scene would unfold.[83] Similarly, by February 1941, Hurrell told his parents that he had 'got that celebration of ours all mapped out' whilst, by December 1942, Private William Richards had it 'all planned out what I'm going to do when I do come home ... we sure will have a good time, just the three of us', he told his wife and son.[84] These idealisations could project weeks or months into these men's return, most commonly taking the form of wishing to be left alone by everyone in order to indulge in marital harmony.[85]

Finally, those prisoners who had good reason to believe they would be imminently repatriated – the protected personnel and sick or wounded – found it particularly hard to separate out their captive and civilian existences. When he was told, just one month after being captured, of the Germans' intention to send home chaplains, King recorded how the repatriation rumours 'only stir up the mud' and

[79] IWM PP MCR 426, Dispatch Rider L. F. Barter, diary entry 'Christmas Day 1944'.
[80] Nell, diary entries, 23 October 1944 and Christmas Day.
[81] For achieving immediacy through such means, see Fitzpatrick, *Oceans of Consolation*, p. 494.
[82] Barrington, diary entry, 5 March 1943.
[83] Angove, diary entries, c. July and 14 August 1942.
[84] Hurrell, letter to his parents, 3 February 1941; IWM 08/12/1, Private W. Richards, letter to his wife, 4 December 1942.
[85] For such examples, see Hyde, letter to his wife, 30 October 1943; Ball, letters to his wife, 28 October 1941 and 16 August 1942; Lambert, letter to his wife, 27 March 1944. For other plans, see Fayers, letter to his wife, 26 October 1944; Taylor, letters to his wife, 4 January and 12 April 1943; Blyth, letter to his wife, 3 December 1944.

set me off day-dreaming. 'What will England look like when I get there? Will R. be at Waterloo to meet me? Will it be Waterloo? And shall I be able to warn them I am coming? Where shall we go: to O.H. [Orchard House – King's home]? And then what?' And so it goes on & on, till it hurts a lot & serves no useful purpose.[86]

For those they left behind, these repatriates brought home much closer. When he left Oflag VIID (Tittmoning) for France, in September 1941, King recorded how 'Everyone was in the yard to see us off, for were we not to be a link between them & home?'[87] Similarly, when others left Oflag IXA/H (Spangenberg), Mansel noted, 'Lot of goodbye saying – most peculiar feeling, telling someone to look in on home – brings it all so much nearer and makes it less of a dream.'[88] Although these prisoners did not return to Britain in 1941, when groups were repatriated, they brought POWs' civilian world closer. One of the prisoners from Oflag VIIB (Eichstätt), who was included in the October 1943 exchange between Britain and Germany, subsequently visited the relatives of some POWs who remained at the camp, including those of Mansel. Mansel considered it 'simply extraordinary to think of someone I was chatting to such a short time ago actually sitting down to lunch at Holm Place [Mansel's home]. Two worlds linked up in some unbelievable way.'[89]

Through these various imagined and real homecomings, which took place throughout the course of the war, POWs lived in close proximity to their loved ones. These might have helped men to better endure captivity, but these examples also hint at how they had unsettling effects: how frustrated hopes made it harder for these men to accept and adapt to their imprisoned lives. Such disruptive consequences of prisoners' relationships with home are similarly evidenced in other areas, as the next section shows.

Reconfiguring Familial Roles

Whilst POWs made sense of their wartime imprisonment through their loved ones at home, the importance of their familial relationships could also make captivity harder to bear. The pain caused to POWs by those at home was referenced in Chapter 2 in relation to 'mail bag splitters'. This section focusses more on how having loved ones at home inadvertently had detrimental effects on POWs, although some of the emotions experienced in this context were similar to those discussed earlier, such as guilt, feelings of being forgotten and fears of sexual betrayal.

---

[86] King, diary entry, 31 July 1940; see also diary entry, 25 July 1940.
[87] King, diary entry, 26 September 1941.   [88] Mansel, diary entry, 27 September 1941.
[89] Mansel, diary entry, 4 January 1944.

The mechanisms POWs used to derive comfort from their loved ones could also have negative causes or consequences.[90] Fantasies of home were important in allowing POWs to mentally escape captivity, but thinking of home too much was also deemed dangerous. Whilst Sunday was a popular day to drift back home, King also pointed out that 'a Sunday ration of sentiment is all they [POWs] can safely allow themselves in the week'.[91] When he let his imagination 'browse upon peace and homecoming and family', he concluded, to do so was 'sentimental extravagance which is more than unprofitable in the long run. To live within the bounds of daily trivialities may be cowardly; but it is certainly less exhausting.'[92] Other men's comparisons of their wife or sweetheart to a ghost suggests that the latter's continuous presence could be troubling. Parker may have spent Christmas 1941 thinking about home, but he was 'glad when it came to night time and went to sleep', although, even then, he described to his sweetheart how 'you haunted my thoughts'.[93] Fayers told his wife, after spending just over a year in captivity, how he could not 'concentrate, nor reason, nor follow a book that is anything but simple. Every thought and action has, I find, a small ghost of you lurking behind it.' Nell similarly recorded in his diary how 'Day and night she [his fiancée] haunts me. As soon as I fall asleep she is in my arms. Consequently I am nearly always sleeping. It's not good for me, I know, but I can't help it.' He added how he found having a photograph of his fiancée unsettling: 'receiving this snap hasn't done me much good', he later wrote. 'It has unbalanced me. I am restless and can't eat. All I want to do is to dream that I am holding that delicious bundle in my arms.'[94]

Medical officers pointed out how the arrival of mail and parcels might have been valued for negative as well as positive reasons. Imprisoned medical officer Philip Newman explained in an article he wrote on captivity for the *British Medical Journal* following a successful escape from incarceration, 'deeply within the prisoner, but seldom expressed, there lies the fear of becoming a forgotten man.' Proof of this fear, Newman explained, could be found 'in the meticulous care with which every word of letters is read and sifted. Hours are spent in making an elaborate checking and filing system for incoming and outgoing mail, and statistics

---

[90] Roper also notes how thoughts of home could bring pain ('Nostalgia as an Emotional Experience in the Great War', 441).

[91] King, diary entry, 15 September 1940. For a similar example, see Taylor, letter to his wife, 27 April 1944.

[92] King, diary entry, 1 January 1941; see also diary entry, 25 December 1941.

[93] Parker, letter to his sweetheart, 26 December 1941.

[94] Fayers, letter to his wife, 26 November 1944; Nell, diary entries, 11 and 17 August 1944; see also diary entry, 31 December 1943. On thoughts of home causing First World War soldiers 'psychic risks', see Duffett, *The Stomach for Fighting*, p. 200.

are kept of its arrival.'[95] Gibbens similarly asserted that food parcels had 'regressive associations' because they were valued 'as proof that the prisoner is not forgotten at home.'[96]

These regressive associations are starkly evident in how POWs referred to themselves when parcels arrived in the camps. When Lance Bombardier Edward Stirling and his fellow POWs were told that they would get a Red Cross parcel the following morning, this married father of three described how 'we went to bed like kiddies waiting for Santa Claus'.[97] Nineteen-year-old Panter-Brick, meanwhile, described in a letter how receiving a whole Red Cross parcel was 'such a windfall that we are like children.'[98] Quarrie described the 'scenes inside our rooms' after they had been issued with Red Cross parcels, as 'truly amazing: we chattered like a lot of children at a Christmas party'.[99] Similar comparisons were made in relation to next-of-kin parcels. Forty-five-year-old husband and father Hawarden wrote that 'thoughts of what is going to be in it remind one of Christmas time when a child begins to unpack his Christmas stocking.'[100] Likewise, Lambert, also a husband and father in his forties, reported how 'all the chaps are just like kids at Xmas, when parcels come for them.'[101]

Portraying themselves as children also links to how POWs were unable to fulfil their familial and manly duties whilst in captivity. Three responsibilities are singled out in their personal narratives, the first being that of provider. The language these men used to describe the arrival of parcels shows how their self-conceptions had shifted from that of family provider to filial dependant. Second Lieutenant Basil Brooke spelt this out explicitly in his diary: 'How ashamed we feel to have to write and ASK for food parcels etc: how small we feel not to be self contained in possessions.'[102]

---

[95] P. H. Newman, 'The Prisoner-of-War Mentality: Its Effect after Repatriation', *British Medical Journal*, 1, 4330 (1 January 1944), 9. Stewart made a similar point. He wrote in reference to receiving letters, 'I suppose it soothes one's personal pride to know that you are being thought of by someone else' (Stewart, diary entry, 22 February 1945).

[96] Gibbens, 'The Psychology of the Prisoner-of-War', p. 12. Brian Feltman also writes of the anxieties and fears German POWs held in the United Kingdom during the First World War had of being forgotten and looks at how these could be alleviated by receiving letters from home and parcels from charitable associations, ('Letters from Captivity', pp. 98–103).

[97] IWM 99/22/1, Lance-Bombardier E. C. Stirling, diary entry, 8 December 1942.

[98] Panter-Brick, letter to his family, 5 January 1941, in Panter-Brick, *Years Not Wasted 1940–1945*, p. 24.

[99] Quarrie, diary entry, 12 October 1941. For a similar example, see East, diary entry, 6 November 1943.

[100] Hawarden, diary entry, 26 March 1942.

[101] Lambert, letter to his wife, 24 October 1943. For a similar example, see Mansel, diary entry, 30 November 1943.

[102] Brooke, diary entry, 6–13 October 1940.

This dependence on loved ones to provide for them is also apparent in how POWs reacted to the receipt of mail. The rationing of letter-forms to prisoners of war meant they were unable to send home the same number of letters as they received – a point that exasperated Hurrell. He wrote to his sweetheart: 'I do so wish I could write you more often ... you can imagine how I feel when I received yours, written, in numerous cases every three or four days always so sincere and cheerful – and then consider the measly amount you receive in return – I could tear the place down.'[103] For some men, letter rations forced them to choose between who they could provide for: their partners or their mothers, a dilemma most acutely felt by men in the ranks. Parker tried to justify to his sweetheart his decision to send one letter to his mother and the other to his wife with the words 'which I think is only fair, don't you?' Similarly, Richards would write one letter-form to his wife and then one postcard to his mother, explaining to his wife that was 'the only way I can do it.' It seems that his wife might have been unimpressed with this arrangement, for a few months later Richards again advised her, 'I write the letter to you, and the card to Mum, I think I am entitled to write to my Mother now and again.'[104] Finally, with both the monotony of prison life and censorship often preventing the discussion of significant events when they did happen, these men were also reliant on home to provide them with news before they, in turn, could construct their own letter. 'Write soon dear', Blyth urged his wife, 'and give me something to write about.'[105]

The second role POWs had to relinquish was family protector. Soldiers have often drawn a sharp gendered dichotomy between their masculinised, combat world and normal, peacetime, feminised life at home, a point borne out by the domestic fantasies discussed earlier in this chapter.[106] Prisoners of war were on the wrong side of this dichotomy: their loved ones, rather than themselves, were now on the front line.

[103] Hurrell, letter to Pamela (his future wife), 26 October 1944. For similar examples, see Ball, letter to his wife, 9 August 1942; Matthews, letter to his wife, 23 March 1941; Mansel, diary entries, 29 October 1941, 14 May and 30 November 1943, 5 February and 10 November 1944; Burnaby-Atkins, letter to his parents, 15 May 1942; Nell, diary entry, 3 April 1944; Fayers, letters to his wife, 26 May and 26 September 1944; Lambert, letter to his wife, 20 August 1944.

[104] Parker, letter to his sweetheart, 29 January 1944; Richards, letters to his wife, 14 September 1941 and 17 May 1943. Greaser Claude Bloss's wife hinted at a similar tension in one of her letters to Bloss. She wrote, 'your Mum thinks you are writing too many letters to me as they never hear from you' (Bloss, letter from his wife, 9 October 1941).

[105] Blyth, letter to his wife, 11 November 1943. For a similar example, see Parker, letter to his sweetheart, 17 October 1941; Nell, diary entries, 22 October 1944, 13 January and 14 February 1945.

[106] On this dichotomy, see Joshua S. Goldstein, *Gender and War: How Gender Shapes the War System and Vice Versa* (Cambridge: Cambridge University Press, 2001), p. 301.

As the war progressed, prisoners were increasingly exposed to aerial bombardment, largely from Allied aircraft, but, during the early years, at the time when British civilians were most in danger, it was unlikely that British POWs would be caught up in air attacks.[107] Matthews described how this felt when he wrote to his wife, from Stalag XXIA (Schildberg), soon after the Blitz had started in 1940, 'I am humiliated beyond words that you and the children are in England while I am so far away that blackouts are unnecessary.' He added in a subsequent letter, 'Never did I dream it would be my lot to live as a husband & father in relative safety waiting month after month for news of you & the children on the battlefield.'[108] Similarly, when Bloss heard it was 'noisey [sic]' where his wife and mother lived, in Grays in Essex, he felt 'restless and worried' and 'above all so darn helpless.'[109] This worry was compounded by the delays in receiving letters, as Bloss explained to his wife: 'they are always about a month old when I get them and it's that month that worries me.'[110] His concerns were again heightened in June 1944, when he heard of a 'new weapon these people are shooting over our country'. He wrote to his wife at the end of the month informing her that he was now 'anxiously wait[ing] for your June letters.'[111] This 'new weapon' was the V-1. The first four missiles had landed in south-east England just two weeks before Bloss sent his letter.[112] Similarly, on 25 July 1944, Mansel wrote in his diary of how 'This V1 is worrying me like hell'. He was 'terribly anxious to get letters written after the darned thing was put into commission.'[113] Mansel's mother lived in Windlesham in Surrey, one of the two counties to suffer most in the 'flying bomb' attacks.[114]

Feelings of helplessness in protecting their loved ones were, in a sense, doubly felt because POWs were also dependent on those at home to win the war for them. Burnaby-Atkins, who had been captured less than a year into the war, wrote home in July 1944 of how 'we all feel so out of things

[107] *Report of the International Committee of the Red Cross*, vol. I, pp. 311–14.
[108] Matthews, letters to his wife, 17 September and 27 October 1940.
[109] Bloss, letter to his wife, 24 January 1943. Gray's railway station, churches and high school were all damaged from bombing in the Second World War; see W. R. Powell (ed.), *A History of the County of Essex: Volume 8* (1983), pp. 35–56, www.british-history .ac.uk/report.aspx?compid=63840, last accessed 27 June 2012.
[110] Bloss, letter to his wife, 2 April 1943. For similar examples, see Abbott, diary entry, 14 February 1941; Fayers, diary entry, 27 June 1944.
[111] Bloss, letter to his wife, 28 June 1944.
[112] Steven J. Zaloga, *V-1 Flying Bomb 1942–52. Hitler's Infamous 'Doodlebug'* (Oxford: Osprey, 2005), pp. 18–21.
[113] Mansel, diary entry, 25 July 1944.
[114] Up to 6,184 people were killed and nearly 18,000 injured in the V-1 attacks, mainly in London, Kent and Surrey (Robert Bartlett, *The Working Life of the Surrey Constabulary 1851–1992* (The Open University), www.open.ac.uk/Arts/history-from-police-archives/ RB1/Pt2/pt2Fbombs.html, last accessed 9 November 2012).

having only had a very short time of the war + are now doing sweet nothing while people at home [are] ALL working.'[115] Mansel viewed himself, despite forging documents every day, from morning until night, as 'sitting back and watching the rest of the family doing not only their very full share [in the war] but mine as well.'[116] When Canon King received a letter from his wife that gave the impression she was 'happily busy in her police work', he revealed in his diary the shame he felt through his invocation of Savile Lumley's famous 1915 poster, which had been aimed at shirkers in the First World War.[117] King mused, 'while she helps to win the war, I just sit about the place here, & wait! I fear I shall be able to give no sort of reputable answer when my children ask "What did you do in the great war, Daddy?" Mamma will have done all the doing.'[118] For others, so deeply felt were these role reversals that they predicted they would continue after the war. When Barrington described in his diary a letter received from his wife, in which she told him of her promotion to Fire Station Mobilising Officer and her role as lecturer to firemen, he added in brackets, 'this is a good life in preparation for wearing the skirts.'[119]

Even though they were 'out of things', to paraphrase Burnaby-Atkins, prisoners of war were experiencing their own set of hardships and challenges, but these were not understood by loved ones at home. This point was alluded to in Chapter 2, when discussing POWs' replication of 'mail bag splitters'. Historians have noted the extent to which combatants needed recognition from those at home for the sacrifices they were making. Military historian David French has identified that appreciation by friends and family of what British soldiers were enduring and achieving was vital in sustaining them in the Second World War.[120] POWs were denied this: their friends and families were presented with overly sanitised versions of their conditions in captivity.[121] These men used their diaries

---

[115] Burnaby-Atkins, letter to his parents, 3 July 1944.

[116] Mansel, letter to his father, 29 April 1942; 'Introduction', in E. G. C. Beckwith (ed.), *The Mansel Diaries*, p. ix.

[117] IWM Art Poster 0311, Savile Lumley, 'Daddy, what did You do in the Great War?' (1915), Parliamentary Recruiting Committee Poster No. 79.

[118] King, diary entry, 22 February 1943.   [119] Barrington, diary entry, 26 August 1943.

[120] French, *Raising Churchill's Army*, p. 144.

[121] Other combatants were also affected by overly sanitised representations of war. See, for example, Robert H. Abzug's study on the GIs who liberated concentration camps. They attempted to tell those at home of what they had witnessed, but were greeted with disbelief, disgust or silence (*Inside the Vicious Heart. Americans and the Liberation of Nazi Concentration Camps*. Oxford: Oxford University Press, 1985, pp. 127–40, 169–70). Audoin-Rouzeau has also written about how the civilian population was ill-informed about the horror of battles of the First World War, and the resulting bitterness of French combatants (*Men at War, 1914–1918*, pp. 113, 133).

to set the record straight. In the early months of his imprisonment, Hawarden recorded how parents and wives had been told by the Red Cross not to send prisoners any more cigarettes or parcels as these were being received on a weekly basis. He clarified the situation for the public audience that would eventually read his diary: 'This . . . is entirely wrong. I would be nearer the mark if I said that we have had on average one parcel per month and this is divided between eight or ten men and, as for cigarettes, we have received sixteen per man'.[122] Articles in the press were also seized upon as misrepresenting the reality of conditions. Mansel vented his frustration in his diary when he heard in February 1941 that 'Country Life says we get scrambled eggs for breakfast! What does an egg look like?'[123] Similarly, Angove was irritated to hear 'some fool' had written a book in England on POWs which said that they were 'if anything slightly overfed' and spoke of 'swimming pools and tennis courts' and 'luxurious cinemas'. Even though Angove was held in Oflag XIIB (Hadamar), which had been deemed 'excellent' and 'good' in its recent ICRC reports, he retorted, 'I do object to one of our own people, painting a rosy picture of overfed & comfortable POWs, who, it would seem won't want to come home & work for a living after such a comfortable and carefree existence.' This misunderstanding exercised Angove greatly; just two months later in his diary, he spelt out his diet for the day, informing his mother that 'I tell you these things, because we hear of people at home who seem to think we live on the fat of the land, have no barbed wire or machines guns all round us & that we go to the local pubs & cinemas, or swimming pools & such like. I would assure them that such is not the case.'[124] Angove's explanation also provides a reason as to why so many POWs reproduced their diet in their logbooks, as described in Chapter 2.

Perhaps most criticised for the picture of captivity it painted was *The Prisoner of War*, a monthly magazine produced by the British Red Cross between May 1942 and September 1945. It was sent to all next of kin, circulated to public libraries and delivered to any Members of Parliament on request.[125] According to the official record of the activities of the British Red Cross Society during the war, the purpose of the magazine was 'the enlightenment and guidance of next-of-kin', and

---

[122] Hawarden, diary entry, 23 November 1940. For similar frustrations with the Red Cross, see King, diary entry, 22 December 1940.

[123] Mansel, diary entry, 5 February 1941; see also diary entry, 25 March 1941.

[124] Angove, diary entry, 20 October 1944. ACICR, C SC, Germany, Oflag XIIB, 8 August 1944; ACICR, C SC, Germany, Oflag XIIB, 22 November 1944; Angove, diary entry, 14 December 1944.

[125] Hately-Broad, *War and Welfare*, pp. 183–4, 205, fn 92.

a typical issue contained summaries of reports on camp conditions, photos of camps and extracts from POWs' letters. Although the magazines included references to the unsatisfactory conditions of camp life, precisely to guard against accusations that the magazines only publicised the brighter aspects, its articles are striking for their upbeat and cheery tone.[126] Prisoners were unimpressed. When Bloss' wife told him in 1942 that she was receiving a free book from the Red Cross about camp life, he gave it short shrift in his reply to her: 'You say the Red Cross sent you a book, well I hope you like fiction stories.' Stoddart advised his parents that the Red Cross publications were 'pretty ironic from what I hear.' Burnaby-Atkins wrote home, 'Funny you should hear [a] glowing account of this camp – as far as I can see Red X always paints a pretty picture.'[127] Evans, meanwhile, used the first uncensored letter he was able to write to his wife on the day of his release from captivity, ahead of his repatriation, to set the record straight in unequivocal terms, 'In your last letter ... you stated that concentration camp no. 70 was a great improvement on 51 (according to B.R.C. news), I must contradict that as 70 was hell – football and hockey was the last thing we thought of!'[128] These men were not alone. An analysis of RAF mail in January 1945 indicated that 'by far the greater part of the criticism directed against the Red Cross results from incomplete and often misleading quotations from letters sent in to the POW magazines.'[129]

The final manly role that the POWs dwelt on being unable to fulfil was that of procreator. Whilst it was common during the Second World War for British soldiers on overseas posting to fear their wives' unfaithfulness in their absence, many would have had their own sexual opportunities whilst abroad.[130] For non-working POWs, confined in camps, there were

---

[126] P. G. Cambray and G. G. B. Briggs, *Red Cross and St. John: the Official Record of the Humanitarian Services of the War Organisation of the British Red Cross Society and Order of St. John of Jerusalem 1939-1947* (London: Sumfield and Day, 1949), pp. 229–30; Hately-Broad, *War and Welfare*, p. 183. Hately-Broad discusses the balancing act for the editors of *The Prisoner of War* between being accused of not presenting a true picture of camp life and of causing unnecessary distress to relatives (*War and Welfare*, p. 184). Mark Rawlinson describes the coverage of Red Cross magazines as 'being unremittingly upbeat' (*British Writing of the Second World War*. Oxford: Oxford University Press, 2000, p. 177, fn 52).

[127] Bloss, letter from his wife, 3 May 1942, letter to his wife, 1 July 1942; Stoddart, letter to his parents, 16 March 1943; Burnaby-Atkins, letter to his parents, 29 December 1942.

[128] Evans, letter to his wife, 21 March 1943.

[129] TNA AIR 40/2361, 'Summary of Mail from RAF Prisoners of War in Germany', 22 January 1945.

[130] On British soldiers fearing their wives' unfaithfulness, see Kaushik Roy, 'Discipline and Morale of African, British and Indian Army Units in Burma and India during World War II: July 1943 to August 1945', *Modern Asian Studies*, 44 (2010), 1264–5; French, *Raising Churchill's Army*, p. 144; Allport, *Browned Off and Bloody-Minded*, p. 293; see

no such heterosexual outlets. This reversed the construction of male combatants as dominant sexual actors whose female partners were submissive and receptive: POWs were now the submissive partners and dependent on their wives or sweethearts' abstinence.[131] Both Bloss and Fayers hinted at their sexual vulnerability when writing respectively to their wives: 'Please be a good girl ... because our future happiness depends on you' and 'the dreams I left are all in your hands'.[132] The unmarried Phillips spelt out the situation more explicitly in a letter, written to a childhood friend, from Oflag IXA/H (Spangenberg): 'One of the biggest worries of a p.o.w is the thought of all the eligible young men of every nationality who must be kicking about England while we're caged up in monastic seclusion.' Being in 'monastic seclusion' was probably particularly galling for Phillips at this time. He wrote this letter one week after his twenty-fifth birthday, having spent his twenty-fourth year celibate. The childhood friend to whom the letter was addressed, Philippa, was also the lady whom Phillips hoped to marry.[133]

These potentially negative consequences of men's dependence on home were so great that some doubted whether being involved in a romantic relationship was actually beneficial. Towards the end of the war, Nell thought that having a fiancée was 'certainly a lot to go back to', but he would 'have been much happier if I hadn't had a girl waiting for me. This constant fear that I may lose her is the most demoralising thing I've ever experienced.'[134] When he contemplated the same point, but from his bachelor perspective, Mansel declared that it was 'from the selfish point of view that I wish I was married – it must be hell for the wives of POWs'. He then followed this train of thought: 'and hell for the POW who doesn't really know how his family is – whether his very young children will recognise him when he returns. There are some poor devils who can't even be sure of their wives.' By the end of the paragraph he had swung a volte-face and concluded, 'I think I'm best unhitched.'[135] Hyde summed up the dilemma of a POW's dependence on his loved one

---

also Garton, 'War and Masculinity in Twentieth-century Australia', 93. According to historian Harold Smith, it was accepted that a husband would engage in sexual activity whilst in the armed forces (*Britain in the Second World War. A Social History*. Manchester: Manchester University Press, 1996, p. 14; see also p. 80). On army service offering 'unique opportunities for erotic exploration', see Allport, *Browned Off and Bloody-Minded*, pp. 120–1.

[131] For this construction, see Goldstein, *Gender and War*, p. 374.

[132] Bloss, letter to his wife, 31 March 1941; Fayers, letter to his wife, 4 February 1944.

[133] The private collection of Veronica Forwood, Lieutenant J. S. Phillips, letter to Philippa Cook, 23 December 1942. With thanks to Veronica Forward for this information.

[134] Nell, diary entry, 13 January 1945; see also diary entries, 22 February and 4 March 1945.

[135] Mansel, diary entry, 16 February 1941.

quite succinctly in a letter to his wife. He mused, 'I don't know whether it is a good thing for a Kriegie to be in love or not. Personally, I find that while the thought of you, my memories of you, and the idea of our future make life here bearable; all the time I am so desperately impatient to be with you once more. What a trick!'[136] It was a trick. POWs turned to home to help them to endure captivity, but at times this made captivity even harder to bear.

Conclusion

In their imagination, prisoners remained in close geographical proximity to home. Letters and parcels enabled loved ones to pass through the barbed wire and join these men in captivity: in POWs' fantasies, they drifted back to civvy street. Through their imagination and use of synchronicity, POWs also overcame the temporal distance that lay between them and their families. In other words, 'escapism', rather than 'escapes', was absolutely crucial to how POWs made sense of their imprisonment. This helped POWs to endure captivity, a point most powerfully illustrated by the way in which this emotional support was represented as helping men to replenish their physical reserves.

Emotional proximity was also primed by POWs living in constant anticipation of an imminent return home. In these expectations, prisoners demonstrated their attachment to their loved ones, by relating the end of the war to a wedding anniversary or birthday. They also showed their desire to resume their civilian lives, by hoping their homecoming would take place in time to be present at the next familial occasion. Imagining their return home was part of these optimistic anticipations: plans were laid down for homecoming two or even three years before it finally materialised.

Proximity to home also had negative consequences. Anticipations of homecoming left POWs unable to order and separate out their captive and civilian existences, making it harder for them to settle down to POW life. Their very dependence on loved ones made POWs conscious that they were unable to fulfil their manly roles of provider, protector and procreator. POWs turned to home to help them to withstand captivity but, at times, loved ones made the experience even harder to bear.

The next chapter turns to look at what potentially could happen when captivity became unbearable. It focusses on the mental repercussions, when no sense could be found in the experience: what happened to those POWs who went 'round the bend'.

---

[136] Hyde, letter to his wife, 8 October 1943.

5   Going 'Round the Bend'

> Sing a song of Stalag
> Days that never end
> Tons of Balmy Kriegies
> Nearly round the bend
> When the gates are opened
> The Government will sing
> 'If that's the cream of Britain
> O death where is thy sting?'[1]

Going 'round the bend' is the favoured phrase of the POWs who feature in *Captives of War* for describing how their minds became disturbed during captivity. It was an old naval term 'for anybody who is mad', but, as this chapter will show, gained widespread currency in prisoner-of-war camps in the Second World War.[2] This opening epigraph, 'Sing a Song of Stalag', appealed enough to Clague and Gallagher for them to write it into their respective logbooks. This ditty creates a paradoxical effect. It has a light-hearted feel, borrowing the tune of a well-known nursery rhyme, but its words conjure up a pitiful image: of thousands of prisoners of war slowly going 'round the bend' with the monotony of captivity.

This chapter explores what it meant to go 'round the bend', that is the psychological disturbances POWs suffered in captivity. It initially provides a brief overview of the research carried out into the mental effects of imprisonment during the First World War. Whilst research and results were conflicting, some doctors recognised a clear link between psychological disturbances and captivity, which proved influential on officials from the ICRC. However, it had no consistent name or diagnosis. This chapter then moves on to the Second World War. It looks at the causes and symptoms of the psychological disturbances POWs suffered, the

---

[1] Clague, logbook, p. 35; Gallagher, logbook, p. 91. Clague attributes the poem to M. A. Clarke; Gallagher to anon.

[2] Frank C. Bowen, *Sea Slang. A Dictionary of the Old-timers' Expressions and Epithets* (London: Sampson Low, Marston & Co., 1929), p. 114.

154

prognosis and finally the treatment available. A significant minority of prisoners suffered from psychological disturbances, but, without any sort of diagnosis, little clarity and much ambiguity surrounded the form these disturbances took.

Barbed-Wire Disease

During the First World War, psychiatrists and doctors were divided as to whether being in wartime captivity caused the development of a specific mental illness. On the one hand, studies by German psychiatrists and doctors concluded no correlation between the two existed. Amongst 12,000 British and French POWs, Dr Fritz Mohr did not find a single case of 'neurosis'.[3] Psychiatrist Friedrich Mörchen observed only eight cases of 'post-traumatic neurosis' amongst 60,000 French prisoners. Many had gone through quite severe artillery fire at Verdun, but, he argued, the feeling of relief at being out of the firing line was responsible for the prisoners' nervous well-being.[4] Professor Karl Wilmanns found only five cases amongst some 80,000 enemy prisoners, whilst Dr F. Lust, who surveyed 20,000 Allied sick or wounded POWs passed for intern-ment in a neutral country, considered 'hysterical' cases extremely rare, but thought the 'neurasthenic complex' common. Symptoms included headaches, giddiness, sleeplessness, irritability and a lack of concentra-tion: it was the 'real prisoner of war disease', he declared.[5]

The conclusions of those who failed to find any correlation between captivity and mental illness is, in many ways, unsurprising. It was a logical extension to some of the prevailing ideas around war neuroses in the First World War. During the first two years of the Great War, mental casualties were attributed to 'shell-shock' quite literally because shelling was con-sidered their cause.[6] In the relative peace and security of a POW camp, how, then, could prisoners correspondingly suffer?[7] There was also no functional gain to be had for POWs who developed neuroses, which was also thought to be a determining factor in the development of mental

---

[3] Paul Lerner, *Hysterical Men: War, Psychiatry, and the Politics of Trauma in Germany, 1890–1930* (Ithaca, NY: Cornell University Press, 2003), p. 68.

[4] Paul Lerner, 'From Traumatic Neurosis to Male Hysteria', in Mark S. Micale and Paul Lerner (eds.), *Traumatic Pasts. History, Psychiatry, and Trauma in the Modern Age, 1870–1930* (Cambridge: Cambridge University Press, 2001), p. 165.

[5] Cited in Lerner, *Hysterical Men*, p. 68; Gibbens, 'The Psychology of the Prisoner-of-War', p. 31.

[6] Binneveld, *From Shellshock to Combat Stress*, p. 3.

[7] A prisoner-of-war camp was believed to protect its inhabitants from mental illness; see Edgar Jones and Simon Wessely, 'British Prisoners-of-War: From Resilience to Psychological Vulnerability: Reality or Perception', *Twentieth Century British History*, 21, 2 (2010), 166.

illness: neurotic or psychotic behaviour would not allow prisoners to escape from their captivity, unlike enabling a fighting man to flee from the front.[8]

However, such views were far from unanimously held. The phrase 'barbed-wire disease' appeared in German in 1916 in the title of a newspaper article published in a German civilian internment camp in Wakefield, West Yorkshire. Prisoners in other camps in Britain used the descriptions 'camp disease', 'mental depression' or 'mental derangements', but 'barbed-wire disease' received official recognition.[9] As the Great War progressed into a third year, the ICRC became concerned about the effects of captivity on prisoners' mental health and it persuaded governments and national Red Cross societies to take action.[10] At an Anglo-German conference on the treatment and conditions of prisoners of war, held at The Hague in July 1917, 'barbed-wire disease' was added as a new term to the list of categories determining prisoners' eligibility for internment in Switzerland and their eventual repatriation.[11]

After the war, 'barbed-wire disease' was further popularised and more comprehensively scrutinised by surgeon and Swiss embassy official Adolf Lukas Vischer, who visited British camps holding German combatant and civilian internees during the First World War.[12] He wrote *The Barbed Wire Disease. A Psychological Study of Prisoners of War* (referred to in Chapter 2), which was initially published in German in 1918, and translated into English in 1919.[13] Vischer classified 'barbed-wire disease' as a 'psychoneurosis'. According to him, it was caused by the 'abnormal' conditions in which prisoners of war found themselves, namely being deprived of their liberty, being crowded together and being uncertain of the duration of their internment.[14] Its effects were akin to a piece of barbed wire winding 'like a red thread through the mental processes' of the prisoner. Symptoms included irritability, difficulty in concentrating, restlessness, a failure of memory, moodiness, depression and unpleasant dreams. He believed almost all those who had been POWs for longer than six months were afflicted. Vischer also noticed discrepancies between

---

[8] Lerner, *Hysterical Men*, p. 68.   [9] Panayi, *Prisoners of Britain*, p. 126.

[10] Matthew Stibbe, 'The Internment of Civilians by Belligerent States during the First World War and the Response of the International Committee of the Red Cross', *Journal of Contemporary History*, 41, 1 (2006), 15–16.

[11] Richard B. Speed, *Prisoners, Diplomats, and the Great War: A Study in the Diplomacy of Captivity* (New York: Greenwood Press, 1990), p. 37; ACICR C G1 A 09–08, 'Draft of an Agreement between the German and British Governments Concerning Combatant and Civilian Prisoners of War', The Hague, 2 July 1917.

[12] Panayi, *Prisoners of Britain*, p. 124.

[13] Vischer, *The Barbed Wire Disease*; Panayi, *Prisoners of Britain*, p. 124.

[14] R. Bing and A. L. Vischer, 'Psychology of Internment Based on the Observation of Prisoners of War in Switzerland', *The Lancet*, 193, 4991 (26 April 1919), 696.

how much barbed-wire disease affected different prisoners or internees depending on their background. He thought civilian internees experienced it more acutely than military prisoners: their self-reliant, independent characters made them unprepared for camp life, unlike officers and other ranks who had already become accustomed to a barrack existence. Reservists suffered more than regulars, again because, he believed, the former were less prepared for camp life than the latter, whilst those in labour camps were best off. These men were not so 'thickly aggregated' and were 'engaged in productive work'.[15]

The idea that 'nervous troubles' arose in wartime captivity was also acknowledged in the 1929 Geneva Convention. However, rather than referencing 'barbed-wire disease', as the 1917 Anglo-German agreement had, the Convention specifically mentioned 'psychasthenia of prisoners of war'.[16] 'Psychasthenia' had been referenced in the Franco–German bilateral agreements during the First World War.[17] It was a mental condition coined by a French psychologist, Pierre Janet, at the end of the nineteenth century. According to Janet, psychasthenia resulted from a disturbance of the mind's 'function of reality' which, according to him, was 'the most difficult mental operation, since it is the one which disappears first and most frequently'. In other words, Janet thought the mind had a natural tendency to roam through the past and future and not to concentrate on the present.[18] From the evidence presented in the previous chapter, which showed the extent to which POWs drifted from their present world into their past and future civilian lives, it is easy to understand how such a theory lent itself well to their experiences.

The literature of the British military-medical establishment, published at the beginning of the Second World War, reproduced both sides of the debate. The sole mention in the fifth edition of David Henderson and Robert Gillespie's well-respected *Text-Book on Psychiatry*, published in

---

[15] Vischer, *The Barbed Wire Disease*, pp. 2–3, 16, 53, 55–6.

[16] Annex to 'Convention Relative to the Treatment of Prisoners of War', Geneva, 27 July 1929, www.icrc.org/ihl.nsf/WebART/305-430099?OpenDocument, last accessed 15 February 2012.

[17] In May 1917, the German and French governments recognised in a bilateral exchange agreement 'barbed-wire psychoses (psychasthenia of prisoners of war)' [la psychose grave du fil de fer (psychasthénie des prisonniers de guerre)] as a new category for repatriation (Edouard Favre, *L'Internement en Suisse des Prisonniers de Guerre Malades ou Blessés 1917*. Second Rapport. Berne: Bureau du Service de l'Internement, 1918, p. 7; Stibbe, *British Civilian Internees in Germany*, p. 137). According to historian Annette Becker, 'psychoses des barbelés' (barbed-wire disease) did not appeal to French prisoners of war in the First World War because it suggested psychological weakness (*Oubliés de la Grande Guerre*, p. 134).

[18] Henri F. Ellenberger, *The Discovery of the Unconscious. The History and Evolution of Dynamic Psychiatry* (New York: Basic Books, 1970), pp. 375–7.

1940, was Lust and Mörchen's research that psychoneuroses affected only a tiny minority of prisoners of war.[19] Meanwhile, psychiatrist Emanuel Miller's edited collection of essays, published in 1940 and designed to inform the present generation of military medical officers on the variety of viewpoints surrounding shell-shock, cited both Vischer's evidence on barbed-wire disease, and the research of Wilmanns and Mörchen, that psychoneuroses amongst prisoners were extremely rare.[20]

Whilst conclusions were varied, a clear link between captivity in the First World War and psychological disturbances was recognised by some doctors and officials, but it was not defined by a consistent name or diagnosis. It seems unlikely that any of the POWs who features in *Captives of War* was aware of this previous research.[21] Yet, as the next section shows, their writings leave little doubt that prisoners in the Second World War also experienced or witnessed psychological disturbances peculiar to wartime imprisonment. None of these POWs was formally diagnosed with any mental condition and this might give cause for the reader to ask, when reading their narratives, whether these men *really* were psychologically disturbed, or whether what they were suffering from can actually be considered a particular mental condition. If this should prove unclear in this chapter, so it was for the men involved.

Manifestations of Being 'Stalag Happy'

In October 1940, Brooke recorded in his diary how 'Every so often a fit of depression seems to take the camp. Everyone together seems to become moody + get on each other's nerves. One of these depressions are [*sic*] on now.'[22] The following year, in a letter to his parents, Hurrell wrote, 'There are times when we get absolutely browned off probably "barbed wire fever" we get over it alright though.'[23] On 1 May 1942, Canon King described how 'Bad patches of ennui have a habit of cropping up from time to time.'[24] In a letter home, written at the end of the same year,

---

[19] David Henderson and Robert Gillespie, *A Text-Book of Psychiatry for Students and Practitioners* (London: Oxford University Press, 1940), p. 531.

[20] Emanuel Miller, 'Preface', in Emanuel Miller (ed.), *The Neuroses in War* (London: Macmillan and Co., 1940), p. ix; Eric Wittkower and J. P. Spillane, 'A Survey of the Literature of the Neuroses in War', in E. Miller (ed.) *The Neuroses in War* (London: Macmillan and Co., 1940), p. 15.

[21] In his MD thesis, Trevor Gibbens refers frequently to Vischer's work, but it is not clear whether he learnt of his research before or after captivity, Gibbens, 'The Psychology of the Prisoner-of-War'.

[22] Brooke, diary entry, 6–13 October 1940.

[23] Hurrell, letter to his parents, stamped 28 August 1941.

[24] King, diary entry, 1 May 1940.

Panter-Brick explained to his family, 'in this life everyone has spells of inertia and melancholy – the "blues", which may last hours or days. I'm in one now'.[25] Along with these four, twenty-three other men who feature in *Captives of War* described, in their personal narratives, the psychological disturbances they experienced whilst held behind barbed wire.

Twenty-five POWs also recorded their fellow inmates being affected. In 1943, Booth noted that Oflag VIIB (Eichstätt) had been hit by a 'curious wave of hysteria', where 'most people seem[ed] to have been affected to a greater or lesser extent.'[26] In the same year, Driver George Didcock commented in his diary how life in his camp was 'making some go silly.'[27] At the same camp, in 1944, Mansel believed the 'number of chaps who have had temporary lapses since we have been in this camp is rather alarming.'[28] In the final months of the war, when describing in his logbook the desperate conditions at Stalag 357 (Fallingbostel), where the billets were damp, prisoners lacked adequate footwear and men fought for refuse discarded from the kitchens, Gallagher added, 'men standing up to it pretty well. Only two deaths and several gone "around the bend".'[29]

These men used a number of terms to describe what they were experiencing and observing: 'barbed-wire fever', 'depression', 'ennui', 'the blues', 'hysteria', 'temporary lapses', 'silly' and 'around the bend'. Others refer to 'kriegy weariness', 'doolalliness', 'a bit nuts' and 'mental disorders'.[30] Literary scholars Carol Acton and Jane Potter have written of the importance of being aware of the 'alternative or euphemistic terms' that were employed during wartime 'to avoid the stigma of naming breakdown.'[31] As discussed later in this chapter, remarkably little stigma appears to have been attached to those who experienced psychological disturbances in POW camps: instead, these labels can be interpreted as an indication of the uncertainty of these men in naming what they were going through. For this reason, throughout this chapter, I have preserved the exact terms prisoners and their doctors used, and drawn upon the unscientific term 'psychological disturbances' when making independent references to this subject.

---

[25] Panter-Brick, letter to his family, 1 December 1943 in Panter-Brick, *Years Not Wasted 1940–1945*, p. 60.

[26] Booth, diary entry, 14 August 1943.

[27] Didcock, diary entry, 24 June 1943; see also diary entry, 27 January 1944.

[28] Mansel, diary entry, 6 February 1944. Mansel defined these temporary lapses as people doing 'something peculiar'.

[29] Gallagher, logbook, dated entry 12 December 1944.

[30] Mansel, diary entry, 10 November 1944; Howard, logbook, dated entry 22 October 1944; Ball, letter to his wife, 27 February 1943.

[31] Acton and Potter, 'These Frightful Sights Would Work Havoc with One's Brain', 69.

Other prisoners referred to new terms that gained popularity in POW camps, specifically to accommodate this new phenomenon they were witnessing. In April 1944, Hawarden noted in his diary that 'War time usually brings out fresh words and phrases. Two in common use at the moment are: – "Stalag Happy" and "Hairy Pie"' (presumably 'Hairy Pie' related to some of the ill-prepared meals POWs had to consume or, perhaps, something a little cruder).[32] Gallagher provided a definition of 'Stalag Happy' in his list of 'Kriegie vocabulary'. It was, he wrote, 'Silly, daft, screwy' and 'More common in army camps.'[33] 'Round the bend', as noted at the start of this chapter, also gained widespread use in POW camps. Taylor indicated this by including the term in his 'Gefangenschaft Glossary', along with the following definition: 'everyone thinks everyone else is'; so did Angove, when he commented how a 'number of men' have 'gone round the bend', and then qualified this description with the words 'as we say here'.[34]

Just as the names used to describe these psychological disturbances were varied, so were the symptoms. For Stewart, 'going round the bend' took the form of losing his 'sense of humour altogether, felt depressed & lethargic & on the few occasions I got off my bed sat silent & moping.'[35] Canon King characterised people who suffered from 'gefengeneritis', in which he included himself, as 'liv[ing] at the mercy of their moods; & . . . incapable of settling down to anything for more than 10 minutes, pleasures even not excepted.'[36] Mansel gave a full commentary in his diary on how his various roommates were affected in early 1941. From Oflag IXA/ H (Spangenberg) he wrote, on 7 February 1941,

I'm certain some are slowly going mad – Batch, Tony, Shortman etc. Poor Roddie is desperately depressed – no letters chiefly – but he sees no point in remaining alive. . . . Frank is letting himself go, I'm afraid – sits and broods, doing nothing, except patience.[37]

The following month, when he and a number of his fellow POWs had been moved to Stalag XXA (Thorn), he was now unsure whether

Frank won't be the first in our room for this place to break. He gets more sullen and bad-tempered every day. Never goes out of the room except for appel [sic] and the abort, and if not on his bed, or someone else's, asleep, he will be sitting on a stool, huddling the stove, face in his cupped hands, brooding.[38]

---

[32] Hawarden, diary entry, 30 April 1944.

[33] Gallagher, logbook, p. 57. For similar examples, see Campbell, diary entry, 7 May 1944; East, diary entry, 24 August 1944.

[34] Taylor, logbook, unpaginated; Angove, diary entry, 24 August 1943. For a similar example, see Gallagher, logbook, p. 57;

[35] Stewart, diary entry, 12 February 1945.   [36] King, diary entry, 16 July 1944.

[37] Mansel, diary entry, 7 February 1941.   [38] Mansel, diary entry, 17 March 1941.

In April, Mansel then described how 'Poor Peter is in the most depressed and browned off state today . . . [he] spends his day, jumping on and off his bed where he lies staring longingly at snapshots of his fiancée or blankly staring into space.' Mansel then appealed to Peter directly: 'Don't let yourself go'. Speaking to Peter in his diary, rather than in person, is a little odd. Perhaps it indicates Mansel's desperation not to see his friend 'break' but also his powerlessness to prevent it: it was only in his diary where Mansel could make this plea.[39]

Prisoners also referred to other symptoms: irritability, lethargy, an inability to concentrate, fits of temper, absent-mindedness and memory loss.[40] It seems these symptoms could come on quite suddenly and last several days.[41] They could be experienced anything from once a week to every two months.[42] Not only were these symptoms described in these personal narratives, they were also reflected in the way in which those narratives were written. At the start of his captivity, between 6 and 19 August 1940, Mansel went through 'such a feeling of depression, general browning off' that he was unable to write his daily notes.[43] Much later in the war, Nell noted how bad his writing was getting, and then commented, 'We write they say as we live. I am nervous so I must write nervously.'[44]

Many of these symptoms are also well-captured in one of Anderson and Westmacott's sketches of prison camp life. The cartoon, shown in Figure 5.1, is of a POW who is 'a little depressed', sitting isolated on his stool. His pyjamas and slippers reveal he is unwilling to leave his bed. The snail crawling in front of him possibly represents his feelings of sluggishness, whilst the camp newspaper discarded at his feet signals this prisoner's inability to concentrate. The most striking aspects of this illustration are the rats, spiders, bats and snakes emerging from the coils

[39] Mansel, diary entry, 13 April 1941; see also diary entry, 5 November 1944.
[40] On irritability, see Fairclough, letter to his wife, 3 June 1943. On lethargy, see King, diary entry, 23 February 1944; Stewart, diary entry, 12 February 1945. On an inability to concentrate, see Jabez-Smith, diary entry, 19 June 1944; King, diary entry, 16 July 1944; Stewart, diary entry, 21 January 1945. On 'fits of temper', see Taylor, diary entry, 28 December 1942; Mansel, diary entry, 10 November 1944. On absent-mindedness, see Mansel, diary entry, 17 February 1944. One of the overriding conclusions of a questionnaire completed by 300 officers in Oflag VIIB was that 'memory and concentration have suffered'; see Captain A. R. Dearlove, 'Enforced Leisure: A Study of the Activities of Officer Prisoners of War', *British Medical Journal*, 1, 4394 (24 March 1945), 408.
[41] Mansel, diary entry, 6 February 1944; Taylor, diary entry, 8 November 1942; Stewart, diary entry, 12 February 1945.
[42] The Army Medical Services Museum, RAMC 466/49, Conference of Military Psychiatrists. Appendix A, Captain Mustardé, 'Adjustment and Mal-adjustment within the Camp', 7–8 October 1944.
[43] Mansel, diary entry, '1st Interval from Aug: 6th to Aug: 19th'.
[44] Nell, diary entry, 10 July 1944.

Figure 5.1: 'Please don't speak to me now – I feel a little depressed.' In Robert Anderson and David Westmacott's *Book of Prison Camp Sketches*. This illustration, by Warrant Officers Robert Anderson and David Westmacott, which was part of their series of sketches on prison camp life in Germany, sets out a variety of symptoms that psychologically disturbed POWs experienced. The prisoner's clothes suggest he is lethargic, the discarded newspaper that he cannot concentrate and the animals emerging from the barbed wire that his mind is being heckled.

Source: Robert Anderson and David Westmacott, *Handle with Care: A Book of Prison Camp Sketches Drawn and Written in Prison Camps in Germany* (Belper, Derby: JoTe Publications, 2005; first published in 1946), p. 29.

of barbed wire, all heckling the POW's mind from a variety of angles. They induce a strong somatic response in the viewer: one can feel this psychological disturbance much better than one can then describe the feeling.

The prisoners who have recorded these observations are mostly officers, warrant officers and senior NCOs: proportionately, more of them referred to psychological disturbances than did those from the non-commissioned ranks, and all but two of the junior NCOs or privates who wrote about these disturbances did so whilst held in camps in Italy or central camps in Germany, as opposed to in working camps.[45] Three conditions intrinsic to life in central POW camps were singled out by prisoners as largely responsible for these disturbances. The first was the physical presence of barbed wire. Mansel suggested that walking around the camp was a cause of 'wire-itis'. When parole walks were curtailed at Oflag VIIB (Eichstätt), he was indignant: 'It is high time they are restarted since to some of the long term prisoners I would have said they are essential in order to get rid to some extent of "wire-consciousness" and claustrophobia. I am sure that many of the mental disorders are due to these causes.'[46] It was also reported to the ICRC that walking around the edge of the barbed-wire fence was recognised as a symptom of psychological disturbance; at Stalag XVIIB, near the village of Gneixendorf in Lower Austria, such men came to be known as 'barb wire Johnsons'.[47]

The second condition, and linked to this, was the inability of POWs to get away from each other; some of the frustrations that resulted from this were discussed in Chapter 3. Exposure to ceaseless noise and being in constant company were considered to take its toll, as Mansel reported on 19 July 1944:

---

[45] Of the twenty-seven men who expressed a concern in their personal narratives that they were affected by mental disturbances, twelve were officers, three warrant officers, two senior NCOs, three junior NCOs and seven servicemen without rank. Of the twenty-five men who expressed a concern in their personal narratives that others were mentally disturbed, fourteen were officers, five warrant officers, two junior NCOs and four servicemen without rank. Didcock is one exception who, when held at a working camp attached to Stalag VIIIB (Lamsdorf), wrote in his diary on 27 January 1944, 'Fed up with this life, I am sure some of the fellows in camps are going mad' (Didcock, diary entry, 27 January 1944). Campbell is also likely to have been in a working camp when he wrote about prisoners being 'stalag happy', although I cannot be certain as his references are undated (Campbell, diary).

[46] Mansel, diary entries, 12 December 1944 and 8 January 1945.

[47] ACICR, B G 14, box 428, file R.VIII. J. Townsend Russell, 'Relief to Prisoners of War, Insular and Foreign Operations, American Red Cross, on Interviews with Members of the Armed Forces Repatriated from German Prison Camps via the SS Gripsholm on September 26, 1944 and those Liberated from the Rumanian Prisoner of War Camps', American Red Cross, Washington DC, 10 October 1944, p. 7.

Tony was saying that after considering every argument that has been put to him on the subject, he is still convinced that there is no form of life of any sort of description to compare with this for sheer mental strain – the entire cause being our thickness on the ground, having to live year in and year out in a crowd of people in a small room, not even with a bed to oneself, let alone a room, with the same old arguments and topics of conversation, the same old irritants turning up day after day and you can't find anywhere to go to get away from people. . . . In many ways I agree with him. The strain is frightful.[48]

As a result, 'silent rooms' were considered to hold great value. Stewart explained, 'I honestly believe that without them a far larger number of people would have gone off their head.'[49] Following news of the deaths of his father and brother, in 1942 and 1944, respectively, the SBO of Oflag VIIB (Eichstätt) put Mansel's name forward for a stay in the officers' 'holiday camp', so that he could 'think in some sort of peace' and without 'wire-consciousness'.[50]

The final and probably most significant cause of psychological disturbance was considered to relate to the empty time or monotony of captivity. As Howard described it on 22 October 1944, 'It is slackness that is the greatest enemy of any prisoners. Having it for a period of four years is no joke and it is the main cause of doolalliness here.'[51] In the same year, Jabez-Smith similarly recorded, 'The last few days I have been rather depressed – the sort of irrational discontent which periodically afflicts those who have to think how they will occupy the day.'[52] Work, therefore, was considered to offer prisoners some protection against psychological disturbance, as were other activities put on in central camps.[53] These men recorded how they disciplined themselves with exercise, study, hobbies, music or, quite simply, getting up in the morning, washing and shaving; many also noted how it sometimes took a great deal of willpower to force oneself into action.[54] Consequently, psychological disturbance was

---

[48] Mansel, diary entry, 19 July 1944. For similar examples, see Booth, diary entry, 5 July 1942; King, diary entry, 11 April 1941.

[49] Stewart, diary entry, 21 January 1945. For a similar example, see Angove, diary entry, 24 August 1943.

[50] Mansel, diary entry, 30 August 1944.

[51] Howard, logbook, entry dated 22 October 1944.

[52] Jabez-Smith, diary entry, 7 August 1944. For a similar example, see Angove, diary entry, 19 August 1942.

[53] Jarvis, letter to his parents, 27 February 1944; Glass, diary, Chapter XXXI – Sickness and Working Parties. On RAMC protected personnel not suffering as much because of being employed in medical duties, see TNA WO 32/10757, Consulting Psychiatrist to the Army, 'Rehabilitation of British Prisoners of War Returned to this Country', 21 August 1943. See also Wylie, *Barbed Wire Diplomacy*, p. 215.

[54] Brook, diary entry, 21–27 July 1941; Taylor, diary entries, 8 November and 15 December 1942; King, diary entries, 3 August 1940 and 28 May 1944; Angove,

conceived as something to be 'guarded against', as Taylor put it; succumbing to it took the form of having 'let themselves go', in Angove's words.[55]

One other cause of psychological disturbance applied to POWs. Chapter 1 discussed the way POWs' optimistic anticipations of an early homecoming could lead to despair when their hopes were not realised: POWs' letters and diaries echo the peril this could pose to prisoners' minds.[56] Lieutenant Gibbens, in his Doctorate of Medicine thesis, recorded this was a particular problem for protected personnel. According to him, they lived under 'greater uncertainty' due to 'the possibility of repatriation', and this actually balanced out any immunity their professional work might offer them from the onset of 'barbed-wire neuroses'.[57]

All these comments indicate that psychological disturbances were very specific to captivity. Prior battle experiences were not referred to by these men as contributing to this form of mental suffering. In fact, according to Taylor, the effect of captivity on a man's mind was 'even more marking than the fighting itself'.[58] When these prisoners experienced battle conditions again – they were exposed to bombing from their own side at the end of the war as neither Britain nor Germany could agree to exchange information regarding the location of POW camps – the psychological disturbances that they endured were given a different name, 'bomb happy', indicating it was perceived as a different condition.[59] Yet,

diary entries, 24 March and 24 August and 19 December and Boxing Day 1943, 9 November 1944; Mansel, diary entries, 19 August 1940 and 27 February 1943.

[55] Taylor, diary entry, 15 December 1942; Angove, diary entry, 6 June 1944. For similar examples, see Mansel, diary entries, 7 February and 13 April 1941; Dearlove, 'Enforced Leisure', 408.

[56] Bloss, letter to his wife, 23 July 1943; Stewart, diary entry, 13 February 1945; Glass, diary entry, 20 June 1942; Mansel, letter to his mother, 21 May 1944; Nell, diary entry, 21 October 1944.

[57] Gibbens, 'The Psychology of the Prisoner-of-War', pp. 19, 63. Evidence from medical staff in concentration camps or imprisoned in the Far East, where there was no chance of an early departure, do reveal that doctors and nurses were amongst the best adjusted of those in captivity; see V. A. Kral, 'Psychiatric Observations under Severe Chronic Stress', *American Journal of Psychiatry*, 108 (1951), 187; Stewart Wolf and Herbert S. Ripley, 'Reactions among Allied Prisoners of War Subjected to Three Years of Imprisonment and Torture by the Japanese', *American Journal of Psychiatry*, 104, 3 (1947), 187.

[58] Taylor, diary entry, 15 December 1942.

[59] On Allied bombing, see Mason, *Prisoners of War*, p. 96. On 'bomb happy', see Stewart, diary entry, 15 February 1945. Gibbens recorded after the war how being bombed by one's own people had a 'remarkably demoralising' effect (SOFO Box 32, Item 46, T. C. N. Gibbens, *'Captivity'. Trevor Gibbens's Experiences as a Prisoner of War in Germany 1940–1945*, p. 73). 'Bomb happy' was also used by the army and the RAF for men who had reached their own psychological breaking point (French, *Raising Churchill's Army*, p. 138; Francis, *The Flyer*, p. 111).

although specific to captivity, the variety of symptoms and names recorded in these personal narratives illustrate the ambiguity with which these psychological disturbances were experienced.

The Prognosis

Four imprisoned British medical officers attempted to theorise these disturbances that they witnessed in captivity. Some of the observations of one, Lieutenant Trevor Gibbens, have been referenced in previous chapters. Before the war, Gibbens had been employed at the prestigious Maudsley psychiatric hospital, and he spent his last eighteen months of captivity working full time as a medical officer at the camp hospital attached to Stalag 344, which had been Stalag VIIIB (Lamsdorf), but was renumbered in 1943.[60] After his return to Britain, Gibbens submitted a Doctorate of Medicine thesis on 'The Psychology of the Prisoner-of-War' to the University of Cambridge in 1947, in which he detailed his findings.[61] Another doctor to record his observations was Major Philip Newman. He had been captured whilst succouring the wounded from his unit in Rosendael in France. He had treated POWs in various hospitals in France, Belgium and Germany before his escape in early 1942 from Sotteville camp near Rouen in France, to where he had been moved in 1941 as part of the same repatriation party that had included King.[62] The third was medical officer Captain Archie Cochrane. He worked mostly with tuberculosis patients and psychoneurotics of all nationalities in POW treatment centres set up in the towns of Hildburghausen and Elsterhorst, located respectively in the centre and east of Germany.[63] Both Newman and Cochrane published their views on the mental effects of captivity in medical journals shortly after their release.[64] The final doctor was Matthews. His letters home form one of the collections of correspondence that inform this book, but he also compiled an unpublished report on the 'mental health' of prisoners of

---

[60] SOFO Box 32, Item 46, Gibbens, 'Captivity', p. 76. For background on the Maudsley, see Thalassis, 'Treating and Preventing Trauma', pp. 58, 83.

[61] Gibbens, 'The Psychology of the Prisoner-of-War'.

[62] Philip Newman, Safer than a Known Way. An Escape Story of World War II (London: William Kimber, 1983), pp. 31–57.

[63] A. L. Cochrane, 'The Medical Officer as Prisoner in Germany', The Lancet, 246, 6370 (29 September 1945), 411; Archibald L. Cochrane with Max Blythe, One Man's Medicine. An Autobiography of Professor Archie Cochrane (Cardiff: British Medical Journal, 2009), pp. 72–84.

[64] Newman, 'The Prisoner-of-War Mentality', 8–10; Cochrane, 'Notes on the Psychology of Prisoners of War', 282–4.

war in Stalag Luft III (Sagan), which was sent to the War Office during his captivity.[65]

Just as the other POWs did, these doctors had different terms for what they witnessed. Newman described a 'mental attitude' building up within prisoners; Cochrane called it 'gefangenitis', chiefly because he liked the term; Gibbens used 'barbed-wire disease', whilst Matthews wrote of 'mental instability' and 'mental aberrations'.[66] They all agreed that the progression of prisoners' psychological disturbances could be divided roughly into a series of phases. Newman, Cochrane and Gibbens each recorded four 'phases'. For Newman, these were 'quite definite in occurrence' but 'nebulous' in length. According to Cochrane, each phase varied with each year spent in captivity. Gibbens, meanwhile, found that the second stage occurred two to six months into captivity and lasted about eighteen months. Matthews identified just two phases, separated by the two-year imprisonment mark.[67]

The initial phase was one of 'adaptation' in Cochrane's words; 'confusion' as Gibbens described it; or the 'breaking-in period' according to Newman.[68] Gibbens explained that, during this period, the 'abnormal aggression' of warfare was followed by an 'equally abnormal depression and humiliation' as well as compensatory tendencies, such as self-justification and contempt for commanders.[69] Newman branded this first stage as the 'most unpleasant of the four stages' in which the captive realises the extent of his loss.[70]

Following this was what Gibbens described as the 'stage of recovery'. It was brought about by a variety of factors: leading a simple life, having all distractions removed, having one's self-expression inhibited and being isolated in a 'functionless' group. At this time, a POW accepted his fate and tried to salvage life by putting up photographs, building a home, reconstructing daily habits and, in so doing, he reconstructed his way of living 'in a deeper sense, his beliefs, ideals and ambitions.' He felt

---

[65] TNA WO 32/10757, Major G. B. Matthews, 'Report on the Mental Health of Prisoners of War', Stalag Luft III, 17 February 1944.

[66] Newman, 'The Prisoner-of-War Mentality', 8; Cochrane, 'Notes on the Psychology of Prisoners of War', 282; Gibbens, 'The Psychology of the Prisoner-of-War', p. 29; WO 32/10757, Matthews, 'Report on the Mental Health of Prisoners of War', 17 February 1944.

[67] Newman, 'The Prisoner-of-War Mentality', 8; Cochrane, 'Notes on the Psychology of Prisoners of War', 284; Gibbens, 'The Psychology of the Prisoner-of-War', pp. 24–9; WO 32/10757, Matthews, 'Report on the Mental Health of Prisoners of War', 17 February 1944.

[68] Cochrane, 'Notes on the Psychology of Prisoners of War', 284; Gibbens, 'The Psychology of the Prisoner-of-War', p. 24; Newman, 'The Prisoner-of-War Mentality', 8.

[69] Gibbens, 'The Psychology of the Prisoner-of-War', p. 24.

[70] Newman, 'The Prisoner-of-War Mentality', 8.

'chastened and reborn' and seized on this opportunity, with books on philosophy being in great demand.[71] Newman described this second stage as the 'period of convalescence'.[72] Similarly, Cochrane summed up this time, which he thought took place in the second year of captivity, as 'the best'.[73]

Matthews, however, did not identify a similarly positive effect of captivity. He attributed 'the manifestation of mental instability' in prisoners of war to four 'outstanding' causes. One of these was the lack of privacy (apart from when undergoing the punishment of solitary confinement – the benefits of which Booth highlighted, as seen in Chapter 3). The second was frustration with being penned in by barbed wire, being constantly supervised by guards and having to follow endless restrictive regulations. Another cause was leading a monotonous life in a drab, unchanging environment. The final was prisoners' depressing surroundings, such as eating and sleeping in a bare room devoid of any amenities. These resulted in 'mental aberrations', of which Matthews gave one example: 'melancholic irritation'. The 'aberrations' that occurred during the first two years of captivity were part of the adaptation process and were potentially transient. The longer the imprisonment, the more persistent these would become, with those imprisoned for more than two years facing, Matthews believed, the danger of 'permanent mental deterioration.'[74]

Cochrane also identified the third year of captivity as a defining one: this was when the 'strain' began to take its toll. He considered this to be caused by 'aggression slowly turning inwards'. He explained:

Sex and food deprivation produced no major conflict in themselves; they merely caused aggressive hate directed towards the Germans, and this increased aggression, perpetually tantalized [*sic*] by the barbed wire and the ever-present guard, could find few outlets compatible with survival as a prisoner. Hence the conflict and the neurosis.[75]

Gibbens christened this the 'crisis stage'. After eighteen months to two years of captivity, the picture of home had begun to fade, replaced by elaborate fantasies which, in turn, the prisoner realised were no longer true and so he had to concentrate on the reality of the camp. After reaching this point, the prisoner would begin to deteriorate from 'barbed-wire disease', which was 'based upon a refusal to hope'. It was

---

[71] Gibbens, 'The Psychology of the Prisoner-of-War', pp. 25–7.
[72] Newman, 'The Prisoner-of-War Mentality', 8.
[73] Cochrane, 'Notes on the Psychology of Prisoners of War', 284.
[74] WO 32/10757, Matthews, 'Report on the Mental Health of Prisoners of War', 17 February 1944.
[75] Cochrane, 'Notes on the Psychology of Prisoners of War', 284.

less painful to inhibit desire than to suffer disappointment … Constantly maintained inhibition produces fatigue and the increase in phantasy life leads to loss of attention, poor concentration and poor memory. At times an incident will reveal the degree of flagging in work or interest, and self-conscious attempts are made to regain the initiative, the outcome of which was either an increasingly rigidity, or childish passivity.[76]

Newman described the third phase through which a prisoner passed as the 'lengthy period of boredom'. This was the period when sexual deprivation, the fear of being forgotten by friends and relatives at home and a lack of stimulation and responsibility became fundamental factors in the formation of a 'prisoner-of-war attitude'. He thought it was up to the prisoner to counteract these by playing a constructive role in camp life.[77]

According to Cochrane, by the fourth year, no one would be left 'unscathed' whilst Gibbens described this final phase as when 'deterioration' from 'barbed-wire disease' began. 'Interest' now became 'restricted', with Gibbens giving the example of fourth-year prisoners paying little attention to war news. This resembles how, in the final year of the war, long-term prisoners abandoned their confidence that it would end imminently, as discussed in Chapter 1. Gibbens also recorded prisoners experiencing a loss of attention, poor concentration and poor memory. Newman, by contrast, recorded phase four as taking place during the repatriation period. This part of his observations are discussed in detail in Chapter 7.[78]

These medical officers did not see these periods of mental decline as occurring identically within each and every prisoner. Gibbens, in line with Vischer's observations, considered that proportionately fewer regular troops developed 'psychoses', probably because they 'adapt all too well'.[79] Regulars, he explained, had suffered a 'greater loss of self-respect on capture', but they 'inverted' this 'into a high prisoner morale with … every type of resistance to authority.'[80] Newman, meanwhile, believed that officers were most affected by the 'prisoner-of-war mentality'. He partly attributed this to each officer being 'unemployed and therefore has to rely on his own resources to dispose of his time', and partly to the way in which the 'contrast between [their] normal life

---

[76] Gibbens, 'The Psychology of the Prisoner-of-War', pp. 28–9.

[77] Newman, 'The Prisoner-of-War Mentality', 8.

[78] Cochrane, 'Notes on the Psychology of Prisoners of War', 284; Gibbens, 'The Psychology of the Prisoner-of-War', p. 29; Newman, 'The Prisoner-of-War Mentality', 9.

[79] Gibbens, 'The Psychology of the Prisoner-of-War', pp. 73–4. Vischer observed that reservists suffered more from barbed wire disease than regulars (*The Barbed Wire Disease*, p. 55).

[80] Gibbens, 'The Psychology of the Prisoner-of-War', p. 140.

and prison life is greater'.[81] This explanation appears to have a class dimension to it. The implication is that life in captivity was more manageable for other ranks, who were largely drawn from the lower-echelons of society, because it contrasted less with their pre-war working-class lives.[82] Another medical officer noted that various personality types were differently affected. Captain Mustardé was one of the protected personnel repatriated in 1943. Soon after his return to the United Kingdom, he presented to a conference of military psychiatrists, where Mustardé explained that those 'worse affected' by 'barbed-wiritis' were

normally of that bouncing full-of-energy type – the extroverts, as I would class them . . . They were of the type that makes good organisers and daring leaders, but in captivity, with all avenue for direction of their energies cut off, they had nothing to fall back on and became moody and depressed.

On the other hand, he explained, least affected were

the introverts, while still sharing in the irksomeness and monotony of the life, were able to find some consolation and preoccupation with their own thoughts, regardless of the physical limitations imposed on them. They were the people who had always been silent and moody, the sober fellows, the introspective, self-sufficient type, and in captivity they merely carried on being self-sufficient and apparently as nearly unaffected psychologically as one could be.[83]

Since the 'daring leaders' or 'good organisers' were attributes also found in the officer class, Mustardé's thinking might also have had a class dimension to it. Both Newman and Mustardé's observations provided an explanation as to why officers were most affected by psychological disturbance that did not question officers' integrity or superiority. This is similar to the First World War, where men and officers who developed mental illnesses were diagnosed differently: officers in a way that avoided labelling them in disreputable manner, and so allowing them to retain their dignity.[84]

---

[81] Newman, 'The Prisoner-of-War Mentality', 8.

[82] According to French, 'Most regular recruits were from working-class backgrounds' (*Raising Churchill's Army*, p. 124). Three-quarters of recruits for the rank-and-file regular army were unskilled, urban labourers. These figures relate to 1 January to 30 September 1920 and are the only post-war figures available (K. Jeffrey, 'The Post-war Army', in F. W. Beckett and K. Simpson (eds.), *A Nation in Arms. A Social Study of the British Army in the First World War*. Manchester: Manchester University Press, 1985, pp. 223–4).

[83] RAMC 466/49, Conference of Military Psychiatrists. Appendix A, Captain Mustardé, 'Adjustment and Mal-adjustment within the Camp', 7–8 October 1944.

[84] See Fiona Reid, *Broken Men: Shell Shock, Treatment and Recovery in Britain, 1914–1930* (London: Continuum, 2010), p. 17; Thalassis, 'Treating and Preventing Trauma', p. 45; Bourke, *Dismembering the Male*, p. 112.

Nevertheless, despite these differences according to a man's recruitment into the armed forces, his rank and personality type, there was also
an underlying agreement amongst these medical officers that, as prisoners' time in captivity wore on, no one would be left 'unscathed', as
Cochrane put it.[85] This point is echoed in other personal narratives.[86]
Barrington accounted for the behaviour of one fellow prisoner with
reference to the length of time he had spent behind barbed wire.
In 1943, prisoners often quoted Stalin's maxim: that the attack on Italy
would take place 'before the leaves fall'. Barrington described how this
caused one man to 'pretend he has been watching [a tree] all day &
counting how many leaves have fallen. Then … he will suddenly shout
"Tin hat issue tomorrow, come & get measured for your rifle!"'
Barrington qualified this behaviour with the words, 'he has been a POW
for four years almost,' adding 'I think I too should be a bit mad after 4
years of this.'[87] Wild also described in a letter to his wife how he employed
one of the 'semi-mentals' at Fort XIV in Stalag XXA (Thorn) to look
after the camp garden, adding that 'these cases are a bit of a problem
these days, increasing as they are after four years', whilst Canon King
similarly put down 'four years of this life' as to why the nerves had 'beaten
the will'.[88]

Prisoners also commented on how, as their time in captivity length-
ened, they found it increasingly difficult to discern how much they had
been affected because, by this time, psychological disturbance seemed
endemic. 'I don't think I do queer things or show any signs of going round
the bend', stated Angove; 'I don't doubt that we are all a bit loopy', wrote
Wild; 'I'm still fairly normal, at least I think I am', assured Taylor in
a letter to his wife. 'Actually', Mansel asserted in his diary, 'I think half of
us, if not the majority, are slowly going mental – tho' <u>we</u> think we're
sane.'[89]

As a result, POWs compared their own mental state with those who
were untainted by captivity. Some turned to civilians back at home for

---

[85] Cochrane, 'Notes on the Psychology of Prisoners of War', 284.
[86] Only Stewart suggests that long-term POWs were less affected. He believed that two
years in captivity became 'beneficial rather than detrimental'. However, he wrote this on
26 April 1945, so he was possibly buoyed by the end of the war being imminent. Some of
his other diary entries, cited elsewhere in this chapter, appear to contradict this attitude
he latterly held (Stewart, diary entry, 26 April 1945).
[87] Barrington, diary entry, 13 July 1943.
[88] Wild, letter to his wife, 16 June 1944; King, diary entry, 28 May 1944. For a similar
example, see Mansel, diary entry, 12 December 1944.
[89] Angove, diary entry, 26 December 1943; see also diary entry, 24 February 1945; Wild,
letter to his wife, 16 June 1944; Taylor, letter to his wife, 26 September 1943; Mansel,
diary entry, 14 February 1941; see also diary entry, 6 February 1944. For a similar
example, see Nell, diary entry, 15 January 1945.

comparison, demonstrating another way in which POWs straddled the divide between their camps and the home front. After almost three years of internment, Bloss wrote to his wife from Milag asking: 'Do I make many mistakes dear? Please tell me because I want to try and analise [*sic*] what effect three years of captivity has had on me. Tell me the nature of the mistake such as if I leave small words out, write a word twice etc.'[90] Others decided they would leave it until the end of the war to receive their wives' assessments.[91] Those POWs who had been imprisoned over a long period also turned to their newly captured comrades for an accurate assessment of their mental state. Burnaby-Akins and Stewart, both captured in June 1940, compared themselves with the recent arrivals to Oflag VIIB (Eichstätt) in summer 1944 and January 1945. They were both, broadly, reassured.[92]

The idea that psychological disturbances in captivity were ubiquitous is revealed in another cartoon by Anderson and Westmacott, shown in Figure 5.2. A prisoner applies to be included in the next POW exchange. The RAMC doctor, however, responds to him with the words 'Mad? Why, you're no more mad than I am!!' One infers from his facial expression that this means they are all 'mad'.

This omnipresence of psychological disturbances reinforces one other feature of these personal narratives: there seemed to have been no hesitancy from POWs in referring to them. The majority of these references appeared in letters home or diary entries that were written with a public audience in mind.[93] These POWs' frankness is remarkable given the stigma attached to soldiers who suffered from war neuroses during this era.[94] There is a number of possible reasons for their forthrightness. First, those who developed psychological disturbances in captivity could not be accused of shirking or malingering from armed combat. Second, officers being particularly susceptible to psychological disturbance, given their non-working status, made it more likely that sufferers would be accepted

---

[90] Bloss, letter to his wife, 23 April 1943.   [91] Taylor, letter to his wife, 20 October 1944.

[92] Burnaby-Atkins, letter to his mother, 30 June 1944; Stewart, diary entry, 28 January 1945. Stanley Cohen and Laurie Taylor have noted a similar trait in long-term inmates of a maximum security wing: they measured their sanity against their interviewers (*Psychological Survival. The Experience of Long-Term Imprisonment.* Harmondsworth: Penguin Books, 1972, p. 105).

[93] One exception here is Mansel. In a letter to his father he wrote that there was 'not the slightest danger of my mind slipping that way' (Mansel, letter to his father, 10 December 1941); in a letter to his mother he wrote, 'I have not been a patient in the depression ward because, thank God, I've seldom suffered very much from it (Mansel, letter to his mother, 10 July 1943).

[94] Binneveld argues that the British armed forces were particularly intolerant of psychological problems, even up to the Falklands war (*From Shellshock to Combat Stress*, pp. 103, 106).

Figure 5.2: 'Mad? Why, you're no more mad than I am!!' In Robert Anderson and David Westmacott's *Book of Prison Camp Sketches*. This illustration, by Warrant Officers Robert Anderson and David Westmacott, which was part of their series of sketches on prison camp life in Germany, shows a prisoner applying for repatriation on the grounds of being 'mad'. The words of the medical officer (denoted by the rod of Asclepius on his lapels, which is a symbol of medicine), plus his facial expression, suggests he is just as affected.

Source: Robert Anderson and David Westmacott, *Handle with Care: A Book of Prison Camp Sketches Drawn and Written in Prison Camps in Germany* (Belper, Derby: JoTe Publications, 2005; first published in 1946), p. 49.

and tolerated, otherwise the integrity or superiority of the officer classes would have been thrown into question. Third, as discussed in Chapters 2 and 4, POWs had often felt misunderstood regarding the adversities they faced, thus these references to psychological disturbances might have been a means of conveying their hardships to those outside captivity. Finally, literary scholars Carol Acton and Jane Potter have written of the importance of 'cultural context' in giving individuals permission to talk about their own 'breakdowns'.[95] The isolated and unique society of a POW camp seems to have fostered a sympathetic and permissive cultural context that enabled prisoners to refer to how they were going 'round the bend'.

[95] Acton and Potter, 'These Frightful Sights Would Work Havoc with One's Brain', 77.

The uniqueness of the POW society is evidenced in one other way. Chapter 2 discussed how POWs made their peculiar way of life part of their distinctive identity. It seems their psychological disturbances was one of those idiosyncrasies they embraced. 'People, I find', wrote Fayers in his diary on 21 October 1944

take an eccentric pride in their claims to be 'round the bend'. Bill sez 'it's nice round the bend' and invites others to join him. Des and Cater slanged and swore at each other between every mouthful the other day apparently to prove to their new kriegie that they are 'gone', and Johnnie doesn't claim it but anyone who takes football as seriously as he does is obviously 'gone'.[96]

Campbell also recorded that

the conception of the 'mad English' really does hold good on the continent. The Germans are bewildered by us. The French and Italians seem to expect it of us: only the Dutch appear to see through it and to some extent copy it. Of course it is a myth, carefully fostered for the sole purpose of confusing the enemy (and in the end doing us no good at all perhaps therein lies proper madness).

He gave some examples of 'Gefangener Madness' or 'Stalag Happy', such as 'a party, sitting in the middle of the road, playing cards and smoking, without either cards or cigarettes. Another party, carrying a railway line, jitter-bugging.'[97] Although these were undoubtedly put-on acts of 'madness', they show how POWs had no inhibitions when it came to behaving as if they were 'round the bend'.[98]

Treatment

As stated earlier, none of the POWs whose personal narratives have been drawn upon in *Captives of War* was formally diagnosed with any mental condition. However, for those Allied POWs who were more seriously affected and diagnosed as 'mentally ill', there were three potential courses of action.[99] Firstly, they could be included in a repatriation exchange given that the 1929 Geneva Convention recognised 'psychasthenia' as grounds for an early return home. Evidence is incomplete on the numbers included in each repatriation exchange, since case records from Germany were usually destroyed during each transport until the final one of 1945.[100]

---

[96] Fayers, diary entry, 21 October 1944.   [97] Campbell, diary.
[98] This behaviour is also reminiscent of 'Crazy Week' at Stalag 383, see Gillies, *The Barbed-Wire University*, pp. 77–8.
[99] ACICR, B G 14, box 414, Dr A. Cramer, membre du CICR, 'Note pour la Délégation due Comité International de la Croix Rouge, Londres', 4 octobre 1943.
[100] Gibbens, 'The Psychology of the Prisoner-of-War', p. 129.

However, according to figures presented to the UK Parliament, the numbers repatriated on these grounds in the first years of the war were extremely small: just thirty-two British POWs, classified as suffering from 'mental and nervous affections', had been repatriated from Germany by December 1943.[101] After that year, numbers increased. At least seventy-six 'mentally ill' British and American POWs were included in the September 1944 exchange at Gothenburg.[102] In the final exchange of January 1945, somewhere between seventy 'mental patients' and 130 'psychiatric cases' are recorded as having returned to Britain.[103]

The Mixed Medical Commissions commented on the rise in cases they were seeing as the war progressed. The reports they made, in 1944, referred to 'barbed-wire disease' (*la maladie des barbelés*) often being found in British officers who had been in captivity for four years, and 'whose nerves were in the process of totally giving way' (*les nerfs sont en train de céder totalement*).[104] In a memorandum addressed to all the belligerent governments in February 1944, the ICRC stressed that the class of 'captivity psychosis' or 'barbed-wire sickness' should be specifically included within the wider category of 'mental cases' eligible for repatriation.[105] Another Commission, in 1944, confirmed that doctors throughout the camps were increasingly finding POWs who had been captured in 1940 and 1941 suffering from another condition, a 'psychological imbalance' (*un déséquilibre psychique*), and that an

---

[101] Hansard HC Deb., 17 December 1943, vol. 395 cols 1819-20W.

[102] No single figure is given for the overall number included in this exchange. Sixty-two British POWs had been declared eligible for repatriation by one of the Mixed Medical Commissions and seventy-six of the 360 American and British prisoners held in one of the seven trains transporting the group to their first stop, the German port of Sassnitz, were classified as mentally ill and, in one of the three ships transporting them onwards to Sweden, out of 282 grand blessés, 59 were diagnosed as mentally ill (ACICR, B G 14, box 424, 'Summary of the Medical Diagnosis in Relation to the Decisions of the Mixed Medical Commission B, 14.4.44 to 12.5.44, on British Prisoners of War'; ACICR, B G 14, box 428, file R.VIII, 'Repatriement de Grands Blessés et Maladies, de Personnel Sanitaire et d'Internes Civils, allemands, americains et britanniques. Echange Effectué à Travers la Suede, avec Enregistrement dans le Port de Goeteborg, les 8, 9 et 10 septembre 1944').

[103] According to Gibbens, the number was 130, whilst the SBO at the Lazaret of Stalag 344 recorded that '70 odd mental patients' were repatriated in January 1945; see Gibbens, 'The Psychology of the Prisoner-of-War', p. 64; 89/16/1–89/16/2(P), Warrant Officer H. C. M. Jarvis, scrapbook, 'Extracts from Diary (entry 12 January 1945) kept by Lt-Col. T. H. Wilson, Senior British Medical Officer, Lazarett, Stalag 344'.

[104] ACICR, B G 14 box 424, Extraits du Rapport 'Commission Médicale Mixte A. Voyage en Allemagne du 14.4.44–12.5.44. Conférence Préliminaire des Deux Commissions Médicales Mixtes à Constance le 14 avril 1944'.

[105] Historical background to 'Direct Repatriation and Accommodation in Neutral Countries', 'Convention (III) Relative to the Treatment of Prisoners of War', Geneva, 12 August 1949, www.icrc.org/ihl.nsf/COM/375-590130?OpenDocument, last accessed 15 February 2010.

increasing number of men had been returning to the Commission over the past few months, although it was unable to find anything objectively wrong.[106]

These Commissions also noted their difficulty in deciding who should be repatriated. The president of one of the Commissions commented on the troubles doctors were having in defining 'barbed-wire disease', and deciding whether the set of symptoms with which men were presenting required their repatriation.[107] This was so challenging that the ICRC declared in July 1944 that it was necessary for the Commission to produce detailed psychiatric reports to guard against the difficult cases being left to arbitrary decisions.[108]

The situation was also further complicated by the appearance of an apparently new type of case in 1944. POWs began to present to doctors with depression, thinness, paleness and wasted muscles; they were also tired and without energy.[109] This was labelled by one of the Commissions as a 'vegetative reaction to captivity' (*la reaction dite vegetative de captivité*), and these cases were significant enough in number to warrant the creation of a new bilateral agreement on POWs eligible for repatriation.[110] In September 1944, the Mixed Medical Commissions in Great Britain, the United States, Canada and Germany agreed that all cases of serious 'psychasthenia' were to be repatriated, under which heading came the subcategory of 'barbed wire psychosis', but they also formally recognised the new and separate category of 'vegetative neurosis', defined as those POWs who simply could not bear the life of captivity.[111]

These reports of the Mixed Medical Commissions reveal the confusion surrounding the diagnostic categories available for defining psychological disturbances resulting from captivity and also that, over time, more and more prisoners were presenting themselves to the Commissions. In both

---

[106] ACICR, B G 14, box 424, 'Rapport sur le Travail de la Commission Médicale Mixte B du 14.4.44–12.5.44 en Allemagne'.

[107] ACICR, B G 14, box 424, Extraits du Rapport 'Commission Médicale Mixte A. Voyage en Allemagne du 14.4.44–12.5.44. Conférence Préliminaire des Deux Commissions Médicales Mixtes à Constance le 14.4.44'.

[108] ACICR, B G 14, box 414, Dr A. Cramer, membre du CICR, 'Note pour la Délégation du CICR à Berlin', 19 juillet 1944.

[109] ACICR, B G 14, box 424, 'Extraits du Rapport "Commission Médicale Mixte B Voyage en Allemagne du 14.4.44 au 12.5.1944" du 5.6.1944'.

[110] ACICR, B G 14, box 424, 'Rapport sur le Travail de la Commission Médicale Mixte B du 14.4.44–12.5.44 en Allemagne'.

[111] ACICR, B G 14, box 424, letter from Colonel d'Erlach, President of the Mixed Medical Commission A in Germany, to the Presidents of the Mixed Medical Commission in Great Britain, United States and Canada, 3 September 1944; ACICR, B G 14, box 424, Colonel d'Erlach, 'Proposals of the Mixed Medical Commission in Germany to the Mixed Medical Commission in Egypt, Australia, India, South Africa to Ensure the Equality of Judgement', covering letter dated 28 May 1944.

these senses, their observations echo those of the POWs who feature in this study.

A second form of treatment available to acutely affected POWs was to send them to civilian psychiatric hospitals. The available evidence indicates this occurred in both Italy and Germany during the early years of the war. In one of his diary entries written from Campo PG 19 (Bologna), during the summer of 1943, Angove told his mother that she would be 'surprised at the number of men who have had to be removed to hospital under observation'.[112] The camp reports from 1942, for Stalag IXC located near Bad Sulza in Thuringia, central Germany, confirmed that the more severe cases held there were sent to mental asylums.[113] In 1943, from Stalag VIIIB (Lamsdorf), serious psychiatric patients were sent to a ward containing thirty beds in a civilian psychiatric hospital in Loben, a town about twenty miles away. Here, half a dozen English psychiatric patients would reside for two months at a time and British doctors were able to visit them at least twice a month.[114] In the same year, Booth and Mansel also recorded how men from Oflag VIIB (Eichstätt) were held in psychiatric hospitals.[115]

According to the ICRC, these men from Oflag VIIB (Eichstätt) received very good care, although none of the staff was able to speak English.[116] Mansel was not so convinced. He wrote of the 'not very pleasant' treatment administered to them. One of the POWs was treated for 'dual personality' with electric shocks, to fuse together the two parts of his brain that had 'become temporarily estranged.' That patient did recover; for others, the prognosis was not so good.[117] Patients at Loben were also treated with electroconvulsive therapy (ECT), but when one man died there, no more were sent.[118] Wild recorded, shortly after the war, how he had administered the burial of one British POW at the Konradstein mental hospital in Poland in the winter of 1943: the same institution which had seen 1,800 patients shot and buried in a nearby forest during the first three months of the war as part of the Nazis' adult

---

[112] Angove, diary entry, 24 August 1943; see also diary entry, 18 June 1943.

[113] ACICR, C SC, Germany, Reserve Lazaret Stradtroda dépendant de Stalag IXC, 8 juillet 1942; ACICR, C SC, Germany, Reserve Lazarett Stalag IXC, Obermassfeld, 16 April 1942.

[114] Gibbens, 'The Psychology of the Prisoner-of-War', p. 48; ACICR, C SC, Germany, Reserve Lazarett VIIIB, 1 February 1943.

[115] Booth, diary entry, 14 August 1943; Mansel, diary entry, 7 September 1943; see also diary entry, 25 January 1944.

[116] ACICR, C SC, Germany, Oflag VIIB, 20 July 1943.

[117] Mansel, diary entry, 5 September 1944.

[118] Gibbens, 'The Psychology of the Prisoner-of-War', p. 48; SOFO Box 32, Item 46, Gibbens, 'Captivity', p. 75.

'euthanasia' programme.[119] This POW had died fewer than three weeks after admission from septicaemia caused by bed sores, which Wild put down to 'gross neglect'. Following the burial service, Wild went on to meet what he described as a 'pathetic' group of British mental patients, later wondering if any of them survived 'their incarceration in that dismal place.'[120]

The third course of action for mentally ill POWs was their treatment in separate divisions of the camp lazaretts.[121] East recorded in his diary that one of his fellow captives at Stalag IVB (Mühlberg), who had 'gone a little off his head', was sent there after he started claiming other men's tunics.[122] ICRC reports reveal that lazaretts held a handful of cases, but one camp hospital, in particular, offered comprehensive treatment.[123] This was attached to Stalag 344 (Lamsdorf), and is discussed in detail in Gibbens' Doctorate of Medicine thesis. The hospital was described as 'excellent' in an ICRC report. It was one-quarter of a mile from the main stalag, occupying six acres of flat land in a forest clearing and consisting of eleven single-story concrete buildings, six of which were self-contained parallel blocks of wards.[124] 'Block IV' was reserved for psychiatric cases. It originally, like the other barracks, consisted of fifty beds, but was later enlarged, in September 1943, to ninety. The beds remained constantly filled. Also attached to it was a psychiatric outpatients' clinic. In 1944, three doctors, including Gibbens, were solely dedicated to psychiatric work with these patients.[125] In comparison, by 1945, there were around 300 serving psychiatrists for the entire British army, which by then numbered almost 3 million men. The few POWs who came into contact with 'Block IV' either were extremely well-served compared to non-captured servicemen, or their mental illness was so severe that it commanded much

---

[119] C. R. Browning, *The Origins of the Final Solution. The Evolution of Nazi Jewish Policy, September 1939–March 1942* (Jerusalem: Yad Vashem, 2004), pp. 186–7.

[120] IWM 66/185/1, Reverend R. D. F. Wild, unpublished account of captivity, book 9, 'Winter 1943', 3–5.

[121] ACICR, B G 14, box 414, Dr A. Cramer, membre du CICR, 'Note pour la Délégation due Comité International de la Croix Rouge, Londres', 4 octobre 1943.

[122] East, diary entry, xmas 1943.

[123] See, for example, ACICR, B G 14, box 430, Feuilles du Service Sanitaire, Repatriement des Maladies, Krgf Réserve Lazaret Kloster Haina Stalag IXA. La Section Psychiatrique, 82; ACICR, C SC, Germany, Reserve Lazaret Stradtroda dépendant de Stalag IXC Confidential, 2 septembre 1941.

[124] ACICR, C SC, Germany, Stalag 344, 4 May 1944; T. Duncan M. Stout, *Medical Services in New Zealand and the Pacific. In Royal New Zealand Navy, Royal New Zealand Air Force and with Prisoners of War* (Wellington: War History Branch, Department of Internal Affairs, 1958), p. 137. Gibbens, 'The Psychology of the Prisoner-of-War', p. 47.

[125] Gibbens, 'The Psychology of the Prisoner-of-War', p. 48; IWM 89/16/1, Warrant Officer H. C. M. Jarvis, 'The Barbed Wire Medico', vol. II, p. 521.

more intense supervision.[126] Due to the limited number of beds, only 18 per cent of these admissions were for 'neurosis': the vast majority were for 'psychosis', which was considered a more serious diagnosis. Had beds been available, about seventy neurotic outpatients (about 30 per cent of those being treated) were severe enough to warrant admission.[127]

Those who came to the attention of medical officers, such as Gibbens, were probably the fortunate ones. In fact, Gibbens reports that 50 per cent of patients treated at Stalag 344 (Lamsdorf) eventually recovered or were much improved before repatriation. However, he also noted that other acute cases never received professional attention. A 'large number' of those with 'psychoses' was admitted to hospital as 'emergencies', whilst many patients with 'neuroses' were regarded as malingering by their guards, so were not allowed to return to the stalag from working units, and 'many others' were treated as cases of physical disease.[128]

For other severely affected men, their mental illness resulted in a more terminal conclusion. Evidence gathered at the end of the war indicates a number of them never made it home. Out of the bulk return of POWs at the end of the war in Europe, the most maladjusted were given psychiatric treatment to which, it was pointed out, they showed a relatively good response. One doctor attributed this to either 'the truly neurotically predisposed' not having been captured in the first place, or their being unable to endure the rigours of captive life in Germany.[129] Either conclusion is possible. Only from June 1942 were British army recruits given intelligence and aptitude tests as part of their basic training, to ensure they were capable of absorbing their training and competent to bear lethal weapons.[130] During the early years of the war, therefore, neurotics may have fought to the death more often and so avoided capture. Whilst

---

[126] Harrison, *Bion, Rickman, Foulkes and the Northfield Experiments*, p. 84. Psychiatrists in the British army did work under high pressure; see Thalassis, 'Treating and Preventing Trauma', p. 155.

[127] Gibbens, 'The Psychology of the Prisoner-of-War', p. 71.

[128] Gibbens, 'The Psychology of the Prisoner-of-War', pp. 79, 49.

[129] Maxwell Jones, *Social Psychiatry. A Study of Therapeutic Communities* (London: Tavistock Publications, 1952), p. 24.

[130] French, *Raising Churchill's Army*, p. 67. There is some discrepancy as to who, therefore, was put in the front line before June 1942. The adjutant general wrote of the retreat at Dunkirk that there was 'a number of cases of breakdown of both officers and men' which 'was not surprising as the Army had been through no form of selection except that of natural selection which occurs over a period of time' (LHC, Adam papers, 3/13, General Sir Ronald Adam, 'Narrative Covering Aspects of Work as Adjutant General, WWII', Chapter XII, Some Lessons, p. 5). However, Ben Shephard argues that 'officers were ready to get rid of men whom they thought not up to fighting' ('"Pitiless Psychology": The Role of Prevention in British Military Psychiatry in the Second World War', *History of Psychiatry*, 10, 4 (1999), 511–12; *A War of Nerves*, pp. 189–90).

historian Tom Harrison has concluded, when writing about statistics that showed the percentage of ex-POWs with 'psychiatric disorders' was lower than non-POWs in six out of seven 'disorders' (the exception being 'anxiety neurosis'), 'it is noteworthy that personality disorders and learning difficulties either were not captured or failed to survive concentration-camp conditions. The latter explanation is the most likely.'[131]

Suicide rates might be an indication of the number of mentally disturbed POWs who failed to survive captive life.[132] Mansel, Flying Officer Ronald Grogan and Wild all refer to attempted suicides in their camps, with Grogan and Wild directly linking those they witnessed to the POWs in question being 'round the bend' and having a 'mental breakdown'.[133] Figures collected by the ICRC reveal that rates increased throughout the war until, in October 1944, suicide was the thirteenth commonest cause of death for British POWs. The actual figure, however, is tiny, just twenty-two deaths, a number that is undoubtedly an underestimation and too small from which to extrapolate any meaningful conclusion. The same fourteen camps or lazaretts appear to have reported suicides to the ICRC, each recording one or two such deaths for each quarter from October 1943 onwards. This would suggest either that conditions in these fourteen camps alone were so bad that they repeatedly drove prisoners to suicide, which seems unlikely or, more probably, that only in these camps were officials prepared to report POWs' deaths in this way. This conclusion is supported by the same two camps consistently recording the deaths of some British POWs as due to mental illness. At the lazarett attached to Stalag IXC (Bad Sulza) there was one death due to 'psychosis' (*psychose*) in every quarter between July 1943 and October 1944. At Stalag XXA (Thorn), 'mental illness' (*maladie mentale*) was the cause of death for one British prisoner of war in every available report produced between August 1941 and October 1944.[134] Since one cannot actually

---

[131] Harrison, *Bion, Rickman, Foulkes and the Northfield Experiments*, p. 118. The figures comparing mental disorders between ex-POWs and non-POWs are listed in Francis A. E. Crew, *The Army Medical Services. Administration*, vol. I (London: HMSO, 1953), p. 450.

[132] For the link between suicide and mental disorders, see B. Barraclough, J. Bunch and B. Nelson, 'A Hundred Cases of Suicide: Clinical Aspects', *British Journal of Psychiatry*, 125 (1974), 355–73.

[133] Mansel, diary entry, 8 July 1943; IWM Documents.16146, Flying Officer R. J. Grogan, diary entry, 17 September 1944; Wild, letter to his wife, 27 December 1943; Wild, unpublished memoir, p. 3.

[134] ACICR, B G 14, box 425, Raptriements des Malades, Statistique sur les Causes de Décès dans les Camps de Prisonniers de Guerre, britanniques, 15 août 1941, 15 octobre 1941, 15 janvier 1942; ACICR, B G 14, box 429, Statistique sur les Causes les Plus Frequentes de Décès dans les Camps de Prisonniers de Guerre en Allemagne, britanniques, 15 octobre 1943, 15 janvier 1944, 15 avril 1944, 15 juillet 1944, 15 octobre 1944.

die from such causes, these figures are more revealing of the tendency of individual doctors to interpret and report deaths related to mental illness in particular ways.

These were the most serious cases, but what of those prisoners who had their minds disturbed by wartime imprisonment, but received no such formal scrutiny? As the war progressed, British doctors and SBOs began to call for action to be taken. Matthews urged, from Stalag Luft III (Sagan), that POWs of over two years be transferred to a neutral country. The SBO of that camp, Group Captain Herbert Massey, sent Matthews' report to the Prisoner of War Department at the Swiss embassy in Berlin, insisting that 'the importance of some early agreement' for the 're- or ex- patriation' of prisoners of war who had been in captivity for a long time be 'strongly impressed upon the British Government'. Massey himself had observed 'the number of mental and nervous cases' to be 'steadily increas- ing', with 'a number ... reaching "breaking point".' He was particularly concerned by Matthews' assessment of the effects in some cases being 'lasting'.[135] The SBO of Oflag VIIB (Eichstätt) alerted the British Red Cross to the 'desirability of getting the Ps.O.W. of long captivity sent, if not home, at least to a neutral country', if they were again to be able to 'render useful service in the future.'[136] Towards the end of the war, the SBO, at Oflag IXA/Z at Rotenburg in Hesse in central Germany, was concerned about the 'mental state' of the younger prisoners of war who were 'showing signs, after 4 ½ – 5 years of captivity of serious mental breakdowns.' He reported that very little was being done for them by the Germans and considered 'something should be done as quickly as possi- ble to prevent them from losing their reason.'[137]

These messages received some attention at home. The Directorate for Prisoners of War put forward the argument that 'increasing evidence of mental affection resulting from long captivity' should allow those cap- tured early in the war to be released.[138] The Air Council also called for 'immediate repatriation or accommodation in a neutral country of prison- ers of war who were captured on or before 31st December 1939' to

---

[135] WO 32/10757, Matthews, 'Report on the Mental Health of Prisoners of War', 17 February 1944; TNA WO 32/10757, letter from Group Captain H. M. Massey, Senior British Officer, Stalag Luft III, to The Secretary, Prisoners of War Department, 23 February 1944.

[136] TNA WO 32/10746, Extract of letter from Senior British Officer, Major J. H. V. Higgon, Oflag VIIB, to Major General Sir Richard Howard-Vyse, Chairman of the Prisoner of War Department, 6 November 1944.

[137] TNA WO 208/3294, 'Secret Camp Histories, Oflag IXA/Z, Rotenburg'.

[138] TNA WO 32/10746, Directorate of Prisoners of War, Imperial Prisoners of War Committee, 'Repatriation of Prisoners of War who have been a long time in captivity', 22 March 1945.

prevent the possibility of 'permanent physical and mental harm', although this was a small concession on the RAF's part: just twelve officers and nineteen airmen had been captured in the first four months of the war.[139] These calls reached the highest level possible, but to no end. The War Cabinet was informed by the Foreign Office and War Office that the 40,000 British and Commonwealth POWs in captivity, since 1 July 1940, were suffering from the 'increasingly harmful effects, both mental and physical, of this prolonged captivity.' These were, the two Departments argued, 'strong grounds' for proceeding with an exchange of 3,000 Germans captured before 1 July 1943 with British and Commonwealth prisoners captured before 1 July 1940. Humanitarian grounds, however, were only a secondary consideration for such an exchange: more importantly, it would allow these POWs a 'period of convalescence' before going on to make a 'useful contribution' in the war against Japan.[140] Despite these calls and these varying motives, in the event, no action was taken.

*****

After the war, psychological disturbances arising in wartime captivity received varied recognition. Members of the Mixed Medical Commissions, in 1946, advised that a new definition of mental illness, due to the frequency of its occurrence in POW camps, be incorporated into the revision of the 1929 Geneva Convention. They defined this as 'serious chronic diseases of the neuro-vegetative system, with considerable diminution of mental or physical fitness, noticeable loss of weight and general asthenia.'[141] The 1949 Geneva Convention on the treatment of prisoners of war included those with the condition of 'serious captivity psychoneurosis' as eligible for direct repatriation.[142] In Britain little

---

[139] TNA ADM 116/5353, letter from the Air Council to the Under-secretary of State, War Office, 17 August 1944.

[140] WO 32/10746, 'Repatriation of Able-bodied Long-term Prisoners of War from the British Commonwealth and Germany', Memorandum by the Secretary of State for Foreign Affairs and the Secretary of State for War, 15 January 1945. POWs would not have been liable for foreign service within six months of their return (TNA WO 32/10757, 'Record of a Meeting to discuss the Reception and Rehabilitation of Repatriated Prisoners of War', 9 May 1944).

[141] Translated from *Les maladies chroniques graves du system nerveux vegetative avec diminution considérable de l'aptitude intellectuelle ou corporelle, perte appréciable de poids, asthénia générale*, ACICR, B G 14, box 420, file: Sous-Commission (Accord Type) Réunion des 2 et 3 mai 1946, 'Rapport du les Travaux de la Réunion de la Sous-Commission chargée d'Établir un Projet d'Accord-type Revisé, tenue à Genève les 2 et 3 mai 1946', 21 mai 1946, 18.

[142] 'Convention (III) Relative to the Treatment of Prisoners of War', Geneva, 12 August 1949, www.icrc.org/ihl.nsf/FULL/375?OpenDocument, last accessed 15 February 2010.

changed. The sole reference to prisoners of war in Henderson and Gillespie's *Text-Book on Psychiatry*, that psychoneuroses were rare amongst prisoners of war, remained unaltered, even though the book was reprinted in 1950 as a seventh edition.[143] As Chapter 7 will show, when action was taken by the government, it was on the basis not of the psychological disturbances these men had suffered during captivity, but how they would adapt upon their return.[144] The psychological disturbance these men had experienced whilst behind barbed wire remained without recognition, without clear diagnosis or prognosis and without a specific name.

Conclusion

During and immediately after the First World War, a clear link was drawn by some doctors, and recognised by officials of the ICRC, between wartime imprisonment and psychological disturbance, yet this was given neither a consistent name nor a clear diagnosis. The writings of the POWs who feature in *Captives of War*, along with the observations of imprisoned medical officers, plus those who worked for the ICRC, reveal a similar phenomenon in POW camps during the Second World War. A significant minority of the men who feature in this book went through or observed POWs undergoing psychological disturbances caused by the conditions of captivity, namely being behind barbed wire, the inability to have any solitude, the empty time and the frustrated hopes for an early homecoming.

There was a lack of clarity as to what this mental condition actually entailed. There were many names for it, the most common being 'round the bend'. It also manifested itself in a variety of symptoms. The medical officers each gave it a different diagnosis and prognosis. Some cases were formally treated, with a few being sent to German and Italian mental asylums. All seemed to agree that as time in captivity increased no one would be left unscathed.

Particularly striking about these personal narratives, given the stigma attached to war neuroses in this era, is the readiness of POWs to acknowledge that they and others were psychologically disturbed. Some even embraced these disturbances as one of the peculiar aspects of POW life. The isolated and unique society of a POW camp seems to have fostered

---

[143] David Henderson and Robert Gillespie, *A Text-Book of Psychiatry for Students and Practitioners* (London: Oxford University Press, 1950), p. 600.

[144] See also Shephard, *A War of Nerves*, p. 316; Jones and Wessely, 'British Prisoners-of-War', 183.

a sympathetic and permissive cultural context that enabled POWs to refer to how they were going 'round the bend'.

Despite the fears expressed by these prisoners of war, their medical officers and SBOs, when the end of the war came, the personal narratives studied for *Captives of War* give no indication that their authors had gone permanently 'round the bend'. Those final few months in captivity, however, presented a new set of challenges for many. The following chapter briefly explores how they made sense of these, along with their long-anticipated day of liberation.

6   Liberation

From the moment of their capture, POWs had expected their liberation to take place imminently. By the start of 1945, it was clear, even to the most cautious prisoner of war, that Germany would be defeated at some point that year.[1] This chapter first explores how POWs represented in their personal narratives those final few months in captivity, before going on to look at their reactions to their eventual liberation. These men had difficulty in articulating their feelings towards their release; instead, the format of their diary entries conveys their excitement. This chapter then looks at how, and when, these men ended their diaries, and so brought to completion their narrative representations of their captive lives.

In Germany, life and conditions in POW camps tended to be largely stable until D-Day, after which Europe, and so POWs' lives, were plunged into chaos.[2] For example, between September 1944 and February 1945, only 210,000 food parcels a month were received in camps for British prisoners and internees on the continent, as compared with 640,000 a month for the preceding year.[3] Local food supplies were also strained and there was a severe fuel shortage.[4] The flow of letters between prison camps and home dwindled: January 1945 was the last month when most prisoners' letters were delivered.[5] Camps became even more overcrowded with the capture of more than 21,000 American troops during the Battle of the Bulge, the last major offensive of the Germans against the Allies, in December 1944.[6] In the spring of 1945, material conditions in camps, such as accommodation, food, clothing, general disciplinary issues, mail or recreation, were deemed in the ICRC and Protecting Power reports to be dangerously inadequate in more than one-third of cases, poor in another third, and satisfactory in just under one-third of reports. By comparison, more than 70 per cent of

---

[1] MacKenzie, *The Colditz Myth*, p. 358.   [2] MacKenzie, *The Colditz Myth*, p. 97.
[3] Mason, *Prisoners of War*, p. 442.   [4] MacKenzie, *The Colditz Myth*, p. 177.
[5] See, for example, Bloss, letter to his wife, 8 January 1945; Parker, letter to his sweetheart, 17 January 1945; Wild, letter to his wife, 1 January 1945.
[6] Kochavi, *Confronting Captivity*, p. 97.

reports deemed conditions in camps to be satisfactory or better through-out most of the prior seasons of the war.[7] As discussed in the previous chapter, Allied bombing further intensified the situation.

Probably the greatest hardship and chaos came to those British pris-oners who were involved in The Long March. This began in January and February 1945. The German High Command had no intention of leaving thousands of prisoners to be liberated by its enemy whilst they still might be useful as workers or bargaining chips.[8] Originally it had planned for prisoners held in camps in the east to be marched in orderly columns westwards, towards the designated collection camps of Stalag 344 (Lamsdorf) or Stalag VIIIA, near the town of Görlitz in Lower Silesia, but, due to the Russians breaking so quickly through the German lines, the columns splintered into different directions across Germany.[9] The prisoners had to complete daily distances of between twelve and eighteen miles.[10] They marched in bad weather, with little food, and were repeatedly subjected to Allied bombing.[11] In March and April, camps in the west of Germany were also abandoned, this time in the face of American advances from the west.[12] By the middle of March 1945, it was estimated that one quarter of all the 'United Nations prisoners of war' (excluding Russians) were on the move.[13] Meanwhile, POWs held in western Germany, who were not forced to march, found their camps overflowing with people as they took in these marching prisoners.[14]

A number of the POWs who have featured in the previous chapters of this book switched the form of their personal narrative as they recorded this phase of their imprisoned existence. Bompas, for example, who spent his final few months in Oflag 79 (Brunswick), wrote a diary in his logbook from the end of August 1944. 'From now on', he wrote, 'I think I'll make this more of a diary – things are happening now, and they may be of more interest than the rest of the time together.'[15] Similarly, McDermott-Brown, who remained in Milag until he was liberated, had written, in December 1944, a general account in his logbook of his previous four

[7] Vourkoutiotis, *Prisoners of War and the German High Command*, pp. 165–7.
[8] MacKenzie, *The Colditz Myth*, p. 359.   [9] Rolf, *Prisoners of the Reich*, p. 223.
[10] Hansard HC Deb., 13 February 1945, vol. 408 cols 51–2.
[11] TNA ADM 116/5353, War Office file no: 0103/6753 (P.W.2), Message sent by American Legation at Bern, 28 February 1945.
[12] Rolf, *Prisoners of the Reich*, pp. 237–45.
[13] H. Satow and M. J. Sée, *The Work of the Prisoners of War Department during the Second World War* (London: Foreign Office, 1950), p. 16.
[14] MacKenzie, *The Colditz Myth*, pp. 97, 367; Rolf, *Prisoners of the Reich*, pp. 235–6, 168; Mason, *Prisoners of War*, pp. 459–60.
[15] Bompas, diary entry, 31 August 1944.

years in captivity. In January 1945, however, he started making dated entries, as 'it was our last year & would be exciting.'[16]

Others, who had kept logbooks in captivity, and were then evacuated from their camps to join The Long March, started to keep a diary to record this event. Gunner King's logbook contains a brief diary, commencing on 8 February 1945 and ending in April, which lists the places where he stayed and how far he marched each day.[17] Cooper's diary of his march, starting on 22 January 1945, and ending on 23 April, which largely describes what he ate and the distance he marched, takes up roughly the equivalent space as the rest of his unvarnished diary, which had documented his previous four and a half years in captivity.[18]

The change in personal narratives kept by these POWs indicates these final few months were, for them, the most noteworthy part of captivity. They are also insightful into how some men felt about their previous time behind barbed wire. Whilst, as Chapter 2 showed, POWs used their logbooks to portray a Kriegie way of life and construct a 'Kriegie identity', starting a diary only at the end of the war also indicates the tedium with which many regarded their day-to-day imprisoned existence.

When the day of liberation came, articulations of relief, jubilation or excitement, which might be expected from men who had spent years of the war in captivity, are conspicuously absent. Very few diarists were able to put into words how they felt. On 22 April 1945, the day Stalag 383 (Hohenfels) was liberated, Hawarden recorded that 'To try and write about today's happenings is far beyond my capabilities', even though he had been able to write a diary entry for almost every day of the five years he had spent in captivity. 'Someone, somewhere, sometime', he added, 'an ex-POW with far more literary knowledge than I will be able to express the feelings of one who has been surrounded by wire for almost five years, then to find himself suddenly freed by a couple of Yanks in a jeep.' Hawarden's use of 'sometime' indicates he assumed it would be too much for any POW to immediately assimilate what had

---

[16] McDermott-Brown, logbook, p. 58. For similar examples, see Cunningham, logbook, pp. 81–5; Tipple logbook, pp. 85–106.

[17] King, logbook, pp. 92–104. For similar examples, see Edwards, logbook, pp. 90–9; Macey, logbook, pp. 96–102; Gallagher, logbook, pp. 57–60.

[18] Cooper, diary. On 24 January 1945, Stirling shifted his type of diary from a documentary-style one, written at broad intervals, to an unvarnished one, written daily, where possible (Stirling, diary entries, 24 January to 6 May 1945). There are also many POWs' diaries, held at the Imperial War Museum, that only start as the end of the war approached, see, for example, IWM Documents 17642, J. Alcock, diary; IWM Documents 13058, B. Bagnall, diary; IWM Documents 3121, S. Baker, diary; IWM Documents 14892, J. Bolton, diary; IWM Documents 13096, L. W. G. Coward, diary; IWM Documents 14433, V. W. Croxford, diary; IWM Documents 15113, G. A. Hemsley, diary.

happened on that day.[19] If diary entries describing the liberation days of Angove and Mansel, who were both usually so ready to record their feelings, are any indication, it was beyond any POW's capabilities to express his emotions at this time. 'Believe me this is the most wonderful time of my life, my heart is too full to write all I feel', recorded Angove on 29 March 1945, the day after Oflag XIIB (Hadamar) was liberated. Three days after his liberation, at the officers' 'holiday camp', Mansel wrote home to his mother, 'I do hope that by now you know that I am free! It is the most staggering feeling and one that it is terribly difficult to grasp.'[20]

Instead, numerous diarists reveal the significance of this long-anticipated day through the formatting of their diary entry. The use of capital letters was one way of doing this. 'It is hard to believe that one is actually FREE', proclaimed Casdagli on 28 March 1945, writing from a foreign workers' camp near Lollar, north of Giessen in Germany, where he had travelled to seven days earlier, after being evacuated from Oflag XIIB (Hadamar). 'LIBERATED by Cheshire Regt of 2nd British Army', wrote Flight Sergeant John Beddis on 2 May 1945, after marching for eighteen days. 'RECAPTURED by US 11th Armoured Division', recorded Cooper on 23 April 1945, just outside Winklarn in Bavaria, having spent three months on The Long March.[21]

Many others did not just write one diary entry for their day of liberation, but numerous entries, at different times of the day. On 16 April 1945, writing from Stalag 357 (Fallingbostel), Nell, at '7.30hrs', could 'hear British machine-guns clattering merrily quite close. It seems that our lads are going to be with us this morning! At last!' At '9.05 hrs', he recorded, 'Some of the blokes are lining the wire watching the battle but most are taking the situation in a most unconcerned manner.' At '1000 hrs' they had 'just un-armed the Germans in the camp'; at '1045 hrs' he reinforced the significance of this entry through underlining: 'They're here!! A couple of tanks and an armoured car have just entered the camp! We're all free again.' At '17.30hrs' he was asking, 'How soon will I be in England?'[22] The emotion and excitement that Nell and other POWs felt

[19] Hawarden, diary entry, 22 April 1945.
[20] Angove, diary entry, 29 March 1945; Mansel, letter to his mother, 28 April 1945.
[21] Casdagli, diary entry, 28 March 1945 in Casdagli, *Prouder Than Ever*, p. 181; Beddis, logbook, entry dated 2 March 1945; Cooper, diary entry, 23 April 1945. For similar examples, see Johnson, logbook, entry dated 12 April 1945; McDermott-Brown, logbook, entry dated 27 April 1945; East, diary entry, 23 April 1945; Hainsworth, diary entry, 17 April 1945.
[22] Nell, diary entry, 16 April 1945. For similar examples, see Bompas, diary entries, 11 and 12 April 1945; Laker, diary entry, 8 May 1945; Jabez-Smith, diary entry, 29 April 1945; Stewart, diary entries, '9pm last night' and 29 April 1945.

on this long-anticipated day is conveyed through these timed entries, rather than the words those entries contained.

In the last of the entries written on his liberation day, Nell alludes to how, quite quickly, the excitement of being released was superseded by a desire to return home. Most of these men returned home with impressive swiftness, although many POWs still expressed their impatience that this return was not fast enough.[23] Four thousand POWs in the east, who had had their camps overrun by Russians before the Germans were able to evacuate them, were transported to Odessa on the Black Sea, from where they were shipped back to the United Kingdom.[24] Wild is the only POW featuring in this book to have returned home in this way. The others, along with the majority of British POWs, were collected by the Allies advancing from the West, taken to transit camps, then to the airfields of Belgium or France, before being flown to the United Kingdom. They spent a couple of days at one of the reception camps in south-east England before making their way home. For most, it took two weeks from the day of their liberation to be reunited with their loved ones.[25] By the end of May 1945, the repatriation of Allied POWs to the United Kingdom was concluded.[26]

At various points during this process, the diaries that have featured in *Captives of War* ended. When and how these men were prepared to close the narrative representation of their life in captivity gives us some indication of their state of mind as they left the POW camps behind. For Barrington, the news he learnt after liberation appears to have overrun his desire to continue with his entries. On 12 May 1945, from near Louvain in Belgium, and with difficult landing conditions in England delaying the take-off of planes, Barrington wrote, '1pm stand by! We may be away within an hour.' Two hours later he added '3pm No go! Another impatient night in this Belgian dump relieved by a visit to the local cinema showing an American film + also the news reel of Belsen + Dachau concentration camps, these'. Then his diary abruptly ends.[27] Perhaps words failed him as he became aware of the extent of Germany's camp

---

[23] For those who express their impatience to return home, see Bompas, diary entry, 19 April 1945; Stewart, diary entry, 6 May 1945; East, diary entries, 6 and 9 May 1945. Stoddart records the impatience of others, Stoddart, diary entry, pp. 50–1.

[24] Satow and Sée, *The Work of the Prisoners of War Department during the Second World War*, p. 16; Kochavi, *Confronting Captivity*, pp. 236–7, 246.

[25] MacKenzie, *The Colditz Myth*, p. 387.

[26] Gilbert, *POW*, p. 315. In mid-August it was estimated that 690 British Commonwealth (excluding India) officers and men who were prisoners of war in Germany had not been recovered or accounted for by the Allied forces. This had reduced to 105 missing POWs by November (FO 916/1201, Draft Parliamentary Answer, 21 August 1945; Hansard HC Deb., 27 November 1945, vol. 416 col. 1269W).

[27] Barrington, diary entry, 12 May 1945.

system, and realised what other inmates had endured under the Third Reich.

Many other diarists wrote their final entries after they had arrived in the United Kingdom. Angove looked forward to the future by concluding his diary, just after he had seen the White Cliffs of Dover, with the words, 'England at last & freedom. It's almost too good to be true. And there my diary of POW life ends, nearly 3 years of captivity & starvation, over like a bad dream. And now for the future.'[28] Naylor also indicated he felt a renewed confidence now that he was home and free, describing, in his last entry, his reclaimed manhood when he wrote how he and others caught a train to London 'no longer PoWs, but men on leave.'[29] Eldridge signalled his readiness to embrace his post-captivity life by writing in his diary, when at Beaconsfield reception camp in Buckinghamshire, '31.5.45: Thursday: – ', and nothing more.[30]

Others focussed their final entries on their wives, children, siblings and parents, providing more evidence, in addition to that contained in Chapter 4, of how POWs defined their imprisonment through their separation from home. Hawarden's final entry indicates his experience of captivity would be concluded only once he was reunited with his wife and daughter, but his use of inverted commas indicates the trepidation he felt ahead of their meeting: 'taxied to Victoria Station, train to Bolton, then bus to "home"'.[31] There was seemingly no anxiety from others. From the reception centre at Beaconsfield, where Abbott had a drink and dance in the town, he ended his diary by announcing 'tomorrow is the day I am looking forward to when I meet my wife and two boys.'[32] Mansel's final diary entry was written when he was back at the centre of his family, just eighteen days after he had been freed. He concluded his diary on the anniversary of his younger brother's death with the words 'Clare [his sister] and I played to Mummy and stayed at home.'[33]

White was the last to close his diary. On 16 May 1945, he wrote his final entry, consisting of the words: 'Sit in garden to write this up.' White's entry is interesting. Whilst the other diarists demonstrate their willingness to look away from captivity and towards the rest of their lives, White's words and his action demonstrate his difficulty in moving on from the

---

[28] Angove, diary entry, 4 April 1945.

[29] Naylor, diary entry, 9 May 1945. For other POWs who concluded their diaries upon arrival in the United Kingdom, see Quarrie, diary, p. 149; Stirling, diary entry, 11 May 1945; East, diary entry, 13 May 1945; Brooke, diary entry, 10 May 1945.

[30] Eldridge, diary entry, 31 May 1945.   [31] Hawarden, diary entry, 10 May 1945.

[32] Abbott, diary entry, 9 May 1945. For similar examples, see Hall, diary entry, 12 May 1945; Hainsworth, diary entry, 26 April 1945.

[33] Mansel, diary entry, 13 May 1945.

experience.[34] Now back at home, he was still working on his captive diary by writing it up. By writing about this act in his diary, he indicates his desire to continue writing entries into his diary, even if he no longer had any suitable experiences to include in it.

Whilst White is the only one to allude to it, few, if any, POWs were able to move on from their experience of captivity as simply as shutting these books. The next chapter charts how these men continued to make sense of their wartime experiences in the post-war world. Before moving on to this, the final word should go to those who did not make it back to England. Just under 6 per cent of British army POWs died in captivity or 7,047 men, 2 per cent or 111 men from the Royal Navy and 1.5 per cent or 152 men from the RAF (including the fifty POWs shot in The Great Escape).[35] The fact that so many prisoners from the army died reflects how junior NCOs and privates, or those of equivalent rank, were exposed to some of the worst conditions in captivity, and experienced more harassment and serious violations of the Geneva Convention than officers or the prisoners held by the *Luftwaffe* and *Kriegsmarine*.[36] Of the POWs' diaries, letters and logbooks drawn upon in *Captives of War*, one author never made it home. Campbell was killed on 12 May 1944 by a bomb at the industrial site where he was working at Bruz in Czechoslovakia. His death is given a particular poignancy by his final diary entry, which was written four days earlier: 'NOTHING TO REPORT. All quiet on the Western Front.'[37]

---

[34] White, diary entry, 16 May 1945.

[35] 'Table 9. Total number of prisoners of war of the armed forces of the United Kingdom captured by the enemy as reported to 28th February 1946', in *Strength and Casualties of the Armed Forces*, p. 9. This table does not provide the figure for the number of merchant seamen who died in captivity.

[36] On the disparity of conditions, see Vourkoutiotis, *Prisoners of War and the German High Command*, p. 177.

[37] Campbell, diary entry, 8 May 1944.

7   Resettling

Given the experiences that POWs had in captivity, as set out in the previous chapters, it is most unlikely that any POW, at an emotional level, was able to leave behind his captivity experience upon his arrival back to Britain. It is important, therefore, to ask how ex-prisoners of war made sense of their imprisonment once the guards had disappeared and the barbed wire had been torn down. There are few contemporary personal narratives to help answer this question; as a result, this chapter turns to other sources. It primarily draws upon the numerous medical papers and reports on this subject, produced by psychiatrists during the war and in its immediate aftermath.

This chapter initially sets out when and how the first few escaped and repatriated prisoners, as well as the majority who returned after the war, received psychiatric and medical attention. It goes on to explore the emotional and practical problems that confronted ex-POWs, before finally looking at the extent to which these challenges were eventually overcome as these men entered civilian life. Overall, it demonstrates how ambiguity surrounded POWs' return home, which is reflected in the language of officials and psychiatrists as well as in the attitudes of ex-prisoners of war, and through their effacement of the very experience of captivity itself.

'Are We Regarded as Dead-Beats or as Normal People?'[1]

This question, which Flight Lieutenant Gosman posed to his relatives whilst in captivity in August 1943, was a pertinent one. The year before, army psychiatrists had started formulating their own views on the subject. There had initially been denials, from all sides, that ex-POWs would need support when returning to their civilian lives. As the war progressed, however, evidence began to accumulate, from a variety

[1] TNA AIR 40/2361, 'Summary of Mail from RAF Prisoners of War', August 1943, letter from Flight Lieutenant A. D. Gosman, Stalag Luft III, 25 June 1943.

of sources, of the difficulties ex-prisoners and their families might confront.[2] Distinguished soldiers from the First World War wrote to the War Office, recalling how they had never fully recovered from the psychological effects of captivity.[3] One War Office psychiatrist, Lieutenant Colonel A. T. M. Wilson, researched 'barbed-wire disease' and interviewed men who had been POWs a generation before. He learned these men had received very little support from the state upon their return to England: they had become unemployed, some turned to crime and a sizeable number had never successfully reintegrated into the civilian world. Wilson was determined this would not be repeated.[4] As escapees and groups of repatriates from the current war began to return, they exhibited psychological problems stemming from imprisonment. A May 1942 survey revealed the difficulty the army was having in rehabilitating and employing escapees and repatriates from Italy. During the course of 1943, the authorities noticed a high invaliding rate amongst repatriated officers who had returned to the United Kingdom some months previously, and other disciplinary difficulties from repatriated soldiers who had outstanding military records.[5] Another investigation, conducted by army psychiatrists on 100 POWs who had returned around the start of 1943, revealed 30 per cent of them were exhibiting 'some degree of abnormality' three to six months later.[6] Meanwhile, repatriated officers sent to a special unit in Sanderstead in Surrey in 1943 had their 'deeper psychological background' studied by the psychiatric medical officer, Major W. R. Bion.[7]

To try to understand more about these problems, the government established an experimental rehabilitation scheme for repatriated prisoners of war at the RAMC Depot in Crookham, near Aldershot. The scheme ran from November 1943 to February 1944 and included more than 500 returned regimental stretcher bearers and almost 800 RAMC personnel.[8] Questionnaires were completed in the first week of the scheme and interviews were conducted with 200 RAMC personnel

[2] R. H. Ahrenfeldt, *Psychiatry in the British Army in the Second World War* (London: Routledge & Kegan Paul, 1958), pp. 226–7.

[3] Eric Trist, 'Working with Bion in the 1940s: The Group Decade', in Malcolm Pines (ed.), *Bion and Group Psychotherapy* (London: Routledge & Kegan Paul, 1985), p. 22.

[4] Shephard, *A War of Nerves*, p. 317.

[5] Ahrenfeldt, *Psychiatry in the British Army in the Second World War*, pp. 226–7.

[6] TNA WO 32/10757, 'Conference of Officers Commanding Military Convalescent Depots on the Rehabilitation of Prisoners of War', 30 November 1943.

[7] A. T. M. Wilson, M. Doyle and J. Kelnar, 'Group Techniques in a Transitional Community', *The Lancet*, 249, 6457 (31 May 1947), 735; Trist 'Working with Bion in the 1940s', pp. 19–20.

[8] Wessely and Jones, 'British Prisoners-of-War', 169.

and 200 stretcher bearers.[9] These revealed POWs had developed a 'stalag mentality', disproportionately severe in those who had been prisoners for more than eighteen months. Features of this included 'a very real but unfounded feeling that their physical or mental health has somehow been damaged', which was related to 'depression and guilt' suffered whilst in captivity, and to 'anxieties of re-adaption'.[10] To address these issues, a six-week residential course was designed, during which psychiatrist Lieutenant Wilson reported on these men's mental state. The course showed that, when compared to other RAMC servicemen, these ex-POWs were more likely to go 'absent without leave' or report sick.[11] It was further assumed that other soldiers, who were not RAMC personnel, and who had not been able to work in their own occupations, might show 'even greater signs of abnormal reaction upon return home', although, as Chapter 5 demonstrated, this assumption may have been misplaced: these men's anticipations of an early homecoming had its own negative mental repercussions.[12]

Around this time, features written by ex-POWs on the consequences of captivity began to appear in the press. Captain George Collie, who had escaped from a POW hospital in Paris in 1942, penned an article for *The Fortnightly* magazine on the 'Rip Van Winkle' effect. He explained how thousands of men captured at the fall of France had 'no conception of life in Britain to-day or of the changes in the outlook for the future', and that 'these blanks in the knowledge of events are a serious matter for the prisoner of war', serious enough for Collie to advise comprehensive psychological treatment for all POWs.[13] A few months later, the *British Medical Journal* published Major Philip Newman's article on 'The Prisoner-of-War Mentality'. As well as setting out Newman's thinking on a 'mental attitude' building up inside POWs, as discussed in Chapter 5, Newman also wrote about how this attitude would persist as 'release phenomena'. Newman characterised these phenomena as the psychological equivalent of 'Cassion's disease', more commonly known as 'the bends' or 'decompression sickness', where the body exhibits a variety of symptoms if insufficient time is taken in releasing it from

---

[9] TNA WO 32/10950, 'The Crookham Experimental Rehabilitation Scheme for Repatriated Prisoners of War', February 1944, pp. 2, 4.

[10] TNA WO 32/10950, A. T. M. Wilson, 'Report to the War Office on Psychological Aspects of the Rehabilitation of Repatriated Prisoners of War', February 1944, p. 2.

[11] WO 32/10950, 'The Crookham Experimental Rehabilitation Scheme', p. 4; Wessely and Jones, 'British Prisoners-of-War', 170.

[12] TNA WO 32/10757, 'Rehabilitation of Repatriated Prisoners of War. Minutes of a Meeting Chaired by Lieutenant-General Sir Alexander Hood', 16 September 1943.

[13] George F. Collie, 'Returned Prisoners of War: A Suggested Scheme for Rehabilitation', *The Fortnightly*, 153 (June 1943), 407–11.

high underwater pressure to a normal atmospheric environment. Similarly, after being freed from captivity and having returned home, an ex-POW would exhibit symptoms of restlessness, irritability and even dishonesty. The intensity of these symptoms would vary according to a man's temperament, the length of time he had spent in captivity and the gravity of his imprisoned conditions. Newman predicted these symptoms would pass in the 'great majority' of cases within six months to one year and stressed that these men should 'not be regarded as abnormal'. He also doubted whether they should be offered psychological treatment because 'it may carry with it a public acknowledgement of mental abnormality'. He did, however, recommend an ex-POW club should be established in every town with a population of more than 100,000.[14]

Possibly due as much to the vividness of their metaphors as the substance of their ideas, Collie and Newman's observations received a great deal of attention and were reproduced in the national press and within government circles.[15] Nine replies to Newman's ideas were published in the *British Medical Journal*. Some of these responses considered Newman had not gone far enough. Millais Culpin, a First World War medical officer with some expertise in shell-shock, recommended that extracts from Newman's piece should form a radio broadcast, but Culpin objected to Newman's rationale for not offering psychological treatment to POWs.[16] John Harkness, having been a POW in the Great War, thought that Newman had 'done the prisoners a real service' but had been 'too optimistic about early recovery.' Instead, he considered that 'the very large majority of our returned prisoners of war will be problems for their lifetime.' As a result, they should either be offered a period of 'reasonable financial security' or be assessed for 'disability' and granted a pension.[17] Others absolutely disagreed. In response to Harkness's letter, Major David Charters, writing from captivity where he had spent the past

---

[14] Newman, 'The Prisoner-of-War Mentality', 8–10. The term 'release phenomena' is taken from a subsequent letter; see P. H. Newman, 'Correspondence: Prisoner-of-War Mentality', *British Medical Journal*, 1, 4387 (3 February 1945), 163. See also Jones and Wessely, 'British Prisoners-of-War', 171.

[15] For references to Collie, see 'Returned Men's Rip Van Winkle Feeling', *News of the World*, 7 November 1943; WO 32/10757, 'Rehabilitation of Repatriated Prisoners of War. Minutes of a Meeting Chaired by Lieutenant-General Sir Alexander Hood', 16 September 1943. For references to Newman, see TNA ADM 1/18875, Memorandum from the Director of Tactical, Torpedo and Staff Duties Division, 17 June 1944. For references to both Collie and Newman, see Lieutenant Colonel Gluckstein's speech in the House of Commons, Hansard HC Deb., 2 March 1944, vol. 397 col. 1625–31.

[16] Millais Culpin, 'Correspondence: Returned Prisoners of War', *British Medical Journal*, 1, 4334 (29 January 1944), 158–9.

[17] John Harkness, 'Correspondence: The Prisoner-of-War Mentality', *British Medical Journal*, 1, 4346 (22 April 1944), 568.

three and a half years treating wounded and disabled POWs, maintained that 'if any group of prisoners-of-war was likely to present psychological problems it was the kind of group with which I had to deal', but he denied they would have a 'peculiar mentality' upon repatriation and urged the lay press not to 'discuss the majority as if they were psychopathological problems.'[18] Others took issue with Newman's recommendation on ex-POW clubs. Captain E. R. C. Walker, whose protected personnel status had entitled him to repatriation in 1943, doubted 'the wisdom of the Returned Prisoners-of-War Associations . . . I am sure that most returned prisoners will not want to perpetuate their experience, they will want to relegate it firmly to the past.'[19] Medical officer Major A. W. Vaughan Eley, who had been imprisoned in Italy, agreed: he considered the formation of POW clubs 'inadvisable'. The ex-POW 'will probably', wrote Eley, 'warmly welcome his best friend in his own home, but not, I feel, in any communal atmosphere.'[20]

Wilson took his findings from the First World War, and those that were available from the current war, and compiled them into a February 1944 report on the 'psychological aspects of the rehabilitation of repatriated prisoners of war'. In his report, Wilson estimated that unless action was taken, at least 20 per cent of ex-POWs would fail to readapt within six months and become psychiatrically ill in 'the usual sense of the word.'[21] He made a number of recommendations for the handling of repatriated POWs. The Executive Committee of the Army Council considered the need to provide returning prisoners with help. Some resisted the idea, either seeing POWs as undeserving of special treatment, or believing that special treatment simply was not necessary. Nevertheless, the adjutant general personally took the matter to the secretary of state for war who, the following day, obtained the Cabinet's agreement to a plan that would enable the army to bridge the gap between POW and civil life.[22]

---

[18] Major D. L. Charters, 'Correspondence: Prisoner-of-War Mentality', *British Medical Journal*, 1, 4383 (6 January 1945), 24. It is unclear how Charters received a copy of the *British Medical Journal* whilst in captivity because government advice prohibited the sending of newspapers and periodicals to POWs in enemy countries. Perhaps, because of his protected personnel status, Charters was able to receive journals relevant to his medical professional. On this government advice, see 'Communication with Prisoners of War and Civilians Interned in Europe (Leaflet P 2280E)', General Post Office, May 1943, in IWM 61/161/1, private papers of Warrant Officer H. L. Hurrell.

[19] Walker, 'Impressions of a Repatriated Medical Officer', 515.

[20] A. W. Vaughan Eley, 'Correspondence. The Prisoner-of-War Mentality', *British Medical Journal*, 1, 4341 (18 March 1944), 404.

[21] WO 32/10950, Wilson, 'Report to the War Office on Psychological Aspects of the Rehabilitation of Repatriated Prisoners of War', p. 1.

[22] LHC, Adam papers, 3/13, Adam, 'Narrative Covering Aspects of Work as Adjutant General, WWII', Chapter IX, Demobilisation and Resettlement.

As a result, the creation of twenty Civil Resettlement Units (CRUs) was set in train. These were residential units that ex-POWs from the army could attend after discharge, offering them a 'half-way house to Civvy Street'.[23]

When the bulk of POWs from Germany returned at the end of the war, each was given six weeks of repatriation leave. During this period, he had a full medical examination and was given the opportunity to volunteer to attend a CRU after his demobilisation.[24] The demobilisation scheme at the end of the war staggered men's release from the armed forces. Release groups were based on age and length of service, meaning the older the man and the greater his length of service, the lower his group and the sooner he would be released. Approximately 12,000 POWs were in groups one to seventeen and were first to be released from the armed forces. Their discharge took place as soon as their leave expired.[25] Dates at which subsequent groups were released were staggered. Thus, all other ex-POWs had to report to a special organisation: 45 Division. It was anticipated that the majority of them would be retrained and sent to fight in the war in the Far East.[26] During the summer months, more than 80,000 men passed through this special organisation.[27]

A large proportion of these ex-POWs, almost 20 per cent, was referred for interview by army psychiatrists and the outcomes of these meetings were collated by an adviser in psychiatry, Lieutenant Colonel R. F. Barbour.[28] The most maladjusted 800 of these men went to the ex-prisoners of war unit at the Southern Hospital in Dartford in Kent, led by Dr Maxwell Jones, who had previously pioneered group therapy

---

[23] Frank Beaumont, 'Rip Van Winkle', *Transatlantic*, 30 (1946), 46. This article was written by a group of social scientists. 'Frank Beaumont' was their pen name.

[24] TNA PIN 15/3444, 'Medical Examination of Repatriated Prisoners of War', letter from War Office to General Officers Commanding-in-Chief and General Officers Commanding, 21 December 1944; A. T. M Wilson, E. L. Trist, and Adam Curle, 'Transitional Communities: A Study of the Civil Resettlement of British Prisoners of War', in Guy E. Swanson et al. (eds.), *Readings in Social Psychology* (New York: Henry Holt and Company, 1952), p. 564.

[25] Adam Curle and E. L. Trist, 'Transitional Communities and Social Reconnection; a Follow-Up Study of the Civil Resettlement of British Prisoners of War. Part II', *Human Relations*, 1 (1947), fn *, 246; Allport, *Demobbed*, pp. 23–4.

[26] The army estimated that two-thirds of the 92,500 British POWs from the other ranks could be turned into 'efficient and co-operative soldiers' for the war in the Far East. On release groups, see TNA WO 165/129, Medical Diaries, AMD 11, January to December 1945, Minutes of the 31st Meeting of Command Psychiatrists, 2 June 1945. On army estimates, see TNA WO 32/10757, Record of a Meeting held at Hobart House on 3 June 1944 to discuss Questions Relating to the Sorting, Training and Subsequent Disposal of Return PW.

[27] TNA WO 32/10757, R. F. Barbour, 'Returned Prisoners of War from Germany', 16 October 1945.

[28] Ahrenfeldt, *Psychiatry in the British Army in the Second World War*, pp. 237–8.

treatment with servicemen at the London suburban Mill Hill Emergency Hospital. Smaller groups, also exhibiting acute symptoms, were treated elsewhere, including the Northfield Military Hospital in Birmingham, Kempston Barracks in Bedfordshire and the Larbert POW rehabilitation unit for neurosis in central Scotland.[29] Meanwhile, repatriated naval POWs showing serious symptoms were referred to the neuropsychiatric department at the Royal Naval Barracks in Chatham.[30]

Reallocation into the armed forces was one of two points when doctors and psychiatrists witnessed the adjustment difficulties of prisoners of war; the other was as former POWs left the army and returned to civilian life. Their social reintegration was primarily monitored through attendance at CRUs and a number of studies was written on ex-POWs' behaviour and the CRUs' achievements.

The findings of this chapter are largely based on these various articles and reports written by ex-POWs and psychiatrists, but caution does need to be exercised. It would be wrong to assume that the medical officers and psychiatrists' observations and diagnoses provide accurate portrayals of the attitudes of ex-prisoners of war. The findings that follow need to be considered against the prevailing socio-cultural biases and schools of thought of the time.[31] For example, for a majority of practitioners during the Second World War, personality or constitutional factors (such as genetic or biological) were considered more significant in causing psychiatric breakdown than 'war service' or degrees of stress.[32] It also needs to be borne in mind that many of those cited later in this chapter were psychoanalysts. Major Susan Davidson, at Northfield Military Hospital, trained as a psychoanalyst after the war, and Margaret Bavin, who worked

---

[29] On the Southern Hospital, see Maxwell Jones and J. M. Tanner, 'The Clinical Characteristics, Treatment, and Rehabilitation of Repatriated Prisoners of War with Neurosis', *Journal of Neurology and Psychiatry*, 11 (1943), 53–60. On the Northfield Military Hospital, see Susan Davidson, 'Notes on a Group of Ex-Prisoners of War', *Bulletin of the Menninger Clinic*, 10, 3 (1946), 90–100. On Kempston Barracks, see Major C. Lack, 'The Management of Convalescent Neurotics at the Neurosis Wing, 101 Military Convalescent Depot', *Journal of the Royal Army Medical Corps*, 86, 1 (1946), 32–4. On Larbert POW rehabilitation unit, see Gibbens, 'The Psychology of the Prisoner-of-War', p. 141. This hospital is named in Gibbens' obituary, 'Obituary. Professor Trevor Gibbens', *The Times* (8 November 1983).

[30] W. P. Mallison and W. Warren, 'Repatriation. A Psychiatric Study of 100 Naval Ex-Prisoners of War', *British Medical Journal*, 2, 4431 (8 December 1945), 798–801.

[31] See also Jones and Wessely's argument that diagnoses of mental illness amongst prisoners of war in the twentieth century were culturally determined ('British Prisoners-of-War', 163–83).

[32] Nafsika Thalassis, 'Soldiers in Psychiatric Therapy: The Case of Northfield Military Hospital 1942–1946', *Social History of Medicine*, 20, 2 (2007), 356. Joanna Bourke, *An Intimate History of Killing. Face-to-Face Killing in Twentieth-Century Warfare* (London: Granta Books, 1999), p. 248.

as a civil liaison officer in a CRU, became a member of the British Psychoanalytic Association.[33] Ernest Jones, one of the most influential people in the development of psychoanalysis in Britain, also included POWs in his general writings on psychology and war.[34] Others who worked with or published on returning POWs were either from the Tavistock Clinic or would later join the Tavistock Group.[35] The Clinic was formed in 1920. It used an eclectic mix of psychoanalytic approaches designed to help not the psychotic, but traumatised and neurotic children and adults of limited means.[36] Amongst those from the Tavistock Clinic were Lieutenant Wilson and Brigadier John Rawlings Rees, one of the highest-ranking psychiatrists in the British Army during the Second World War, who included a discussion of POWs in his more general work on war psychiatry.[37] The 'Tavistock Group' was a term coined by Lieutenant Colonel Eric Trist, who was a senior psychologist to the War Office. He, plus army psychiatrists Major Martin Doyle and Lieutenant Colonel Tom Main, who all published research into the efficacy of CRUs, later joined it. Similarly, army psychiatrist Lieutenant Colonel Alfred Torrie, who wrote on the social integration of POWs, became part of this group.[38]

During the war, these army psychiatrists made particular use of ideas and theories concerned with how individual behaviour is shaped by surrounding social relationships. For example, the group put much emphasis on social psychology.[39] Kleinian object-relations was also

[33] Pearl King, 'Activities of British Psychoanalysts during the Second World War and the Influence of Their Interdisciplinary Collaboration on the Development of Psychoanalysis in Great Britain', *International Review of Psychoanalysis*, 16 (1989), 22; Elizabeth R. Zetzel, 'List of Members of the Regional Association, Component and Affiliate Societies of the International Psycho-Analytical Association 1964–1965', *Bulletin of the International Psychoanalytic Association*, 45 (1964), 627–707.

[34] Sonu Shamdasani, 'Jones, (Alfred) Ernest (1879–1958)', Oxford Dictionary of National Biography (Oxford: Oxford University Press, 2004); online edn, September 2010, www.oxforddnb.com/view/article/34221, last accessed 13 September 2016. Jones started practising psychoanalysis as early as 1905 and founded the London Psycho-Analytical Society in 1913, which became the British Psycho-Analytical Society in 1919 (Shapira, *The War Inside*, p. 7).

[35] King, 'Activities of British Psychoanalysts during the Second World War', 16.

[36] Thalassis, 'Treating and Preventing Trauma', 57–8; The Tavistock and Portman NHS Trust, *Our History*, http://tavistockandportman.uk/sites/default/files/files/Our%20history_0.pdf, last accessed 16 November 2015.

[37] King, 'Activities of British Psychoanalysts during the Second World War', 20, 25.

[38] Frances Abraham, 'The Tavistock Group', in Morgen Witzel and Malcolm Warner (eds.), *The Oxford Handbook of Management Theorists* (Oxford: Oxford University Press, 2013), pp. 155–6; H. V. Dicks, *Fifty Years of the Tavistock Clinic* (London: Routledge and Kegan Paul, 1970), pp. 108, 139.

[39] 'Social psychology' can be defined as attempting 'to understand and explain how the thought, feeling, and behaviour of individuals are influenced by the actual, imagined, or implied presence of others' (G. W. Allport, 'The Historical Background of Social

influential and dynamic approaches to psychiatry were also favoured.[40] This context needs to be considered when reading some of these psychiatrists' analyses of the problems POWs were facing. Their observations should be considered as reflecting certain psychological discourses and modes of thought, rather than as providing an accurate testimony to the realities of war.[41]

Equally, the observations of some of the medical officer ex-POWs listed here should not be assumed to be representative simply because these men had been through captivity. The example of Newman, whose initial article drew attention to the needs of repatriated prisoners of war, is a fitting one. Newman's escape from captivity had involved being buried for fifty-six hours underneath the floorboards of one of the huts in his camp at Rouen, whilst the rest of the camp was being moved back to Germany. When he was confident they had left, he resurfaced and walked to freedom across France, the Pyrenees, Spain and into Gibraltar, arriving home in May 1942.[42] With such a prelude to his release, it is not surprising he adopted the metaphor of 'Cassion's disease' to describe returned POWs' experiences.

Difficulties of Re-adjustment

The studies, reports and articles written on ex-POWs suggest three factors were crucial to how they readjusted to freedom. First, attention was drawn to the extent to which POWs had changed in order to adapt to

Psychology', in Gardner Lindzey and Elliot Aronson (eds.), *Handbook of Social Psychology. Vol. I, Theory and Method.* New York: Random House, 1985, p. 3).

[40] One theory behind Kleinian object-relations is that the interactions an infant has with its main object, the mother (or partial objects of the mother – her breast), and other family members, provide a blueprint for all future relationships. See King, 'Activities of British Psychoanalysts during the Second World War', 19; Abraham, 'The Tavistock Group', p. 157; David E. Scharff, 'Object Relations Theory (General)', in Ross M. Skelton (ed.), *The Edinburgh International Encyclopaedia of Psychoanalysis* (Edinburgh: Edinburgh University Press, 2006), p. 334; Shapira, *The War Inside*, p. 93. Dynamic approaches to psychiatry used psychological exploration and self-understanding for therapeutic gain (Richard B. Corradi, 'Psychodynamic Psychotherapy: A Core Conceptual Model and Its Application', The *Journal of the American Academy of Psychoanalysis and Dynamic Psychiatry*, 34, 1 (2006), 93; King, 'Activities of British Psychoanalysts during the Second World War', 19–20).

[41] Shapira criticises the scholarship on the emotions of civilians on the British home front in the Second World War for failing to take into consideration how psychological experts conceptualised and shaped emotions (*The War Inside*, pp. 25–6). King suggests the theories these psychiatrists adopted were the most suitable ('Activities of British Psychoanalysts during the Second World War', 19).

[42] For details of Newman's journey, see Newman, *Safer than a Known Way*, pp. 76–97; IWM Sound Archive 16714/9, oral history with Richard Hutchinson Forbes, undated recording.

and cope with their captive environments, transformations that had, as a result, left them 'uprooted' from their old society.[43] As discussed in Chapter 2, prisoners were aware of how they had altered during captivity: they envisaged, at a humorous level, exhibiting some of their POW mannerisms after returning home. Psychiatrists took a more sober view. They focussed specifically on prisoners' attitude towards authority. In POW camps, it was thought that morale had been sustained by a negative attitude to military authority, where disrespect and sabotage against authority had been actively encouraged, and prisoners had learnt to silently hate authority figures. After repatriation, all ex-POWs would have a tendency to show these phenomena.[44] Thus, the resentment, which had previously been directed towards their enemy, would be transferred to any persons or organisations that seemed to have contributed to their misfortune.[45] Psychiatrists may have put too much emphasis on this negative attitude. As the findings of Chapter 2 showed, British POWs did not universally hate their German captors. Psychiatrists' assumptions may be an illustration of their diagnoses being made with administrative repercussions in mind: it would have been difficult for the UK government to acknowledge that, at an individual level, there could be understanding or cooperation between the warring sides.

Secondly, these reports discussed POWs struggling to come to terms with how much home had changed in their absence. This was, in part, due to the fantasy lives they had led whilst behind barbed wire. Some men had developed overly romanticised pictures of home which contrasted distinctly from the reality that greeted them. As a result, disillusionment set in.[46] Chapter 4 showed how the moment of reunion had been anticipated

---

[43] Adam Curle, 'Transitional Communities and Social Reconnection', in Charles Zwingmann and Maria Pfister-Ammende (eds.), *Uprooting and After* ... (New York: Springer-Verlag, 1973), p. 235. See also WO 32/10950, Wilson, 'Report to the War Office on Psychological Aspects of the Rehabilitation of Repatriated Prisoners of War', p. 1.

[44] Ernest Jones, 'Psychology and War Conditions', *Psychoanalytic Quarterly*, 14, 1 (1945), 13; WO 32/10950, Wilson, 'Report to the War Office on Psychological Aspects of the Rehabilitation of Repatriated Prisoners of War', pp. 2–4; Newman, 'Correspondence: Prisoner-of-War Mentality', 163; RAMC 466/49, Conference of Military Psychiatrists. Appendix A, Captain Mustardé, 'Adjustment and Mal-adjustment within the Camp', 7–8 October 1944.

[45] Major G. C. Pether, 'The Returned Prisoner-of-War', *The Lancet*, 245, 6394 (5 May 1945), 572. For similar analysis, see Francis A. E. Crew, *The Army Medical Services. Administration*, vol. II (London: HMSO, 1955), p. 279.

[46] Wilson, Doyle and Kelnar, 'Group Techniques in a Transitional Community', 738; Brigadier L. Bootle-Wilbraham, 'Civil Resettlement of Ex-Prisoners of War', *Mental Health*, 6, 2 (1946), 39–40; Major W. H. Whiles, 'Neurosis among Repatriated Prisoners of War', *British Medical Journal*, 2, 4428 (17 November 1945), 697; WO 32/10950, Wilson, 'Report to the War Office on Psychological Aspects of the Rehabilitation

and imagined for many years. These plans and imaginings were common enough for army psychiatrists to give them a name: the 'garden gate phantasy'. Yet, when the time came for these plans to be realised, the scenario was not played out as these men had, for so long, expected: repatriated prisoners expressed their irritation that their wives, sweethearts or friends had met them at the train station. Such was the resentment that one repatriate, who prepared some points of advice for the relatives of prisoners of war, suggested they 'let him meet you at home. As a rule, that's where he's always imagined you.'[47]

The extent to which the home situation had changed during the course of a man's captivity left former prisoners feeling 'out of the picture', as Ernest Jones described it – the 'Rip Van Winkle' effect Collie had predicted.[48] When the group of ex-POWs who were admitted to Northfield Military Hospital was asked about the difficulties that brought them there, they referred to their inability to fit into the country and of finding a topic of mutual interest: 'the only thing they knew anything about was P.O.W. life and of this they had no desire to speak.'[49] Army psychiatrist Major W. H. Whiles also reported that the ex-prisoner of war was shy of making a 'fool' of himself, such as asking for items in shops that were no longer available.[50] Margaret Bavin singled out women as a 'particular source of uncertainty and bewilderment'. Women's increased independence was considered to 'constitute a threat to [ex-POWs'] manhood and aroused a fear that their place in the family was no longer necessary.' Bavin also considered that single men felt 'utterly rejected' on finding that their younger brothers and sisters had grown up in their absence and usurped their role.[51] Married fathers had a different problem. When Captain Mustardé, a 'posthumous parent', finally met his two-year-old child, he warned that it was 'not a question of the child getting used to the father as most people foolishly imagine, but of the father getting used to the child.'[52] Bavin proposed this was because 'the

of Repatriated Prisoners of War', p. 2. See also Newman, 'Correspondence: Prisoner-of-War Mentality', 163.

[47] TNA WO 32/10757, Directorate of Army Psychiatry. Technical Memorandum No. 13. The Prisoner of War Comes Home. Notes Prepared for the Information of Army Psychiatrists, prepared by DAP, May 1944.

[48] Adam Curle, 'Transitional Communities and Social Re-connection; a Follow-Up Study of the Civil Resettlement of British Prisoners of War. Part I', *Human Relations*, 1 (1947), 50; Jones, 'Psychology and War Conditions', 13.

[49] Davidson, 'Notes on a Group of Ex-Prisoners of War', 93.

[50] Whiles, 'Neurosis among Repatriated Prisoners of War', 697.

[51] Margaret G. Bavin, 'A Contribution Towards the Understanding of the Repatriated Prisoner of War', *British Journal of Psychiatric Social Work*, 1 (1947), 32, 34.

[52] RAMC 466/49, Conference of Military Psychiatrists. Appendix A, Captain Mustardé, 'Adjustment and Mal-adjustment within the Camp', 7–8 October 1944.

demands of the young and hardly known child conflict[ed] with the father's infantile need to get all the attention.'[53]

Finally, the capacity of the family at home to understand the problems of a POW was deemed of 'outstanding importance'.[54] Wilson considered this so paramount that it was 'necessary to pay as much attention to the education and preparation of the home community as it was to the returning service men.'[55] He and Lieutenant Colonel Eric Trist, along with social anthropologist Major Adam Curle, described resettlement as a two-way process, calling for emotional readjustment amongst all members of the re-formed family and larger community.[56] This onus on those at home may be as indicative of Trist and Wilson's interest in social psychology as of the way POWs reacted to their reception.[57] Assessments may also have been infused with prevalent gender assumptions of the time: that it was the responsibility and duty of women to accommodate and solve the problems of the returning servicemen.[58] Barbour also noted how 'some families fussed, others left well alone, some wives understood an apparent disinterestedness while others suggested that it was due to affections being misplaced.' He concluded that 'previous personality and adaptability of the people at home are probably the most important factors in deciding whether a man will settle quickly or slowly.'[59] Unsurprisingly, therefore, marital disharmony greatly complicated a POW's readjustment.[60] In a study of 100 repatriates who were treated in a psychiatric unit in 1944, marital disharmony was considered

---

[53] Bavin, 'A Contribution Towards the Understanding of the Repatriated Prisoner of War', 33.

[54] RAMC 466/49, Conference of Military Psychiatrists, A. T. M. Wilson, 'Problems of Repatriated Prisoners of War', 7–8 October 1944.

[55] TNA FO 1013/177, A. T. M. Wilson 'Some Problems of Repatriation and Resettlement of German Prisoners of War', September 1947.

[56] Wilson, Trist, and Curle, 'Transitional Communities: A Study of the Civil Resettlement of British Prisoners of War', p. 561.

[57] On Wilson's interest in social psychology and Kurt Lewin, one of its founders, see Dicks, *Fifty Years of the Tavistock Clinic*, p. 103. On Trist's interest in the work of Kurt Lewin, see King, 'Activities of British Psychoanalysts during the Second World War', 21, 23.

[58] This attitude is set out in the memoirs of the adjutant general. He detailed how the war had changed both the serviceman and his wife during their separation, setting out how his wife had become the wage earner, gained independence and acquired a sense of freedom, but follows this with the words: 'Often she could not realise what he had been through' (LHC, Adam papers, 3/13, Adam, 'Narrative Covering Aspects of Work as Adjutant General, WWII', Chapter XI, Demobilisation and Resettlement). For evidence of similar attitudes in the United States and Australia, see Susan Hartmann, 'Prescriptions for Penelope: Literature on Women's Obligations to Returning World War II Veterans', *Women's Studies*, 5 (1978), 223–39; Stephen Garton, *The Cost of War. Australians Return* (Melbourne: Oxford University Press, 1996), p. 177.

[59] TNA WO 32/10757, R. F. Barbour, 'Interim Report on Returned Prisoners of War', 29 August 1945.

[60] TNA WO 32/11125, 'Repatriation of Canadian POW', 1 July 1944, 5.

the main precipitating factor of neurosis in twenty-four men.[61] These men, it seems, were not just the unlucky few. Out of 1,200 repatriates interviewed in 1943, almost 4 per cent were in the process of starting divorce proceedings and a further 1.6 per cent reported marital problems. If this is compared to a national divorce rate in England, which peaked in the post-war years at 13.6 per 10,000 in 1947, divorces amongst ex-POWs were some thirty times higher.[62]

Psychiatrists and ex-POWs also criticised relatives for failing to recognise some of the most profound changes POWs had gone through. They noted how some prisoners believed captivity had promoted positive psychological development and were, as a result, more mature, wise, considerate and self-reliant.[63] Perhaps these changes had been fostered through how POWs learnt to live with scarce resources or en masse, as discussed in Chapters 2 and 3. One difficulty now faced by liberated POWs was how to use this maturity in a society they felt they had outgrown. They searched for a sanction of the values of their prison-camp experience and, when this sanction was not forthcoming, 'the consequent isolation was as painful as the isolation of captivity.'[64] Mustardé explained to military psychiatrists, in 1944, of how captivity had forced POWs to rebuild their philosophy of life up 'from the very foundations', but ex-prisoners of war were dismayed to find, on their return, friends and relatives much the same as they had left them, 'carrying on in the same old way and with the same old muddles and squabbles in evidence.' Despite change having taken place, he added, 'the repatriate sees plainly the old faults that are still there, and feels that those at home might have done a little better in their attempt to bring about the brave new world for which he was fighting, and for which he feels he has given up so much.'[65]

These challenges did not immediately manifest themselves. Wilson had observed that it took between two and four weeks after returning home for

---

[61] Lieutenant Colonel Alfred Torrie, 'The Return of Odysseus. The Problem of Marital Infidelity for the Repatriate', *British Medical Journal*, 2, 4414 (11 August 1945), 192. See also Whiles, 'Neurosis among Repatriated Prisoners of War', 698.

[62] WO 32/10950, Wilson, 'Report to the War Office on Psychological Aspects of the Rehabilitation of Repatriated Prisoners of War', p. 9; Gail Braybon and Penny Summerfield, *Out of the Cage. Women's Experiences in the Two World Wars* (London: Pandora, 1987), p. 272.

[63] T. H. Hawes, 'Letters to the Editor. Returned Prisoners-of-War', *The Lancet*, 245, 6351 (19 May 1945), 643; Bavin, 'A Contribution Towards the Understanding of the Repatriated Prisoner of War', 35.

[64] Wilson, Trist and Curle, 'Transitional Communities: A Study of the Civil Resettlement of British Prisoners of War', p. 561.

[65] RAMC 466/49, Conference of Military Psychiatrists. Appendix A, Captain Mustardé, 'Adjustment and Mal-adjustment within the Camp', 7–8 October 1944.

them to become apparent: the initial excitement of being back at home masked any difficulties. He described symptoms of reintegration beginning to show when POWs entered a 'curious sense of flatness'.[66] These symptoms included a difficulty in concentrating; impatience and irritability, and even dishonesty; fear of enclosed spaces, especially when confined amongst a large crowd; cynicism; self-consciousness; dislike of company; embarrassment in society; rebellious views and a quick and violent temper.[67] According to Wilson, these were 'basic psychological difficulties related to "resocialisation"', indicating the 'deeper conflict going on between [the POW's] need for security and affectionate relationships, and his dread of further rejection by the world from which he was forcibly separated.'[68]

These emotional problems were then compounded by practical ones, which became apparent only weeks after POWs returned home. Quasi-demotion was one such problem, acutely felt by those who had either practised their careers in captivity or who were regular or territorial servicemen. Medical officer Cochrane, for example, described how he discovered, upon his return home, that the experience he had gained whilst in captivity was not recognised, such that he went from working as a physician in POW camps to being the 'dog's body' of a general hospital. He had also missed out on all chances of promotion, courted a risk of psychological problems and lost a vast amount of leave.[69] The same regressive journey was experienced amongst those who remained in the armed forces. POWs were allowed to retain their acting ranks for the duration of their captivity, but were then demoted on their return even if, at the time of capture, they had been just a few days away from becoming substantive (when their acting rank would have been made permanent). This policy of reversion was seen to accentuate 'mental stress', and was particularly resented by POWs who had escaped: they had been rewarded for their initiative and courage with a demotion.[70]

---

[66] A. T. M. Wilson, 'The Serviceman Comes Home', *Pilot Papers*, 1, 2 (1946), 13; TNA LAB 12/352, Minutes of a Meeting with Regional Controllers, Ministry of Labour and National Service, Civil Resettlement Planning Headquarters, 10 May 1945.

[67] Newman, 'The Prisoner-of-War Mentality', 9; Mallison and Warren, 'Repatriation. A Psychiatric Study of 100 Naval Ex-Prisoners of War', 798–9; Lack, 'The Management of Convalescent Neurotics at the Neurosis Wing, 101 Military Convalescent Depot', 34.

[68] Wilson, Doyle and Kelnar, 'Group Techniques in a Transitional Community', 737–8.

[69] Cochrane, 'The Medical Officer as Prisoner in Germany', 412.

[70] Several escaped NCOs also stated that those who were still in enemy hands, and aware that 'escape means reversion', had been discouraged from making an escape attempt by this policy (TNA WO 32/10757, Extract from 'Report on Interviews with Escaped and Repatriated Ps of W', 8 June 1944).

Reallocation was a more common experience, and an equally problematic one. It was assumed by officials that prisoners of war would want to return to the armed forces after their release, and 'would resent the thought that they are no longer fit to help with the war just because they have been prisoners of war', but such an assessment appears to have been at odds with POWs' own aspirations.[71] The War Office's advisory panel, which included repatriated POWs, one of whom was Newman, noted that it was believed in stalags 'almost to a man, that demobilisation or discharge would follow return to this country.' Once these men became aware that their return would more likely be followed by reallocation, the panel feared mass absenteeism might follow.[72] Back at home, similar sentiments prevailed. Those who had been repatriated in 1943 felt so strongly about being returned to service that they wrote to their fellow captives advising them to stay put until the war was over.[73] Half of the repatriates interviewed at Crookham in 1944 believed the handling of returned POWs could be improved by allowing them to be discharged.[74] At the beginning of 1945, Major R. A. C. Radcliffe noted how the idea of serving overseas again was 'not popular' amongst those held in units at 45 Division.[75] Of those retained for Corps training in the summer of 1945, it was concluded that they 'barely faced up to' the prospect of further overseas services: 'they all presume that "something will happen" before their turn comes.'[76]

This attitude is also evidenced amongst those who signed up to stay at a CRU. Attendance at a unit was purely on a voluntary basis. The opportunity for an ex-POW to choose whether to participate in the programme was considered an important principle in the running of CRUs, given the units were supposed to provide returned prisoners with the opportunity to experiment with their freedom.[77] RAF ex-

[71] TNA WO 32/10757, Template Letter from the Director of the Prisoner of War Department, War Office, to the Next-of-Kin of POWs repatriated in May 1944, 27 May 1944. One publication, 'Instructions on How to Treat Prisoners of War', also pointed out that POWs were aggrieved to think there might no longer be a part for them in the war. Instead, each would 'want to show that, given knowledge of weapons, he can be as good a man as you and I – and better' (TNA WO 32/10757, Refresher Training for Repatriated Prisoners of War, War Office, April 1945).

[72] TNA WO 32/10757, 'Advisory Panel on the Problems of the Repatriated', minutes, 4 March 1944, p. 5.

[73] WO 32/10950, 'Extracts from a Questionnaire Given to 200 RAMC and 200 Stretcher Bearer Repatriated Prisoners of War', 21 December 1943.

[74] WO 32/10950, 'The Crookham Experimental Rehabilitation Scheme', p. 4.

[75] TNA WO 32/11125, R. A. C. Radcliffe, 'Welfare and Morale of Returned Prisoners of War', Visit to Units of 45 Division, 5–9 January 1945.

[76] WO 32/10757, R. F. Barbour, 'Interim Report on Returned Prisoners of War', 29 August 1945.

[77] Curle, 'Transitional Communities and Social Reconnection', p. 237.

POWs were reported as volunteering 'man after man' for a resettlement course because they erroneously assumed that it offered them a 'short cut to release' from service.[78] These attitudes reflected soldiers' aspirations more generally: their most important war aim, according to military historian David French, was to return home to their families.[79] They also echo the findings in Chapter 4, that British POWs looked forward to their liberation, not so that they could resume their fighting roles, but so they could return to their loved ones.

The return to military duty and subsequent barrack life tipped some men from dissatisfaction to despair. Surgeon Lieutenant Commanders W. P. Mallison and W. Warren noted in their psychiatric study of 100 naval ex-prisoners of war that 'returning to duty, with its unwelcome separation from home, the inevitable mixing with a crowd of strangers, and the obligation to conform to an impersonal code of behaviour, is an ordeal for the repatriated prisoner.'[80] Of those who attended the ex-prisoners of war unit at the Southern Hospital in Dartford, nothing was said to cause greater symptoms of anxiety amongst the repatriates, which sometimes amounted to 'panic', than the idea that they would be returned to army service.[81] Of the forty-seven cases at the Larbert POW rehabilitation unit, the 'most obvious characteristic' was the group's 'intolerance of army life.' These men stated 'quite frankly that they had done their duty, had no further duty to the nation, wanted to go home and would not improve anywhere else.'[82] The reintegration problems of seven POWs who were admitted to Northfield Military Hospital were also precipitated by a return to army life. They expected to be demobilised upon repatriation and their first thought was to get on with something 'useful'. Instead, they were sent to a Selection and Training Battalion, whose environment reminded them of POW camps. Here they had received instructions from an NCO who had far less experience than the ex-prisoners themselves, were shown Japanese atrocity films and were forced to do physical training before many had been medically examined. The men contrasted this treatment to the 'considerable democratic freedom' they had enjoyed in

---

[78] TNA LAB 12/352, letter from Ministry of Labour and National Service Northern Regional Office, 8 June 1945.

[79] French, *Raising Churchill's Army*, p. 134. See also Shephard, *A War of Nerves*, p. 174. Adrian Gilbert also comes to the conclusion that 'Most former POWs did not make enthusiastic soldiers' (*POW*, p. 319).

[80] Mallison and Warren, 'Repatriation. A Psychiatric Study of 100 Naval Ex-Prisoners of War', 799.

[81] Jones and Tanner, 'The Clinical Characteristics, Treatment, and Rehabilitation of Repatriated Prisoners of War with Neurosis', 59.

[82] Gibbens, 'The Psychology of the Prisoner-of-War', p. 141; 'Obituary. Professor Trevor Gibbens', *The Times* (8 November 1983).

POW camps where, on their committee of representatives, a private had as many rights as a warrant officer, and anyone who failed to come up to the required standard could be voted out. Instead, back in army life, 'they were no longer allowed to think for themselves.'[83]

Such were some of the emotional and practical problems that beset ex-prisoners of war returning to the United Kingdom.[84] In terms of how many were affected by these problems, estimates vary. The experimental rehabilitation scheme at Crookham had found that at least 60 per cent of ex-prisoners were experiencing 'minor psychological disturbances.'[85] POWs who returned at the end of the war in Europe, however, despite the length of time they had spent in captivity, were actually easier to handle than had been anticipated from the behaviour of escapees and repatriates, and there were also fewer disciplinary problems amongst them than had been expected.[86] Out of them, Wilson thought that 'serious difficulty arose' in one-third of families, which would usually diminish after three to nine months.[87] According to Brigadier John Rawlings Rees, the majority of men experienced 'some difficulty' upon their return home, taking approximately six months before they again settled down, whilst one-fifth had a 'marked difficulty' in reintegrating into army or home life.[88] As discussed earlier, some ex-POWs were sent for hospital treatment, but these were far fewer in number. Of those POWs who were repatriated or had escaped, anything from between 2 per cent and 8 per cent required hospital treatment on account of neurosis.[89]

---

[83] Davidson, 'Notes on a Group of Ex-Prisoners of War', 90–100.

[84] Ex-POWs were beset by other practical problems. According to Maxwell Jones, housing difficulties were a 'major cause of trouble in nearly 50 per cent of cases'. Although the housing shortage affected everyone, eating and sleeping in a single room was thought to have a greater demoralising effect upon a POW than others (*Social Psychiatry. A Study of Therapeutic Communities*. London: Tavistock Publications, 1952, p. 20; The Viscount Tarbat, 'The Problem of Resettlement', *The Clarion. The Official Organ of the Returned British Prisoners of War Association*, 2 (1946), unpaginated).

[85] WO 32/10950, 'The Crookham Experimental Rehabilitation Scheme', p. 4.

[86] WO 32/10757, R. F. Barbour, 'Interim Report on Returned Prisoners of War', 29 August 1945. Barbour does not explain this discrepancy. Perhaps it reflects just how unsettled captivity had been for protected personnel, always expecting their return home. Repatriates and escapees also returned to Britain during the war in Europe and many had to be 'reallocated', which, as explained, was problematic for some, whereas soon after the majority returned home, the Second World War ended. The sheer numbers of those who returned at the end of the war in Europe might also have meant they were able to support each other, or that certain behaviours would not have stood out as much to psychiatrists as they did when exhibited within the small groups of escapees or repatriates.

[87] Wilson, 'The Serviceman Comes Home', 13–14.

[88] J. R. Rees, *The Shaping of Psychiatry by War* (New York: W. W. Norton, 1945), p. 102.

[89] TNA WO 32/10757, Letter from Lieutenant-General Alex Hood, Director General of Army Medical Services, to the Director General of Emergency Medical Services, Ministry of Health, 17 October 1944.

Of those who had returned to 45 Division by August 1945, 2 per cent were sent to hospital on psychotic or neurotic grounds.[90]

Not all ex-POWs were considered equally liable to suffer from adjustment difficulties. Regular soldiers were seen to be disproportionately represented amongst those suffering neurotic breakdown: according to Gibbens, they accounted for 30 per cent of cases. As was pointed out in Chapter 5, these men were deemed to have adapted well to captivity, through their enthusiasm for practising all types of resistance to authority. This, however, had the unwanted effect of irreparably shattering their belief in all external forms of authority. These men also had to contend with the prospect of several more years of armed service, making re-adjustment all the more difficult.[91] Another factor thought to make certain ex-prisoners more likely to suffer was that of predisposition to mental illness. Six studies emphasised this was a crucial contributory factor in the development of any post-captivity neurotic condition.[92] Finally, emotional problems were thought to be disproportionately severe in men who had been prisoners for more than eighteen months; two to three years of absence was said to have produced the largest group of difficulties.[93]

These last two points, attributing an ex-POW's problems to predisposition and absence from home, fitted in with prevailing psychiatric thinking at the time. In the Second World War, the term *predisposition* did not necessarily imply a biological approach to mental illness, as it had in the First World War, but rather the cause of the breakdown lay in the patient's past, rooted in their personality or intelligence, and whilst psychiatrists tended to agree intelligence was genetically determined, many

---

[90] TNA WO 32/10757, R. F. Barbour, 'Returned Prisoners of War from Germany', 16 October 1945.

[91] Gibbens, 'The Psychology of the Prisoner-of-War', pp. 74, 140. Cochrane also argued that those 'who best adapted to imprisonment found the greatest difficulty in readapting in England' ('Notes on the Psychology of Prisoners of War', 282).

[92] Manfred Jeffrey and E. J. G. Bradford, 'Neurosis in Escaped Prisoners of War', *British Journal of Medical Psychology*, 20, 4 (1945–6), 430; Whiles, 'Neurosis among Repatriated Prisoners of War', 697; Mallison and Warren, 'Repatriation. A Psychiatric Study of 100 Naval Ex-Prisoners of War', 801; Gibbens, 'The Psychology of the Prisoner-of-War', p. 138; WO 32/10757, R. F. Barbour, 'Interim Report on Returned Prisoners of War', 29 August 1945; WO 32/10950, 'The Crookham Experimental Rehabilitation Scheme', p. 3. See also TNA WO 32/10757, Directorate of Army Psychiatry. Technical Memorandum No. 13. The Prisoner of War Comes Home. Notes Prepared for the Information of Army Psychiatrists, prepared by DAP, May 1944. Jones and Wessely conclude in their research that 'psychiatric disorders found in POWs were explained in terms of a pre-conflict predisposition to, or a history of, mental illness' ('British Prisoners-of-War', 163).

[93] WO 32/10950, Wilson, 'Report to the War Office on Psychological Aspects of the Rehabilitation of Repatriated Prisoners of War', p. 1; Rees, *The Shaping of Psychiatry by War*, p. 102.

considered personalities were formed according to childhood influences.[94] A focus on a serviceman's length of absence from home, meanwhile, was consistent with object-relations psychiatry, in that his problems were primarily attributed to his inability to interact with family members over a long period of time, and not to what he was doing during that time.

The implication of both these conclusions was that the broader experience of captivity had little to do with the problems ex-POWs were facing. This also had the additional consequence of circumventing the issue of captivity in any pension payments. This was something to which the Ministries of Pensions and Labour were both attuned: they both voiced their opposition to segregating and separating ex-POWs from other servicemen in terms of their resettlement provision.[95] Perhaps it was also with these potential economic repercussions in mind that there was almost universal agreement amongst these army psychiatrists that the basic problems POWs faced were different only in the degree, rather than in kind, from those facing all repatriates: according to historian Joanna Bourke, 'military psychiatrists made their diagnoses with economic and administrative repercussions firmly in mind.'[96] Whatever the reason, the role captivity had played as the fundamental cause of ex-POWs' maladjustment was ambiguous. Ambiguity is also evident in the language used in this debate.

The 'Right' Vocabulary and Terminology

Throughout this literature, there is an unwavering assertion that repatriated prisoners of war should not be regarded as psychiatric cases. Yet the language used to describe what, exactly, these men were experiencing

---

[94] Thalassis, 'Treating and Preventing Trauma', pp. 158–9. For predisposition in the First World War, see Ellenberger, *The Discovery of the Unconscious*, p. 168; Reid, *Broken Men*, pp. 22–3.

[95] TNA AIR 49/388, Record of Conference held at the Ministry of Pensions to discuss the Rehabilitation and Resettlement of Repatriated Prisoners of War, 20 June 1944.

[96] Bourke, *An Intimate History of Killing*, p. 245; Garton also discusses the link between the conceptualisation of returning Far East Australian POWs' psychological problems and the provision of special benefits for them, Garton, *The Cost of War*, pp. 219–20. On problems POWs faced being different only in degree, rather than in kind, to those facing all repatriates, see Bootle-Wilbraham, 'Civil Resettlement of Ex-Prisoners of War', 39; Jones and Tanner, 'The Clinical Characteristics, Treatment, and Rehabilitation of Repatriated Prisoners of War with Neurosis', 59; WO 32/10950, Wilson, 'Report to the War Office on Psychological Aspects of the Rehabilitation of Repatriated Prisoners of War', p. 3; WO 32/10757, R. F. Barbour, 'Interim Report on Returned Prisoners of War', 29 August 1945; TNA WO 165/129, Medical Diaries, AMD 11, January to December 1944, Minutes of a Conference of War Office Selection Board Psychiatrists, 23 April 1944.

is striking for both its precision and its vagueness. Wilson insisted that 'these repatriated prisoners of war are not psychiatric cases', but, instead, they were experiencing problems 'of a special type'.[97] Rees said they needed 'careful understanding' and Whiles called for a 'special approach' to avoid their symptoms from becoming worse.[98] In Barbour's words, these men experienced 'a social maladjustment and not a mental state'.[99] The secretary of state for war called the prisoner of wars' 'disability' a 'psychological one of a peculiar kind'.[100] For Newman, 'release phenomena' were a 'normal response of a normal man to release from an abnormal external environment.'[101] In the RAF, meanwhile, it was concluded both that captivity had 'left deep impressions on [POWs'] mental make-up' and that it was necessary to use the word 'resettlement' rather than 'rehabilitation' to describe prisoners' return, because the latter was 'often associated with a medical history and it is necessary at all costs to avoid giving prisoners of war the impression . . . that they are anything but normal'.[102] These descriptions are precise in avoiding certain words, but the adjectives used are inherently vague: 'special', 'peculiar', but still 'normal'. They echo a point historians Christina Twomey and Stephen Garton make in relation to the return of Australian POWs from the Far East, that these men were caught up in a 'conflict between the normal and the exceptional'.[103]

This ambiguous language of psychiatrists, officials and politicians appears to have affected how ex-POWs themselves named their experiences. Whilst the voices of these men in the immediate post-war period are hard to find, one place where they were expressed is in *The Clarion*. A number of local and national ex-POW associations appeared towards the end of the war and in the post-war years. One of the largest was the Returned British Prisoners of War Association (RBPOWA), primarily created in order to provide practical assistance in their rehabilitation.[104]

---

[97] RAMC 466/49, Conference of Military Psychiatrists, A. T. M. Wilson, 'Problems of Repatriated Prisoners of War', 7–8 October 1944.

[98] Rees, *The Shaping of Psychiatry by War*, p. 146; Whiles, 'Neurosis among Repatriated Prisoners of War', 698.

[99] WO 32/10757, R. F. Barbour, 'Interim Report on Returned Prisoners of War', 29 August 1945.

[100] WO 32/10757, Secret Working Paper (44) 456, War Cabinet, 'Rehabilitation of Returned Prisoners of War', Memorandum by the Secretary of State for War, 22 August 1944.

[101] Newman, 'Correspondence: Prisoner-of-War Mentality', 163.

[102] TNA AIR 49/388, RAF POW Resettlement Centres: Reorientation Training, 30 April 1945; TNA AIR 49/388, The Resettlement Training of Returned RAF Prisoners of War, 30 January 1945.

[103] Twomey, 'Emaciation or Emasculation', 302; Garton, *The Cost of War*, pp. 209, 219.

[104] For a more detailed discussion of the work of the RBPOWA, see Clare Makepeace, 'For "ALL Who Were Captured"? The Evolution of National Ex-Prisoner of War

The Clarion was the RBPOWA's newsletter, to which ex-POWs were encouraged to contribute. Charles Chapman, who had been held at Stalag VIIIB (Lamsdorf) and was the publications manager for the RBPOWA, wrote one article in the autumn 1946 issue, in which he urged readers to see a recently released POW film, *The Captive Heart*. Chapman drew upon the secretary of state's description to explain why: 'seeing this film may help some people to realise that many ex-prisoners-of-war still have their problems. Peculiar problems.'[105] In another article, Chapman demanded that returned prisoners of war 'having difficulty in adjusting themselves to the normalities of civilian life must be treated as individuals, with problems, social, physical and psychological, peculiar to themselves.'[106] In a subsequent edition, Brigadier J. G. Smyth, who was on the executive committee of the Association and a vociferous advocate for the needs of ex-POWs, wrote equally vaguely of how 'these men need help and understanding of a particular nature.'[107]

This ambiguous phrasing was no accident. Getting the terminology and vocabulary 'right' was deemed by the deputy adjutant general to have such an important influence on ex-POWs' attitudes that educating the staff of training units in the correct language was 'a matter of the first importance which must be laid down as a disciplinary instruction', although, again, it should be noted that using the 'right' language would also have been important for averting demands for pension payments.[108] He ordered that the words 'mental rehabilitation' should be avoided: 'resettlement training' was the preferred generic term to describe the treatment given to all repatriates, whilst 'reorientation' or 'readjustment' would be used when treatment was aimed at 'a new or improved outlook (as distinct from purely military or physical reconditioning)'.[109]

It was not just the labelling of this mental state that involved treading a delicate line, but also public pronouncements on its nature. When Lieutenant Chapel, an imprisoned medical officer who had been

Associations in Britain after the Second World War', *Journal of War and Culture Studies*, 7, 3 (August 2014), 255–8.

[105] Charles Chapman, 'Come to Think of It', *The Clarion. The Official Organ of the Returned British Prisoners of War Association*, 1 (1946), unpaginated.

[106] C. E. Chapman, 'More about Resettlement', *The Clarion. The Official Organ of the Returned British Prisoners of War Association*, 2 (September–October 1946), unpaginated.

[107] Brigadier J. G. Smyth, 'Memoir to Mary Crossan', *The Clarion. The Official Organ of the Returned British Prisoners of War Association*, Special Issue (April 1948), unpaginated. J. G. Smyth did not experience captivity but two-thirds of his division were captured during the fighting in Burma.

[108] TNA AIR 49/388, Minutes of Meeting to Consider the Question of the Rehabilitation of Returned PW, 1 March 1945.

[109] TNA WO 165/129, Medical Diaries, AMD 11, January to December 1945, Minutes of the 30th Meeting of Command Psychiatrists, 6 April 1945.

repatriated in October 1943, wrote a radio broadcast to inform relatives of what to expect from returning POWs, he was criticised for dwelling too much on the idea that POWs had become 'different'.[110] In a draft of his speech, Chapel had described an ex-POW who developed a 'disturbing habit' of pacing his room each night and referred to how some might be 'full of grouses' or in denial that they had any difficulties. He went so far as to draw a distinction between fighting soldiers, who had 'done a good job', and POWs who had led what they believed to be 'a more or less futile existence.'[111] His speech was never broadcast. It was replaced by a much more anodyne version, read by the adjutant general. This focussed almost entirely on the material provisions and logistical arrangements for returning prisoners of war, with only one sentence referring to the fact that 'things here at home may seem very different from what they were when your men were last here and it is quite likely they may take some time to get used to them.'[112]

In other words, no clear script emerged from officials or psychiatrists that recognised how captivity had affected prisoners of war. Yet this is not to argue that ex-prisoners of war were unfairly denied acknowledgement of their experiences: POWs themselves also minimised their difficulties, even though, at the same time, they desired some sort of recognition of them.[113] Wilson recorded that they showed a 'sensitivity to psychiatric "labelling"' and letters written to the press, by repatriated POWs, demonstrated they were 'touchy' about being labelled 'queer'.[114] This provides an interesting contrast to the sympathetic and permissive culture that appeared to have built up in POW camps towards those who experienced psychological disturbances. Perhaps, this disparity also illustrates how much of a unique society developed in the isolation of the POW camp.

Beyond mental distress, POWs were also reported as being ambivalent towards other aspects of their captivity experience being acknowledged. Chapter 4 set out how the sanitised portrayals of captivity, by organisations such as the British Red Cross, misled relatives about the true nature of wartime incarceration, and how this became a source of

---

[110] TNA WO 32/11125, Memo from P.W.2.d to D. P.W., 16 November 1944.

[111] TNA WO 32/11125, Colonel Chapel, 'A Few Words on Returned Prisoners of War', version 10A, October 1944.

[112] TNA WO 32/11125, Minute from DD of O (D) to the Private Secretary to the Adjutant General, 2 July 1945; TNA WO 32/11125, 'Repatriation and Resettlement of British Prisoners of War', Broadcast by Adjutant General Sir Ronald Forbes Adam, Home Service, 25 April 1945.

[113] Curle and Trist, 'Transitional Communities and Social Re-connection. Part II', 241.

[114] WO 165/129, Medical Diaries, AMD 11, January to December 1945, Minutes of the 31st Meeting of Command Psychiatrists, 2 June 1945; WO 32/10757, Barbour, 'Returned Prisoners of War from Germany', 16 October 1945.

grievance for the men in the camps. For some, this was perpetuated upon homecoming. One wrote of his frustration at the 'wide divergence in the appreciation of the degree of sacrifice made when considered from the point of view of the prisoner and the men at home.'[115] This difficulty was possibly compounded by the fact that the British government explicitly advised ex-prisoners not to discuss their conditions in captivity. Those repatriated from Italy in May 1943 were told by the Foreign Office not to mention their treatment to the press, in order to avoid the possibility of jeopardising any future exchanges or even causing additional hardship to prisoners still in Italian hands. They were also advised not to discuss anything with visitors either, in case they had connections with the press. The British consul-general in Turkey, where this exchange took place, made clear they were to be 'careful not to talk about bad conditions in Italian camps or anything of that kind.'[116] The British consul in Switzerland similarly asked the ICRC to ensure that British prisoners of war leaving Germany in the May 1944 exchange gave no personal interviews to the press, in order to prevent 'the publication of injudicious reports ... of their treatment in Germany, which might adversely affect prisoners remaining there.'[117]

Again, this is not to suggest that prisoners were unwillingly gagged, for they did not want to be treated as returning heroes.[118] When Evans was repatriated from Italy in 1943, he demonstrated how these two states could not co-exist when he told his wife that 'We feel like heros [sic] instead of ex P.O.Ws.'[119] His fellow repatriates also resented the media attention and the welcome parties.[120] As one former POW, Captain Hammersley Johnston advised, 'They don't want to be glamourised for the simple reason that, although they have done their share, it is their comrades who fought the last battle who are the ones to be in the limelight.'[121] However, some felt they deserved a form of

[115] TNA WO 32/11125, Proposal by a Repatriated RAF Officer, sent from E. G. Gepp (DPW) to the Deputy Adjutant General, 23 August 1944.

[116] ACICR, B G 14, box 427, file R.III, letter from E. C. Hole, British Consulate-General, Izmir, to the Senior British Officer, S.S. Citta di Tunisi, 7 May 1943.

[117] ACICR, B G 14, box 428, file R.VII, letter from H. M. Majesty's Consul, British Consulate in Geneva, to Monsieur Claude Pilloud, ICRC, Geneva, 3 May 1944.

[118] ADM 1/18875, Memorandum from the Director of Tactical, Torpedo and Staff Duties Division, 17 June 1944.

[119] Evans, letter to his wife, 28 March 1943.

[120] WO 32/10950, 'The Crookham Experimental Rehabilitation Scheme', p. 13.

[121] TNA ADM 1/18875, Captain H. Johnston 'Remarks on Handling Repatriated Prisoners of War', 17 June 1944. On Johnston's captivity, see ADM 1/18875, Memorandum from the Director of Tactical, Torpedo and Staff Duties Division, 17 June 1944.

public acknowledgement. Mustardé, who may have heard the consul-general's warnings during his repatriation in May 1943, considered that the

ordinary POW is a funny mixture, and although shrinking from the actinic glare of too public a limelight, he <u>does</u> love to be made a fuss of a little, and he tends to feel that unless he can produce some evidence of change in his personality to show what horror he has come through, people may take it for granted that he has spent a reasonably pleasant sojourn in the enemy's hands.[122]

According to Newman, the repatriated POW did not want 'charitable sympathy but a sympathetic understanding, an acceptance and recognition of his value'.[123] Yet it was left unclear what form this acceptance and recognition should take.[124]

The ultimate ambiguity in references to the immediate legacy of captivity can be found in the effacement of imprisonment itself. At one lecture, Supreme Headquarters Allied Expeditionary Force (SHAEF) prisoner-of-war executive officers were told that 'the name "prisoner of war" is not liked; the word "prisoner" by itself will arouse protests. Remember the fragile self-respect with which you are dealing.'[125] Lieutenant Colonel Dean, representing the Army Selection Training Units, suggested that what 'the majority of P.O.Ws want to do is to be allowed to forget that they were Prisoners of War. They would also appreciate not being classified as such at the various Centres and Units that they go to.' Instead they were to be referred to as 'non-trainees'.[126] Wilson advised those involved with the CRUs that 'care should be exercised in dealing with prisoners of war and in avoiding conditions or names which may suggest his experiences in captivity.'[127]

These assessments appear to have reflected the views which ex-POWs themselves held. An all-ranks advisory panel of repatriated prisoners of war 'felt strongly' that ex-prisoners of war should carry just one document stamped 'Repatriated Prisoner of War' and that this document should be produced only on demand. The government even considered arranging for returned POWs to have a temporary loan of civilian suits, so they

---

[122] RAMC 466/49, Conference of Military Psychiatrists. Appendix A, Captain Mustardé, 'Adjustment and Mal-adjustment within the Camp', 7–8 October 1944.
[123] Newman, 'Correspondence: Prisoner-of-War Mentality', 163.
[124] For other combatants being ambivalent about public recognition, see Goldstein, *Gender and War*, pp. 308–9.
[125] Wellcome Library, GC/135/B.1/1, Lecture to SHAEF P.W. Executive Officers, August 1944, 4.
[126] RAMC 466/49, Conference of Military Psychiatrists, H. S. Dean 'Prisoners of War at the Army Selection Training Units', 7–8 October 1944.
[127] LAB 12/352, Minutes of a Meeting with Regional Controllers, Ministry of Labour and National Service, Civil Resettlement Planning Headquarters, 10 May 1945.

Figure 7.1: 'Get in shape for civvy street – Civil Resettlement Units'.
The poster shows how POWs were doubly invisible in the advertising
material for CRUs. The figure is of a civilian man, who features as a cut-
out person. The small print reads: 'Civil Resettlement Units are open to
repatriated Prisoners of War due for release or discharge from the Army.
The pamphlet "Settling down in Civvy Street" explains the scheme.'
   © Imperial War Museums (Art.IWM PST 2977).

could make their 'initial readjustment incognito.'[128] Similarly, the advertising material for Civil Resettlement Units passed over the very fact these men had been captives. In one poster (Figure 7.1), designed by Abram Ganes, the official poster designer for the War Office, the captive was doubly invisible. The figure is of a civilian man who features as a cut-out person.

The eight-page leaflet 'Settling Down in Civvy Street. Civil Resettlement Units' which accompanied this poster was designed and worded largely by repatriates so that the scheme would appeal to them, and it was given to every returning POW.[129] It did not mention captivity once. This document advised these men where they could find CRUs, how they would run, how they could help the repatriates to find a job and covered issues dealing with pay and health. In providing a rationale for the CRUs, the leaflet explained to ex-prisoners of war that:

> Changes have taken place in civvy street. Your friends have been engaged in war-work. Many are on jobs that didn't exist before. There are ration cards and wartime regulations. Your wives, mothers and sisters have carried the burden of war-work as well as the extra difficulties of wartime housekeeping. It is a different world in many ways from the one you left. You have changed too. You are older than when you joined the Army. You are more experienced. You have seen new countries and different people and you have looked at them through the eyes of a soldier instead of a civilian. You have a new outlook on civil life, a more developed outlook and, quite possibly, a better one than before.[130]

Why these men had changed, were more experienced and had developed a new outlook was left unreferenced. In effect, the years these men had spent behind barbed wire went unacknowledged, seemingly at their own behest.

Resettlement

Although re-entering army life brought its own set of difficulties, the army was also thought to offer ex-POWs a form of emotional security.[131]

---

[128] TNA WO 32/10757, minute from Lieutenant Colonel G. R. Hargreaves, Assistant Director of Army Psychiatry, 10 March 1944; WO 32/10950, Wilson, 'Report to the War Office on Psychological Aspects of the Rehabilitation of Repatriated Prisoners of War', p. 6; TNA WO 32/11125, 'Brief for DPW on War Office Report on the Rehabilitation of Repatriated Prisoners of War', undated.

[129] Curle, 'Transitional Communities and Social Re-connection. Part I', 62; LHC, Adam papers, 3/13, Adam, 'Narrative Covering Aspects of Work as Adjutant General, WWII', Chapter XI, Demobilisation and Resettlement.

[130] TNA LAB 12/352, 'Settling Down in Civvy Street, Civil Resettlement Units', May 1945.

[131] Curle, 'Transitional Communities and Social Re-connection. Part I', 50.

As a result, the adjustment problems prisoners of war experienced were, in fact, considered by psychiatrists to be most severe during the first six months of civilian life.[132] The CRUs were designed to catch the men at this point.[133] They offered ex-POWs 'transitional communities' to take them from service to civilian life.[134] All army men qualified to spend up to three months at a CRU as long as they had spent a minimum of sixty-one days in captivity.[135] Most men stayed for between four and five weeks.[136]

Where possible, the CRUs were set up in large country houses to mark their contrast from army camps, such as the Jacobean stately home Hatfield House in Hertfordshire, or the eighteenth-century mansion Luton Hoo in Bedfordshire. Each unit could accommodate 240 ex-POWs at any one time, but ex-POWs entered in groups of sixty per week so that the older residents could help settle in the newcomers.[137] They were arranged in order to eliminate some of the key challenges POWs faced in their reintegration back into society.[138] The Auxiliary Territorial Service, the women's branch of the British Army, supplied 100 of the 140 staff members of each unit, to re-accustom POWs to a mixed community.[139] Meals were served in a common dining room shared by all ranks, repatriates and staff, which symbolised CRU democracy.[140] There was minimal formal discipline at CRUs, allowing activities to be spontaneous and democratic, and enabling 'flexibility and personal embellishment'.[141] The repatriate attended the CRU nearest his house, so he could return home each weekend and so that his wife and civilian friends could attend the social gatherings that took place in the unit.[142] Group discussions were held to encourage men to disclose their feelings without embarrassment, in the hope they could discuss their problems

[132] Curle and Trist, 'Transitional Communities and Social Re-connection. Part II', 250.

[133] Curle, 'Transitional Communities and Social Re-connection. Part I', 52.

[134] Wilson, 'The Serviceman Comes Home', 25.

[135] TNA WO 32/10757, 'Release and Resettlement – Civil Resettlement for Returned Prisoners of War', Army Council instruction no. 396, 1946; Bootle-Wilbraham, 'Civil Resettlement of Ex-Prisoners of War', 39.

[136] Wilson, Trist and Curle, 'Transitional Communities: A Study of the Civil Resettlement of British Prisoners of War', p. 565.

[137] LHC, Adam papers, 3/13, Adam, 'Narrative Covering Aspects of Work as Adjutant General, WWII', Chapter XI, Demobilisation and Resettlement.

[138] TNA LAB 12/352, Ministry of Labour's Circular to Regional Controllers 'Civil Resettlement Units for Army Personnel', April 1945.

[139] Wilson, 'The Serviceman Comes Home', 18.

[140] Wilson, Trist and Curle, 'Transitional Communities: A Study of the Civil Resettlement of British Prisoners of War', p. 564.

[141] Curle, 'Transitional Communities and Social Re-connection. Part I', 66.

[142] LHC, Adam papers, 3/13, Adam, 'Narrative Covering Aspects of Work as Adjutant General, WWII', Chapter XI, Demobilisation and Resettlement.

more openly at home.[143] Men could also be referred or self-referred to a psychiatrist: two CRUs had a resident psychiatrist; others were paid weekly visits.[144] A series of specialists, from dental officers to Army Education Corps instructors, were available for consultation, but the guidance information handed out at individual CRUs placed great emphasis on these meetings being voluntary, with it being up to the repatriate to initiate contact.[145]

In all these ways, it was anticipated that suspicion of authority would be neutralised, a POW would return to a less regressed social attitude, he would reconnect with home society, he would accept responsibility and display the initiative that was necessary for civilian life and for his personal goals to gain structure.[146] CRUs also offered vocational guidance and access to the labour exchange, with the proximity of the CRU to a man's home allowing him to remain close to possible jobs. There were also workshops where men learnt skills under trained supervision and often gained a hobby for life.[147]

Whilst some units had a mix of ranks, one unit, housed in the mansion house of Kneller Hall, in the London Borough of Richmond, was set aside for officer ex-POWs.[148] Officers volunteered for CRUs in small numbers, although the War Office was of the view that they needed these facilities just as much as those without commissions.[149] In fact, 'generally speaking', Brigadier Lionel Bootle-Wilheim, who worked at the Civil Resettlement headquarters, found that 'their difficulties are more acute than those of the other ranks.' Bootle-Wilheim went on to clarify how this was 'very natural. On the whole, officers, all of whom have been leaders in some capacity during the war, would be less prone to seek help and more liable to try to solve their own problems.'[150] Again, as noted in Chapter 5, the greater susceptibility of officers to psychological difficulties seems to have been explained in a way that protected their superiority. Kneller Hall was one of

---

[143] Bootle-Wilbraham, 'Civil Resettlement of Ex-Prisoners of War', 41.
[144] Bootle-Wilbraham, 'Civil Resettlement of Ex-Prisoners of War', 42; Curle, 'Transitional Communities and Social Re-connection. Part I', 66.
[145] IWM 02(41.15 [5 Civil Resettlement Unit, Acton Place Camp, Suffolk]/5, Guide to No. 5 Civil Resettlement Unit, Acton Place Camp, Suffolk.
[146] Wilson, Trist and Curle, 'Transitional Communities: A Study of the Civil Resettlement of British Prisoners of War', p. 565; Wilson, 'The Serviceman Comes Home', 25.
[147] LHC, Adam papers, 3/13, Adam, 'Narrative Covering Aspects of Work as Adjutant General, WWII', Chapter XI, Demobilisation and Resettlement.
[148] TNA, LAB 12/352, Notes of a Discussion on the Civil Resettlement of Repatriated Officer Prisoners of War, Kneller Hall, 2 October 1945; Bootle-Wilbraham 'Civil Resettlement of Ex-Prisoners of War', 42.
[149] TNA, LAB 12/352, Notes of a Discussion on the Civil Resettlement of Repatriated Officer Prisoners of War, Kneller Hall, 2 October 1945.
[150] Bootle-Wilbraham, 'Civil Resettlement of Ex-Prisoners of War', 42.

the two units that had a resident psychiatrist, which could also indicate either that officers did have greater problems, or that they were given a better service. The former seems more likely, given that, at another unit, which was attended by all ranks, 15 per cent of the intake of other ranks saw the psychiatrist, compared to 25 per cent of the officer intake.[151]

The CRUs existed for two years after the war ended; they started closing in May 1946, with the final one shutting its doors at the end of June 1947.[152] In total, 40,000 to 50,000 ex-POWs, held either in Europe or the Far East, attended one.[153] The RAF similarly established four of its own resettlement centres, which were attended by more than one quarter of some 13,000 returned airmen who had been held captive in either Europe or the Far East.[154] The Royal Navy made no comparable provision.[155] Non-medical cases amongst prisoners of war were not regarded by the Royal Navy as special groups and, because the navy had relatively few POWs, it probably considered the cost of establishing dedicated centres outweighed any gain.[156]

Unfortunately, since there is little testimony from ex-POWs dating from this era, their personal reactions to CRUs are hard to gauge. Again, *The Clarion* provides a brief but inconclusive insight. 'K. S.', who described his return to 'civilisation' as 'terrible', wrote in 'appreciation to the staffs of various CRUs and hospitals which helped me during my two years convalescence' and spoke of 'many who helped, because they understood me, yes, understood me better than I understood myself.'[157] Another POW, conversely, described them as 'sinecure', failing to deal with ex-POWs 'real problems', because of their 'ignorance of our positives, not our negatives'.[158] The latter POW was imprisoned in

---

[151] Wilson, Doyle and Kelnar, 'Group Techniques in a Transitional Community', 737.

[152] Ahrenfeldt, *Psychiatry in the British Army in the Second World War*, p. 240.

[153] Wilson, Trist and Curle, 'Transitional Communities: A Study of the Civil Resettlement of British Prisoners of War', p. 565. There is some discrepancy over this figure. Ahrenfeldt states that 'in all, a total of some 19,000 ex-European, and some 4,500 ex-Japanese, prisoners of war attended C.R.U.s up to the end of March 1947', but this figure is at odds with another statistic he provides: 'some 60% of ex-prisoners of war from Germany entered C.R.U.s' (*Psychiatry in the British Army in the Second World War*, p. 240).

[154] The 13,000 figure consists of 9,374 from Europe and 3,371 from the Far East. The article does not break down the 3,000 who attended an RAF resettlement centre into those from Europe and those from the Far East; see 'Over 13,000 Ex-POWs went through Cosford', *The Clarion. The Official Organ of the Returned British Prisoners of War Association*, 8 (1947), unpaginated.

[155] TNA LAB 12/352, M. L. C. 4/2 War Office Resettlement Units, 28 November 1945.

[156] Jones and Wessely, 'British Prisoners-of-War', 174–5.

[157] K. S., 'Appreciation', *The Clarion. The Official Organ of the Returned British Prisoners of War Association*, 16, (1949), unpaginated.

[158] C. Barclay Miller, 'In THE balance', *The Clarion. The Official Organ of the Returned British Prisoners of War Association*, 4 (1947), unpaginated.

the Far East and so likely faced a different set of challenges upon returning home to those who had been imprisoned in Europe. It is unclear where 'K. S.' was imprisoned.

More systematic evidence comes from a study carried out by army psychiatrists that attempted to assess the efficacy of this programme. Fifty repatriated POWs in one area, who had attended a CRU, along with 100 who had not, were 'intensively studied' some months after they had been demobilised.[159] The results indicated that the programme had been a success: 74 per cent of ex-POWs who had attended a CRU were deemed more settled in civilian life compared to only 36 per cent of those who had elected not to attend a CRU.[160] This was measured by observing and discussing the repatriate's relationship with his family, employers and community life and comparing this against social norms.[161]

A wider objective of CRUs, as distinct from the narrow aim of 'preventing casualties', was to acknowledge and sanction the positive democratic outlook a POW had gained from his experience and sustain this in civilian society.[162] These two groups of POWs were, therefore, compared to a control group of forty families who represented the civilian norm. The findings revealed that POWs who had attended CRUs showed 'more adaptability and co-operativeness' than was normal for their civilian neighbours. In contrast to adhering to conventional roles that sometimes impeded cooperation between a husband and wife, these former prisoners of war were said to have discovered how to get the most out of relationships, and had broken the bonds of conventional restriction. In fact, a 'continuum ... in terms of the degree of flexibility and participation in these relationships' was noticed from those who had attended CRUs, to community members who had not been prisoners of war at all, to those former prisoners who had not attended CRUs.[163]

How much of this was down to the success of the CRU programme is open to debate. There is evidence to indicate that the worst-affected men never attended CRUs. Due to its voluntary nature, those who participated in the programme were a self-selecting group and, according to Lieutenant Colonel Main, scores of men cancelled their acceptance of the offer because they could not face the prospect of discussing their problems with anybody.[164] The background from which the sample of

---

[159] Curle, 'Transitional Communities and Social Re-connection. Part I', 43.
[160] Curle and Trist, 'Transitional Communities and Social Re-connection. Part II', 274.
[161] Wilson, Trist and Curle, 'Transitional Communities: A Study of the Civil Resettlement of British Prisoners of War', p. 568.
[162] Curle, 'Transitional Communities and Social Re-connection. Part I', 52, 63.
[163] Curle, 'Transitional Communities and Social Reconnection', pp. 239–40.
[164] T. F. Main, 'Clinical Problems in Repatriates', *Journal of Mental Science*, 93 (1947), 355.

repatriates for this evaluation study was drawn may have also minimised potential problems. These men all lived in Oxford, where there was full employment, so that the nature of their unsettlement could be isolated from other factors. However, being in employment also affected readjustment. In CRUs in South Wales and Tyneside, where high levels of unemployment prevailed, unsettlement in ex-POW populations was more widespread.[165] Nor did the CRUs deal with any clinical psychiatric cases. These were sent to the hospitals referred to earlier.[166]

The final outcome of these hospital cases was quite positive. A follow-up sample of 100 patients at the Southern Hospital showed that twenty-two had completely recovered, sixty-six improved whilst twelve remained unimproved, and three and a half months after discharge, 90 per cent of these patients reported that they were employed.[167] Of the men sent to Kempston Barracks, more than 90 per cent were returned to duty, whilst just under 3 per cent were readmitted to psychiatric hospitals and another 3 per cent discharged as permanently unfit for further service.[168] Those who received treatment at Northfield Military Hospital all improved.[169]

A final insight into how ex-POWs held in Europe managed any psychological problems can be glimpsed through the work of the RBPOWA.[170] One of the forms of assistance that the RBPOWA offered ex-POWs was free medical and psychiatric treatment for those who experienced 'serious physical and mental lapses'.[171] Between January 1946 and 1947, a total of 560 applications was received from European theatre prisoners of war, with only 150 cases being for some form of neuroses.[172] Again, this could indicate that returning prisoners of war had successfully resettled into society, but, given the total number of applications was so low, it is more likely that this figure reveals a reticence amongst ex-POWs to seek help for what they had been through, as well as, perhaps, an unwillingness to admit any neurotic problems when back in civilian life.

---

[165] Curle and Trist, 'Transitional Communities and Social Re-connection. Part II', 244.
[166] Bootle-Wilbraham, 'Civil Resettlement of Ex-Prisoners of War', 41.
[167] Jones and Tanner, 'The Clinical Characteristics, Treatment, and Rehabilitation of Repatriated Prisoners of War with Neurosis', 55; Jones, *Social Psychiatry*, p. 19.
[168] Lack, 'The Management of Convalescent Neurotics at the Neurosis Wing, 101 Military Convalescent Depot', 32–3.
[169] Davidson, 'Notes on a Group of Ex-Prisoners of War', 100.
[170] A more holistic picture is almost impossible to achieve. In the United Kingdom, the War Pension Computer System is unable to identify whether a War Disablement Pension application was received from an individual who had been a POW in the Second World War. This means that accessing ex-POWs' records would involve a manual search going through thousands of pension files: a process prohibited by cost and data protection concerns, Letter from Kim Humberstone, Service Personnel and Veterans Agency, to the author, dated 3 November 2010.
[171] Chapman, 'More about Resettlement', unpaginated.
[172] Gibbens, 'The Psychology of the Prisoner-of-War', p. 144.

Conclusion

The end of the war was still distant when the army and government authorities first considered whether they would need to offer support to returned prisoners of war. The behaviour of the first groups of escapees and repatriates initially raised concern, along with warnings from veterans of the First World War of the possible consequences if no help was forthcoming for POWs. This caught the attention of one army psychiatrist in particular, Lieutenant Colonel Wilson, who became much involved with the issue, and whose report to the secretary of state for war ultimately garnered the attention of the Cabinet that something needed to be done.

The ways in which POWs had adjusted to captivity – altering their attitude to authority, building up fantasies of home and rethinking their philosophies on life and society – as well as their reception from their family, were considered to cause ex-POWs most difficulty as they re-entered service or civvy street. These were compounded by practical problems, such as demotion and reallocation. At least a significant minority of returning POWs probably experienced mild symptoms resulting from their struggle to reintegrate. A much smaller minority was so severely affected that they required hospital treatment. Some were deemed disproportionately affected: those who had spent more than eighteen months in captivity, regular soldiers and those with a predisposition to mental illness. Evidence indicates that the support offered to these men to help them readjust to civilian life had some success. One study showed that the CRUs could have an extremely positive effect, and most of those who received psychiatric attention appear to have been successfully treated and discharged.

On the face of it, it would appear there were few officially recognised psychiatric casualties amongst ex-POWs, but the consequences of captivity were not well acknowledged. When officials described what, exactly, these men were experiencing upon their homecoming, their language is striking for both its precision in avoiding certain words and the vagueness of the adjectives adopted. Here a picture of ambiguity emerges regarding how the experience of captivity had affected these men, which can also be evidenced in the attitudes of ex-POWs themselves. In some cases, ex-POWs replaced this ambivalence with effacement, wishing their very experience of imprisonment not to be publicly acknowledged.

Conclusion

This book has explored the inner and intimate worlds of British prisoners of war held in Europe during the Second World War in order to understand how these men made sense of a wartime experience that prohibited them from continuing their military service and left them under the power of their enemy, incarcerated in camps and separated from their loved ones.

By drawing upon POWs' correspondence, as well as their diaries and logbooks, *Captives of War* has looked at how captivity was experienced during the time of incarceration. It has charted how prisoners of war interpreted their indeterminate sentence of captivity not as lasting an interminable length, but as ending imminently, with barely anyone doubting that Britain would win the war. It has shown how POWs constructed themselves as superior to their guards, the unique 'Kriegie' identity they embraced, the close bonds they forged in their all-male environment, how they used their imagination to remain close to their loved ones at home and how those who attended CRUs showed greater adaptability and co-operation in their relationships than was normal for their civilian counterparts. This book has also told a bleaker story: one of guilt, isolation, lost manhood and wasted youth, a failure to unite in adversity and of mental strains from which no prisoner could escape. It has shown how ambiguity defined these men's homecoming and how both officials and ex-POWs effaced the very experience of captivity itself.

Beyond this, a number of conclusions can be drawn. Some of these might give historians pause to consider the experience of captivity in other wars or spheres of incarceration in slightly different terms from how it has so far been conceived. Some contribute to how we approach the cultural history of warfare more generally, whilst others add to our understanding of social and gender conventions in mid-twentieth-century Britain.

Firstly, this book has shown the limited attachment of these men to what cultural historian Graham Dawson describes as the 'soldier hero' ideal.[1] Chapter 1 demonstrated that it was in relation to the circumstances of POWs' surrender, rather than the act of surrendering in itself, where these men felt their honour and integrity might be questioned. Chapter 4 discussed how few prisoners wrote during captivity of their wish to return to their fighting roles – many more instead articulated how they looked forward to the end of the war so they could resume their civilian life. This chapter also showed how prominently loved ones at home featured in POWs' lives. Home offered POWs a crucial source of emotional strength, replenished through photographs, letters, parcels and fantasies. These men also conceived of the war ending in time for them to attend the next familial occasion and return to being part of their family life. Chapter 3 also showed how bonding amongst prisoners of war was strengthened by loved ones at home: they were invited to contact each other, mirroring outside captivity the networks established within. Chapter 7 explored how a return to military duty and subsequent barrack life tipped some men from dissatisfaction to despair. These conclusions add to the voices of historians who have argued for the primacy of domestic, rather than military ties of combatants.[2] Aside from warfare, this finding also provides an insight into the importance of emotional expression during this era. Historians have considered romantic love and emotional connectivity to have arisen in marriage in the post-war world.[3] The intensity of the marital relationships expressed in the letters and diaries studied here questions such an understanding.

The attachment of POWs to their civilian identities relates to a second, broad finding of this book, which answers a question that preoccupies historians of captivity: to what extent did POWs, or male civilian internees, suffer a crisis of masculinity? The limited attachment of these men to the 'soldier hero' ideal suggests we should not assume that being in captivity was, in itself, automatically emasculating. Instead, Chapter 4 showed that feelings of emasculation were brought into sharp relief when these men considered the wartime experiences that their wives, mothers and children were or might be having in their absence. They reminded POWs that captivity had dispossessed them of the three Ps of masculinity:

---

[1] Graham Dawson, *Soldier Heroes. British Adventure, Empire and the Imagining of Masculinities* (London and New York: Routledge, 1994), pp. 1–2.

[2] For historians who make this argument with regard to the First World War, see Bourke, *Dismembering the Male*, p. 170; Meyer, *Men of War*, p. 167. For arguments that combatants in the Second World War remained, in their hearts, civilians, determined to return to their ordinary civilian life as soon as the war ended, see French, *Raising Churchill's Army*, pp. 126, 154; James Hinton, *Nine Wartime Lives. Mass-Observation and the Making of the Modern Self* (Oxford: Oxford University Press, 2010), p. 12; Francis, *The Flyer*, p. 12.

[3] On romantic love in the post-war world, see Claire Langhamer, 'Love, Selfhood and Authenticity in Post-war Britain', *Cultural and Social History*, 9, 2 (2012), 278, 293.

family protector, provider and procreator.[4] Masculinity was not lost because these men felt as if they had failed in their military world, but, instead, because they felt they had let down loved ones in their familial, domestic sphere. Prisoners of war also bolstered their sense of masculinity and asserted their male superiority in other, sometimes unlikely situations. Chapter 2 showed how British captives used situations that were intended to quell or compromise them to paint a picture of their continuing to fight the war from behind barbed wire. The chapter also set out how, far from ruing or bemoaning their now subservient position, these men asserted their equality or superiority to their captors through escape attempts or reprisal episodes. Chapter 3 showed that when POWs replaced physically absent women in their camps with female impersonators, they paradoxically enforced the traditional gender hierarchy by claiming that these men could be more feminine than women themselves. At the same time, this chapter showed the fluidity in prisoners' attitudes towards male sexuality, through their contradictory reactions to different forms of male heterosexual and homoerotic behaviour, as well as their muted response to homosexuality.

The third way in which *Captives of War* contributes to understandings of wartime imprisonment, and the experience of wartime more generally, is the way in which it has shown the need to reconfigure both the spatial and temporal dimensions of captivity. Many histories of captivity have been written as if POWs' experiences were sealed off in some sort of barbed-wire vacuum. This book has shown how, in their imagination, POWs were constantly breaching their barbed-wire boundaries, either through letters, parcels and photographs bringing relatives into the camps, or through fantasies which allowed prisoners to leave captivity in all but body. This supports a growing number of histories that reveals how experiences of war often transcended notions of front line and home front.[5]

This research also stresses how the experience of captivity was lived out at a temporal level. The optimistic anticipations, set out in Chapter 1, demonstrate how prisoners of war experienced their indeterminate sentence of captivity as one that would end imminently, with barely anyone doubting that Britain would win the war. This has significance for the

---

[4] For a reference to the 'three Ps' of masculinity, see Heide Fehrenbach, 'Rehabilitating Fatherland: Race and German Remasculinization', *Signs*, 24, 1 (1998), 109.

[5] See, for example, Roper, *The Secret Battle*; Acton, *Grief in Wartime*. Laura Doan, in a review of *The Secret Battle*, writes that the book 'invites readers to rethink the dominant paradigm of spatial configurations of the Western front'. Her observation helped crystallise my thinking ('Book Review: The Secret Battle: Emotional Survival in the Great War. By Michael Roper,' *Twentieth Century British History*, 20 (2009), 429).

temporal experience of combatants in the Second World War more generally. Reading that men captured at Dunkirk or Tobruk expected the BEF would soon liberate them, or that prisoners planned out their moment of reunion with their families years before they were released, conveys a sense of how prolonged the war was for those who lived through it. This protraction was also evidenced in Chapter 3, where the length of the war was shown to have created different war generations, between those who enlisted at the start and towards the end of the war, and divided servicemen's attitudes accordingly.

POWs' experience of the temporal length of their captivity brings me to the fourth lesson that can be drawn. One question central to understanding experiences of captivity is: how did POWs cope with their deprived and confined conditions?[6] This is such a central question to ask of the experience of captivity that it is worth highlighting the most significant answers. Representing themselves as the equal or the superior of their enemy was a way of coping with their enforced subservience. POWs' hopes for an early homecoming explains how these men endured the indeterminate nature of their imprisonment. This might have also given them a sense of control over their destiny, as it enabled them to select their own end to the war. These optimistic anticipations were so important in helping prisoners survive captivity that they, along with the arrival of letters, were given equal significance to food. Meanwhile, prisoners' use of fantasy demonstrates that 'escapism', rather than 'escapes', was crucial in enabling POWs to endure their incarceration.

Captives of War has also presented what may be perceived as less admirable ways in which prisoners coped with captivity. Chapter 3 showed that British prisoners of war did not collectively unite around two of the most significant hardships of imprisonment: length of time in captivity and shortage of food. Whilst men tried to alleviate each other's privations, they were equally ready to steal, be involved in rackets or trade with the enemy. This finding is an important one, since it goes against the expectations we might hold for human behaviour. In Christina Twomey's words, who has identified similar behaviour in internment camps in the Far East, it 'undermine[s] any easy correlation we might be tempted to make between adversity and unity'.[7] This finding also supports conclusions from existing studies on combatants in the First and Second World Wars, which stress the shallow and perfunctory nature of military camaraderie.[8]

---

[6] Joan Beaumont identifies this as central (*Gull Force*, p. 139).
[7] Twomey, *Australia's Forgotten Prisoners*, p. 59.
[8] Francis, *The Flyer*, p. 62; Bourke, *Dismembering the Male*, pp. 144–5.

The fifth point to be taken from *Captives of War* relates to what happened when prisoners were, in a way, unable to cope with captivity and reached the limits of their mental endurance. Most often, in historical studies, mental illness is examined through medical or government records. They provide only oblique access to the patients' experiences and, inevitably, miss those who also suffered but were not formally diagnosed. Chapter 5 offered something different. In the absence of any formal name or diagnosis, it provided unmediated access to the thoughts and emotions of POWs who believed themselves to be psychologically disturbed. Whether they actually were is not the question. 'Going round the bend' was a reality for a significant minority of prisoners of war, and the informality and vagueness that this turn-of-phase encompasses should not encourage us to see this aspect of the captivity experience as factitious, but consider how it was experienced given this lack of clarity.

Chapter 7, meanwhile, showed how the psychological problems experienced upon homecoming were attributed more to the world in which ex-prisoners of war had to 'resettle', than to what they had actually been through whilst in captivity. This stance reflects the dominance of psychological theories of the time and, possibly, points towards the government's desire to circumvent the issue of captivity in any pension payments. It supports the conclusions of other historians in that diagnoses of mental illness were not led by psychological suffering, but, instead, were culturally determined and could be manipulated to effect political ends.[9]

The sixth finding of this book contributes to how cultural historians have drawn upon personal narratives to inform their research. This book has demonstrated the great variation between diaries, depending on the different audiences and purposes they served, and the correspondingly different experiences of captivity they reveal. This variation exists not just between different diaries, but also amongst different entries of the same diary. This variation is so great that it is unhelpful to assume that all diaries form a single genre. In many cases, POWs' diaries and letters were written for the same purpose and the same audience. This also indicates that distinctions historians draw between the genre of diary and correspondence are sometimes arbitrary.[10]

---

[9] See, for example, Jones and Wessely, 'British Prisoners-of-War', 163–83.

[10] For this point, see Doris L. Bergen, 'Book Review. Numbered Days: Diaries and the Holocaust. By Alexandra Garbarini. New Haven, CT, and London: Yale University Press. 2006', *Central European History*, 42, 2 (June 2009), 365; Stowe, 'Making Sense of Letters and Diaries'.

Finally, *Captives of War* highlights an aspect of captivity that remains to be studied. The narrative of this book ends in the late 1940s. One area ripe for further research is how the POW experience has been remembered in post-war society, why it has been remembered in such a way and what effect that remembrance had on society, families and, most importantly, the veterans themselves. During my grandfather's final weeks, it became painfully obvious to my family that there was so much of his experience of captivity that he had never resolved. This was revealed to us at a time when it was too late to help. It angered me – although I doubt my grandfather would have seen it in this way – that so little was done for him, during the sixty-seven years he lived after the war, to help him come to terms with what he had been through and what he had witnessed. My resentment was not so much directed at the lack of psychological

Figure 8.1: Andrew Makepeace aged eighty-seven years at Okrągła Łąka, a village in northern Poland. Sixty years after being released from captivity, my grandfather returned to sites of his captivity in Poland, including the village of Okrągła Łąka, where he worked on a farm. There is still much research to be done on the long-term personal effects of captivity on former POWs and how post-war society helped or hindered them in coming to terms with their experiences.

Source: Author's collection. Image reproduced with permission from Richard Makepeace.

support offered to him; in fact, I do believe that the Civil Resettlement Units were quite remarkable for their time, and my grandfather had attended the unit at Luton Hoo in Bedfordshire. Rather, my annoyance was directed at broader society, a society that seemed uninterested in the particulars of the experiences of all POWs, and much more interested in just those who had 'heroically' escaped. We still know so little about the long-term personal effects of captivity on former POWs and how society helped or hindered them. In the contemporary era, when warfare is being commemorated to an unprecedented degree, it seems particularly important research, if we are to fully support both those who served in the past and who do so in the present.

Appendix 1   Ranks of Soldiers, Sailors and Airmen

The ranks of those who served in the Army, RAF, Royal Navy and Merchant Navy are set out in this appendix; the ranks of the captured servicemen whose personal narratives appear in *Captives of War* are italicised in bold.

Ranks of the British Army in the Second World War[1]

Officers
Field Marshal
General
Lieutenant General
Major General
Brigadier
Colonel
Lieutenant Colonel
Major
Captain
Lieutenant
Second Lieutenant

Other British Army ranks were divided into warrant officers, non-commissioned officers (NCOs) and privates. The most important ***warrant officer*** was the ***regimental sergeant major*** **(RSM)**. Each infantry company had a ***company sergeant major*** **(CSM)**, which was one rank below the RSM in seniority.

Below warrant officers were NCOs, who were ranked in the following order:

Staff Sergeant
Sergeant
Corporal ('***Bombardier***' in the Royal Artillery)
Lance Corporal/Lance Bombardier

---

[1] Allport, *Browned Off and Bloody-Minded*, pp. 328–9.

Those who were staff sergeant or sergeant were senior NCOs; corporals and lance corporals were junior NCOs.

Other soldiers without rank were known either as '*private*' or by a title traditional to their particular unit or arm of service. Those in the Royal Artillery were '*gunners*'; in the rifle regiments '*riflemen*'; in the Royal Armoured Corps and the Royal Tank Regiment '*troopers*'; in the Royal Corps of Signals '*signalmen*' and '*dispatch riders*'. '*Driver*' was a private-equivalent in the Royal Army Service Corps.

Ranks of the Royal Air Force in the Second World War

Commissioned Ranks
Marshal of the Royal Air Force
Air Chief Marshal
Air Marshal
Air Vice Marshal
Air Commodore
Group Captain
Wing Commander
Squadron Leader
Flight Lieutenant
Flying Officer
Pilot Officer

Non-commissioned Officers
Warrant Officer
Flight Sergeant
Sergeant

Those who were flight sergeant or sergeant were senior NCOs. Warrant officers formed a separate class of their own. From May 1940, the Air Ministry awarded qualified aircrew the minimum rank of sergeant; all of the captured flyers in my sample were senior NCOs or above.[2]

Ranks of the Royal Navy in the Second World War

Naval Officers
Admiral of the Fleet
Admiral
Commodore
Captain

[2] Kevin Wilson, *Men of Air. The Doomed Youth of Bomber Command* (London: Phoenix, 2008), p. 63.

Commander
Lieutenant Commander
Lieutenant
Sub-lieutenant
Ensign
Midshipman
Warrant Officer

Naval Ratings
Petty Officer
Leading Seaman/*Leading Telegraphist*
Seaman
Able Seaman
Ordinary Seaman

In this study, where POWs have been classified as senior NCOs and junior NCOs, the rank of petty officer is included in the senior NCO category, and leading telegraphist in the junior NCO category.

Ranks of the Merchant Navy in the Second World War

The ranking system of the Merchant Navy was more trade based compared to the structures of the armed services. The Merchant Navy had different grades of crew according to whether they were primarily assigned to work on deck, in the engine room or in the catering department. Ranks also altered according to the tonnage of the ship. Below is an indication of how the merchant seamen who feature in this study fit within the ship's hierarchy.

The '*4th mate*' was in the deck department, junior to the 3rd mate.

The '*5th engineer*' was in the engineering department, junior to the 4th engineer.

A '*greaser*' was the equivalent of the most senior rating in the Royal Navy, equal in status to corporal.

An '*able seaman*' was one of the most junior ratings on the ship.

'*Cadets*' and '*apprentices*' were in training. It is unclear what Cadet McDermott-Brown and Apprentice Howard were training for.

In this study, POWs have been grouped together according to their rank, the ranks of 4th mate and 5th engineer have been included as officers, greaser as a junior NCO and able seaman as without rank.

Appendix 2 Background Information on the Seventy-Five POWs Whose Letters, Diaries and Logbooks Have Been Drawn Upon in *Captives of War*

This information is not comprehensive, and has been informed by the prisoner's 'Liberated Prisoner of War Interrogation Questionnaire' (where he completed one), his own narrative and supporting information provided by the relevant archive in which his narrative is held.

♦ At the time of capture.

Name	Rank ◆	Branch of service	Military career prior to war	Date and place of capture	Age ◆	Relationship status/children ◆	Camp	Personal narrative
Abbott, E. W.	Private	Army	Reservist	20 June 1940, Calais, France	32	Married, two sons	Stalag XXB (30 June 40–Oct. 40) Work camps (Oct. 40–Feb. 45)	Diary
Allen, C. W. G.	4th Mate	Merchant Navy	Unknown	February 1943, in the Atlantic	Unknown	Unknown	Marlag-Milag Nord	Logbook
Angove, R. L.	Captain	Army	Unknown	1942, Tobruk, Libya	32	Single	Campo PG 66 (20 June 42–7 Nov. 42) Campo PG 35 (7 Nov. 42–7 Aug. 43) Campo PG 19 (13 Aug. 43–11 Sept. 43) Stalag VIIA (13 Sept. 43–20 Sept. 43) Oflag XIIB (2 Oct. 43 onwards)	Diary
Armitage, D. L.	Squadron Leader	RAF	Reservist	21 September 1941, near Boulogne, France	30	Single	Dulag Luft Hospital (21 Sept. 41–28 Sept. 41) Oflag XC (28 Sept. 41–6 Oct. 41) Oflag VIB (6 Oct. 41–Sept. 42) Oflag XXIB (Sept. 42–Apr. 43) Stalag Luft (Apr. 43–28 Jan. 45) (military district unknown)	Letters to his mother

(cont.)

Name	Rank◆	Branch of service	Military career prior to war	Date and place of capture	Age◆	Relationship status/children◆	Camp	Personal narrative
Bains, L. A.	Lance Corporal	Army	Unknown	6 June 1942, Libya	Unknown	Unknown	Marlag (6 Feb. 45–10 Apr. 45) Campo PG 66 (Aug.–Oct. 42) Campo PG 53 (Oct. 42–Sept. 43)	Diary
Ball, E. G.	Sergeant	RAF	Unknown	16 August 1941, Aphoven, Germany	28	Married, one son	Stalag Luft III (22 Aug. 41–9 June 43) Stalag Luft VI (16 June 43–July 44) Stalag Luft IV (July 44–Feb. 45) Stalag 357 (Mar. 45–Apr. 45)	Letters to his wife; logbook
Barrington, E.	Corporal	RAF[1]	None	21 June 1942, Tobruk, Libya	26	Married	Derna (23 June 42–25 June 42) Benghazi (25 June 42–4 July 42) Campo PG 87 (4 July 42–6 July 42)	Diary; logbook

[1] Barrington was captured whilst serving in the RAF police, but was treated by the Italians and Germans as if he was a junior NCO in the army.

							Campo PG 66 (14 July–28 Sept. 42) Campo PG 54 (28 Sept. 42–2 Dec. 42) Campo PG 73 (2 Dec. 42–18 Sept. 43) Stalag IVB (21 Sept. 43–Oct. 43) Work camps attached to Stalag IVD (18 Oct. 43–Apr. 45)	
Barter, L. F.	Dispatch Rider	Army	None	23	31 May 1940, Grombach, Belgium	Single	Hospital, Bruges (July 40–Nov. 40) Stalag IXB (Nov. 40–Jan. 41) Work camps attached to Stalag IXC (Jan. 41–Sept. 44) Stalag IVB (Sept. 44–Apr. 45)	Diary
Beddis, J. H.	Flight Sergeant	RAF	None	19	10 April 1944, Amiens, France	Single	Stalag Luft III (1 May 44–27 Jan. 45) Marlag-Milag Nord (4 Feb. 45–10 Apr. 45) On The Long March	Logbook
Bloss, C. E.	Greaser	Merchant Navy	Unknown	26	8 June 1940, off Narvik, Norway	Married, wife expecting a child	Ilag XIII (July 40–June 41) Stalag XB (June 41–Sept. 41) Milag (Sept. 41–Apr. 45)	Letters to his wife

(*cont.*)

Name	Rank◆	Branch of service	Military career prior to war	Date and place of capture	Age◆	Relationship status/children◆	Camp	Personal narrative
Blyth, F. G.	Lance Corporal	Army	None	10 September 1943, Italy	28	Married, one daughter	Stalag VIIIA (20 Sept. 43–23 Sept. 43) Stalag VIIIB (23 Sept. 43–12 Nov. 43) Stalag 344 (9 Dec. 43–22 Jan. 45) On The Long March	Letters to his wife
Bompas, W. M. G.	Lieutenant	Army	Unknown	3 December 1942, Tebourba, Tunisia	22	Unknown	Campo PG 98 (Dec. 42–1 Jan. 43) Campo PG 21 (Jan. 43–Sept. 43) Stalag VIIB (Sept. 43–Dec. 43) Oflag VIIIF (Dec. 43–May 44) Oflag 79 (May 44–Apr. 45)	Logbook; diary
Booth, E.	Major	Army	Unknown	23 May 1940, France	Unknown	Married, at least one son	Oflag VIIC (June 40–Oct. 41) Oflag VIB (Oct. 41–Sept. 42) Oflag VIIB (Sept. 42–May 45)	Diary
Brook, A. G.	Rifleman	Army	Unknown	3 April 1941, Agedabia, Libya	22	Unknown	Derna, Barce and Benghazi	Diary

							Campo PG 78 (22 Apr. 41–1 July 42); Work camps attached to Campo PG 68 (1 July 42–mid-Jan. 43); Campo PG 122 (mid-Jan. 43–mid-Feb. 43); Campo PG 54 (mid-Feb. 43–12 Aug. 43); Stalag IIID (11 Sept. 43–23 Sept. 43); Work camps attached to Stalag IVD (Nov. 43–13 Apr. 45)	
Brooke, B. A.	Second Lieutenant	Army	Regular	12 June 1940, St Valery, France	22	Unknown	Oflag VIIC/H (July 40–Apr. 41); Stalag XXID (Apr. 41–July 41); Oflag VB; Oflag VIIC/Z (July 41–Oct. 41); Oflag VIB (Oct. 41–Oct. 42); Oflag VIIB (Oct. 42–Apr. 45); Stalag VIIA (Apr. 45–liberation)	Diary
Buckley, P. N.	Lieutenant Commander	Royal Navy	Unknown	6 July 1940, south-west of	31	Unknown	Stavanger Hospital (July 40–Aug. 40)	Logbook

(cont.)

Name	Rank♦	Branch of service	Military career prior to war	Date and place of capture	Age♦	Relationship status/ children♦	Camp	Personal narrative
				Stavanger, Norway			Oslo Hospital (Aug. 40) Stargard Hospital (Aug. 40–Sept. 40) Stalag XXA (Sept. 40–Nov. 40) Oflag IXA (Nov. 40–Jan. 41) Stalag XB (Jan. 41 to June 42) Marlag 'O' (June 42 to April 45)	
Burnaby-Atkins, F. J.	Second Lieutenant	Army	Unknown	12 June 1940, France	19	Single	Oflag VIIC/H (7 July 40–5 Mar. 41) Stalag XXID (20 Mar. 41–6 May 41) Oflag VB (13 June 41–30 Sept. 41) Oflag IVB (17 Oct. 41–31 Aug. 42) Oflag VIIB (3 Sept. 42–15 Mar. 45) On The Long March	Letters to his parents
Campbell, S.	Lance Bombardier	Army	Territorial Army	1942, Tobruk, Libya	23	Married	Campo PG 70 Stalag IVG Work camps Died 12 May 44	Letters to his wife and mother; diary

Name	Rank	Service		Captured	Age	Personal	Camps	Source
Casdagli, A. T.	Major	Army	None	1 June 1941, Crete, Greece	35	Married, one son	Salonika (11 June 41–22 July 41), Oflag XC (29 July 41–8 Oct. 41), Oflag VIB (9 Oct. 41–15 Jan. 42), Oflag IXA/H (15 Jan. 42–2 Mar. 44), Oflag XIIB (2 Mar. 44–21 Mar. 45), Foreign workers' camp, Lollar (22 Mar. 45–liberation)	Diary
Clague, A.	Warrant Officer	RAF	Unknown	19 August 1941, off the Dutch coast	25	Unknown	Dulag Luft (24 Aug. 41–30 Aug. 41), Stalag VIIIB (3 Sept. 41–6 May 41), Stalag Luft III (9 May 41–6 June 41), Stalag Luft VI (27 June 43–15 July 43), Stalag 357 (17 July 43–release)	Logbook
Coles, C. L.	Lieutenant	Royal Navy	Reservist	23 February 1943, off Bizerta, Tunisia	25	Had a sweetheart	Campo PG 35 (1 Apr. 43–12 Sept. 43), Campo PG 19, Stalag VIIA, Oflag VA, Marlag 'O' (31 Oct. 43–10 Apr. 45)	Logbook

(cont.)

Name	Rank ◆	Branch of service	Military career prior to war	Date and place of capture	Age ◆	Relationship status/ children ◆	Camp	Personal narrative
Cooper, D. R.	Gunner	Army	Unknown	27 May 1940, near Hazelbrouck, France	21	Unknown	Stalag XXA (July 40–Jan. 42) Work camps attached to Stalag VIIIB (Jan. 42–Jan. 45) On The Long March	Diary
Cunningham, P. A.	Flight Lieutenant	RAF	None	23/24 June 1944, shot down during raid on Scholven-Buer, Germany	20	Had a sweetheart	Stalag Luft III (1 July 44–27 Jan. 45) Marlag-Milag Nord (5 Feb. 45–10 Apr. 45)	Logbook
Didcock, G.	Driver	Army	None	North Africa, date unknown	31	Engaged	Italy Stalag IVB (22 July 43–9 Aug. 43) Stalag VB (10 Aug. 43–6 Sept. 43) Work camps attached to Stalag VIIIB (7 Sept. 43–release)	Diary
Dover, J. F.	Regimental Sergeant Major	Army	Unknown	8 April 1941, Tobruk, Libya	33	Married	Campo PG 78 (15 May 41–3 Oct. 43) Stalag VIIA (9 Oct. 43–4 Nov. 43) Stalag XIA (6 Nov. 43–22 Feb. 45) Stalag 357 (22 Feb. 45–8 Apr. 45)	Diary

Name	Rank	Service	Pre-war status	Capture	Age	Marital status	Camps	Source
East, A. J.	Warrant Officer	RAF	Unknown	1 September 1943, near Nordhausen, Germany	35	Married	Dulag Luft Stalag IVB (12 Sept. 43–14 May 45)	Diary
Edwards, A. G.	Flying Officer	RAF	Unknown	21 November 1942, near Paris, France	29	Married, one daughter	Dulag (23 Nov. 42–5 Dec. 42) Stalag Luft III (7 Dec. 42–26 Jan. 45) Marlag (4 Feb. 45–10 Apr. 45) Bad Schwartau (24 Apr. 45–2 May 45)	Logbook
Eldridge, J.	Rifleman	Army	Unknown	29 April 1941, Salonika, Greece	29	Unknown	Stalag XVIIID (5 Sept. 41–30 May 42) Stalag XVIIIB (31 May 42–13 June 42) Stalag XVIIID (13 June 42–6 Dec. 42) Stalag XVIIIB (6 Dec. 42–16 Mar. 43) Work camps attached to Stalag XVIIIB (16 Mar. 43–13 Apr. 45)	Diary
Evans, J. W.	Lieutenant	Royal Navy	Regular	22 September 1942, off Tobruk, Libya	Unknown	Married, two daughters	Campo PG 51 (26 Nov. 42) Campo PG 70 (2 Jan. 43–6 Mar. 43) Repatriated from Italy	Letters to his wife
Fairclough, R.	Flight Lieutenant	RAF	Joined RAF shortly before outbreak of war	25 April 1942, the Netherlands	25	Married	Stalag Luft III	Letters to his wife

(cont.)

Name	Rank◆	Branch of service	Military career prior to war	Date and place of capture	Age◆	Relationship status/children◆	Camp	Personal narrative
Fayers, R. J.	Flying Officer	RAF	Unknown	25 November 1943, Frankfurt, Germany	26	Married	Dulag Luft (27 Nov. 43–6 Dec. 43) Stalag Luft I (10 Dec. 43–May 45)	Letters to his wife and mother; diary
Figg, T. A.	Bombardier	Army	Territorial Army	31 May 1940, Merville, France	21	Single	Stalag VIIIB Work camps	Letters to his parents
Gallagher, G. B.	Warrant Officer	RAF	Unknown	17 April 1942, near Amiens, France	26	Unknown	Dulag Luft (20 Apr. 43–7 May 43) Stalag Luft I (10 May 43–27 Oct. 43) Stalag Luft VI (Nov. 43–16 July 44) Stalag 357 (17 July 44–Apr. 45)	Diary; logbook
Glass, J. K.	Driver	Army	Unknown	23 January 1942, Libya	31	Had a sweetheart	Campo PG 98 (Jan. 42–Mar. 42) Campo PG 65 (Mar. 42–June 43) Campo PG 53 (2 June 43–20 Sept. 43) Stalag VIIA (22 Sept. 43–Oct. 43) Stalag XVIIA (Oct. 43–Nov. 43) Work camps (27 Nov. 43–22 Feb. 45) Escaped 22 Feb. 45	Diary

Name	Rank/Role	Service	Pre-war service	Date and place captured	Age	Marital status	Camps	Source
Graydon, R. A.	5th Engineer	Merchant Navy	Unknown	Off South America	Unknown	Unknown	Bremen, Germany Milag	Logbook
Grogan, R. J.	Flying Officer	RAF	None	16 June 1944, over Essen, Ruhr, Germany	23	Married	Stalag Luft III (28 June 44–2 Jan. 45), Stalag XIII (16 Jan. 45–4 Apr. 45), On The Long March	Diary
Hainsworth, P.	Driver	Army	Territorial Army	28 June 1942, Libya	22	Married	Derna and Benghazi, Campo PG 51 (2 Aug. 42–1 Sept. 42), Campo PG 73 (2 Sept. 42–22 Sept. 43), Stalag IVB (25 Sept. 43–14 Oct. 43), Work camps attached to Stalag IVG (15 Oct. 43–13 Apr. 45), On The Long March (13 Apr. 45–17 Apr. 45)	Letters to his mother; diary
Hall, G. W.	Sergeant Navigator	RAF	Unknown	18 April 1943, during a raid on Ludwigshafen, Germany	23	Unknown	Stalag Luft III (Apr. 43–June 43), Stalag Luft VI (June 43–July 44), Stalag XXA (July 44–Aug. 44), Stalag 357 (Aug. 44–May 45)	Diary
Hawarden, A.	Sergeant Major	Army	Reservist	29 May 1940, Berques, France	44	Married, one daughter	Stalag XXA (June 40–16 Sept. 42), Stalag 383 (20 Sept. 42–Apr. 45)	Diary

(cont.)

Name	Rank◆	Branch of service	Military career prior to war	Date and place of capture	Age◆	Relationship status/children◆	Camp	Personal narrative
Howard, A. C.	Apprentice	Merchant Navy	Joined Merchant Navy in 1939	8 October 1940, South Atlantic	18	Single	Camps in France at Bordeaux and Drancy Stalag XB/Ilag/Marlag (Apr. 41–Feb. 42) Milag (Westertimke, Feb. 42–Jan. 45)	Logbook
Hurrell, H. L.	Warrant Officer	RAF	Reservist	15 October 1940, near Berlin, Germany	24	Had a sweetheart	Dulag Luft (27 Oct. 40–20 Nov. 40) Stalag Luft I (21 Nov. 40–27 Apr. 42) Stalag Luft III (28 Apr. 42–12 Oct. 42) Stalag Luft I (13 Oct. 42–1 May 45)	Letters to Pamela (his future wife) and parents; logbook
Hyde, N. C.	Wing Commander (Officer)	RAF	Regular	9 April 1941, Flensburg, Germany	30	Married, two children and wife expecting a third	Dulag Luft (11 Apr. 41–3 June 41) Stalag Luft I (10 June 41–5 Aug. 41) Oflag XC (5 Aug. 41–7 Sept. 41) Oflag IVB (8 Sept. 41–3 Sept. 42) Oflag XXIB (5 Sept. 42–15 Apr. 43) Stalag Luft III (16 Apr. 43–28 Jan. 45) Marlag-Milag Nord (8 Feb. 45–10 May 45)	Letters to his wife

Name	Rank	Service		Capture	Age	Status	Camps	Sources
Jabez-Smith, A. R.	Second Lieutenant	Army	Territorial Army	26 May 1940, Calais, France	Unknown	Single	Oflag VIIC/H (18 June 40–3 Mar. 41) Stalag XXID (4 Mar. 41–20 June 41) Oflag VB (20 June 41–17 Oct. 41) Oflag VIB (17 Oct. 41–29 Aug. 42) Oflag VIIB (15 Sept. 42–13 Apr. 45) Stalag VIIA (29 Apr. 45)	Letters to his family; diary
Jarvis, H. C. M.	Warrant Officer	RAF	Unknown	15 September 1942, Oldenburg, Germany	21	Had a sweetheart	Stalag VIIIB (23 Sept. 42–12 Dec. 43) Lazarett attached to Stalag 344 (12 Dec. 43–3 Mar. 45)[2] Stalag VIIIB (8 Mar. 45–7 May 45)	Letters to his parents; logbook
Jenkins, J. E.	Captain	Army	None	20 June 1942, Tobruk, Libya	26	Single	Derma (23 June 42–2 July 42) Benghazi (2 July 42) Campo PG 75 (3 July 42–4 Aug. 42) Campo PG 21 (4 Aug. 42–24 Sept. 43) Liberated with Italy's surrender	Diary

[2] Jarvis worked here, although he was not a member of the RAMC.

(cont.)

Name	Rank ◆	Branch of service	Military career prior to war	Date and place of capture	Age ◆	Relationship status/ children ◆	Camp	Personal narrative
Johnson, R. G.	Lieutenant	Army	Regular	July 1940, location unknown	30	Married, one son	Oflag VIIC Stalag XXID Oflag VB Oflag VIB Oflag VIIB Oflag VIIIF Oflag 79	Logbook
Kennedy, J. F.	Flying Officer	RAF	None	August 1943, bailed out in the sea near Leghorn, Italy	31	Married	Stalag Luft III On The Long March	Logbook
King, C. G.	Gunner	Army	Territorial	24 May 1940, near Lille, France	20	Not married	Cambrai (May–June 40) Schubin (June 40) Oflag VIIC (May 41) Stalag VIIIB (May 42) Stalag Luft III (May 43) Stalag VIIIC (July 44) The Long March to a camp at Bad Orb (March 45)	Logbook
King, J. H.	Canon (RAChD)	Army	None	12 June 1940, St Valery, France	29	Married, two daughters	Oflag VIIC (until 25 Jan. 41) Oflag VIID (25 Jan. 41–26 Sept. 41)	Diary

							Heilag-Rouen (3 Oct. 41–14 Dec. 41) Stalag XXIA (23 Dec. 41–21 Mar. 42) Oflag IXA/H (23 Mar. 42–14 Sept. 42) Stalag XIIIC (14 Sept. 42 onwards)	
Laker, E. G.	Lance Corporal	Army	Unknown	24 October 1942, El Alamein, Egypt	Unknown	Unknown	Campo PG 66 (Nov. 42–Dec. 42) Campo PG 70 (7 Dec. 42–Oct. 43) Work camps attached to Stalag IVC (Oct. 43–May 45)	Diary
Lambert, G. T.	Commander	Royal Navy	Regular	19 August 1942, Dieppe, France	41	Married, one son, one daughter	Oflag VIIB (Sept. 42–10 July 43) Marlag 'O' (10 July 43–Apr. 45) Oflag XC (Apr. 45–May 45)	Letters to his wife
Macey, H. C.	Petty Officer	Royal Navy	Unknown	June 1942, Mediterranean	Unknown	Unknown	Campo PG 52 Stalag VIIIB Marlag-Milag Nord	Logbook
Mansel, J. W. M.	Captain	Army	Territorial Army	21 May 1940, Bellancourt District, France	30	Single	Oflag IXA/H (2 June 40–4 Mar. 41) Stalag XXA (6 Mar. 41–June 41)	Letters to his family; diary

(cont.)

Name	Rank♦	Branch of service	Military career prior to war	Date and place of capture	Age♦	Relationship status/children♦	Camp	Personal narrative
							Oflag IXA/H (June 41–10 Oct. 41) Oflag VIB (10 Oct. 41–5 Sept. 42) Oflag VIIB (15 Sept. 42–Mar. 45) Zweilager 383 (Mar. 45–25 Apr. 45)	
Matthews, G. B.	Major (RAMC)	Army	Territorial Army	28 May 1940, France	38	Married, two daughters	Oflag VIIC/H (3 July 40–30 July 40) Stalag XXIB (6 Aug. 40–24 Aug. 40) Stalag XXIA (17 Sept. 40–10 Oct. 41) Stalag XXIC (10 Oct. 41–28 Oct. 41) Stalag XXIA (28 Oct. 41–3 Feb. 42) Stalag XIIIC (22 Feb. 42–15 Apr. 42) Oflag IVC (18 Apr. 42–19 July 42) Stalag Luft III (2 Aug. 42 onwards)	Letters to his family
McDermott-Brown, L.	Cadet	Merchant Navy	Unknown	13 July 1940, Indian Ocean	15	Single	Repatriated Sept. 44 Wilhelmshaven (Oct. 40)	Logbook

Name	Rank	Service	Force	Date and place of capture	Age	Marital status	Camps	Documents
							Tost, Poland (Dec. 40); 'Gedlizte' (Apr. 41); Sandbostel (June 41); Milag (Mar. 42–Apr. 45)	
Naylor, J. S.	Reverend (RAChD)	Army	Territorial Army	28 June 1942, Tobruk, Libya	42	Married, two daughters	Campo PG 75 (5 July 42–13 Sept. 42); Campo PG 78 (14 Sept. 42–20 July 43); Campo PG 19 (21 July 43–11 Sept. 43); Stalag VIIA (14 Sept. 43–20 Sept. 43); Strasbourg (21 Sept. 43–9 Oct. 43); Oflag VA (9 Oct. 43–29 Mar. 45); Stalag VA (30 Mar. 45–21 Apr. 45)	Diary; logbook
Nell, D.	Sergeant	Army	Regular	28 June 1942, Marsa Matruh, Egypt	29	Engaged	Campo PG 70 (Aug. 42–24 Sept. 43); Stalag IVB (28 Sept. 43–Sept. 44); Stalag 357 (Sept. 44–25 Apr. 45)	Diary
Panter-Brick, K.	Private	Army	Territorial Army	19 May 1940, Cassel, France	19	Single	Stalag XXA (to July 40)	Letters to his family; diary

Name	Rank◆	Branch of service	Military career prior to war	Date and place of capture	Age◆	Relationship status/children◆	Camp	Personal narrative
							Work camps attached to Stalag XXA (July 40–Dec. 42) Straflager (4 Mar. 43–11 May 43) Stalag XXA (12 May 43–Mar. 44) Work camps (Apr. 44–Jan. 45) On The Long March	
Parker, E. E.	Gunner	Army	Unknown	April 1941, North Africa	Unknown	Had a sweetheart	Campo PG 118 (until 31 Oct. 41) Campo PG 78 (Jan. 42–19 Aug. 43) Campo PG 19 (19 Aug. 43–20 Oct. 43) Oflag VIIA (20 Oct. 43–27 Oct. 43) Oflag V (to release)	Letters to his sweetheart and mother
Pexton, L. D.	Sergeant	Army	Regular	20 May 1940, Cambrai, France	32	Married	Stalag XXA (7 June 40–29 July 40) Stalag XXIB (29 July 40–6 Aug. 40) Work camps	Diary
Phillips, J.	Lieutenant	Army	None	1 June 1941, Crete, Greece	21	Single	Kokkinia Hospital (3 June 41–11 June 41)	Letters to a close friend

Name	Rank	Service		Captured	Age		Camps	Source
Quarrie, R. G. M.	Lieutenant	Army	Unknown	1 June 1941, Crete, Greece	23	Unknown	Avaroff Prison (20 Aug. 41–7 Sept. 41) Dulag 183 (10 Sept. 41–5 Oct. 41) Stalag VIIIB (15 Oct. 41–15 Feb. 42) Oflag IXA/H (18 Feb. 42–27 Mar. 45) Salonika (5 June 41–20 July 41) Oflag XC (2 Aug. 41–10 Oct. 41) Oflag VIB (12 Oct. 41–9 Sept. 42) Oflag VIIB (12 Sept. 42–15 Apr. 45) On The Long March (after 15 Apr. 45)	Diary
Richards, W.	Private	Army	Unknown	26 May 1940, Amiens, France	21	Married, one son	Stalag XXA (to June 40) Stalag XXIB (June 40–Aug. 40) Work camp, Kuhndorf (Jan. 41–Nov. 41) Work camps attached to Stalag VIIIB (Jan. 42–Jan. 45) Stalag VIIA (Apr.–May 45)	Letters to his wife

(cont.)

Name	Rank◆	Branch of service	Military career prior to war	Date and place of capture	Age◆	Relationship status/ children◆	Camp	Personal narrative
Scott, J. W.	Trooper	Army	Unknown	5 June 1942, Libya	22	Unknown	Campo PG 66 (Aug. 42–Oct. 42) Campo PG 53 (Oct. 42–Sept. 43) Stalag VIIA (Sept. 43–Nov. 43) Work camps attached to Stalag XVIIA (Nov. 43–Mar. 45)	Diary
Shipp, H. F.	Leading Telegraphist	Royal Navy	Unknown	9 January 1940, off Hiligoland Bight, Germany	31	Unknown	Oflag IXA (19 Jan. 40–12 Feb. 40) Work camps attached to Stalag IXC (12 Feb. 40–24 May 40) Stalag XXIB/H (25 May 40–24 June 40) Stalag XXID (24 June 40–28 Jan. 41) Marlag (30 Jan. 41–28 Apr. 45)	Logbook
Stewart, F. J.	Second Lieutenant	Army	None	15 June 1940, St Valery, France	23	Single	Oflag VIIC/H (July 40–Mar. 41) Stalag XXIB (Mar. 41–Apr. 41) Stalag XXXA (Apr. 41–June 41)	Diary

Name	Rank	Service	Type	Date and place of capture	Age	Family	Camps	Source
							Oflag VB (June 41–Oct. 41) Oflag VIB (Oct. 41–Sept. 42) Oflag VIIB (Sept. 42–14 Apr. 45) Stalag VIIA (23 Apr. 45–May 45)	Diary
Stirling, E. C.	Lance Bombardier	Army	Regular	21 June 1942, Tobruk, Libya	29	Married, three children	Benghazi (30 June 42–18 Oct. 42) Benito Camp and Busetta Hospital (19 Oct. 42–5 Nov. 42). Campo PG 155 (23 Nov. 42–5 Dec. 42) Campo PG 68 (8 Dec. 42–24 Dec. 42) Campo PG 52 (24 Dec. 42–4 Apr. 43) Campo PG 73 (7. Apr. 43–July 43) Stalag VIIIB (Aug. 43–15 Sept. 43) Work camps attached to Stalag VIIIB (19 Sept. 43–6 Jan. 45) Theresienstadt concentration camp (27 Feb. 45–4 Apr. 45)	

Name	Rank ◆	Branch of service	Military career prior to war	Date and place of capture	Age ◆	Relationship status/ children ◆	Camp	Personal narrative
Stoddart, K. B.	Lieutenant	Army	None	18 June 1942, El Adem, Libya	22	Single	Campo PG 21 (20 Aug. 42–Sept. 43) Stalag VIIA (8 Oct. 43–28 Nov. 43) Oflag VIIIF (15 Dec. 43–4 May 44) Oflag 79 (5 May 44 to release)	Letters to his parents; diary
Taylor, H. R.	Sub-lieutenant	Royal Navy	Reservist	21 July 1942, Calais, France	29	Married	Hardingham Hospital (21 July 42–23 July 42) Military prison (23 July 42–24 July 42) Dulag Nord (25 July 42–31 July 42) Marlag 'O' (31 July 42 to release)	Letters to his wife; diary; logbook
Tipple, E.	Able seaman	Merchant Navy	Joined prior to outbreak of war	20 November 1940, Indian Ocean	34	Unknown	Bordeaux (5 Feb. 41–12 Mar. 41) Stalag XB (15 Mar. 41–28 Nov. 41) Milag (28 Nov. 41–21 May 45)	Logbook
Upshall, L. G. F.	Lieutenant	Army	Unknown	April 1941, Greece	Unknown	Unknown	Oflag VIIB	Logbook

Name	Rank	Service	Unit	Date/place of capture	Age	Marital status	Camps	Source
Webster, D. H.	Warrant Officer	RAF	Unknown	14 January 1943, near Tripoli, Libya	21	Had a sweetheart	Tripoli Hospital (15 Jan. 43–19 Jan. 43), Caserta Hospital (23 Jan. 43–15 Feb. 43), Campo PG 66 (15 Feb. 43–12 May 43), Campo PG 70 (12 May 43–28 Sept. 43), Stalag IVB (3 Oct. 43–20 Feb. 45), Wahren Lazarett (20 Feb. 45–9 Apr. 45)	Letters to his family
White, J. G.	Corporal	Army	Unknown	22 June 1940, La Capelle, France	27	Unknown	Stalag XXA (24 July 40–Mar. 41), Stalag XXB (Mar. 41–Dec. 41), Work camps attached to Stalag VIIIB (Dec. 41–Aug. 42), Stalag 383 (27 Aug. 42–18 Apr. 45), Stalag VIIA (18 Apr. 45–1 May 45)	Diary
Wild, R. D. F.	Reverend (RAChD)	Army	Territorial Army	25 May 1940, Cassel, France	30	Married	Oflag VIIC (29 May 40–18 Oct. 41), Oflag VIB (18 Oct. 41–4 Nov. 41), Stalag XXA (6 Nov. 41–Jan. 45)	Letters to his wife

(cont.)

Name	Rank◆	Branch of service	Military career prior to war	Date and place of capture	Age◆	Relationship status/ children◆	Camp	Personal narrative
Wylie, N. R.	Signalman	Army	Unknown	12 June 1940, St Valery, France	26	Unknown	Stalag XXA (10 July 40–14 Oct. 40) Work camps attached to Stalag XXA (14 Oct. 40–12 Dec. 40) Stalag XXB (12 Dec. 40–Jan. 45) On The Long March	Diary

Bibliography

Primary Sources

Unpublished Primary Sources

Letters, Diaries, Logbooks and other Private Papers
Imperial War Museum (Department of Documents), London
IWM Documents.17642, J. Alcock, diary
IWM Documents.3746, C. W. G. Allen, logbook
IWM 66/174/1, R. L. Angove, diary
IWM Documents.13058, B. Bagnall, diary
IWM Documents.883, L. A. Bains, diary
IWM Documents.3121, S. Baker, diary
IWM 05/57/1 (+ con shelf), E. G. Ball, letters to his wife and logbook
IWM 88/58/1 (P), E. Barrington, diary and logbook
IWM PP/MCR/426, L. F. Barter, diary
IWM 61/157/1, J. H. Beddis, logbook
IWM Documents.14385, L. Blakey, diary
PP/MCR/408, C. E. Bloss, letters to and from his wife
IWM 05/57/1, F. G. Blyth, letters to his wife
IWM Documents.14892, J. Bolton, diary
IWM 86/89/1, W. M. G. Bompas, logbook (containing his diary)
IWM P370, E. Booth, diary
IWM Documents.20269, A. M. Boyd, diary
IWM 80/38/1, A. G. Brook, diary
IWM Documents.2485, B. A. Brooke, diary
IWM 81/5/1, P. N. Buckley, logbook
IWM Documents.2728, C. N. S. Campbell, diary
IWM P463, A. T. Casdagli, diary
IWM 75/71/1, Mrs D. Cooper, diary of D. R. Cooper
IWM Documents.13096, L. W. G. Coward, diary
IWM Documents.14433, V. W. Croxford, diary
IWM Documents.19672, P. A. Cunningham, logbook
IWM 10/6/1, G. Didcock, diary
IWM 99/82/1, J. F. Dover, diary
IWM 87/34/1, A. J. East, diary
IWM Documents.8127, A. G. Edwards, logbook

IWM 03/10/1, J. Eldridge, diary
IWM 99/8/1-8, J. W. Evans, letters to his wife and private papers
IWM 88/22/2, R. J. Fayers, letters to his wife and mother, and diary
IWM (not yet catalogued), T. A. Figg, letters to his parents and private papers
IWM 95/30/1, J. K. Glass, diary
IWM Documents.17336, A. J. Graham, diary
IWM 2996, R. A. Graydon, logbook
IWM Documents.16146, R. J. Grogan, logbook (containing his diary)
IWM Documents.172, G. W. Hall, diary
IWM 66/132/1, A. Hawarden, diary and private papers
IWM Documents.15113, G. A. Hemsley, diary
IWM 86/35/1, J. D. Hewitt, private papers containing the logbook of J. W. Scott
IWM Documents.16596, H. Higton, diary
IWM 01/8/1, R. A. Hilton, private papers
IWM 88/5/1, A. C. Howard, logbook
IWM 61/161/1, H. L. Hurrell, letters to his sweetheart and parents, and private papers
IWM 88/14/1, N. C. Hyde, letters to his wife
IWM 89/16/1-2(P), H. C. M. Jarvis, letters to his parents and logbook
IWM Documents.9020, R. G. Johnson, logbook
IWM Documents.7927, M. L. Jones, diary
IWM Documents.16311, J. F. Kennedy, logbook
IWM 85/50/1, C. G. King, logbook
IWM 66/185/1, J. H. King, diary
IWM Documents.2824, W. Kite, diary
IWM 85/18/1, E. G. Laker, diary
IWM 90/19/1, G. T. Lambert, letters to his wife
IWM 95/3/1, H. C. Macey, logbook
IWM 99/68/1-2, J. W. M. Mansel, letters to his family, diary and private papers
IWM 03/12/1, G. B. Matthews, letters to his family
IWM Documents.234, L. McDermott-Brown, logbook
IWM P 382 (+ Con Shelf), J. S. Naylor, diary and logbook
IWM PP/MCR/215, D. Nell, diary
IWM 85/20/1, E. E. Parker, letters to his sweetheart and mother
IWM 86/89/1, L. D. Pexton, diary
IWM 08/12/1, W. Richards, letters to his wife
IWM P308, H. F. Shipp, logbook
IWM 88/20/1, F. J. Stewart, diary
IWM 99/22/1, E. C. Stirling, diary
IWM 79/32/1, E. Tipple, logbook
IWM 74/22/1, Miss M. Trevor, private papers
IWM 05/3/1, L. G. F. Upshall, logbook
IWM 95/39/1, R. Watchorn, logbook
IWM 01/25/1, J. G. White, diary

IWM 66/185/1, R. D. F. Wild, letters to his wife and unpublished account of captivity, written in 1945–6.
IWM 83/33/1, N. R. Wylie, diary

The National Army Museum, London
NAM 2001-01-352-01, E. W. Abbott, diary
NAM 2001-09-300, A. R. Jabez-Smith, letters to his family, diary and other private papers

The Second World War Experience Centre, West Yorkshire
SWWEC 99.117, D. L. Armitage, letters to his mother
SWWEC 1999.14, F. J. Burnaby-Atkins, letters to his parents and private papers
SWWEC 2008.134, A. Clague, logbook
SWWEC 2001.927, C. L. Coles, logbook
SWWEC 2003.2426, R. Fairclough, letters to his wife
SWWEC 2001.1043/2001.1048, P. Hainsworth, letters to his mother, diary and private papers
SWWEC 99.201, J. E. Jenkins, diary
SWWEC 2009.21, R. G. M. Quarrie, diary
SWWEC 2006.690.3-5, H. R. Taylor, letters to his wife, diary and logbook
SWWEC 2007.153/2007.158/2007.531, D. H. Webster, letters to his family and private papers

University of Leeds Special Collections
Liddle ARMY 023, S. Campbell, letters to his wife and mother, and diary
Liddle RAF 042, G. B. Gallagher, diary and logbook

Private Collections
Private collection of Veronica Forwood, J. Phillips, letters to his close friend Philippa Cook
Private collection of Simon Stoddart, K. B. Stoddart, letters to his parents and diary
Private collection of Mrs Sandra Hawarden-Lord, A. Hawarden, diary

Memoirs and other Retrospective Sources
Liddle Hart Centre for Military Archives, King's College, London
LHC, Adam papers, 3/13, General Sir Ronald Adam, 'Narrative Covering Aspects of Work as Adjutant General, WWII'

The Soldiers of Oxfordshire Museum
SOFO Box 32, Item 46. T. C. N. Gibbens. *'Captivity'. Trevor Gibbens's Experiences as a Prisoner of War in Germany 1940–1945*

Imperial War Museum

IWM Sound Archive 16714/9, oral history with Richard Hutchinson Forbes, undated recording

IWM Sound Archive 4790/6, oral history interview with H. C. Macey, recorded 1981

Private Collections

Private collection of Andrew McIrvine, autobiography of Brian McIrvine

Government, Military and Parliamentary Papers

The Army Medical Services Museum

RAMC 466/49, Conference of Military Psychiatrists, 7–8 October 1944

Author's Correspondence

Letter from Kim Humberstone, Service Personnel and Veterans Agency, to the author, dated 3 November 2010

The National Archives, London

Records of the Admiralty

ADM 1/18875, Memorandum from the Director of Tactical, Torpedo and Staff Duties Division, 17 June 1944

ADM 1/18875, Captain H. Johnston 'Remarks on Handling Repatriated Prisoners of War', 17 June 1944

ADM 116/5353, letter from the Air Council to the Under-secretary of State, War Office, 17 August 1944

ADM 116/5353, War Office file no: 0103/6753 (P.W.2), Message sent by American Legation at Bern, 28 February 1945

Records of the Air Ministry

AIR 40/2361, 'Summary of Mail from RAF Prisoners of War', August 1943

AIR 40/2361, 'Summary of Mail from RAF Prisoners of War in Germany', 22 January 1945

AIR 49/388, Record of Conference Held at the Ministry of Pensions to Discuss the Rehabilitation and Resettlement of Repatriated Prisoners of War, 20 June 1944

AIR 49/388, The Resettlement Training of Returned RAF Prisoners of War, 30 January 1945

AIR 49/388, Minutes of Meeting to Consider the Question of the Rehabilitation of Returned PW, 1 March 1945

AIR 49/388, RAF POW Resettlement Centres: Reorientation Training, 30 April 1945

Records of the Boards of Customs

CUST 106/369, 'Communication with Prisoners of War Interned Abroad', General Post Office, December 1940

CUST 106/369, 'Communication with Prisoners of War and Civilians Interned Abroad', General Post Office, August 1941

Records of the Foreign Office

FO 916/38, Telegram from the American Embassy at Berlin, 23 March 1941
FO 916/1201, Draft Parliamentary Answer, 21 August 1945
FO 1013/177, A. T. M. Wilson, 'Some Problems of Repatriation and Resettlement of German Prisoners of War', September 1947

Records of the Ministry of Labour

LAB 12/352, Ministry of Labour's Circular to Regional Controllers 'Civil Resettlement Units for Army Personnel', April 1945
LAB 12/352, 'Settling Down in Civvy Street, Civil Resettlement Units', May 1945
LAB 12/352, Minutes of a Meeting with Regional Controllers, Ministry of Labour and National Service, Civil Resettlement Planning Headquarters, 10 May 1945
LAB 12/352, Letter from Ministry of Labour and National Service Northern Regional Office, 8 June 1945.
LAB 12/352, Notes of a Discussion on the Civil Resettlement of Repatriated Officer Prisoners of War, Kneller Hall, 2 October 1945
LAB 12/352, M. L. C. 4/2 War Office Resettlement Units, 28 November 1945

Records of the Ministry of Pensions

PIN 15/3444, 'Medical Examination of Repatriated Prisoners of War', Letter from War Office to General Officers Commanding-in-Chief and General Officers Commanding, 21 December 1944

Records of the War Office

WO 32/10746, 'Prisoners of War Captured before 14 April 1940, Repatriation of Prisoners of War Who Have Been a Long Time in Captivity'
WO 32/10746, Extract of Letter from Senior British Officer, Major J. H. V. Higgon, Oflag VIIB, to Major General Sir Richard Howard-Vyse, Chairman of the Prisoner of War Department, 6 November 1944
WO 32/10746, 'Repatriation of Able-Bodied Long-Term Prisoners of War from the British Commonwealth and Germany', Memorandum by the Secretary of State for Foreign Affairs and the Secretary of State for War, 15 January 1945, submitted to the War Cabinet
WO 32/10746, Directorate of Prisoners of War, Imperial Prisoners of War Committee, 'Repatriation of Prisoners of War Who Have Been a Long Time in Captivity', 22 March 1945
WO 32/10757, The Repatriate Prisoner of War from the Medical Aspect, Australian Military Forces, undated

WO 32/10757, Consulting Psychiatrist to the Army, 'Rehabilitation of British Prisoners of War Returned to this Country', 21 August 1943

WO 32/10757, 'Rehabilitation of Repatriated Prisoners of War. Minutes of a Meeting Chaired by Lieutenant-General Sir Alexander Hood', 16 September 1943

WO 32/10757, 'Conference of Officers Commanding Military Convalescent Depots on the Rehabilitation of Prisoners of War', 30 November 1943

WO 32/10757, Major G. B. Matthews, 'Report on the Mental Health of Prisoners of War', Stalag Luft III, 17 February 1944

WO 32/10757, letter from Group Captain H. M. Massey, Senior British Officer, Stalag Luft III, to the Secretary, Prisoners of War Department, 23 February 1944

WO 32/10757, 'Advisory Panel on the Problems of the Repatriated', minutes, 4 March 1944

WO 32/10757, Minute from Lieutenant Colonel G. R. Hargreaves, Assistant Director of Army Psychiatry, 10 March 1944

WO 32/10757, Directorate of Army Psychiatry. Technical Memorandum No. 13. The Prisoner of War Comes Home. Notes Prepared for the Information of Army Psychiatrists, prepared by DAP, May 1944

WO 32/10757, 'Record of a Meeting to Discuss the Reception and Rehabilitation of Repatriated Prisoners of War', 9 May 1944

WO 32/10757, Template Letter from the Director of the Prisoner of War Department, War Office, to the Next-of-Kin of POWs Repatriated in May 1944, 27 May 1944

WO 32/10757, Record of a Meeting Held at Hobart House on 3 June 1944 to Discuss Questions Relating to the Sorting, Training and Subsequent Disposal of Return PW

WO 32/10757, Extract from 'Report on Interviews with Escaped and Repatriated Ps of W', 8 June 1944

WO 32/10757, 'British Ex-Prisoners of War. Rehabilitation of those Returning to Civil Life', 16 August 1944

WO 32/10757, Secret Working Paper (44) 456, War Cabinet, 'Rehabilitation of Returned Prisoners of War', Memorandum by the Secretary of State for War, 22 August 1944

WO 32/10757, Letter from Lieutenant-General Alex Hood, Director General of Army Medical Services, to the Director General of Emergency Medical Services, Ministry of Health, 17 October 1944

WO 32/10757, Refresher Training for Repatriated Prisoners of War, War Office, April 1945

WO 32/10757, R. F. Barbour, 'Interim Report on Returned Prisoners of War', 29 August 1945

WO 32/10757, R. F. Barbour, 'Returned Prisoners of War from Germany', 16 October 1945

WO 32/10757, 'Release and Resettlement – Civil Resettlement for Returned Prisoners of War', Army Council Instruction no. 396, 1946

WO 32/10950, 'Extracts from a Questionnaire Given to 200 RAMC and 200 Stretcher Bearer Repatriated Prisoners of War', 21 December 1943

WO 32/10950, A. T. M. Wilson, 'Report to the War Office on Psychological Aspects of the Rehabilitation of Repatriated Prisoners of War', February 1944

WO 32/10950, 'The Crookham Experimental Rehabilitation Scheme for Repatriated Prisoners of War', February 1944

WO 32/11125, 'Brief for DPW on War Office Report on the Rehabilitation of Repatriated Prisoners of War'

WO 32/11125, 'Repatriation of Canadian POW', 1 July 1944

WO 32/11125, Proposal by a Repatriated RAF Officer, sent from E. G. Gepp (DPW) to the Deputy Adjutant General, 23 August 1944

WO 32/11125, Colonel Chapel, 'A Few Words on Returned Prisoners of War', version 10A, October 1944

WO 32/11125, Memo from P.W.2.d to D. P. W., 16 November 1944

WO 32/11125, R. A. C. Radcliffe, 'Welfare and Morale of Returned Prisoners of War', Visit to Units of 45 Division, 5–9 January 1945

WO 32/11125, 'Repatriation and Resettlement of British Prisoners of War', Broadcast by Adjutant General Sir Ronald Forbes Adam, Home Service, 25 April 1945

WO 32/11125, Minute from DD of O (D) to the Private Secretary to the Adjutant General, 2 July 1945

WO 165/129, Medical Diaries, AMD 11, January to December 1943, Memorandum for Deputy Director of Medical Services, Eastern Command, 10 January 1943

WO 165/129, Medical Diaries, AMD 11, January to December 1944, Minutes of a Conference of War Office Selection Board Psychiatrists, 23 April 1944

WO 165/129, Medical Diaries, AMD 11, January to December 1945, Minutes of the 30th Meeting of Command Psychiatrists, 6 April 1945

WO 165/129, Medical Diaries, AMD 11, January to December 1945, Minutes of the 31st Meeting of Command Psychiatrists, 2 June 1945

WO 208/3291, 'Secret Camp Histories, Oflag VIIB Eichstatt'

WO 208/3294, 'Secret Camp Histories, Oflag IXA/Z, Rotenburg'

WO 208/3295, 'Secret Camp Histories, Oflag XIIB, Hadamar'

WO 344/1/1, Liberated Prisoner of War Interrogation Questionnaire of E. W. Abbott

WO 344/7/1, Liberated Prisoner of War Interrogation Questionnaire of R. Anderson

WO 344/9/1, Liberated Prisoner of War Interrogation Questionnaire of D. I. Armitage

WO 344/15/1, Liberated Prisoner of War Interrogation Questionnaire of E. G. Ball

WO 344/19/1, Liberated Prisoner of War Interrogation Questionnaire of E. Barrington

WO 344/19/2, Liberated Prisoner of War Interrogation Questionnaire of L. F. Barter

WO 344/23/1, Liberated Prisoner of War Interrogation Questionnaire of J. H. Beddis

WO 344/31/2, Liberated Prisoner of War Interrogation Questionnaire of C. E. Bloss

WO 344/32/2, Liberated Prisoner of War Interrogation Questionnaire of W. M. G. Bompas

WO 344/41/2, Liberated Prisoner of War Interrogation Questionnaire of A. G. Brook

WO 344/41/2, Liberated Prisoner of War Interrogation Questionnaire of B. A. Brooke

WO 344/46/2, Liberated Prisoner of War Interrogation Questionnaire of P. N. Buckley

WO 344/62/2, Liberated Prisoner of War Interrogation Questionnaire of A. Clague

WO 344/68/2, Liberated Prisoner of War Interrogation Questionnaire of C. L. Coles

WO 344/72/1, Liberated Prisoner of War Interrogation Questionnaire of D. R. Cooper

WO 344/80/1, Liberated Prisoner of War Interrogation Questionnaire of P. A Cunningham

WO 344/94/2, Liberated Prisoner of War Interrogation Questionnaire of J. F. Dover

WO 344/99/1, Liberated Prisoner of War Interrogation Questionnaire of A. J. East

WO 344/100/1, Liberated Prisoner of War Interrogation Questionnaire of A. G. Edwards

WO 344/106/1, Liberated Prisoner of War Interrogation Questionnaire of R. J. Fayers

WO 344/107/2, Liberated Prisoner of War Interrogation Questionnaire of T. A. Figg

WO 344/115/1, Liberated Prisoner of War Interrogation Questionnaire of G. B. Gallagher

WO 344/119/2, Liberated Prisoner of War Interrogation Questionnaire of J. K. Glass

WO 344/127/1, Liberated Prisoner of War Interrogation Questionnaire of R. J. Grogan

WO 344/128/2, Liberated Prisoner of War Interrogation Questionnaire of P. Hainsworth

WO 344/129/1, Liberated Prisoner of War Interrogation Questionnaire of G. W. Hall

WO 344/137/2, Liberated Prisoner of War Interrogation Questionnaire of A. Hawarden

WO 344/156/1, Liberated Prisoner of War Interrogation Questionnaire of H. L. Hurrell

WO 344/156/3, Liberated Prisoner of War Interrogation Questionnaire of N. C. Hyde

WO 344/161/2, Liberated Prisoner of War Interrogation Questionnaire of H. C. M. Jarvis

WO 344/177/2, Liberated Prisoner of War Interrogation Questionnaire of E. G. Laker

WO 344/178/1, Liberated Prisoner of War Interrogation Questionnaire of G. T. Lambert

WO 344/209/2, Liberated Prisoner of War Interrogation Questionnaire of J. W. M. Mansel

WO 344/231/2, Liberated Prisoner of War Interrogation Questionnaire of J. S. Naylor

WO 344/232/1, Liberated Prisoner of War Interrogation Questionnaire of D. Nell

WO 344/251/2, Liberated Prisoner of War Interrogation Questionnaire of J. Phillips

WO 344/262, Liberated Prisoner of War Interrogation Questionnaire of R. G. M. Quarrie

WO 344/267/2, Liberated Prisoner of War Interrogation Questionnaire of W. Richards

WO 344/280/2, Liberated Prisoner of War Interrogation Questionnaire of J. W. Scott

WO 344/286/1, Liberated Prisoner of War Interrogation Questionnaire of H. F. Shipp

WO 344/304/1, Liberated Prisoner of War Interrogation Questionnaire of F. J. Stewart

WO 344/305/1, Liberated Prisoner of War Interrogation Questionnaire of E. C. Stirling

WO 344/319/2, Liberated Prisoner of War Interrogation Questionnaire of E. Tipple

WO 344/337/2, Liberated Prisoner of War Interrogation Questionnaire of D. H. Webster

WO 344/340/1, Liberated Prisoner of War Interrogation Questionnaire of D. Westmacott

WO 344/341/2, Liberated Prisoner of War Interrogation Questionnaire of J. G. White

WO 344/356, Liberated Prisoner of War Interrogation Questionnaire of N. R. Wylie

WO 366/26, Colonel H. J. Phillimore, 'Prisoners of War', 1949

Wellcome Library (Archives and Manuscripts Department), London

GC/135/B.1/1, Lecture to SHAEF P. W. Executive Officers, August 1944

Papers of the International Committee of the Red Cross
Archives of the International Committee of the Red Cross, Geneva

ACICR, B G 14, box 413, file IV, Note pour M. Pictet de Marti, Délégue du CICR, 30 janvier 1942

ACICR, B G 14, box 414, Letter from A. S. Greenwood, Man of Confidence, Reserve Lazarett, Freising, to Secretary ICRC, 5 September 1943

ACICR, B G 14, box 414, Dr A. Cramer, membre du CICR, 'Note pour la Délégation du Comité International de la Croix Rouge, Londres', 4 octobre 1943

ACICR, B G 14, box 414, Letter from Senior British Medical Officer at Stalag VIIIB to the Protecting Power, 7 October 1943

ACICR, B G 14, box 414, Dr A. Cramer, membre du CICR, 'Note sur la Question du Rapatriement', 20 janvier 1944

ACICR, B G 14, box 414, Dr A. Cramer, membre du CICR, 'Note pour la Délégation du CICR à Berlin', 4 février 1944

ACICR, B G 14, box 414, Dr A. Cramer, membre du CICR, 'Note pour la Délégation du CICR à Berlin', 19 juillet 1944

ACICR, B G 14, box 420, file: Sous-Commission (Accord Type) Réunion des 2 et 3 mai 1946, 'Rapport du les Travaux de la Réunion de la Sous-Commission chargée d'Établir un Projet d'Accord-type Revisé, tenue à Genève les 2 et 3 mai 1946', 21 mai 1946

ACICR, B G 14 box 424, Extraits du Rapport 'Commission Médicale Mixte A. Voyage en Allemagne du 14.4.44-12.5.44. Conférence Préliminaire des Deux Commissions Médicales Mixtes à Constance le 14 avril 1944'

ACICR, B G 14, box 424, 'Summary of the Medical Diagnosis in Relation to the Decisions of the Mixed Medical Commission B, 14.4.44 to 12.5.44, on British Prisoners of War'

ACICR, B G 14, box 424, 'Rapport sur le Travail de la Commission Médicale Mixte B du 14.4.44-12.5.44 en Allemagne'

ACICR, B G 14, box 424, Dr Rubli et Dr Waldhart, 'Commission Médicale Mixte en Allemagne (avril 1944)', 15 mai 1944

ACICR, B G 14, box 424, Letter d'Erlach à A. Cramer, membre du CICR, 22 mai 1944

ACICR, B G 14, box 424, Colonel d'Erlach, 'Proposals of the Mixed Medical Commission in Germany to the Mixed Medical Commission in Egypt, Australia, India, South Africa to Ensure the Equality of Judgement', covering letter dated 28 May 1944

ACICR, B G 14, box 424, 'Extraits du Rapport "Commission Médicale Mixte B Voyage en Allemagne du 14.4.44 au 12.5.1944" du 5.6.1944'

ACICR, B G 14, box 424, Letter from Colonel d'Erlach, President of the Mixed Medical Commission A in Germany, to the Presidents of the Mixed Medical Commission in Great Britain, United States and Canada, 3 September 1944

ACICR, B G 14, box 425, Raptriements des Malades, Statistique sur les Causes de Décès dans les Camps de Prisonniers de Guerre, britanniques, 15 août 1941, 15 octobre 1941, 15 janvier 1942

ACICR, B G 14, box 426, file R.I., 'Some Notes on the Treatment of Prisoners of War', Major G. J. Dean, 24 April 1942

ACICR, B G 14, box 427, file R.III., Letter from E. C. Hole, British Consulate-General, Izmir, to the Senior British Officer, S.S. Citta di Tunisi, 7 May 1943

ACICR, B G 14, box 427, file R.IV, Letter from the Senior British Officer of Oflag IXA/Z to ICRC, 9 November 1942

ACICR, B G 14, box 427, file R.IV, Lettre de Dr A. Cramer, membre du CICR, à Monsieur H. B. Livingston, Consul Britannique, 9 juin 1944

ACICR, B G 14, box 427, file R.IV, Lettre de 'Commando der Wehrmacht' au CICR, 23 août 1944

ACICR, B G 14, box 428, file R.VII, Letter from H. M. Majesty's Consul, British Consulate in Geneva, to Monsieur Claude Pilloud, ICRC, Geneva, 3 May 1944

ACICR, B G 14, box 428, file R.VIII, 'Repatriement de Grands Blessés et Maladies, de Personnel Sanitaire et d'Internes Civils, allemands, americains et britanniques. Echange Effectué à Travers la Suede, avec Enregistrement dans le Port de Goeteborg, les 8, 9 et 10 septembre 1944'

ACICR, B G 14, box 428, file R.VIII, J. Townsend Russell, 'Relief to Prisoners of War, Insular and Foreign Operations, American Red Cross, on Interviews with Members of the Armed Forces Repatriated from German Prison Camps via the SS Gripsholm on September 26, 1944 and those Liberated from the Rumanian Prisoner of War Camps', American Red Cross, Washington, DC, 10 October 1944

ACICR, B G 14, box 429, Statistique sur les Causes les Plus Frequentes de Décès dans les Camps de Prisonniers de Guerre en Allemagne, britanniques, 15 octobre 1943, 15 janvier 1944, 15 avril 1944, 15 juillet 1944, 15 octobre 1944

ACICR, B G 14, box 430, Feuilles du Service Sanitaire, Repatriement des Maladies, Kriegsgefangener Réserve Lazaret Kloster Haina Stalag IXA. La Section Psychiatrique

ACICR C G1 A 09-08, 'Draft of an Agreement between the German and British Governments Concerning Combatant and Civilian Prisoners of War', The Hague, 2 July 1917

ACICR, C SC, Germany, Luftlager III, 13 September 1942

ACICR, C SC, Germany, Marlag und Milag Nord, 28 June 1943

ACICR, C SC, Germany, Oflag VIIB, 20 July 1943

ACICR, C SC, Germany, Oflag IXA/H, 16 October 1940

ACICR, C SC, Germany, Oflag IXA/H, 27 May 1941

ACICR, C SC, Germany, Oflag XIIB, 8 August 1944

ACICR, C SC, Germany, Oflag XIIB, 22 November 1944

ACICR, C SC, Germany, Oflag 79, 19 September 1944

ACICR, C SC, Germany, Reserve Lazarett VIIIB, 1 February 1943

ACICR, C SC, Germany, Reserve Lazaret Stradtroda dépendant de Stalag IXC Confidential, 2 septembre 1941

ACICR, C SC, Germany, Reserve Lazarett Stalag IXC, Obermassfeld, 16 April 1942

ACICR, C SC, Germany, Reserve Lazaret Stradtroda dépendant de Stalag IXC, 8 juillet 1942

ACICR, C SC, Germany, Stalag Luft I, 9 March 1944

ACICR, C SC, Germany, Stalag XXA, Camp pour officiers britanniques, 1 avril 1941

ACICR, C SC, Germany, Stalag XXA, 7 September 1941

ACICR, C SC, Germany, Stalag XXIA, 5 February 1942

ACICR, C SC, Germany, Stalag 344, 4 May 1944

ACICR, C SC, Germany, Zweiglager du Stalag XXID/Z, 6 octobre 1943

ACICR, C SC, Italy, Campo PG 66, 22 November 1942

ACICR, C SC, Italy, Campo PG 70, 15 November 1942

Theses

Gibbens, Trevor C. N., 'The Psychology of the Prisoner-of-War', unpublished M. D. thesis, University of Cambridge (1947)

Published Primary Sources

Letters, Diaries and other Contemporary Sources

Anderson, Robert and David Westmacott, *Handle with Care: A Book of Prison Camp Sketches Drawn and Written in Prison Camps in Germany* (Belper, Derby: JoTe Publications, 2005; first published in 1946)

Beckwith, E. C. G. Editor, *Selections from The Quill. A Collection of Prose, Verse and Sketches by Officers Prisoner-of-War in Germany, 1940–1945* (London: Country Life, 1947)

Casdagli, A. T., *Prouder Than Ever. My War + My Diary + My Embroidery*, compiled by Alexis Penny Casdagli (London: Cylix Press, 2014)

Panter-Brick, Keith, *Years Not Wasted 1940–1945. A POW's Letters and Diary* (Sussex: The Book Guild Ltd, 1999)

Memoirs and other Retrospective Sources

Brickhill, Paul, *The Great Escape* (London: Faber & Faber, 1951)

Cochrane, Archibald L., with Max Blythe, *One Man's Medicine. An Autobiography of Professor Archie Cochrane* (Cardiff: British Medical Journal, 2009)

Morgan, Guy, *Only Ghosts Can Live* (London: Crosby Lockwood & Son Ltd, 1945)

Newman, Philip, *Safer than a Known Way. An Escape Story of World War II* (London: William Kimber, 1983)

Pritte, T. C. F. and W. Earle Edwards, *South to Freedom. A Record of Escape* (London: Hutchinson & Co., 1946)

Reid, Patrick Robert, *The Colditz Story* (London: Hodder & Stoughton, 1952)

Williams, Eric, *The Wooden Horse* (London: Collins, 1949)

Government and Parliamentary Publications

Crew, Francis A. E., *The Army Medical Services. Administration*, volume I (London: HMSO, 1953)

Crew, Francis A. E., *The Army Medical Services. Administration*, volume II (London: HMSO, 1955)

Guide to No. 5 Civil Resettlement Unit, Acton Place Camp, Suffolk (held at IWM 02(41.15 [5 Civil Resettlement Unit, Acton Place Camp, Suffolk]/5)

Hansard, House of Commons Debates, 17 December 1943, volume 395, columns 1819–20W

Hansard, House of Commons Debates, 2 March 1944, volume 397, columns 1625–31

Hansard, House of Commons Debates, 17 November 1944, volume 404, columns 2352–70

Hansard, House of Commons Debates, 13 February 1945, volume 408, columns 51–52

Hansard, House of Commons Debates, 27 November 1945, volume 416, column 1269W

IWM Art Poster 0311, Savile Lumley, 'Daddy, what did You do in the Great War?' (1915), Parliamentary Recruiting Committee Poster No. 79

Prisoner of War Enquiry Centre, *A Handbook for the Information of Relatives and Friends of Prisoners of War* (London: HMSO, 1943)

Prisoners of War British Army, 1939–1945 (HMSO, 1945; Polstead: J. B. Hayward in association with the Imperial War Museum Department of Printed Books, 1990)

Prisoners of War Naval and Air Forces of Great Britain and the Empire, 1939–1945 (HMSO, 1945; Polstead: J. B. Hayward in association with the Imperial War Museum Department of Printed Books, 1990)

Satow, H. and M. J. Sée, *The Work of the Prisoners of War Department during the Second World War* (London: Foreign Office, 1950)

Statistical Digest of the War. Prepared in the Central Statistical Office (London: HMSO, 1951)

Strength and Casualties of the Armed Forces and Auxiliary Services of the United Kingdom 1939 to 1945 (London: HMSO, 1946)

Publications of the International Committee of the Red Cross

Annex to 'Convention Relative to the Treatment of Prisoners of War', Geneva, 27 July 1929, www.icrc.org/ihl.nsf/WebART/305-430099?OpenDocument, last accessed 15 February 2012

'Convention for the Amelioration of the Condition of the Wounded and Sick in Armies in the Field', Geneva, 27 July 1929, www.icrc.org/ihl.nsf/FULL/300? OpenDocument, last accessed 8 February 2013

'Convention Relative to the Treatment of Prisoners of War', Geneva, 27 July 1929, www.icrc.org/ihl.nsf/FULL/305?OpenDocument, last accessed 8 February 2013

'Convention (III) Relative to the Treatment of Prisoners of War,' Geneva, 12 August 1949, www.icrc.org/ihl.nsf/FULL/375?OpenDocument, last accessed 15 February 2010

Favre, Edouard, *L'Internement en Suisse des Prisonniers de Guerre Malades ou Blessés 1917*. Second Rapport (Berne: Bureau du Service de l'Internement, 1918)

Historical Background to 'Direct Repatriation and Accommodation in Neutral Countries', 'Convention (III) Relative to the Treatment of Prisoners of War', Geneva, 12 August 1949, www.icrc.org/ihl.nsf/COM/375-590130?OpenDoc ument, last accessed 15 February 2010

Report of the International Committee of the Red Cross on Its Activities during the Second World War, September 1939 to 30 June 1947, volume 1 (Geneva: International Committee of the Red Cross, 1948)

Other Journal Articles and Books

Ahrenfeldt, R. H., *Psychiatry in the British Army in the Second World War* (London: Routledge & Kegan Paul, 1958)

Bavin, Margaret G., 'A Contribution Towards the Understanding of the Repatriated Prisoner of War', *British Journal of Psychiatric Social Work*, 1 (1947), 29–35

Beaumont, Frank, 'Rip Van Winkle', *Transatlantic*, 30 (1946), 41–6

Bing, R. and A. L. Vischer, 'Psychology of Internment Based on the Observation of Prisoners of War in Switzerland', *The Lancet*, 193, 4991 (26 April 1919), 696–7

Bootle-Wilbraham, Brigadier L., 'Civil Resettlement of Ex-Prisoners of War', *Mental Health*, 6, 2 (1946), 39–43

Bowen, Frank C., *Sea Slang. A Dictionary of the Old-Timers' Expressions and Epithets* (London: Sampson Low, Marston & Co., 1929)

Chapman, Charles, 'Come to Think of It', *The Clarion. The Official Organ of the Returned British Prisoners of War Association*, 1 (1946), unpaginated

Chapman, C. E., 'More about Resettlement', *The Clarion. The Official Organ of the Returned British Prisoners of War Association*, 2 (September–October 1946), unpaginated

Charters, Major D. L., 'Correspondence: Prisoner-of-War Mentality', *British Medical Journal*, 1, 4383 (6 January 1945), 24

Cochrane, A. L., 'The Medical Officer as Prisoner in Germany', *The Lancet*, 246, 6370 (29 September 1945), 411–12

Cochrane, A. L., 'Notes on the Psychology of Prisoners of War', *British Medical Journal*, 1, 4442 (23 February 1946), 282–4

Collie, George F., 'Returned Prisoners of War: A Suggested Scheme for Rehabilitation', *The Fortnightly*, 153 (June 1943), 407–11

Culpin, Millais, 'Correspondence: Returned Prisoners of War', *British Medical Journal*, 1, 4334 (29 January 1944), 158–9

Curle, Adam, 'Transitional Communities and Social Re-connection; a Follow-Up Study of the Civil Resettlement of British Prisoners of War. Part I', *Human Relations*, 1 (1947), 42–68

Curle, Adam, 'Transitional Communities and Social Reconnection', in Charles Zwingmann and Maria Pfister-Ammende (eds.) in *Uprooting and After ...* (New York: Springer-Verlag, 1973), pp. 234–40

Curle, Adam and E. L. Trist, 'Transitional Communities and Social Re-connection; a Follow-Up Study of the Civil Resettlement of British Prisoners of War. Part II', *Human Relations*, 1 (1947), 240–88

Davidson, Susan, 'Notes on a Group of Ex-Prisoners of War', *Bulletin of the Menninger Clinic*, 10, 3 (1946), 90–100

Dearlove, Captain A. R., 'Enforced Leisure: A Study of the Activities of Officer Prisoners of War', *British Medical Journal*, 1, 4394 (24 March 1945), 406–9

Eley, A. W. Vaughan, 'Correspondence. The Prisoner-of-War Mentality', *British Medical Journal*, 1, 4341 (18 March 1944)

Harkness, John, 'Correspondence: The Prisoner-of-War Mentality', *British Medical Journal*, 1, 4346 (22 April 1944), 568

Hawes, T. H., 'Letters to the Editor. Returned Prisoners-of-War', *The Lancet*, 245, 6351 (19 May 1945), 643

Henderson, David and Robert Gillespie, *A Text-Book of Psychiatry for Students and Practitioners* (London: Oxford University Press, 1940)

Henderson, David, and Robert Gillespie, *A Text-Book of Psychiatry for Students and Practitioners* (London: Oxford University Press, 1950)

Jeffrey, Manfred and E. J. G. Bradford, 'Neurosis in Escaped Prisoners of War', *British Journal of Medical Psychology*, 20, 4 (1945–6), 422–35

Jones, Ernest, 'Psychology and War Conditions', *Psychoanalytic Quarterly*, 14, 1 (1945), 1–27

Jones, Maxwell, *Social Psychiatry. A Study of Therapeutic Communities* (London: Tavistock Publications, 1952)

Jones, Maxwell and J. M. Tanner, 'The Clinical Characteristics, Treatment, and Rehabilitation of Repatriated Prisoners of War with Neurosis', *Journal of Neurology and Psychiatry*, 11 (1943), 53–60

Kral, V. A. 'Psychiatric Observations under Severe Chronic Stress', *American Journal of Psychiatry*, 108 (1951), 185–92

Lack, Major C., 'The Management of Convalescent Neurotics at the Neurosis Wing, 101 Military Convalescent Depot', *Journal of the Royal Army Medical Corps*, 86, 1 (1946), 32–4

Main, T. F., 'Clinical Problems in Repatriates', *Journal of Mental Science*, 93 (1947), 354–63

Mallison, W. P., and W. Warren, 'Repatriation. A Psychiatric Study of 100 Naval Ex-Prisoners of War', *British Medical Journal*, 2, 4431 (8 December 1945), 798–801

Mass Observation, *Meet Yourself on Sunday* (London: The Naldrett Press, 1949)

Miller, C. Barclay, 'In the Balance', *The Clarion. The Official Organ of the Returned British Prisoners of War Association*, 4 (1947), unpaginated

Miller, Emanuel, 'Preface', in Emanuel Miller (ed.), *The Neuroses in War* (London: Macmillan and Co., 1940), pp. vii–ix

Newman, P. H., 'The Prisoner-of-War Mentality: Its Effect after Repatriation', *British Medical Journal*, 1, 4330 (1 January 1944), 8–10

Newman, P. H., 'Correspondence: Prisoner-of-War Mentality', *British Medical Journal*, 1, 4387 (3 February 1945), 163

'Over 13,000 Ex-POWs Went through Cosford', *The Clarion. The Official Organ of the Returned British Prisoners of War Association*, 8 (1947), unpaginated

Pether, Major G. C., 'The Returned Prisoner-of-War', *The Lancet*, 245, 6394 (5 May 1945), 571–2

Rees, J. R., *The Shaping of Psychiatry by War* (New York: W. W. Norton, 1945)

Smyth, Brigadier J. G., 'Memoir to Mary Crossan', *The Clarion*, Special Issue (April 1948), unpaginated

S., K., 'Appreciation', *The Clarion. The Official Organ of the Returned British Prisoners of War Association*, 16, (1949), unpaginated

The Viscount Tarbat, 'The Problem of Resettlement', *The Clarion. The Official Organ of the Returned British Prisoners of War Association*, 2 (July–August 1946), unpaginated

Torrie, Lieutenant Colonel Alfred, 'The Return of Odysseus. The Problem of Marital Infidelity for the Repatriate', *British Medical Journal*, 2, 4414 (11 August 1945), 192–3

Twist, Eric, 'Working with Bion in the 1940s: The Group Decade', in Malcolm Pines (ed.) *Bion and Group Psychotherapy* (London: Routledge & Kegan Paul, 1985), pp. 1–46

Vischer, A. L., *The Barbed Wire Disease. A Psychological Study of Prisoners of War* (London: John Bale & Co., 1919)

Walker, E. R. C., 'Impressions of a Repatriated Medical Officer', *The Lancet*, 243, 6249 (15 April 1944), 514–15

Whiles, Major W. H., 'Neurosis among Repatriated Prisoners of War', *British Medical Journal*, 2, 4428 (17 November 1945), 697–8

Wilson, A. T. M., 'The Serviceman Comes Home', *Pilot Papers*, 1, 2 (1946), 9–28

Wilson, A. T. M., M. Doyle and J. Kelnar, 'Group Techniques in a Transitional Community', *The Lancet*, 249, 6457 (31 May 1947), 735–8

Wilson, A. T. M., E. L. Trist and Adam Curle, 'Transitional Communities: A Study of the Civil Resettlement of British Prisoners of War', in Guy E. Swanson, Theodore M. Newcomb and Eugene L. Hartley (eds.) *Readings in Social Psychology* (New York: Henry Holt and Company, 1952), pp. 561–79

Wittkower, Eric and J. P. Spillane, 'A Survey of the Literature of the Neuroses in War', in Emanuel Miller (ed.) *The Neuroses in War* (London: Macmillan and Co., 1940), pp. 1–32

Wolf, Stewart and Herbert S. Ripley, 'Reactions among Allied Prisoners of War Subjected to Three Years of Imprisonment and Torture by the Japanese', *American Journal of Psychiatry*, 104, 3 (1947), 180–93

Newspapers and Newsletters

'Exchange of War Prisoners. German Answer to Latest Approach', *The Times* (18 April 1945)

'Obituary. Professor Trevor Gibbens', *The Times* (8 November 1983)

'Returned Men's Rip Van Winkle Feeling', *News of the World* (7 November 1943)

Secondary Literature

Books and Articles

Abraham, Frances, 'The Tavistock Group', in Morgen Witzel and Malcolm Warner (eds.), *The Oxford Handbook of Management Theorists* (Oxford: Oxford University Press, 2013), pp. 155–73

Abzug, Robert H, *Inside the Vicious Heart. Americans and the Liberation of Nazi Concentration Camps* (Oxford: Oxford University Press, 1985)

Acton, Carol, 'Writing and Waiting: First World War Correspondence between Vera Brittain and Roland Leighton', *Gender and History*, 11, 1 (1999), 54–83

Acton, Carol, *Grief in Wartime. Private Pain, Public Discourse* (Basingstoke: Palgrave Macmillan, 2007)

Acton, Carol, '"Stepping into History": Reading the Second World War through Irish Women's Diaries', *Irish Studies Review*, 18, 1 (2010), 39–56

Acton, Carol and Jane Potter, '"These Frightful Sights Would Work Havoc with One's Brain": Subjective Experience, Trauma, and Resilience in First World War Writings by Medical Personnel', *Literature and Medicine*, 30, 1 (2012), 61–85

Allport, Alan, *Demobbed: Coming Home after World War Two* (New Haven, CT: Yale University Press, 2009)

Allport, Alan, *Browned Off and Bloody-Minded: The British Soldier Goes to War 1939–1945* (New Haven, CT: Yale University Press, 2015)

Allport, G. W., 'The Historical Background of Social Psychology', in Gardner Lindzey and Elliot Aronson (eds.), *Handbook of Social Psychology, Theory and Method*, volume 1 (New York: Random House, 1985), pp. 1–46

Anderson, Benedict, *Imagined Communities. Reflections on the Origins and Spread of Nationalism* (London: Verso, 1983)

Archer, Bernice, *A Patchwork of Internment. The Internment of Western Civilians under the Japanese, 1941–1945* (London: RoutledgeCurzon, 2004)

Audoin-Rouzeau, Stéphane, *Men at War, 1914–1918. National Sentiment and Trench Journalism in France during the First World War.* Translated by Helen McPhail (Oxford: Berg, 1992)

Baker, Paul and Jo Stanley, *Hello Sailor! The Hidden History of Gay Life at Sea* (London: Longman, 2003)

Barraclough, B., J. Bunch and B. Nelson, 'A Hundred Cases of Suicide: Clinical Aspects', *British Journal of Psychiatry*, 125 (1974), 355–73

Beaumont, Joan, 'Rank, Privilege and Prisoners of War', *War and Society*, 1 (1983), 67–94

Beaumont, Joan, *Gull Force. Survival and Leadership in Captivity 1941–1945* (Sydney: Allen & Unwin, 1985)

Beaumont, Joan, Lachlan Grant and Aaron Pegram, 'Remembering and Rethinking Captivity', in Joan Beaumont, Lachlan Grant and Aaron Pegram (eds.), *Beyond Surrender. Australian Prisoners of War in the Twentieth Century* ([e-book] Carlton, Victoria: Melbourne University Press, 2015), unpaginated

Becker, Annette, *Oubliés de la Grande Guerre. Humanitaire et Culture de Guerre. Populations Occupées, Déportés Civils, Prisonniers de Guerre* (Paris: Noêsis, 1998)

Becker, Annette, 'Art, Material Life and Disaster. Civilian and Military Prisoners of War', in Nicholas J. Saunders (ed.), *Matters of Conflict. Material Culture, Memory and the First World War* (London: Routledge, 2004), pp. 26–34

Beckwith, E. G. C. (ed.), *The Mansel Diaries. The Diaries of Captain John Mansel, Prisoner of War and Camp Forger in Germany 1940–45* (Privately published, 1977)

Bergen, Doris L., 'Book Review. Numbered Days: Diaries and the Holocaust. By Alexandra Garbarini. New Haven, CT, and London: Yale University Press. 2006', *Central European History*, 42, 2 (June 2009), 364–6

Bet-El, Ilana R, *Conscripts. Forgotten Men of the Great War* (Stroud: Sutton Publishing, 1999)

Biess, Frank, *Homecomings: Returning POWs and the Legacies of Defeat in Postwar Germany* (Princeton, NJ: Princeton University Press, 2006)

Binneveld, Hans, *From Shellshock to Combat Stress. A Comparative History of Military Psychiatry* (Amsterdam: Amsterdam University Press, 1997)

Blodgett, Harriet, 'Preserving the Moment in the Diary of Margaret Fountaine', in Suzanne L. Bunkers and Cynthia A. Huff (eds.), *Inscribing the Daily. Critical Essays on Women's Diaries* (Amherst: University of Massachusetts Press, 1996), pp. 156–68

Bloom, Lynn Z., '"I write for Myself and Strangers": Private Diaries as Public Documents', in Suzanne L. Bunkers and Cynthia A. Huff (eds.), *Inscribing the Daily: Critical Essays on Women's Diaries* (Amherst: University of Massachusetts Press, 1996), 23–37

Boag, P., *Re-dressing America's Frontier Past* (Berkeley: University of California Press, 2011)

Bourke, Joanna, 'Disciplining the Emotions: Fear, Psychiatry and the Second World War', in Roger Cooter, Mark Harrison and Steve Sturdy (eds.), *War, Medicine and Modernity* (Stroud: Sutton Publishing, 1998), pp. 225–38

Bourke, Joanna, *Dismembering the Male. Men's Bodies, Britain and the Great War* (London: Reaktion, 1999)

Bourke, Joanna, *An Intimate History of Killing. Face-to-Face Killing in Twentieth-Century Warfare* (London: Granta Books, 1999)

Bourke, Joanna, 'New Military History', in Matthew Hughes and William J. Philpott (eds.), *Palgrave Advances in Modern Military History* (Basingstoke: Palgrave Macmillan, 2006), pp. 258–80

Bourke, Joanna, 'Pain: Metaphor, Body, and Culture in Anglo-American Societies between the Eighteenth and Twentieth Centuries', *Rethinking History*, 18, 4 (2014), 475–98

Boxwell, David A., 'The Follies of War: Cross-Dressing and Popular Theatre on the British Front Lines, 1914–18', *Modernism/modernity* 9, 1 (2002), 1–20

Braybon, Gail and Penny Summerfield, *Out of the Cage. Women's Experiences in the Two World Wars* (London: Pandora, 1987)

Browning, C. R., *The Origins of the Final Solution. The Evolution of Nazi Jewish Policy, September 1939–March 1942* (Jerusalem: Yad Vashem, 2004)

Cambray, P. G. and G. G. B. Briggs, *Red Cross and St. John: the Official Record of the Humanitarian Services of the War Organisation of the British Red Cross Society and Order of St. John of Jerusalem 1939-1947* (London: Sumfield and Day, 1949)

Carr, G. and H. Mytum (eds.), *Cultural Heritage and Prisoners of War. Creativity behind Barbed Wire* (New York: Routledge, 2012)

Carroll, Tim, *The Great Escapers: The Full Story of the Second World War's Most Remarkable Mass Escape* (Edinburgh: Mainstream, 2004)

Cohen, Stanley and Laurie Taylor, *Psychological Survival. The Experience of Long-Term Imprisonment* (Harmondsworth: Penguin Books, 1972)

Conway, Martin A., Lucy V. Justice and Catriona M. Morrison, 'Beliefs about Autobiographical Memory … and Why They Matter', *The Psychologist*, 27, 7 (2014), 502–5

Corradi, Richard B, 'Psychodynamic Psychotherapy: A Core Conceptual Model and Its Application', *The Journal of the American Academy of Psychoanalysis and Dynamic Psychiatry*, 34, 1 (2006), 93–116

Crang, Jeremy A., *The British Army and the People's War* (Manchester: Manchester University Press, 2000)

Culley, Margo, 'Introduction', in Margo Culley (ed.), *A Day at a Time. The Diary Literature of American Women from 1764 to the Present* (New York: The Feminist Press at the City University of New York, 1985)

Davis, Natalie Zemon, *Society and Culture in Early Modern France. Eight Essays by Natalie Zemon Davis* (Cambridge: Polity Press, 1987)

Dawson, Graham, *Soldier Heroes. British Adventure, Empire and the Imagining of Masculinities* (London and New York: Routledge, 1994)

Dicks, H. V., *Fifty Years of the Tavistock Clinic* (London: Routledge and Kegan Paul, 1970)

Doan, Laura, 'Book Review: The Secret Battle: Emotional Survival in the Great War. By Michael Roper', *Twentieth Century British History*, 20 (2009), 428–30

Donnelly, Katherine Fair, *Recovering from the Loss of a Parent* (New York: Berkley Publishing, 1993)

Doyle, Peter, *Prisoner of War in Germany* (Oxford: Shire Publications, 2008)

Doyle, Robert C., *Voices from Captivity. Interpreting the American POW Narrative* (Lawrence: University of Kansas Press, 1991)

Duffett, Rachel, *The Stomach for Fighting: Food and the Soldiers of the Great War* (Manchester: Manchester University Press, 2012)

'Editor's Foreword' in Ted Beckwith (ed.), *The Mansel Diaries. The Diaries of Captain John Mansel, Prisoner of War and Camp Forger in Germany 1940–45* (London: Wildwood House, 1977), pp. vii–viii

Ellenberger, Henri F., *The Discovery of the Unconscious. The History and Evolution of Dynamic Psychiatry* (New York: Basic Books, 1970)

Fehrenbach, Heide, 'Rehabilitating Fatherland: Race and German Remasculinization', *Signs*, 24, 1 (1998), 107–27

Feltman, Brian K., 'Letters from Captivity: The First World War Correspondence of the German Prisoners of War in the United Kingdom', in Jennifer D. Keene and Michael S. Neiberg (eds.), *Finding Common Ground. New Directions in First World War Studies* (Boston: Brill, 2011), pp. 87–110

Feltman, Brian K., *The Stigma of Surrender. German Prisoners, British Captors, and Manhood in the Great War and Beyond* (Chapel Hill: University of North Carolina, 2015)

Fitzpatrick, David, *Oceans of Consolation. Personal Accounts of Irish Migration to Australia* (Cork: Cork University Press, 1994)

Flaherty, Michael G. 'The Erotics and Hermeneutics of Temporality', in Carolyn Ellis and Michael G. Flaherty (eds.) *Investigating Subjectivity. Research on Lived Experience* (Newbury Park: Sage Publications, 1992), pp. 141–55

Francis, Martin, 'A Flight from Commitment? Domesticity, Adventure and the Masculine Imaginary in Britain after the Second World War', *Gender and History*, 19, 1 (2007), 163–85

Francis, Martin, *The Flyer. British Culture and the Royal Air Force, 1939–1945* (Oxford: Oxford University Press, 2008)

French, David, *Raising Churchill's Army. The British Army and the War against Germany 1919–1945* (Oxford: Oxford University Press, 2000)

Fuller, J. G., *Troop Morale and Popular Culture in the British and Dominion Armies, 1914–1918* (Oxford: Clarendon Press, 1990)

Fussell, Paul, *Wartime. Understanding and Behaviour in the Second World War* (Oxford: Oxford University Press, 1989)

Gabriel, Martha A., 'Anniversary Reactions: Trauma Revisited', *Clinical Social Work Journal*, 20, 2 (1992), pp. 179–92

Garbarini, Alexandra, *Numbered Days. Diaries and the Holocaust* (New Haven, CT: Yale University Press, 2006)

Garber, Marjorie, *Vested Interests. Cross-Dressing and Cultural Anxiety* (New York: Routledge, 1992)

Garton, Stephen, *The Cost of War. Australians Return* (Melbourne: Oxford University Press, 1996)

Garton, Stephen, 'War and Masculinity in Twentieth-Century Australia', *Journal of Australian Studies*, 56 (1998), 86–95

Gerster, Robin, *Big-Noting: The Heroic Theme in Australian War Writing* (Melbourne: Melbourne University Press, 1987)

Gilbert, Adrian, *POW: Allied Prisoners in Europe, 1939–1945* (London: John Murray, 2006)

Gilbert, Martin, *The Second World War. A Complete History* (London: Phoenix, 2009)

Gilbert, Sandra M. and Susan Gubar, *No Man's Land: The Place of the Woman Writer in the Twentieth Century*, volume 2, *Sexchanges* (New Haven, CT: Yale University Press, 1989)

Gillies, Midge, *The Barbed-Wire University. The Real Lives of Prisoners of War in the Second World War* (London: Aurum Press Ltd, 2011)

Goffman, Erving, *Asylums: Essays on the Social Situation of Mental Patients and Other Inmates* (Harmondsworth: Penguin, 1968)

Goldstein, Joshua S., *Gender and War: How Gender Shapes the War System and Vice Versa* (Cambridge: Cambridge University Press, 2001)

Hanna, A, 'A Republic of Letters: The Epistolary Tradition in France during World War I', *The American Historical Review*, 108 (2003), 1338–61

Harrison, Tom, *Bion, Rickman, Foulkes and the Northfield Experiments. Advancing on a Different Front* (London: Jessica Kingsley Publishers, 2000)

Hartmann, Susan, 'Prescriptions for Penelope: Literature on Women's Obligations to Returning World War II Veterans', *Women's Studies*, 5 (1978), 223–39

Haslam, S. Alexander and Stephen D. Reicher, 'When Prisoners Take Over the Prison: A Social Psychology of Resistance', *Personality and Social Psychology Review*, 16, 2 (2012), 154–79

Hately-Broad, Barbara, *War and Welfare, British Prisoner of War Families 1939–45* (Manchester: Manchester University Press, 2009)

Hinton, James, *Nine Wartime Lives. Mass-Observation and the Making of the Modern Self* (Oxford: Oxford University Press, 2010)

Hogan, Rebecca, 'Engendered Autobiographies: The Diary as a Feminine Form', in Shirley Neuman (ed.), *Autobiography and Questions of Gender* (London: Frank Cass & Co. Ltd, 1991), pp. 95–107

Holden, Wendy, *Shell Shock* (London: Channel 4 Books, 1998)

Houghton, Frances, '"To the Kwai and Back": Myth, Memory and Memoirs of the "Death Railway" 1942–1943', *Journal of War and Culture Studies*, 7, 3 (2014), 223–35

Houlbrook, Matt, *Queer London. Perils and Pleasures in the Sexual Metropolis, 1918–1957* (Chicago: University of Chicago Press, 2005)

Jeffrey, K., 'The Post-war Army', in F. W. Beckett and K. Simpson (eds.), *A Nation in Arms. A Social Study of the British Army in the First World War* (Manchester: Manchester University Press, 1985), pp. 211–34

Jolly, Margaretta, 'Love Letters versus Letters Carved in Stone: Gender, Memory and the "Forces Sweethearts" Exhibition', in Martin Evans and Ken Lunn (eds.), *War and Memory in the Twentieth Century* (Oxford: Berg, 1997), pp. 105–21

Jones, Edgar and Simon Wessely, *Shell Shock to PTSD. Military Psychiatry from 1900 to the Gulf War* (Hove: Psychology Press, 2005)

Jones, Edgar and Simon Wessely, 'British Prisoners-of-War: From Resilience to Psychological Vulnerability: Reality or Perception', *Twentieth Century British History*, 21, 2 (2010), 163–83

Jones, Heather, *Violence against Prisoners of War in the First World War: Britain, France, and Germany, 1914–1920* (Cambridge: Cambridge University Press, 2012)

Kaushik, Roy, 'Discipline and Morale of African, British and Indian Army Units in Burma and India during World War II: July 1943 to August 1945', *Modern Asian Studies*, 44 (2010), 1255–82

King, Pearl, 'Activities of British Psychoanalysts during the Second World War and the Influence of Their Interdisciplinary Collaboration on the Development of Psychoanalysis in Great Britain', *International Review of Psychoanalysis*, 16 (1989), 15–32

Kochavi, Arieh, *Confronting Captivity: Britain and the United States and Their POWs in Nazi Germany* (Chapel Hill: University of North Carolina Press, 2005)

Koreman, Megan, 'A Hero's Homecoming: The Return of the Deportees to France, 1945', *Journal of Contemporary History*, 32, 1 (1997), 9–22

Kühne, Thomas, 'Comradeship: Gender Confusion and Gender Order in the German Military, 1918–1945', in Karen Hagemann and Stefanie Schüler-Springorum (eds.), *Home/Front. The Military, War and Gender in Twentieth-Century Germany* (Oxford: Berg, 2002), pp. 233–54

Kühne, Thomas, *Belonging and Genocide. Hitler's Community, 1918–1945* (New Haven, CT: Yale University Press, 2010)

Langhamer, Claire, 'Love, Selfhood and Authenticity in Post-war Britain', *Cultural and Social History*, 9, 2 (2012), 277–97

Leed, Eric, *No Man's Land. Combat and Identity in the First World War* (Cambridge: Cambridge University Press, 1979)

Lejeune, Philippe, *On Diary*, edited by Jeremy D. Popkin and Julie Rak, translated by Katherine Durnin (Manoa: University of Hawaii, 2009)

Lerner, Paul, 'From Traumatic Neurosis to Male Hysteria', in Mark S. Micale and Paul Lerner (eds.) *Traumatic Pasts. History, Psychiatry, and Trauma in the Modern Age, 1870–1930* (Cambridge: Cambridge University Press, 2001), pp. 140–71

Lerner, Paul, *Hysterical Men: War, Psychiatry, and the Politics of Trauma in Germany, 1890–1930* (Ithaca, NY: Cornell University Press, 2003)

Lieblich, Amia, *Seasons for Captivity. The Inner World of POWs* (New York and London: New York University Press, 1994)

Longden, Sean, *Dunkirk: The Men They Left Behind* (London: Constable, 2008)

Mackenzie, S. P., 'The Shackling Crisis: A Case Study in the Dynamics of Prisoner-of-War Diplomacy in the Second World War', *International History Review*, 17, 1 (1995), 78–98

MacKenzie, S. P., *The Colditz Myth: British and Commonwealth Prisoners of War in Nazi Germany* (Oxford: Oxford University Press, 2006)

Makepeace, Clare, 'For "ALL Who Were Captured"? The Evolution of National Ex-Prisoner of War Associations in Britain after the Second World War', *Journal of War and Culture Studies*, 7, 3 (August 2014), 255–8

Mason, W. Wynne, *Prisoners of War. Official History of New Zealand in the Second World War 1939–45* (London: Oxford University Press, 1954)

Meyer, Jessica, *Men of War: Masculinity and the First World War in Britain* (Basingstoke: Palgrave Macmillan, 2009)

Monteath, Peter, *P.O.W. Australian Prisoners of War in Hitler's Reich* (Sydney: Macmillan, 2011)

Monteath, Peter, 'POW "Holiday Camps" in the Third Reich', *European History Quarterly*, 44, 3 (2014), 480–503

Monteath, Peter, 'Beyond the Colditz Myth: Australian Experiences of German Captivity in World War II', in Joan Beaumont, Lachlan Grant and Aaron Pegram (eds.), *Beyond Surrender. Australian Prisoners of War in the Twentieth Century* ([e-book] Carlton, Victoria: Melbourne University Press, 2015), unpaginated

Moore, Bob and Kent Fedorowich (eds.), *Prisoners of War and Their Captors in World War II* (Oxford: Berg, 1996)

Moore, Bob and Barbara Hately-Broad, 'Living on Hope and Onions: The Everyday Life of British Servicemen in Axis Captivity', *Everyone's War: The Journal of the Second World War Experience Centre*, 8 (2003), 39–45

Moore, Bob and Barbara Hately 'Captive Audience: Camp Entertainment and British Prisoners-of-War in German Captivity, 1939–1945', *Popular Entertainment Studies*, 5, 1 (2014), 58–73

Newlands, Emma, *Civilians into Soldiers. War, the Body and British Army Recruits, 1939–45* (Manchester, Manchester University Press, 2013)

Nichol, John and Tony Rennell, *The Last Escape. The Untold Story of Allied Prisoners of War in Germany, 1944–45* (London: Viking, 2002)

Nussbaum, Felicity, 'Toward Conceptualizing Diary', in James Olney (ed.), *Studies in Autobiography* (New York: Oxford University Press, 1988), pp. 128–40

Panayi, Panikos, *Prisoners of Britain. German Civilian and Combatant Internees during the First World War* (Manchester: Manchester University Press, 2012)

Passerini, Luisa, *Europe in Love, Love in Europe. Imagination and Politics in Britain between the Wars* (London: I. B. Tauris Publishers, 1999)

Pattinson, Juliette, Lucy Noakes and Wendy Ugolini, 'Incarcerated Masculinities: Male POWs and the Second World War', *Journal of War and Culture Studies*, 7, 3 (2014), 179–90

Plain, Gill, 'Before the Colditz Myth: Telling POW Stories in Postwar British Cinema', *Journal of War and Culture Studies*, 7, 3 (2014), 269–282

Rachamimov, Iris, *POWs and the Great War: Captivity on the Eastern Front* (Oxford: Berg, 2002)

Rachamimov, Iris, 'The Disruptive Comforts of Drag: (Trans)Gender Performances among Prisoners of War in Russia, 1914–1920', *American Historical Review*, 111, 2 (2006), 362–82

Rachamimov, Iris, 'Camp Domesticity. Shifting Gender Boundaries in WWI Internment Camps', in Gilly Carr and Harold Mytum (eds.), *Cultural Heritage and Prisoners of War. Creativity behind Barbed Wire* (New York: Routledge, 2012), pp. 291–305

Rawlinson, Mark, *British Writing of the Second World War* (Oxford: Oxford University Press, 2000)

Reid, Fiona, *Broken Men: Shell Shock, Treatment and Recovery in Britain, 1914–1930* (London: Continuum, 2010)

Reiss, Matthias, 'Bronzed Bodies behind Barbed Wire: Masculinity and the Treatment of German Prisoners of War in the United States during World War II', *The Journal of Military History*, 69, 2 (2005), 475–504

Reiss, Matthias, 'The Importance of Being Men: The Afrika-Korps in American Captivity', *Journal of Social History*, 46, 1 (2012), 23–47

Robb, Linsey, *Men at Work: The Working Man in British Culture* (Basingstoke: Palgrave Macmillan, 2015)

Rolf, David, *Prisoners of the Reich: Germany's Captives 1939–1945* (Sevenoaks: Coronet 1989)

Roper, Michael, *The Secret Battle. Emotional Survival in the Great War* (Manchester: Manchester University Press, 2009)

Roper, Michael, 'Nostalgia as an Emotional Experience in the Great War', *The Historical Journal*, 54, 2 (2011), 421–51

Rose, Sonya O., *Which People's War?: National Identity and Citizenship in Britain 1939–1945* (Oxford: Oxford University Press, 2003)

Rothfels, Nigel, *Savages and Beasts. The Birth of the Modern Zoo* (Baltimore, MD: John Hopkins University Press, 2008)

Scharff, David E., 'Object Relations Theory (General)', in Ross M. Skelton (ed.), *The Edinburgh International Encyclopaedia of Psychoanalysis* (Edinburgh: Edinburgh University Press, 2006), pp. 333–4

Shapira, Michal, *The War Inside. Psychoanalysis, Total War, and the Making of the Democratic Self in Postwar Britain* (Cambridge: Cambridge University Press, 2013)

Shephard, Ben, '"Pitiless Psychology": The Role of Prevention in British Military Psychiatry in the Second World War', *History of Psychiatry*, 10, 4 (1999), 491–524

Shephard, Ben, *A War of Nerves: Soldiers and Psychiatrists in the Twentieth Century* (Cambridge, MA: Harvard University Press, 2001)

Smith, Harold L., *Britain in the Second World War. A Social History* (Manchester: Manchester University Press, 1996)

Smith, Helen, *Masculinity, Class and Same-Sex Desire in Industrial England, 1895–1957* (Basingstoke: Palgrave Macmillan, 2015)

Sontag, Susan, *On Photography* (London: Allen Lane, 1978)

Spark, Seumas, 'Australian Prisoners of War of Italy in World War II: Public and Private Histories', in Joan Beaumont, Lachlan Grant and Aaron Pegram (eds.), *Beyond Surrender. Australian Prisoners of War in the Twentieth Century ([e-book] Carlton*, Victoria: Melbourne University Press, 2015), unpaginated

Speed, Richard B., *Prisoners, Diplomats, and the Great War: A Study in the Diplomacy of Captivity* (New York: Greenwood Press, 1990)

Stibbe, Matthew, 'The Internment of Civilians by Belligerent States during the First World War and the Response of the International Committee of the Red Cross', *Journal of Contemporary History*, 41, 1 (2006), 5–19

Stibbe, Matthew, *British Civilian Internees in Germany: The Ruhleben Camp, 1914–1918* (Manchester: Manchester University Press, 2008)

Stibbe, Matthew, 'Gendered Experiences of Civilian Internment during the First World War: A Forgotten Dimension of Wartime Violence', in Ana Carden-Coyne (ed.), *Gender and Conflict since 1914. Historical and Interdisciplinary Perspectives* (Basingstoke: Palgrave Macmillan, 2012), pp. 14–28

Stout, T. Duncan M., *Medical Services in New Zealand and the Pacific. In Royal New Zealand Navy, Royal New Zealand Air Force and with Prisoners of War* (Wellington: War History Branch, Department of Internal Affairs, 1958)

Summerfield, Penny and Corinna Peniston-Bird, *Contesting Home Defence. Men, Women and the Home Guard in the Second World War* (Manchester: Manchester University Press, 2007)

Summers, Julie, *Stranger in the House: Women's Stories of Men Returning from the Second World War* (London: Simon and Schuster, 2008)

Tajfel, Henri, 'Experiments in Intergroup Discrimination', *Scientific American*, 223 (November 1970), 96–102

Thalassis, Nafsika, 'Soldiers in Psychiatric Therapy: The Case of Northfield Military Hospital 1942–1946', *Social History of Medicine*, 20, 2 (2007), 351–68

Towle, Philip, 'Introduction', in Philip Towle, Margaret Kosuge and Yoichi Kibata (eds.), *Japanese Prisoners of War* (London: Hambledon Press, 2000), pp. xiii–xv

Turner, Victor W., *The Ritual Process. Structure and Anti-structure* (London: Routledge & Kegan Paul, 1969)

Twells, Alison, '"Went into Raptures": Reading Emotion in the Ordinary Wartime Diary, 1941–1946', *Women's History Review*, 25, 1 (2015), 143–60

Twomey, Christina, '"Impossible History": Trauma and Testimony among Australian Civilians Interned by the Japanese in World War II', in Joy Damousi and Robert Reynolds (eds.), *History on the Couch. Essays in History and Psychoanalysis* (Melbourne: Melbourne University Press, 2003), pp. 155–65

Twomey, Christina, *Australia's Forgotten Prisoners. Civilians Interned by the Japanese in World War Two* (Cambridge: Cambridge University Press, 2007)

Twomey, Christina, 'Emaciation or Emasculation: Photographic Images, White Masculinity and Captivity by the Japanese', *Journal of Men's Studies*, 15, 3 (2007), 295–310

Twomey, Christina, 'Double Displacement: Western Women's Return Home from Japanese Internment in the Second World War', *Gender and History*, 21, 3 (2009), 670–84

Ullman, Sharon R., *Sex Seen: The Emergence of Modern Sexuality in America* (Berkeley: University of California Press, 1997)

Ursano, Robert J., James R. Rundell, M. Richard Fragala, Susan G. Larson, John T. Jaccard, Harold J. Wain, George T. Brandt and Brucinda L. Beach, 'The Prisoner of War', in Robert J. Ursano and Ann Norwood (eds.), *Emotional Aftermath of the Persian Gulf War. Veterans, Families, Communities, and Nations* (Washington, DC: American Psychiatric Press, 1996), pp. 443–76

Vance, Jonathan F., 'Men in Manacles: The Shackling of Prisoners of War, 1942–1943', *Journal of Military History*, 59 (1995), 483–504

Vickers, Emma, *Queen and Country. Same-Sex Desire in the British Armed Forces, 1939–45* (Manchester: Manchester University Press, 2015)

Vourkoutiotis, Vasilis, *Prisoners of War and the German High Command: The British and American Experience* (Basingstoke: Palgrave Macmillan, 2003)

Waxman, Zoe, *Writing the Holocaust. Identity, Testimony, Representation* (Oxford: Oxford University Press, 2006)

Wiener, Wendy J. and George C. Rosenwald, 'A Moment's Moment: The Psychology of Keeping a Diary', in R. Josselson and A. Lieblich (eds.), *The Narrative Study of Lives*, volume 1 (London: Sage Publications, 1993) pp. 30–58

Wilcox, Helen, 'Civil War Letters and Diaries and the Rhetoric of Experience', in Laura Lunger Knoppers (ed.), *The Oxford Handbook of Literature and the English Revolution* (Oxford: Oxford University Press, 2012), pp. 238–52

Wilkinson, Oliver, 'Captivity in Print. The Form and Function of POW Camp Magazines', in Gilly Carr and Harold Mytum (eds.), *Cultural Heritage and Prisoners of War. Creativity behind Barbed Wire* (New York: Routledge, 2012), pp. 227–43

Wilkinson, Oliver, 'Diluting Displacement. Letters from Captivity', in Sandra Barkhof and Angela K. Smith (eds.), *War and Displacement in the Twentieth Century. Global Conflicts* (London: Routledge, 2014), pp. 70–88

Wilson, Anita, '"Absolutely Truly Brill to See from You": Visuality and Prisoners' Letters', in David Barton and Nigel Hall (eds.), *Letter Writing as a Social Practice* (Amsterdam: John Benjamins Publishing Co., 1999), pp. 179–97

Wilson, Kevin, *Men of Air. The Doomed Youth of Bomber Command* (London: Phoenix, 2008)

Winter, Jay and Blaine Baggett, *The Great War and the Shaping of the 20th Century* (London: Penguin Studio, 1996)

Woollacott, Angela, 'Sisters and Brothers in Arms: Family, Class, and Gendering in World War I in Britain', in Miriam Cooke and Angela Woollacott (eds.), *Gendering War Talk* (Princeton, NJ: Princeton University Press, 1993), pp. 128–47

Wylie, Neville, *Barbed Wire Diplomacy. Britain, Germany, and Politics of Prisoners of War, 1939–1945* (Oxford: Oxford University Press, 2010)

Zaloga, Steven J., *V-1 Flying Bomb 1942–52. Hitler's Infamous 'Doodlebug'* (Oxford: Osprey, 2005)

Zetzel, Elizabeth R., 'List of Members of the Regional Association, Component and Affiliate Societies of the International Psycho-Analytical Association 1964–1965', *Bulletin of the International Psychoanalytic Association*, 45 (1964), 627–707

Films and Television Programmes

Colditz. Series 1 and 2. First broadcast between 1972 and 1974 by the BBC (BBC and Universal TV, 1972–74; BBC World Wide, 2010), DVD

The Colditz Story. Directed by Guy Hamilton (Ivan Foxwell Productions, 1955; Optimum Releasing Ltd, 2007), DVD

The Great Escape. Directed by John Sturges (MGM Studios, 1963; Sony Pictures Home Entertainment, 2006), DVD

The Wooden Horse. Directed by Jack Lee (Canal +, 1950; Optimum Releasing Ltd, 2007), DVD

Theses and Dissertations

Croft, Hazel, 'War Neurosis and Civilian Mental Health in Britain during the Second World War', unpublished PhD thesis, Birkbeck College, University of London (2016)

Thalassis, Nafsika, 'Treating and Preventing Trauma: British Military Psychiatry during the Second World War', unpublished PhD thesis, University of Salford (2004)

Websites

Bartlett, Robert, *The Working Life of the Surrey Constabulary 1851–1992*, www.open .ac.uk/Arts/history-from-police-archives/RB1/Pt2/pt2Fbombs.html, last accessed 9 November 2012

Eldredge, Sears A., *Captive Audiences/Captive Performers: Music and Theatre as Strategies for Survival on the Thailand–Burma Railway 1942–1945* (Macalester College, 2014), http://digitalcommons.macalester.edu/thdabooks/24, last accessed 31 March 2016

Powell, W. R. (ed.), *A History of the County of Essex: Volume 8*, 1983, www.british-history.ac.uk/report.aspx?compid=63840, last accessed 27 June 2012

Shamdasani, Sonu, 'Jones, (Alfred) Ernest (1879–1958)', in *Oxford Dictionary of National Biography* (Oxford: Oxford University Press, 2004) Online edition, September 2010, www.oxforddnb.com/view/article/34221, last accessed 10 August 2010

Stowe, Steven, 'Making Sense of Letters and Diaries', *History Matters: The U.S. Survey Course on the Web*, http://historymatters.gmu.edu/mse/letters/, July 2002, last accessed 25 October 2015

The Tavistock and Portman NHS Trust, *Our History*, http://tavistockandport man.uk/sites/default/files/files/Our%20history_0.pdf, last accessed November 16, 2016

Index